KUNDUN

KUNDUN

-

A Biography of the Family of the

DALAI LAMA

-

MARY CRAIG

COUNTERPOINT
WASHINGTON, D.C.

Front cover photograph shows Dekyi Tsering (the Great Mother) and her children pictured in the early 1950s. From left to right: Dekyi Tsering, Tsering Dolma, Thubten Jigme Norbu, Gyalo Thondup, Lobsang Samten, HH the Dalai Lama, Jetsun Pema and Tendzin Choegyal.

Text copyright © 1997 by Mary Craig
Illustrations copyright © 1997 by Anne Jennings Brown

First paperback edition 1998

First published in Great Britain in 1997 by HarperCollins*Publishers*

LIBRARY OF CONGRESS CATALOGING-IN-PUBLICATION DATA
Craig, Mary.
Kundun : a biography of the family of the Dalai Lama / Mary Craig.
1. Bstan-'dzin-rgya-mtsho, Dalai Lama XIV, 1935–   —xFamily.
I. Title.
BQ7935.B777C73 1997
294.3'923'0922—dc21   [B]   97–28904

ISBN 1–887178–91–0

COVER DESIGN: JENNY DOSSIN

COUNTERPOINT
P.O. Box 65793
Washington, D.C. 20035–5793

Counterpoint is a member of the Perseus Books Group.

3   5   7   9   10   8   6   4

For Anne with love

I have always felt that if I had been born in a rich or aristo-cratic family, I would not have been able to appreciate the feelings and sentiments of the humble classes of Tibetans. But owing to my lowly birth, I can understand them and read their minds, and that is why I feel for them so strongly and have tried my best to improve their lot in life.

The Fourteenth Dalai Lama

I think of Tibet as a beautiful country, and so it is, but the greatest beauty to me is that the people live a life dedicated to religion. You know it when you meet them without being told. There is a warmth that touches you, a power that fills you with new strength, a peace that is gentle. I remember such people, and I feel sad that now it is so seldom one meets their like.

Thubten Jigme Norbu, eldest brother of the Dalai Lama

A small child running out of a burning building is powerless to put the fire out by himself. All he can do is yell, 'Fire', in the hope that some bigger, stronger people will listen and take action. That's exactly what we Tibetans are doing. Our home is disintegrating and our relatives are in there.

Tendzin Choegyal, younger brother of the Dalai Lama

Contents

Acknowledgements

- I should like first of all to thank the Dalai Lama, for the many hours I was privileged to spend with him, and for his patience and good humour at all times.
- Thanks are due also to the family for their friendship and co-operation, especially to Tendzin Choegyal, Rinchen Khando Choegyal, Jetsun Pema, and Namlha Taklha in Dharamsala. And to Khando Chazotsang – whom I first knew in Dharamsala and later went to stay with at her home in Utah.
- Special thanks to Jetsun Pema who arranged for me to meet her elusive older brothers, Thubten Jigme Norbu and Gyalo Thondup, when they were in Dharamsala for the sixtieth birthday celebrations of His Holiness in July 1995. And to Gyalo Thondup for the unexpected and very welcome six-hour interview he gave me later in New Delhi.
- Still in Dharamsala, thanks are due to: His Holiness's Secretary, Tenzin Geyche Tethong, for his unfailing help and support; my old friend, Tenzin Atisha at the Department of Information; and Tashi Tsering of the Tibetan Library (and Amnye Machin Foundation) for pointing me in the direction of crucial Foreign Office papers in the British Library.
- Nearer home, I am grateful to Mrs Kesang Taklha, His Holiness's Representative in London, to Phuntsok Tashi Taklha for his rèminiscences, and to Tseten Samdup at the Office of Tibet, who was always on hand (at least by telephone, fax or e-mail) to encourage and advise. Phuntsog Wangyal at the Tibet Foundation contributed much fascinating material and even more intriguing insights.
- My gratitude to Hugh Richardson for his invaluable memories of former days in Tibet, and for his kindness and courtesy in receiving me at his home in St Andrews.
- Finally, I owe a huge debt of gratitude to my friend, Anne Jennings Brown, who not only provided the illustrations for the book, but also constantly spurred me on when I showed signs of flagging. She came with me three times to Dharamsala and read the manuscript in all its

various stages. Tendzin Choegyal and Khando Chazotsang also read the completed manuscript, and I am deeply grateful to them both. It was Tendzin Choegyal's suggestion that one day I should return to Dharamsala to help him with his memoirs that sparked off the idea for this book. He has been endlessly helpful.

List of Illustrations

The Tibetan artefacts depicted on the first page of each chapter are as follows:

p. 189   Temple horn. Conch shell encased in silver. Used in temple or-
chestras, also to invoke water or rain.

p. 198   Tsampa bowl. To hold salted tea mixed with yak's butter and
roasted barley flour (tsampa), the staple diet of Tibetans. Dark
wood encased in silver.

p. 212   Knife and sheath. Steel blade with silver hilt, and sheath hung
from the belt.

p. 226   Metal soup ladle, with hanging loop for when travelling.

p. 241   One of a pair of woman's silver hair ornaments decorated with
coral & turquoise, suspended either side of the face. Worn by the
nobility in Lhasa and central Tibet.

p. 255   Rosary of 108 prayer beads made of human bone, inlaid with silver, brass, copper, coral and turquoise.

p. 270   Silver costume ornament to hold a chatelaine or draped string of
beads.

p. 290   The cranium of a deceased high lama (or wise man), lined with silver and filled with consecrated liquid in specific rituals.

p. 305   Ceremonial silver teapot used by high lamas and the nobility.

p. 320   Reliquary box with glass window to view small image or relic. Silver and turquoise.

p. 334   Reliquary box, worn around the neck. Silver with turquoise. Central Tibet.

p. 347   Decorative belt-hanging. Brocade with silver mount and turquoise.
Eastern Tibet.

p. 356   Small reliquary box to hold religious charms. Silver and turquoise.
Southern and western Tibet.

Foreword

By His Holiness the Dalai Lama

In the early years of my life, Tibet was a land where people were free to live according to their own traditions. What the Tibetan way of life lacked in terms of modern amenities it more than made up for in terms of contentment. Our physical needs were adequately met and our ancient culture, strongly influenced by Buddhism, brought us peace of mind. The water was pure, the air was clean and the land was vast. Our low population had little cause for fear or anxiety. Farmers and nomadic herdspeople were amply productive and no one went hungry. Education and spiritual training were available in the monasteries and nunneries. Entry to them was unrestricted and the monks and nuns received universal respect. People could come and go as they pleased, which they regularly did, mostly on pilgrimage or trading expeditions. Even our wild animals ran free due to the long-standing prohibition on hunting. In short, Tibet was a land of peace, because there was harmony between people and animals, between sentient beings and the environment.

Unfortunately, in our natural isolation, we took this peace and harmony for granted. When the storm of the Chinese invasion broke over Tibet, it took us by surprise. The subsequent occupation has been ruthless and unrelenting. From the broken promises to respect our customs and way of life to the physical destruction of our cultural monuments, artefacts and our natural environment, the occupying forces have shown little regard for anything Tibetan. After more than forty years of upheaval, there cannot be a single Tibetan family whose lives have not been turned upside down.

In telling the story of my family members, Mary Craig reveals something of the tragedy that befell our nation. Beginning with the happy days at home as ordinary farmers, she describes the great changes that took place when I was recognized as the Dalai Lama and we moved to Lhasa. Sadly those good times were short-lived. I was barely fifteen when the Chinese invaded and there were the first signs that the way of life we had known was coming to an end. Gradually, our carefree attitudes gave way to tension and anxiety. Finally, in 1959, I and those members of my direct family who remained in Tibet escaped to India as refugees.

As the Dalai Lama, I have a special responsibility towards Tibet and its people. I do not claim to have high realizations or any other quality, but I firmly believe that there is a special karmic bond between the Tibetan people and myself. Because of this I was born at this critical juncture when we Tibetans are facing great trouble and there is a need to work hard. My predecessor, the Thirteenth Dalai Lama, felt himself to be very much alone, whereas I have had the good fortune to have received the help and support of my brothers and sisters.

Historically and according to international law Tibet is an independent country under illegal Chinese occupation. However, although we have the right to reclaim our independence, I have adopted a 'middle-way' approach of reconciliation and compromise. While it is the overwhelming desire of the Tibetan people to regain their national independence, I have repeatedly and publicly stated that I am willing to enter into negotiations on the basis of an agenda that does not include independence. The continued occupation of Tibet poses an increasing threat to the very existence of a distinct Tibetan national and cultural identity. Therefore, I consider that my primary responsibility is to take whatever steps I must to save my people and our unique cultural heritage from total annihilation.

Tibet's religious culture, its medical knowledge, peaceful outlook and respectful attitude to the environment contain much that can be of widespread benefit to others. Therefore, those of us in exile have had a responsibility to preserve what we could, not only for the benefit of our brothers and sisters who remain in Tibet, but also for the world at large. In re-establishing our religious and cultural institutions we have ensured the survival of these traditions, at least for the time being. But, in the long run, we will be able to maintain them in a dynamic way only if we return to the freedom of our own land.

No matter how successful those of us in exile have been, we are but a fraction of the entire population of six million Tibetans. They continue to live under dreadful conditions. The Chinese may have brought elements of modernization and economic improvement to Tibet, but, as the saying goes, man does not live by bread alone. People need mental freedom, a conducive atmosphere in which to exercise their creative talents, and, above all, personal responsibility, the ability to determine their own future. Unfortunately, these basic rights are absent in Chinese-occupied Tibet.

It would be easy to be pessimistic. Recently, new measures have been adopted by the Chinese authorities to tighten political control in Tibet. A new crackdown has been launched against advocates of human rights and independence. People suspected of harbouring religious and nationalistic feelings are falling victim to a new wave of political persecution. Existing monasteries have been raided by the police. The construction or rebuilding of monasteries and nunneries has been prohibited and the admission of new monks and nuns stopped. Tibetans who used to work as guides for foreign tourists have been dismissed. Tibetan children are no longer allowed to study in our institutions in exile and those already doing so have been ordered to return. At the same time, the flow of Chinese settlers into Tibet continues inexorably.

Nevertheless, it is important to be optimistic. All is not lost. We Tibetans are resilient, patient and resourceful. Ours is a just cause. We continue to be confident that truth will ultimately triumph and our land and people will once more be free. Would the Chinese consider the Tibetan question so sensitive if our cause was dead? Under difficult circumstances we have kept the Tibetan spirit and a sense of hope alive. However, it is clear that these efforts alone will not be sufficient to bring about a final positive solution. Therefore, I appeal to readers of this book to support the Tibetan people, so that ultimately they may again live in peace with dignity.

8 January 1997

Preface

While I was writing *Tears of Blood*, my book on the Chinese occupation of Tibet, I made several visits to Dharamsala, the hill station in Northern India which is the home of the Dalai Lama and his administration-in-exile. It became almost a second home to me and I made many enduring friendships there. The more I learned about Tibet and Tibetans, the more I was hooked. So much so that when Giles Semper, my then editor at HarperCollins, suggested a second book on Tibet, I jumped at the chance. It occurred to me then that, while there had been many books written about the Dalai Lama himself, no one, so far as I knew, had ever written about his immediate family, his mother, father, four brothers and two sisters. I wrote to His Holiness to see whether he would agree to a book on the family, and was delighted to find that he thought the idea a good one.

That was 1993. Since then I have made many more visits to Dharamsala, consolidating old friendships and making new ones. Those of the family who live there could not have been more co-operative, and gradually I became immersed in their very different lives. The rags-to-riches-and-back-again theme is perennially fascinating, and there were so many facets to it. How do people cope with such huge and traumatic changes? How did an ordinary peasant family adapt to having a Dalai Lama in its midst? How did they learn to turn themselves into a royal family? How did they then cope with losing everything and becoming refugees? How did people steeped in the isolationism of the most mysterious land on earth adapt to life in a modern, bustling land such as India? How easily did they survive the culture shock of exchanging their own medieval world, unchanged through the centuries, for the dislocated post-modern societies of the West? Were they able to reinvent themselves, to find a role for themselves in these very different societies? Or did they themselves experience a certain dislocation?

The thread running through all their lives is, of course, Tibet. The various members of the Dalai Lama's family are linked together by their love of and loyalty to their country – and by their devotion to the Dalai Lama, to whom they refer as His Holiness, or Kundun – the Presence – rather than brother. Their lives are woven and meshed into the fabric of the Tibetan experience, the experience of a country, rich in its beliefs and culture, which was overthrown by a ruthless and powerful invader and is now threatened with the extinction of its identity. It is not possible to tell their stories without telling the story of Tibet.

This has been an absorbing book to research and write. If I have one regret at the end of it, it is that I came on the scene too late to meet the remarkable Dekyi Tsering (Amala), mother of the family and designated Great Mother of Tibet. The more I learned about her, the more I regretted not having met her. I have walked in her garden, lived in her house, even slept in the room where she died. I have a picture of her hanging in my hallway at home. But what wouldn't I give to have actually known her? The family were well blessed to have such a truly extraordinary woman as mother.

Mary Craig 1996

THE FAMILY OF THE DALAI LAMA, KNOWN AS THE YAPSHI TAKLHA FAMILY

CHOEKYONG TSERING (PALA)
1899–1947
*later known as Yapshi Kung,
the Kung, the Duke, and as
Gyayap Chenmo (Great Father)*

=

DEKYI TSERING (AMALA)
1900–1982
*known as Sonam Tsomo
(before her marriage) and later as
Gyayum Chenmo (Great Mother)*

TSERING DOLMA
1919–1964
*also known as
Achala (Elder
Sister)*
=
PHUNTSOK
TASHI

- TENZIN
  NGAWANG
  1941–1994
- KHANDO
  TSERING
  1945–

**THUBTEN
JIGME NORBU**
1922–
*known at differ-
ent periods as
Cho-la (Elder
Brother), Jigme,
Taktser Rinpoche
and Norbu*
=
KUNYANG

- LHUNDUP
  NAMGYAL
- KUNYA
  GYALTSEN
- JIGME
  KUNDUN

**GYALO
THONDUP**
1928–
*often referred
to as GT*
=
ZHU DAN
*known as
Dekyi Dolkar*
D. 1986

- YANGZOM
  DOLMA(d.)
- TENZIN
  KHEDUP
- NGAWANG
  TEMPA

**LOBSANG
SAMTEN**
1933–1982
=
NAMGYAL
LHAMO
*known as
Namlha*

- TENZIN
  CHUKI
- TENZIN
  NAMDHAK

**LHAMO
DHONDUP**
1935–
*His Holiness the
Fourteenth Dalai
Lama, also referred
to as Kundun,
Tenzin Gyatso,
Yeshi Norbu*

**JETSUN
PEMA**
1940–
=
(1) LHUNDUP
GYALPO
D. 1984

- TENZIN
  CHOEDON
- KELSANG
  YANGZOM
- TENZIN
  CHOEDHAK

(2) TEMPA
TSERING

**TENDZIN
CHOEGYAL**
1946–
*also referred
to as Ngari Rinpoche
and TC*
=
RINCHEN
KHANDO

- TENZIN
  CHOEZOM
- TENZIN
  LODOE

Death of a Dalai Lama

In my lifetime conditions will be as they are now, peaceful
and quiet. But the future holds darkness and misery. I have
warned you of these things.

The Last Political Testament of the Thirteenth Dalai Lama

On the twenty-second day of the tenth month of the Year of the Waterbird
(roughly 17 December 1933 on the Western Calendar), Choekyong Tsering, a farmer from the village of Taktser in the far north-east of Tibet, rode
home from market with news that would plunge his family and neighbours into deep shock. Thubten Gyatso, the Thirteenth Dalai Lama, secular and spiritual ruler of Tibet, was dead.

Arguably the greatest of all the Dalai Lamas, Thubten Gyatso had 'returned to the Heavenly Fields' at the age of fifty-eight after being ill for
only twelve days with what had seemed like an ordinary cold. A strong-
minded champion of his country's independence, he had ruled Tibet as a
benevolent autocrat since 1895. In 1911, after a Revolution in China
which had deposed the Manchu Emperor, he had lost no time in declaring
Tibet's independence from China, and thereafter distanced himself steadily from the new Chinese Republic, preferring to form closer ties with the
Government of Great Britain in India.[1] A political realist at the helm of a
near-medieval, semi-feudal theocracy, he was aware that if Tibet was to
survive, it must come into the modern age; and had forced through a
number of reforms in the teeth of fierce opposition from an entrenched

monastic and aristocratic Establishment. He had overhauled Tibet's anti-quated penal system and abolished capital punishment; standardized taxa-tion; extended education; introduced electricity, postal services, telegraph and telephone systems and a mint for producing currency. He had reorga-nized the small Tibetan army along British lines,[2] having its military bands play such un-Asian tunes as 'It's a Long Way to Tipperary', 'Auld Lang Syne' and 'God Save the King',[3] and adopting British words of com-mand for its drill. One way or another, the Thirteenth Dalai Lama had been determined that his country should be able to hold its own in the modern world. Had he lived a few years longer, who knows what the sub-sequent history of Tibet might have been?

In 1931, two years before his untimely death, the Great Thirteenth had published an urgent warning to his countrymen (aimed, more specifically, at the officials and the powerful monks) that preserving Tibet's indepen-dence in the modern world would require selflessness and dedication. The future lay in their hands:

> I urge you all to rise up together and work for the common good in accordance with your individual capacity...Together we can win out in the end. Avoid ri-valry and petty self-interest, and look instead to what is essential.[4]

Warning that the recent spread of revolutionary Communism to neigh-bouring Mongolia posed a threat to Tibet, and describing how monasteries (and monks) there were being destroyed, he prophesied:

> It will not be long before we find the red onslaught at our own front door. It is only a matter of time before we come into a direct confrontation with it, ei-ther from within our own ranks or else as a threat from an external (Commu-nist) nation.
>
> And when that happens we must be ready to defend ourselves. Otherwise our spiritual and cultural conditions will be completely eradicated.[5]

This prophecy, followed so closely by its author's death, struck fear into the hearts of the Tibetans. Until now, they had believed themselves pro-tected by the impregnable mountain ranges which surrounded them. If their mountains could no longer protect them, who then could save them?

But in Tibet's capital, Lhasa, the predominant emotion was grief. Losing a Dalai Lama was, for this most religious people on earth, like losing an important part of themselves. Whole families went into mourning, weep-ing openly on the streets:

the drums on the Potala Palace roof beat a sorrowful dirge, spreading the news...throughout Lhasa. Prayer flags and other house decorations were taken down, and people dressed in traditional mourning: dark colours, with no aprons and no ear-rings or other jewellery. Singing, dancing and playing music were banned, butter lamps burned on household altars and on house roofs, and people offered prayers in the holy Tsuglakhang Temple.[6]

When the traditional 49-day period of mourning was over and people resumed their normal lives, there was still, as one man wrote, 'a place in our hearts which was empty, and we prayed and hoped he would return to us soon'.[7]

Already there was speculation about where and how soon the dead leader's reincarnation would be found. In Buddhist belief, rebirth follows death: a good life merits rebirth on to a higher plane of existence, (a bad one on to a lower), until at last goodness may lead to enlightenment – the realization of things as they actually are, without delusion – and absorption into the light of Ultimate Reality. Human beings who have reached the enlightened state yet choose to go on being reborn in order to help others to reach it are known as *bodhisattvas*; and every Dalai Lama is a *bodhisattva*. Each one is a reincarnation of his predecessor, a re-embodiment of Chenrezig, the Lord of Mercy and Compassion, the patron deity of Tibet, who centuries ago vowed to continue returning to earth in human form until all sentient beings were saved.[8] Each Dalai Lama has the power to choose where and to whom he will be reborn.

What fortunate Tibetan couple would, probably in a few months' time, give birth to the boy-child in whom the spiritual consciousness of the late leader would once again be incarnated? Where and how would he be found? Every pregnant woman in the land must have prayed she might be the chosen one.

Since to the Western mind, the whole Dalai Lama business seems unutterably exotic, it may help to look briefly at how the institution came into being and what it had come to mean. The Dalai Lamas do not stretch back into the mists of time, they have been around only since the sixteenth century; and their story is tied up with that of their country.

The Tibetans emerged with a flourish on to the world scene in the early seventh century, when their king, Songtsen Gampo, invaded the Chinese Empire and laid the foundations of what was to become one of the most powerful nations in Asia. Over the next two centuries, the Tibetan Empire came to include Nepal, Bhutan, Upper Burma, Turkestan and parts of Western China. In AD 763, showing a military genius matched only by that of Genghis Khan and his successors four centuries later, Tibetan armies marched to the gates of the Chinese capital (present-day Xian) and dictated terms of peace to the emperor, exacting from him an annual tribute of fifty thousand rolls of silk. A later peace treaty signed between the two countries in AD 821 did not, as the Chinese claim today, result in some kind of 'union' between them. On the contrary, its principal passage makes it quite clear that here were two separate, equally powerful empires:

> Tibet and China shall abide by the frontiers of which they are now in occupation. All to the east is the country of great China; and all to the west is, without question, the country of great Tibet. Henceforth, on neither side shall there be waging of war nor seizing of territory...
>
> This solemn agreement has established a great epoch when Tibetans shall be happy in the land of Tibet, and Chinese in the land of China.[9]

Long before the seventh century, wandering holy men from India had brought Mahayana Buddhism to Tibet[10] – but its impact had been slight. The real spark to Tibet's future[11] came from King Songtsen Gampo's two Buddhist wives, Wen Chang, a Chinese princess, and Bhrikuti, a Nepalese. The Chinese bride brought as part of her dowry a large bronze statue of Buddha which had originally come from India. To house it, a temple (the Jokhang, meaning House of the Lord) was built in Lhasa and became one of the most sacred sites in the whole of Asia. Having converted the king, his wives spread the Buddhist teachings wherever they went. Though still little more than a court religion, with the weight and prestige of the State behind it, Buddhism slowly and painfully absorbed and displaced Tibet's indigenous shamanism, Bön. The monastic system which would eventually give the country its political and cultural identity was established.

This golden age of Tibetan history ended in about AD 914, when a usurper king suppressed Buddhism and brought about the monarchy's collapse. For about three hundred years Tibet disintegrated into a ferment of feuding kingdoms. Yet somewhere along that chaotic road, Buddhism made a spectacular comeback, reintroduced in the eleventh century by the Indian scholar-saint, Atisha. By the twelfth century, it was universally adopted. Tibetans turned their backs on their martial past and became the sole inheritors of the peaceful Buddhist tradition, which, under Muslim pressure, had already disappeared from North-West India and Central Asia.[12]

In the early thirteenth century, Tibet came into the orbit of the legendary Genghis Khan, becoming part of the huge Mongol Empire which came to dominate most of Asia and much of Europe besides. That the Mongols did not actually invade Tibet – apart from the north-eastern area nearest to Mongolia – was mainly because the Tibetans achieved a sort of symbiotic relationship with the Khans: spiritual teaching in exchange for military protection. This Chö-Yon (priest/patron) relationship, in which neither party was considered superior to the other – suited the needs of both. When, a few decades later, the great Kubilai Khan conquered the Chinese Empire and made it the centre of his Yuan Dynasty he embraced Tibetan Buddhism for himself and his court and continued the relationship on the same mutually acceptable terms. This is the basis of China's present insistence that Tibet is part of China, yet it is a fact that no Mongol ruler ever made any attempt to impose direct rule over Tibet. 'Tibet did not even pay tax to the Mongol Empire, and it certainly was never considered part of China by the Mongol Emperors.'[13] Ten years before the end of the Mongol Dynasty in China (1386) Tibet had severed its political ties with the Empire, though the priest/patron relationship with the Mongol Khans remained.

A century passed and Tibet again relapsed into civil disorder, while in the monasteries discipline grew slack. A saviour came on the scene in the fourteenth century: Tsong-khapa (1357–1419), a monk from the north-eastern Amdo region. Tsong-khapa reasserted a long-lost monastic discipline, built the Ganden monastery outside Lhasa, and unified Buddhist doctrine by drawing up a canon of written scriptures to replace the hither-to oral tradition. Those who adopted Tsong-khapa's reforms were known as Gelugpa or Virtuous Ones – their aim being a life of simple austerity, in tune with the teachings of the Buddha.

Tsong-khapa was succeeded as head of the Gelugpa sect by one of his disciples, and it was after the latter's death in 1475 that the *tulku* system which came to be the hallmark of Tibetan Buddhism was finally established. For almost two hundred years the Tibetans had believed that the spiritual essence of holy men or great teachers (known as lamas)[14] was reincarnated in their successors who then became known as Incarnations or *tulkus*.[15] This now became an article of faith.

The *tulku* system was raised a notch higher in 1517 when the Tibetan teacher Sonam Gyatso converted Altan Khan, a descendant of the Great

Kubilai. At the court of the Khan, the warrior chieftain and the lama swore eternal friendship and bestowed magnificent titles on each other, Sonam Gyatso receiving that of Dalai Lama, a Mongolian term meaning Broad Ocean – interpreted to mean 'the teacher whose wisdom is as vast as the Ocean'.

Accepting the title not only for himself but also retrospectively for his two predecessors, Sonam Gyatso would henceforth be known as the Third Dalai Lama. The title remained a purely spiritual one until 1642 when, after a vicious civil war in Tibet, another Khan, Gushri, installed the energetic and visionary Fifth Dalai Lama as the first King of a unified Tibet, investing him with absolute secular as well as spiritual power. To consolidate his position, the new ruler made his way to Peking, where the Manchu (Ch'ing) Dynasty had recently been established. He was received as both sovereign and equal. It is recorded that the Emperor of China 'went out of his capital to meet his visitor, and that he had an inclined pathway built over the city wall so that the Dalai Lama could pass into the city without going through a gate in the wall, for pedestrians use the walls of Peking and it was felt to be unfitting that His Holiness should pass beneath a place trodden by people's feet'.[16]

The Fifth Dalai Lama – 'the Great Fifth' – was thus the first in a new line of religious kings, the first to be called His Holiness the Ruler. It was he who put Lhasa on the map and restructured the whole Tibetan system of government, ensuring that from now on all positions of importance would be filled jointly by lay officials and monks.

Few of his successors, however, lived long enough to enjoy power – for two centuries after the death of the Great Fifth in 1682, no Dalai Lama ruled Tibet for more than a few years.[17] Since they were discovered as young children, usually from peasant or middle-class families, a Regent was appointed to rule until they were old enough to take over, usually at the age of eighteen. The Regents acquired considerable power – which they were disinclined to relinquish when the time came. Could it have been coincidental that between the seventh and thirteenth holders of the office, only one ('the Great Thirteenth') reached his majority? It was generally assumed that the others were poisoned by the reigning Regent – with a little help from the Chinese who would naturally prefer a Regent who was secretly on their pay-roll to an unknown who was king, pope and incarnate god rolled into one. The Great Thirteenth himself had survived an assassination attempt shortly after his accession. In what has been described as 'the case of the accursed shoes',[18] the retiring Regent apparently attempted to regain power through black magic, preparing a powerful mantra which consisted of the figure of a man with outstretched arms and legs. Surrounding this figure were various written mantras and inside its body the words *Thubten Gyatso* and *chiwa* were written: Thubten Gyatso was the personal name of the Thirteenth Dalai Lama and *chiwa* was his birth year. This black mantra was put inside the sole of a beautiful pair of new boots.[19]

It is unclear whether the boots were actually sent to the Dalai Lama, though his British friend, Sir Charles Bell (the Government of India's Political Officer in Sikkim) believed they were.[20] At all events, the 22-year-old ruler knew there had been an attempt on his life and that his ex-Regent was implicated. The latter was placed under house-arrest and soon afterwards he too mysteriously died![21]

Given this inauspicious start to the Great Thirteenth's reign, it was hardly surprising that his sudden death should herald accusations of foul play. The young monk, Kunphela, a favourite of the late ruler, and in the running for the job of Regent, found himself arrested on suspicion of poisoning his master. Though the case against him remained unproved, he was sentenced to exile for life.

The Great Thirteenth's warnings about the future were well founded. After the overthrow of the Empire in China, the first attempt at democracy by the ruling Kuomintang (KMT, Nationalist) Party had disintegrated into civil conflict, with a number of warlords striving for power. The Chinese Communist Party had been formed in 1921, and Chiang Kai-shek, who became leader of the Kuomintang in 1926, at first supported them. But Chiang had turned on the Communists, and was now engaged in a fight to the death with them. The danger, as the Great Thirteenth well knew, was coming closer.

But the warnings went unheeded, his death in 1933 being followed by a bitter power-struggle in Tibet, with rival groups striving to have their own candidate declared Regent by the National Assembly.[22] Though it was known that the late ruler had hoped for the appointment of a Regent with some knowledge and understanding of the larger world outside, the monk die-hards in the Government insisted that Regents must continue to be incarnate lamas chosen from one of The Three Seats, the powerful Lhasa monasteries, Drepung – the largest, with 10,000 monks, Sera (about 7500), or Ganden (6000) – i.e. from men totally lacking in worldly or administrative know-how. A young, inexperienced Incarnate named Ret-ing was selected by lottery – a choice tragic in its consequences. Under his leadership, the reforms of the Great Thirteenth would go to the wall; the economic surpluses would disappear, the ethical standards would slip and the efficient little British-style army would be left to disintegrate, with its trained officers sidelined into civil jobs.

But, in those early days after the Thirteenth Dalai Lama's death, these matters seemed of little importance beside the two urgent tasks facing the new Regent: first, to build a splendid gold mausoleum in memory of the late ruler; and then, most important of all, to undertake the search for his successor.

NOTES

1. In 1910, the Chinese had occupied Tibet's capital, Lhasa, and the Dalai Lama had fled to British India to avoid capture. While there he formed a deep and abiding friendship with the Political Officer for Sikkim, Sir Charles Bell.

2. Nobody had known which army model to choose. The Thirteenth Dalai Lama employed a few foreign instructors, and had one regiment trained by the Russ-ian instructors, another by the Japanese and a third by the British. The British model proved to be the most viable.

3. This was also used as the Tibetan National Anthem.

4. *The Last Political Testament of the Thirteenth Dalai Lama*, trans. Glenn H. Mullin.

5. *The Last Political Testament of the Thirteenth Dalai Lama*.

6. Melvyn C. Goldstein, *A History of Modern Tibet, 1913–1951: The Demise of the Lamaist State*, University of California Press, 1989.

7. Jamyang Norbu, *Warriors of Tibet: the story of Aten and the Khampas' fight for the freedom of their country*, Wisdom Publications, 1979, repr. 1986.

8. The *Bodhisattva* prayer is as follows:
   For as long as space endures,
   And for as long as living beings remain
   Until then may I, too, abide
   To dispel the misery of the world.

9. Hugh E. Richardson, *Tibet and its History*, Appendix 1, Shambhala, 1984.

10. Mahayana Buddhism is based on unselfishness and compassion for all sentient beings, and on the belief in karma, the law of cause and effect which says that

whatever happens to us is the result of our actions in the past. Sentient beings are condemned by karma to be reborn within a world of pain and suffering until they achieve enlightenment. This comes through the practice of patience, tolerance, kindness and compassion, combined with a 'right' way of seeing things as they are.

11. Louis Magrath King, Historical Introduction to *We Tibetans* by Rinchen Lhamo, Potala Books, 1985.

12. See David Snellgrove and Hugh Richardson, *A Cultural History of Tibet*, Prajna Books, 1980.

13. *Tibet, A Source Book*, All-Party Indian Parliamentary Forum for Tibet, 1994.

14. Westerners often speak as though 'lama' is just another name for 'monk'. It is true that some lamas are monks. But not all monks are lamas, for to become a lama (teacher, spiritual guru) takes twenty to twenty-five years of study. It is a peculiarly Tibetan Buddhist belief that important lamas are reincarnated and can choose the manner of their rebirth.

15. The *tulku* system had been developed in an attempt to maintain the authority of the highest priesthood, which was celibate, and to ensure that the 'wisdom memory' of those who had been enlightened was not lost. It incorporated the belief that those who become fully realized, enlightened persons can choose to return to life again and again in order to help all living beings.

16. Magrath King.

17. See Goldstein, chapter 1.

18. W. D. Shakabpa, *Tibet: A Political History*, Potala Books, 1984, p. 195.

19. Shakabpa, p. 195.

20. Sir Charles Bell, *Portrait of the Dalai Lama*, London, 1946.

21. 'Demo Rinpoche . . . is said to have been killed by being immersed in a huge copper vat until he drowned.' Goldstein, chapter 1.

22. In the Tibetan system of government, the Dalai Lama – or the Regent during his minority – was at the top of a pyramid. He was assisted by a Cabinet, known as the Kashag, consisting of four ministers, of whom three were laymen and one – the most senior – a monk. Next in importance came the National Assembly, a Parliament which was summoned by the Kashag only at times of grave national emergency. It consisted of fifty lay and monastic officials and was presided over by a Council of four senior monks. (Its deliberations were based not only on civil law but also on Buddhist moral law and so focused not only on the people's material well-being in this life but also on their spiritual welfare in the next.) Lay ministers and all Government officials were appointed from land-owning families – the latters' tenure of land being subject to their

providing at least one member of the family for unpaid Government service. Tibet was therefore ruled jointly by high lamas and the two hundred aristocratic families of Tibet, the one group providing checks and balances on the other.

2

The Search

> The connection of every Tibetan with the Dalai Lama is a
> deep and inexpressible thing. To us, the Dalai Lama symbol-
> izes the whole of Tibet: the beauty of the land, the purity of
> its rivers and lakes, the sanctity of its skies, the solidity of its
> mountains, and the strength of its people. But even more, he
> is the living embodiment of the eternal principles of Bud-
> dhism, and also the epitome of what every Tibetan, from the
> most debauched harlot in Lhasa to the saintly ascetic, is
> striving for – freedom, the total freedom of Nirvana.
>
> *Jamyang Norbu, Warriors of Tibet*

The search for a new Dalai Lama is an undertaking without parallel anywhere else in the world. The succession is neither hereditary nor elective;
with every Dalai Lama a fresh start is made. The quest begins within
about a year of the former ruler's death. But it is not straightforward. It is
not, as Basil Gould[1] tried to explain to a doubtless bemused British Government in 1941,

> a case of considering which of many children born at or about a certain time
> would be likely to make a suitable successor but of searching – as it were for a
> hidden treasure – for a child, exact age unknown, whose whereabouts would
> be indicated by divination and by signs and whose identity would be revealed
> by the possession of certain bodily characteristics and of marvellous mental
> and spiritual powers.[2]

In 1934, the Tibetan Government instructed its local authorities to look out for any remarkable boy-babies in their areas, particularly if they displayed the characteristic marks of a Dalai Lama:

> the legs' skin ought to be striped as a tiger's; the eyes wide and the brows turned outwards; the ears large; two fleshly excrescences should be found near the shoulder-blades, as a token of the two extra arms of Chenrezig, the god whose earthly embodiment the Dalai Lama is supposed to be; last, the palms should bear the pattern of a sea-shell.[3]

The late ruler had left certain clues of his own. His body was embalmed, clothed in rich gold brocades and seated cross-legged on his throne in the Norbulingka Palace, facing towards the south. All that day the people of Lhasa filed past, offering white ceremonial scarves in homage. Next morning, the attendants noticed that the head of the corpse had turned several degrees towards the north-east. Gently they returned it to its original position, and all through that second day the people continued their mournful file-past. Next morning, the head had once again slewed round towards the north-east.

Was it a sign that the reincarnation would be found in the north-east? Over the next few months, a succession of omens seemed to reinforce the message.

> The three state Oracles turned eastward in trance...a patch of snapdragons sprouted from the east end of the platform used for public sermons in Lhasa's main square; overnight a giant star-shaped fungus grew on the east side of the north-east pillar of the shrine in the Potala where the Dalai Lama's jewel-inlaid tomb was under construction. And as had frequently happened in the past when a high incarnate lama died, the people of Lhasa beheld auspicious cloud formations, now and again pierced by rainbows, rising over the barren wall of mountains ringing the north-east end of the city.[4]

In old Tibet, such signs and wonders were part of the very fabric of life.

When 1934 and part of 1935 passed without news, despondency grew in Lhasa and throughout Tibet. Then in the summer of 1935 Regent Reting and a party of high officials made a pilgrimage to the sacred lake of Lhamoi Lhatso, about ninety miles south-east of Lhasa. Mountains and lakes were held in awe in the land of mystery and magic that was Tibet, for they seemed to radiate a supernatural life of their own; they were reputed to put strange thoughts into the head and fill the ear with sounds. Some lakes were so numinous that they were consulted as oracles. Of them all, the mountain lake Lhamoi Lhatso inspired the most awe, and was always consulted about the whereabouts of the next Dalai Lama. For its guardian spirit was the goddess Palden Lhamo, who had promised the first Dalai Lama in a vision that she would watch over his successors. (Almost sixty years earlier the birthplace of the Great Thirteenth had been indicated in this same lake.)

Different people saw different things in the still blue waters – and some, it must be said, saw nothing at all. On this occasion, Regent Reting had a vision. But he kept quiet about it until the following year, by which time he had had time to reflect on what he had seen and to discuss its possible meaning with a few selected lamas and Oracles. Summoning the National Assembly, Reting announced that in the lake of Lhamoi Lhatso he had seen, clearly delineated, three Tibetan letters, *ah*, *ka* and *ma*; a monastery with roofs of jade-green and gold, with a twisting road leading eastwards to a bare pagoda-shaped hill and a small one-storey house with oddly-shaped guttering and turquoise tiles. He said he was now sure that the letter Ah stood for the province of Amdo in the north-east, a huge area populated mainly by Tibetans but currently ruled over by a Muslim warlord in the name of Nationalist China.

The Regent's words caused a stir. Although the earlier signs had all pointed to the possibility of the rebirth taking place in the north-east, some of the delegates were appalled at the idea of sending a search party into an area currently under the control of China. The question of the Tibetan borderlands was explosive, and some of the delegates saw no point in handing China a tailor-made excuse to meddle in Tibet's affairs. But a sacred vision was a sacred vision, and in the end the Assembly agreed that a search party must go to Amdo.

In the autumn of 1936, therefore, three teams of about forty set off for eastern Tibet, each of them led by a high lama and including both monks and lay government officials. They were despatched across the rugged Tibetan plateau, one to Amdo in the north-east, another due east and a third to the south-east, each group charged with identifying two or three likely boys and bringing them back to Lhasa for a final selection. It might well be years before any of them returned.

Over the next two years the Lhasa grapevine buzzed with reports that three, five or even more boys had been discovered in this, that or the other place. The Regent and his Government stayed silent.

Could there be many Tibetan baby boys with tiger-striped legs, long eyes, big ears, extra flesh on the shoulder-blades and a conch-shell imprint on the palm of their hand? Unlikely though it would seem, when the search party reached Amdo in the winter of 1936 they heard of several.[5] They learned from the Panchen Lama, Tibet's second highest spiritual leader, who was now in Amdo,[6] that during a public blessing ceremony at the Kumbum Monastery, he had picked out three possibles. And despite the strong suspicion that the Chinese might have been whispering in the Panchen Lama's ear, nevertheless, the advice of so august a figure could not be disregarded.

After a delay caused by heavy snowfalls, the search party, headed by Kesang Rinpoche,[7] Abbot of Lhasa's Sera Monastery, set off for Kumbum – where, to their satisfaction, they saw the three-tiered pagoda-style building with the jade-green and gold roofs of the Regent's vision. Did the *ka*, the second letter of that vision, stand for Kumbum? If so, all that was now needed was to identify a twisting road leading eastwards, a bare hill and a house with unusual tiles and guttering – and their mission might well be over.

After about six weeks they had amassed twelve names plus the three on the Panchen Lama's list. Of these three, one turned out to have died, but the other two were very serious, top-priority contenders. One was two-year-old Lhamo Dhondup, youngest son of the Amdo farmer, Choekyong Tsering, from the village of Taktser.

Taktser lay high on the Tibetan plateau, about nine thousand feet above sea-level, one of six villages under the jurisdiction of Kumbum monastery and lying on the caravan route between Siling, the seat of the Chinese administration, and Amdo's second largest monastery, Tashi Tashikiel. Along this route, in the winter of 1937, Kesang Rinpoche and his retinue slowly picked their way, having first visited Siling to pay their respects to General Ma Pu-feng, the wily Muslim warlord who ruled the area in China's name. They had decided on their plan of action: they would pose as traders, and on reaching the farmhouse where the child lived, Kesang Rinpoche's servant would pretend to be in charge, while the lama himself would dress as a servant, to gain easy access to the kitchen where the child would probably be playing.

Everything went as planned. The cavalcade approached Taktser, higher than the other villages round about, but otherwise a typical Amdo village with about thirty or so small-holdings jostling each other on a hillside, surrounded by bigger mountains and dominated by the snow- and ice-covered Mount Ami-chiri (or Kyeri). There, suddenly, was the pagoda-shaped hillock and facing it, among a group of three flat-roofed, white-washed buildings slightly higher than the rest, was the single-storey house they sought. With mounting excitement, they saw that it had turquoise tiles and strangely-shaped guttering made of gnarled juniper branches.

At the gate, decorated Tibetan-style with fluttering prayer-flags, the strangers were greeted by the farmer and his wife who offered them hospitality for the night. The 'leader', Lobsang Tsewang, was taken into the house, while his 'servant', Kesang Rinpoche, went into the kitchen. There he found two-year-old Lhamo Dhondup, who immediately ran to him and climbed onto his knee:

> The lama was disguised in a cloak lined with lambskin, but round his neck he was wearing a rosary which had belonged to the Thirteenth Dalai Lama. The little boy seemed to recognize the rosary, and he asked to be given it. The lama promised to give it to him if he could guess who he was, and the boy replied that he was Sera-aga, which meant, in the local dialect, 'a lama of Sera'. The lama asked who the 'master' was and the boy gave the name of Lobsang. He also knew the name of the real servant, which was Amdo Kesang.[8]

Gyalo Thondup, the child's nine-year-old brother, remembers the day clearly:

> With a group of about ten other boys from our village, I used to go to a Chinese school six miles away. We had a two hours' walk every morning and the same back again in the afternoon. On that day, I returned to find people and horses everywhere. I was fascinated by the sight of one tall, dark man wearing long ear-rings. Now in Amdo we did have some men who wore ear-rings, but none with long ear-rings like that. I'd never seen such a thing in my life. I dashed into the kitchen to ask my mother who all these people were. She said they were a group of travellers, businessmen, on their way to the Shartsong hermitage about fifteen miles away. They were Central Tibetans, she told me, rich traders travelling through this area via the Kumbum Monastery. There seemed to be a lot of servants and one of them stayed in the kitchen with my mother, helping her stack up logs for the stove, or carrying my little brother, Lhamo Dhondup, around the kitchen in his arms. My little brother seemed to have taken to him. My mother was busy making tea, heating water, preparing food for them all.[9]

Next morning, the 'traders' went on their way. When they returned soon afterwards, asking if they could again stay for one more night, they were greeted like old friends.

The searchers returned in triumph to their base at Kumbum Monastery and sent a coded telegram to Lhasa about their discovery. (The Panchen Lama's other remaining nominee had proved to be a nonstarter, bursting into tears and fleeing in terror at the sight of the monks – unlikely behaviour for a potential Dalai Lama!) In reply, they were told to continue their examination of the Taktser boy who sounded 'most interesting'.[10]

A few weeks later, as a stream of high lamas and dignitaries left Kumbum Monastery for phase two of the operation, three thousand monks blew a farewell on their conch-shell trumpets, a sound of good omen in Tibet. Just as they were approaching Taktser, they met a man who advised them to go by the lower road. This brought them by way of the little hermitage of Karma Rolpai Dorje on the hill above the village. Here the Thirteenth Dalai Lama had rested in 1909 on his way back to Lhasa after a four-year exile in Mongolia. He had been welcomed by the monks, and received homage from the villagers among whom had been the future farmer Choekyong Tsering, then nine years old. It was recalled that, gazing down on the village below, the Great Thirteenth had remarked on the beauty of the place. He had even left behind a pair of boots, as if intending to return.[11] It occurred to more than one of the searchers that it was not at Kumbum but here at Karma Rolpai Dorje that they had found the *ka, ma* of the Regent's vision, the place to which the Great Thirteenth wanted to return.

It was afternoon when the procession reached the farmhouse. Approaching the front entrance, they mentally registered the turquoise tiles and gnarled guttering, and asked to see the child. The farmer and his wife, awe-struck by the size and grandeur of this cavalcade, had already begun to wonder if perhaps Lhamo Dhondup, like his older brother, Jigme, might be the reincarnation of some great lama. They had always felt the child was special, but it would almost certainly not have occurred to them that he might be the most special reincarnation of them all.

'When they came back that time,' remembers Gyalo Thondup,

we noticed something very strange. The old servant wasn't a servant any more; and the young man who was supposed to be in charge was no longer in charge but seemed to be acting as assistant to the old man. It seemed as though the old man was actually in charge of the whole party. It was very puzzling – until they disclosed their real identity and purpose to my parents. They said my little brother was just possibly the reincarnation of the late Dalai Lama and they asked my parents' permission to put him to the test. Well, of course, they agreed without hesitation. They felt very privileged. The group then went into the kitchen where my little brother was delighted to see his old friend again.[12]

Everything was done according to time-honoured practice. Children considered as possible reincarnations of high lamas are generally expected to remember objects and people from their previous lives and can often recite scriptures they cannot possibly have seen or heard. In this case, the tests involved matched pairs of articles, one of which had belonged to the late Dalai Lama. 'A Living Buddha, thus returning to earth,' explains Sir Charles Bell, 'proves his identity by recognizing his rosary, bell and other religious implements, as well as servants, ponies, etc. that were with him in his previous existence.'[13] So, pairs of articles were laid out on a long trestle table in the farmhouse. They included two black and two yellow rosaries. When the boy was brought in and asked to choose, he chose the two that had belonged to the late ruler.

Next day, they offered him the late Dalai Lama's walking-stick and Kesang Rinpoche's. He looked carefully at these and started to take the fake one. The search team thought he was going to make a mistake, but the boy changed his mind, put the wrong one back and took the correct one. Later, when they thought about this near miss, they realized that the duplicate walking-stick had in fact also belonged to the Dalai Lama, who had given it to a lama, who had in turn given it to Kesang Rinpoche. So the Taktser boy had made no mistake in the three tests. The last test involved the small *damaru* drum the Thirteenth Dalai Lama had used to summon his servants. It was very plain, while the duplicate one was spectacularly beautiful, with ivory, gold and turquoise and a long, multi-coloured brocade tassel. Kheme later said he was very nervous about this test. However, the child again chose correctly, taking it immediately in his right hand and beginning to play it.[14]

His mother, in conversation with a friend, recalled the incident of the drum:

When the time came for me to take him to bed he clutched a small drum which the Thirteenth Dalai Lama had used for calling his attendants, and he beat it exactly as the monks do during prayers. He refused to be parted from it, and I was much embarrassed by the self-will shown by my usually biddable child. The lamas, however, told me to let him keep it.[15]

By now the men from Lhasa were in no doubt at all that they had found the child they were seeking. (He even had the tiger-striped legs and significantly large ears.) But when they returned a few days later to Kumbum, they dared not admit the fact, since the last thing they wanted was for the Chinese authorities in Siling to suspect the truth just yet. Unfortunately, there was only one telegraph line in Tibet, and as it was routed via the trading station, Kalimpong, in India, messages took a long time to get through. And although their telegram to Lhasa elicited the coded reply that the Taktser boy was obviously the right one and should be brought forthwith to the Holy City, they knew very well that once Ma Pu-feng got wind of this, he would demand a king's ransom before he let the boy go, and even then would insist on a huge Chinese military escort to go with him to Lhasa.

The fact was that the Chinese, whose representatives in Lhasa the Great Thirteenth had promptly expelled in 1912 when the Manchu Empire collapsed, had long been looking for an excuse to return.[16] The Kuomintang Government of General Chiang Kai-shek had already attempted to re-assert Chinese influence over Tibet by sending an official condolence Mission to Lhasa after the Dalai Lama's death.[17] The Tibetan Government had wanted to refuse, but were persuaded by the senior monks that the Mission's purpose was purely religious. Such thinking was ludicrously naïve – the Mission's real objective being to find out whether, unlike the old Dalai Lama who had turfed them out, the new people in power might be intimidated or suborned back into the Chinese fold. Though General Huang Mu-sung, the Mission's leader, was reluctantly obliged to return home after delivering his condolences, he contrived to leave behind two officials with a wireless transmitter, the only one in the whole of Tibet.

Secrecy regarding the child was vital, though it is clear that the British in India knew what was going on. A coded telegram from the Government of India External Affairs Department to the Secretary of State for India on 6 June 1938 announced that, according to a usually reliable source, 'The reincarnation of the Dalai Lama has been discovered in Amdo country... [and that] steps are being taken to recognize the child officially'. A further telegram, dated 16 August, is more specific: the child has been located in the Kokonor area of Amdo, i.e. in Chinese territory:

IT IS HOPED THAT THE CHILD MAY BE BROUGHT SECRETLY TO TIBET DUR-
ING THE WINTER. MEANWHILE, FOR FEAR OF CHINESE INTERFERENCE,
GREATEST SECRECY IS BEING MAINTAINED AND IT IS POSSIBLE THAT AS A
PRECAUTION THE TIBETAN GOVERNMENT MAY ANNOUNCE THE DISCOVERY
OF SEVERAL POSSIBLE CANDIDATES.[18]

The Tibetans did indeed take this precaution; but one by one the other candidates were ruled out. None but Lhamo Dhondup had chosen even two
items on the list right – and he had made no mistakes at all. The Tibetans
were forced to admit to Ma Pu-feng that the Taktser boy had indeed done
rather better in the tests than the others, while insisting that candidates
from other regions had still to be considered and that no definite conclusion could be reached until all the finalists had been brought to Lhasa.

Ma, being nobody's fool, took precautions of his own. 'One day,' recalls
Gyalo Thondup,

> I came home from school to find a number of armed soldiers from Siling in-
> stalled there. They said they had come to take my parents and little brother
> away. I began to howl, because it meant that I was going to be left there on my
> own, but the soldiers didn't care. My mother was trying to make arrange-
> ments for my uncle and aunt next door to look after me. She was very upset
> and frightened; and I was bawling my head off. The officer in charge merely
> said he was obeying orders from the Governor General – to take my parents
> and younger brother to Siling. There could be no arguing with that. They left
> within a day or two. Of course, when Kesang Rinpoche heard what had hap-
> pened, he dashed straight down to Siling to see Ma Pu-feng. He learned to his
> relief that my family were not in prison, they were being housed in a rather
> nice guest-house in the town. Ma asked Kesang Rinpoche if the boy really was
> the Dalai Lama, but Rinpoche said that he was only one candidate and noth-
> ing had been decided yet. He asked Ma to release the family, to let them go
> back home or at least to Kumbum Monastery.

Shortly after that, the family took their youngest child to Kumbum, and a
group of riders was despatched to bring Gyalo Thondup from Taktser to
join them. He and his parents would soon afterwards leave the monastery
and go home, but two-year-old Lhamo Dhondup would not. His brief
childhood was already over.

NOTES

1. B. J. (later Sir Basil) Gould was British India's Political Officer in Sikkim, and as such had an advisory role in Bhutan and a 'vaguely diplomatic' one in Tibet. He was in Lhasa with a small British Mission from 1936 to 1937 and returned there in 1939 for the installation of the new Dalai Lama.

2. Report by Mr B. J.Gould, C.M.G., C.I.E., On the Discovery, Recognition and Installation of the Fourteenth Dalai Lama. White Paper for official use only, 1941.

3. Giuseppe Tucci, *To Lhasa and Beyond, Diary of the Expedition to Tibet in the year 1928*, Snow Lion Publications, 1983 (first published 1956).

4. John Avedon, *In Exile from the Land of Snows*, Michael Joseph, 1984.

5. Kham is the eastern part of Tibet, Do-kham or Amdo the north-east. Both areas are inhabited by the distinctive race of Tibetans known as Khampas.

6. The Panchen Lama's monastery of Tashilhunpo near Shigatse owned huge estates. It had never been the custom for landowners and big monasteries to pay much revenue to the Government, but because of the expense of maintaining a standing army, the Thirteenth Dalai Lama had revised the taxation system to collect money from both groups. For centuries the Chinese had made a point of playing off the Panchen Lama against the Dalai Lama, and had acquired influence in the former's court. After the Dalai Lama's flight to British India in 1910 (following a Chinese occupation of Lhasa), the Tashilhunpo officials became very friendly with the Chinese. When, later, the new taxes were imposed, they saw it as a kind of revenge, possibly the thin end of the wedge. So in 1923, the pro-Chinese courtiers ran away to China, and persuaded the 40-year-old Ninth Panchen to go with them. There was great disquiet throughout Tibet at this, the Tibetans fearing that the Chinese would exploit the situation and use it as a pretext for invading Tibet.

   In 1935, when it was known that the Panchen Lama wished to return home, this became a dangerous political issue, since the Chinese had obtained a large measure of control over him and his court and were insisting on his return to Tibet with a large Chinese military escort. This, of course, was seen by the Tibetans as illustrating China's determination to extend its influence over Tibet, and they were resolved to resist it. There was grave danger of a clash between the two countries, but the situation was defused both by the outbreak of the Sino-Japanese War in June 1937 and by the Ninth Panchen Lama's death while still on Chinese territory, on 1 December 1937.

7. An incarnate lama – *tulku* – is addressed as Rinpoche, or 'Precious One'.

8. Fourteenth Dalai Lama, *My Land and My People: Memoirs of the Dalai Lama of Tibet*, Potala, 1962.

9. Author interview with Gyalo Thondup, Dharamsala, July 1995.

10. Goldstein, *A History of Modern Tibet*, p. 318.

11. *My Land and My People.*

12. Author interview with Gyalo Thondup, Dharamsala, July 1995.

13. Bell, *Portrait of the Dalai Lama.*

14. Goldstein, p. 319.

15. Great Mother in conversation with Lady Gould, Isle of Wight, 1960, as reported to the author.

16. The Emperor's representatives or *ambans* had been expelled from Lhasa in 1912 after the fall of the Manchu Dynasty. The Thirteenth Dalai Lama had declared Tibet's complete independence of China.

17. The Chinese Nationalists took over the Imperial concept of an empire led by the majority Han Chinese, comprised of the Han and the four minority nationalities: Tibetans, Manchus, Mongolians and the Muslims of East Turkestan. The concept never wavered, even though Tibet, Manchuria and Outer Mongolia were functioning independently of China.

18. Oriental and India Office Collections, Political (External) Files and Collections, L/P&S/12/4178 File 15 (1). Death of the XIIIth Dalai Lama and question of successor, December 1933 – October 1940.

3

In the Land of Horses

For many in Tibet, material life was hard, but they were not
victims of desire; and in simplicity among our mountains
there was more peace of mind than there is in most of the
cities of the world.

The Fourteenth Dalai Lama

Amdo in the far north-east beyond the Yangtse River, was one of the three
provinces that traditionally made up Tibet: U-Tsang (Central Tibet), the
land of *dharma* – the theory and practice of Buddhism; Do-toe (Kham), the
land of people; and Do-may (Amdo), the land of horses. Like frontier-lands
everywhere, Amdo had had a chequered history. There, where the mountains of the high plateau swept down towards the plains of western China,
Tibet's borders were uncertain. It was a wild, windswept region of vast
steppes from which soared some of the highest mountains in the world; a
beautiful country of lush grasslands, conifer forests, giant rhododendron
bushes and innumerable salt lakes, one of which was the inland sea
known as Kokonor, the Blue Lake, so vast (97 km across) that a caravan
would take a month to cross it. To the Chinese, Kokonor was Ching 'hai;
they gave its name to the whole region and claimed it as their own.

Before the seventh century, the population had been entirely Tibetan,
but since then many Chinese and Chinese Muslims had come to the area,
and the indigenous Tibetans had moved up to ever higher altitudes. Since
the middle of the eighteenth century, the province had been ruled by

fiercely independent *gyalpos* (kings) and warlords often supported by China. (The Amdowas had not in fact been ruled as a united people by any one leader since the fall of the Tibetan Empire in the ninth century.)[1] At the time of the search for the Fourteenth Dalai Lama, the area was controlled by the Muslim warlord, Ma Pu-feng, ostensibly in the name of China, although in most respects he was answerable only to himself.

This is the area which Western scholars regard as the cradle of the Tibetan race. The majority of its people had never considered themselves Chinese, their culture and religious beliefs being unmistakably Tibetan, and their loyalty to the Dalai Lama never in doubt.

The Fourteenth Dalai Lama has a clear memory of this land of his childhood where sedge, rock jasmine, rhubarb and gentian grew on the steppes and many medicinal plants were found among the alpines that grew above the treeline:

> To the south of the village, there was a mountain that was higher than the rest. Its name was Ami-chiri, but the local people called it The Mountain Which Pierces The Sky, and it was regarded as the abode of the guardian deity of the place. Its lower slopes were covered by forests; above them a rich growth of grass could be seen; higher still, the rock was bare; and on the summit was a patch of snow which never melted. On the northern face of the mountain, there were junipers and poplars, peaches, plums and walnuts, and many kinds of berries and scented flowers. Clear springs of water fell in cascades, and the birds and wild animals – deer, wild asses, monkeys and a few leopards, bears and foxes – all wandered unafraid of man; for our people were Buddhists who would never willingly harm a living creature.[2]

Born into this earthly paradise, Lhamo Dhondup was the fifth surviving child of farmer Choekyong Tsering, whose family had lived in the area for many generations. (No one could move far away in a country without roads, where ponies and mules provided the only means of transport.) He had a sister sixteen years older than himself and three older brothers. The farmer had married seventeen-year-old Sonam Tsomo, oldest of the five daughters of Chodang Phuntsok Nima and his wife Dolma Tso from Churkha, a small village just south of Kumbum Monastery and twenty-five kilometres from Taktser. Sonam Tsomo was a good-natured, attractive girl with thick, black, glossy hair that was the envy of the other village girls. In accordance with Amdo custom, the families, both small, independent farmers, had arranged the marriage, though Sonam's grandparents were known to have protested that Taktser men worked their women too hard. Once the families had reached agreement, the astrologers were consulted, to make sure that the couple were compatible.[3] It took almost two years before they could agree on an auspicious date for the wedding. But eventually, the signs were judged to be right and on the eleventh day of the eleventh month of Fire Serpent Year (1917), Choekyong Tsering and Sonam Tsomo were married.[4]

The bride's preparations for her wedding day were laid down by tradition:

> One by one she slipped into silk blouses of red, green and white colours carefully selected to suit her complexion. Then she donned a jade-green chuba made of pure Mongolian silk and fashioned in the Amdo style. She combed her long black hair as usual into three plaits, two in the front and one in the back. From her ears she hung long ear-rings of coral, turquoise and silver. Finally, she put on a vase-shaped head-dress studded with jewels, which reached down to her waist. While she dressed, a neighbour sat cross-legged on a low, carpet-covered platform, singing traditional Amdo wedding songs in a deep, husky voice.[5]

First of all, a ceremonial engagement party took place in the altar room of the bride's house. Prayers were said, blessings invoked, and representatives of the groom's family presented a series of gifts to the bride's: tea, rice, butter, tsampa,[6] salt and lengths of silk. Most important was the *nurin* – 'breast-price' – symbolizing a payment to the bride's mother for having nourished her. The occasion was rounded off by much drinking of *chang*, the fermented barley-beer beloved of Tibetans. The guests agreed that the *chang* was so good it was in itself an auspicious sign.

That evening, a group of gaily-dressed horsemen came from Taktser to the bride's home, bringing with them a white mare on whose back the bride would be led to her new home after the wedding next day; plus a white stallion and a black heifer for her grandparents who, as senior family members, would accompany her. The leader of the group also carried the *sipaho*, an arrow-shaped banner with a painted scroll hanging from its point on which were astrological symbols depicting the stars and planets and mystical symbols for protection against evil spirits.

After a short service next day, in which a lama besought the household deity to accept the bride into her new family, the groom's representative 'touched the back of Sonam Tsomo's neck with an arrow decorated with five strips of different-coloured silk and announced to everyone present that from then on she belonged only to her husband'.[7]

The journey to the bridegroom's home, punctuated by cheerful farewell sessions with vast quantities of food and *chang* for friends and relatives along the route, took seven hours and was a very convivial occasion.

All this time, the bride, wrapped in a fur-lined cloak, kept her face covered, for the groom – whom she had not yet met – must be the first man to set eyes on her. At last the party reached Taktser and the square, single-storey farmhouse, built of stone and mud, and newly white-washed for the occasion. The door leading to the interior courtyard swung open to receive them; the bride dismounted on to a platform of barley and tea and was led across the flagstoned yard to a stack of wood, around which she walked three times in a clockwise direction:

> Moving to the kitchen door, she stood with her back to it, facing east as her horoscope had indicated, and proceeded to wash her face; then she went inside to make tea. Some of the guests tried to steal a look at her while praising the tea she had brewed, but she kept her face hidden behind one of the sleeves of her blouse, which had been cut quite full. A few mischievous older guests tugged playfully on her arm, saying, 'Let's have a look! We won't be here long, so let's see your face before we leave!' She was embarrassed but tried not to show it.[6]

Only after this, in a ceremony for family and friends in the altar room, was Sonam Tsomo placed beside her husband, and the couple set eyes on each other for the first time. She thought he was 'very handsome'; what he thought about her is not on record. Afterwards, they went up on to the roof to burn incense and offer prayers for the success of the marriage.

After three hectic days of dancing and feasting, Sonam Tsomo went back to Churkha with her family. She returned alone one month later and, on approaching the gate of her new house, was greeted by her husband's elder brother, holding a white porcelain bowl of milk:

> Into this she placed the thumb and fourth finger of her right hand, then withdrew them and flicked little droplets into the air three times. Then she went into the kitchen and brewed tea, the first steaming cup of which she placed on the altar as an offering. From that time on she was considered a regular member of the Taktser household, and the next day began to take part in the housework and other routines.[9]

The backcloth to her new life was a village like her own, mainly given over to pasturage – one village was much like another in Amdo. Since most Tibetans lived in villages separated by large distances (unlike the Chinese who tended to live in large, enclosed towns, with their farms on the outside), the people were sturdily self-reliant. The staple crops were wheat and barley; vegetables such as peas, potatoes, onions, turnips and radishes being also grown for domestic use. They drank butter-tea and *chang*, the barley beer. As in Churkha, the people of Taktser were simple peasant folk. The men all wore fur hats, high leather boots and the ubiquitous *chuba*, a voluminous outer garment belted just below the waist. The women wore long, sleeveless, woollen versions of the *chuba* with bright silk or cotton blouses.

Sonam Tsomo's new family was of pure Tibetan stock, their forefathers having reputedly come from Phenpo near Lhasa, part of the army sent by King Trisong Detsen in the middle of the eighth century to protect Tibet's frontiers against invaders. As the Amdo garrison had never been recalled, the soldiers' descendants had gone on living in the area, for centuries serving as unpaid, elected headmen of their villages. Though their speech was still peppered with words and phrases from the ancient Lhasa dialect, they spoke Tibetan in the Amdo dialect, which, since 1910 when the Chinese had reoccupied the area, now contained a strong admixture of Chinese.

The Taktser house was a large-ish farmhouse built for Sonam Tsomo's mother-in-law by her older brother, an important local *tulku* known as Taktser Rinpoche. Many years earlier, he had escaped with his life during a violent insurrection by local Chinese Muslims, in the course of which Kumbum Monastery and many of its surrounding villages had been destroyed. The farmhouse in which his family had lived for generations was burned to the ground, while he himself was hidden by a friendly Muslim butcher and enabled to escape to nearby Outer Mongolia disguised as a beggar. Discovering in himself the gifts of a natural healer, he achieved fame and fortune not only in Mongolia but in Tsarist Russia, returning eventually to Kumbum a wealthy man with a caravan load of treasures, including cuckoo clocks and musical boxes, the like of which the Tibetans had never seen. One of his first acts was to rebuild Kumbum Monastery, and then, finding his sister and her husband without a home, to restore the burned-out farmhouse.

This was now the family home. When the new bride arrived there, Taktser Rinpoche renamed her Dekyi Tsering, which means Ocean of Luck. (It was not unusual for a bride's name to be changed upon her marriage. Tibetan names can be frequently changed, usually on recovery from an illness, following the visit of a great lama, etc.) Her father-in-law, Tashi Dhondup, was a gentle, kind-hearted man, but her mother-in-law, Lhamo Dolma, a gaunt, pock-marked virago with a vile temper, was impossible to like.[10] Dekyi Tsering was scared of her and would sometimes run out of the house to escape her intolerable nagging. Within two years, however, both parents-in-law died and Choekyong Tsering became the owner of the farmhouse.

Nineteen-year-old Dekyi Tsering was used to hard work. At home, she and her sisters had worked in the fields, milked the cows, done the hundred-and-one household chores. They were a close-knit family and had shared their labours, sitting down together in the evening to sing as they sewed and mended a pile of clothes. But in Taktser, with more exhausting work and no companionship, the new bride found her grandparents' forebodings about Taktser men well justified. After a mere four hours' sleep, she would rise each morning before cock-crow to make a fire with juniper logs in the large brick stove in the kitchen. Over it she would set big copper kettles full of water for washing and for the morning tea. In Taktser, time was measured in the age-old manner, as her eldest son would write later:

> We did not need to measure time of day, but we needed to measure it for cooking. One method was to fill a special pot with water; the pot had a small hole in it, and it allowed the water to escape drop by drop. My mother would know to put in so much water to measure the time needed to cook such and such a meal. If we needed to be wakened up at such and such an hour, my mother would light a stick of incense of the right length. When it burned down to the end it would burn through a thread that held a stone above an old metal pot, and we would be awakened by the clanging and clattering as the stone fell. During the day we knew the hour by the sun, at night by the stars. Our lives in Tibet were spent without haste.[11]

Next she would go into the altar room, wash her hands, twist new wicks out of cotton, fill the containers with butter she had already melted over the stove, and light the butter-lamps. (All Tibetan families, even the very poorest, had an altar in their homes, and an image of the Buddha before which butter-lamps burned continuously.) With the rest of the household, she would perform the daily ritual of prostrating three times and saying prayers for the happiness of all sentient beings, before going outside and filling the clay incense burner in the courtyard with glowing coals and herbs such as dried Alpine roses. Only then could tea be served and the day begin.

At daybreak, Choekyong Tsering would lead his horses out to water. After breakfast, he went out to the fields, where, with the aid of three or four hired labourers and perhaps a mule or an ox, he grew barley, buck-wheat, oats, jute and potatoes. His wife, meanwhile, swept and garnished the house. There were six rooms: a large kitchen, the altar room, one bed-room, a guest room, a store-room for provisions and, at the back of the house, a cow byre. Next she prepared lunch for her husband and the other men and took it out to them in a basket carried on her back or in a shoul-der sling. That done, she would return home, exchange the basket for a water-carrier and fetch water from the well at the far side of the village. (In winter she would repeat this procedure more than twice a day and in sum-mer, often in appalling heat, at least four times.) She then churned butter and cooked the evening meal. In summer they lived mainly on vegetables and salad, a particular favourite being a kind of radish pickled in a tub with sour gherkins; in colder weather there was a thick vegetable soup known as *thukpa*, potatoes, tsampa and tea. Potatoes were eaten at almost every meal, but meat – mutton or beef – was a rare luxury, except in the autumn when the sheep were slaughtered, or occasionally in summer after the wolves had killed an animal and abandoned some of the carcass. The staple food, whatever the season, was tsampa, or barley-flour. Like Ti-betans everywhere, they ate it dry or mixed with liquid – milk or brick-tea specially brought from China[12] – into a kind of dough to which they added butter and salt.

The evening meal could take place only after the animals had been at-tended to. Whilst the farmer led the horses and mules out to drink, his wife would milk the cows in the stone-flagged byre at the back of the house. After the meal until round about midnight was the time for em-broidering, mending and baking. Dekyi Tsering baked bread rolls and pas-tries in an old iron tin scattered with glowing coals; and her reputation as a pastrycook was second to none in the village. As to her sewing, it was said that she could have embroidered a bird on the wing.

The produce of the farmer's fields was used mainly to feed his family, the grain being ground in the mill by the village stream in nearby Balangt-sa. Choekyong Tsering would take it there, pulling the mule laden with the grain sacks behind him. (As payment he would give the miller one-tenth of the ground flour.) Occasionally he would trade grain or a few sheep with passing nomads, or barter them in the nearby markets of Siling or Kumbum for Chinese brick-tea, sugar, cotton fabric and iron tools. A kitchen garden provided them with peas, mustard, potatoes, tomatoes, garlic, onions, radishes and a few green vegetables. But as crops of any kind were liable to be ruined by heavy hailstorms or severe drought, families tended to rely on animals as a source of produce: a couple of yaks,[13] cows, sheep, goats, dzomos (a cross between a yak and a cow which gave a high yield of milk), free-range chickens and pigs.

And horses. Amdo produced what were arguably the sleekest, most powerful horses in the world; in the grasslands, horses were not a luxury but a way of life. They were Choekyong Tsering's passion; and he visited the horse-markets (entailing an absence of several days) whenever occasion arose. Dekyi Tsering had soon discovered that her husband, whom she had been warned was a wild, headstrong youth, overindulged by his doting mother, cared more for the horse-markets than for labouring in the fields. The sheer drudgery of the latter he preferred, where possible, to leave to the hired help. Not that he was idle – no Tibetan peasant was ever that. In the evenings, when his hands weren't busy with such routine tasks as spinning sewing-thread and making boot-laces, he would be passing a rosary through his fingers and murmuring prayers. But it seemed to his wife that horses were all he really cared about – his knowledge of horse-flesh being wedded to a rare talent for healing – and that most of the responsibility for house and family was left to her.

The couple had a total of sixteen children, of whom only seven survived beyond infancy. The first (born in 1919) was a girl, Tsering Dolma, born, as her brothers and sisters would be, on a straw pallet on the floor of the cow byre. (In Kham and Amdo, babies were always born in the place where the animals were kept.) Lhamo Dolma, the bad-tempered mother-in-law, was still alive and when the child turned out to be a girl, her disappointment was epic: 'When my mother had a daughter,' says Gyalo Thondup, 'my grandmother was so furious that she refused to eat, she just hid herself away and wept all day long. She would not speak to my mother or look at the child.'[14] It seems that she cried herself more or less literally to death!

Three years later (1922), when his grandmother was already dead, a son was born, an occasion, as everywhere in the East, for great rejoicing. His parents called him Tashi Tsering, but he does not remember ever being called by those names. As a small boy he was known as Cho-la, an honorific meaning 'Eldest Son'. Tibetan children are frequently not given their permanent names till later on, in connection with some great occasion. Until then, they may be addressed as 'Boy', 'Girl', 'Child' – or 'Eldest Son', 'Eldest Daughter'.

Cho-la (under his later name of Thubten Jigme Norbu, given to him by the Thirteenth Dalai Lama)[15] would one day write a moving account of his childhood in Taktser. If there was a family atmosphere there, the explanation was simple, he says: there were a lot of family members around – and, as in most Tibetan villages, people thought of themselves as related to each other even when they weren't.

> The Tibetan village is spread out among the fields and meadows. Each house has a stone wall around it, with a gate leading into an inner courtyard. Inside these courtyards the great black mastiffs are allowed to roam at night. Some houses are all by themselves, but mostly they cluster together, perhaps three or four of them separated from the next cluster by open country. In [Taktser] our own family cluster was the largest, having seven or eight houses in it. A number of the men were called 'brother' by my father, but they really were not. Their mothers I called 'Grandmother'. One was blind, and whenever I went to see her she let her hands feel all over my face as she talked to me. Another 'Grandmother', who lived next door, sometimes used to fight with her son's wife, and that used to give me bad dreams. But one in particular I liked to visit…She always carried her beads in her hand and when she was doing nothing else she would murmur invocations to the gods…I liked to play with her and try to take her beads away from her. Then she would put them in a bag and I would try to take the bag. She was old and very kind to us.[16]

Tsering Dolma was the apple of her father's eye, a tomboy who shared his passion for horses – though she was more like her mother in temperament, outspoken, hard-working and kind-hearted. When Cho-la was small, she used to carry him around on her back and as he grew older, huddled together under the bedclothes in the light of a flickering oil-lamp, she would tell him the stories and folk-tales she had heard from her mother and grandmother. Stories, for example, dating back to the fourteenth century, of the heroic Prince Gesar, the legendary prince of Ling, and the many wars and battles he waged against neighbouring tribes and kingdoms. The epic of Prince Gesar was immensely popular in eastern Tibet, abounding as it did with stories of valour and daring, with the gods, titans, demons and imps that Gesar – 'Great Lion of the World' – had to do battle with. A saga which harked back to the many wars in the Amdo region between

Tibetans and Chinese. The memories of these far-off battles still survived in Amdo in a number of significant placenames, such as Gyatrag-thang, Field of Chinese Blood, and Gyadu-thang, Field of Chinese Corpses. The Amdowas, so many of whom were descended from the old Tibetan warriors, had long memories.[17]

The children spent much time with their mother: their father was often away, and in any case women play a significant role in every Tibetan household. 'At first light she went up onto the flat roof of our house taking some charcoal or yak-dung fire with her, and when I was old enough I would go too. There she lit a little fire and made offerings of cedar or juniper wood, and of a little food such as tsampa flour, dried fruits and butter. Every house in the village did the same thing, and it is done all over Tibet each morning as the sun strikes the snowy peaks of the mountains. From every roof a wavering wisp of smoke rises up to the sky, and the air is filled with sweet smells and the sound of prayers.' When that was done, they came downstairs, their mother lit the butter lamp and put it on the altar where it burned all day. The whole family would gather there, morning and evening, for prayers.

Sometimes a monk would come to the house to say prayers. 'Then he would wash my sister and me with holy water, to remove all the bad things in us. My father used to like to invite him to stay for several days so that he could read from the religious books to us and do honour to our ancestors.' But the children were not expected to sit still and listen. Nobody minded if they ran off to play.

Religion was a focal point even in the children's play. They played at building temples of clay, arranging offerings in front of them and making the prostrations that they knew instinctively how to perform. One of their favourite places was the household shrine which stood in the main courtyard. 'It was a clay tower containing various sacred images, and it was the centre of certain rites concerning the protection of the home. It was equally the centre of attraction for my friends and me, and there was no place to play that we liked better. We were not particularly conscious of its religious significance – we were simply aware that somehow this was a warm and friendly place.'

With the other village children, Cho-la and Tsering Dolma would roam far and wide through woods and meadows which were green in summer and rich with wild flowers, deep in snow during the bitterly cold winters. Cho-la's childhood hero was the village shepherd to whose hire all the villagers contributed. 'Every morning when we were at breakfast he would pass our house with the village flocks and herds. Small groups of cows and sheep joined him from every yard as he passed on his way...Our sheep and cows would all be waiting impatiently in the yard to surge out and join him.'

The villagers' cattle were taken to pasture every day of the year, except on those winter days when violent snowstorms swept the land; yet even in mid-winter there was pasture, the winds being so fierce that they drove the snow off the meadows and enabled both cattle and sheep to find roots and herbs to feed on. Although Cho-la was strictly forbidden to follow the herdsman into the mountains where the sheep and cattle were grazing, as he grew older it was one of his favourite pastimes. Especially if his father was away, he and his friends would follow the herdsman like some Pied Piper, enjoying long days, free from parental interference, playing their wildest, noisiest games, exploring the treasures and secrets of the mountains. 'We all used to steal some food from our homes, some potatoes, dry bread and some cheese, put it in string bags and tie the bags to our waists. This way our hands were free.' On good days, when they felt hungry they would pick and eat the raspberries, strawberries and bilberries which at times grew in profusion in the woods. They would stay out all day, returning only when the herdsman brought the cattle back at dusk. As afternoon approached, and Cho-la thought of the inevitable scolding awaiting him at home, he would run and gather a few particularly luscious berries 'as a propitiatory offering for my parents'. The herdsman ignored the children; he would sit on a stone, lost in thought and looking dreamily up at the sky. 'And I would sometimes think I saw his lips move as though he were talking to the clouds, the trees, the birds and the water.' It was Cho-la's first introduction to the contemplative life; and the summit of his childhood ambition was to become the next herdsman of Taktser.

But mostly the children stayed in the courtyards of their houses, playing games like hopscotch and trials of skill involving coins, coloured stones and sheep's bones.

We also had a ball of wool into which we stuck hens' feathers, and this had to be kept in the air as long as possible by kicking it up with the instep. A kind of football game we played, with a leather ball stuffed with wool, was by no means difficult. The ball was supposed to be round but it never was.[18]

In winter, when for five months the ground was covered with snow, the children would build huge snowmen, with pieces of burnt wood for eyes; and on the mountainsides, they 'slid down the slopes so often that in the end we had slides as highly polished as mirrors'. Often they would make warm burrows for themselves in the haystacks left over from the autumn grain harvest. In fact, one of Cho-la's earliest memories is of 'a day in late autumn when all the colours in the fields and on the sides of the mountains were changing. My sister and I went into the fields to play almost every day because the straw that had been cut was piled up and we had made a little house by burrowing into the pile and making little rooms. Into one room we had brought some flat stones, making a table. Other smaller stones we used as dishes. This particular day, as usual, we brought a few grains of barley and some peas, and we pretended we were having our meal. But as winter was approaching it was cold even inside our straw house, so we lit a fire to keep us warm. Of course, the whole pile of straw was soon alight, and our parents came running to beat it out with sticks and blankets. We were more frightened of the beating we might get than of the danger, but everyone was too busy putting the fire out to do more than shout at us. We were never allowed to play in the straw again and it was the last house we made together.'[19]

Cho-la was in awe of his father – who had inherited his mother's unpleasant temper. At heart, he knew him to be a good-natured man who disliked having to punish his children – 'soon afterwards he would find some opportunity for surreptitiously giving me an apricot, or he would ask me casually if I would like to go with him to the fields'. But his father's temper was legendary and Cho-la, who was frequently in trouble, used to beg his mother to intercede for him. Once, however, even his mother disowned him. He had got hold of a very fine large potato which he decided to roast over the butter-lamp in the altar room. As soon as opportunity arose, he crept into the chapel and began his illicit cookery:

It was already beginning to bake on one side and a wonderful smell tickled my nostrils, when suddenly I heard footsteps in the covered way outside, and in a panic at the thought of being caught I made a sudden grab at the potato, knocking both it and the butter-lamp onto the floor where lay the open match-box which my parents used to light the lamp. The matches caught fire, and in an instant a big sheet of flame leapt up, and the spilled butter on the wooden floor began to burn too. I shrieked in my fright, and there was my mother to the rescue again. She had been about to hang clothes in the yard to

33

dry and instead she now used them to beat out the fire...When the job was done she turned on me with a face far more angry than I usually saw and gave me a couple of stinging clouts.[10]

Ashamed of himself and terrified of what his father would say – and do – when he came home, Cho-la fled to the neighbouring wood and stayed there until it grew dark and the night-owls started hooting. Then, even more frightened of the owls than of his father, he slunk homewards.

> When I got to the farmstead door I stood there for a while hesitating. I was afraid to knock. And then it suddenly opened, and there was my father on his way to search for his missing son. My distress didn't save me. He put me across his knee, bared my bottom, and with his hard and heavy hand he gave me a thorough drubbing. If I had set the house on fire as a result of my naughtiness I could hardly have been thrashed more thoroughly than I was because I had desecrated the sacred butter-lamp and the picture of Buddha before which it burned.

Today, 'Cho-la' is an old man and has forgotten many things. But he has never forgotten that particular night: the night-owls' screeching and the beating handed out by his father.

Though children under the age of ten were thought too young for hard labour in the fields, Tsering Dolma and Cho-la helped with such tasks as weeding, and in spring when their father ploughed the land, would follow him to gather up the sweet white tubers turned up by the ploughshare. Tsering Dolma helped her mother with the cooking and made sure the stove was adequately supplied with fuel. 'Sometimes we used yak dung, horse and sheep dung being used mainly in the fields, but we also had plenty of wood. It was not large wood, for we used to get it from the bushes that covered the hills near by, but it was good fuel and we were never without warmth.' It was a life filled with 'a hundred thousand pleasures', many of them four-legged. One of Cho-la's tasks was 'to take any food that was left over and mix it in a small bucket with some meat and bread, then take it out to our watchdog. We also used to feed the pigs, and when a sow gave birth we had to look after all the piglets to make sure they did not wander away too far.'

During the sheep-shearing season in early summer, the children had to help in earnest, holding the feet of the panicky animals as they were being shorn. 'We liked shearing time, when the wool piled up in the yard into white mountains waiting to be packed into jute sacks, work which was invariably accompanied by a good deal of shouting and jollity.'[21] Later in the year, with less outdoor work to be done, the sacks would be brought out and the wool soaked in great wooden tubs before being washed, teased and hung up to dry. When some of it had been spun, 'my mother would colour the thick ropes with dyes made from the bark of trees, earth and plants'. The favourite dye was the reddish brown obtained from the wild rhubarb growing on the mountainsides, prized not only for its colour but for the acid it contained which could be mixed with other colours.

Certain colours could be found only in the markets, and Choekyong Tsering travelling in caravan with other villagers, would set off to buy the dyes, taking with him donkeys laden with goods for barter. Each man brought grain and wool and cloth which they or their wives had woven. Naturally, Choekyong Tsering would also visit the horse-fair, where horses were taken in part-exchange, the difference being made up in sheepskins, wool or barley.

When the farmer arrived home – 'it was always good to hear my father's voice calling out as he rode back through the gate into the courtyard' – he was greeted boisterously by the family mastiff, Kyimo, 'a huge black beast with shaggy matted hair that hung down to the ground'; and more restrainedly by the cat, Shimi. (These, like the children's names, were generic, Kyimo meaning 'bitch' and Shimi simply 'cat'.) When Tsering Dolma was a baby, this cat had scratched her eyeball so badly that she had had to be fitted with a glass eye – later she always wore dark glasses. The same cat had once savaged a little musk-deer Cho-la had tended:

> I loved my little musk-deer very much and I even took it to bed with me under the warm covering. In the morning it would wake me up by licking my cheek with its gentle tongue. But one morning...I woke up...and found I was cuddling its lifeless body. And then I saw that there was blood around. In the night that wretched cat had bitten through my poor musk-deer's throat.

It was a bitter experience and, though Tibetans are taught from infancy to eschew all violence against sentient beings, Cho-la's emotions got the better of him. 'For the first time in my life I felt a desire for vengeance and would have liked to see that cat suffer a similar bloody end.'

The maternal grandparents often came from Churkha, a day's journey away, and though their arrival meant the young couple having to crowd in with the children, sleeping in the kitchen on the heated platform around the stove, they were always welcome guests. At other times, the house was like a busy market, as traders and craftsmen of all kinds arrived to display their wares. Cho-la and Tsering Dolma loved the traders coming, but the door was usually locked to keep the children out. Cho-la tried his utmost to get in but 'the best I could do was to make a little tear in the cloth of the small window panels, and stare inside at all the treasures laid out there'. With the fruit-sellers they had more luck – when the traders laid the fruit on the floor for inspection, 'we usually managed to sneak a few apples away without being noticed'.

A regular visitor was the weaver, who went from farm to farm, staying for several days, setting up his loom in the yards and weaving pieces of cloth about eight inches wide and many feet in length. Dekyi Tsering made the whole family's clothes herself, using the sewing-thread spun by her husband during the long winter evenings. But for special occasions and religious festivals, a tailor would be summoned; and when these special clothes had been made, Dekyi Tsering would get out the ornaments which Taktser women saved for great occasions – long ornate head-dresses which they wore over their shoulders like a back-pack – 'for example, three red ribbons on which, silver coins, shells, corals and turquoise stones were sewn to make very colourful finery'.²¹

In summer, the family went barefoot, but in the harsh winters they wore out so many boots that the cobbler was another regular caller: he had to make several visits to sew new leather soles onto the sturdy fabric tops. Choekyong Tsering bought cow leather for the boots at the Balangtsa market and soaked and softened it ready for the cobbler to cut out. He also made the thread for tying the boots from the jute grown along the edges of his fields.

In addition, there were the carpenter and the carpet-maker, the potter (providing earthenware jars for storing water) and the itinerant glue-vendors who made their own glue from cow hooves, bones and skin, peddling it from village to village, house to house, and usually paid in food-grains. All of them – and any passing caravan driver besides – were given overnight hospitality, with their animals, in the guest-room next to the cow shed, where they slept on a broad bench against the wall. Dekyi Tsering was never known to turn anyone away. All devout Buddhists were expected to give alms to beggars, but she went far beyond the call of duty. If she met a beggar on the road, she would make sure he had adequate food and clothing.

Her one desire in life, says Phuntsok Tashi, her future son-in-law, was for people to be happy. 'My mother,' the Dalai Lama would write,

> was undoubtedly one of the kindest people I've ever known...Once, I remember being told, there was a terrible famine in nearby China. As a result, many poor Chinese people were driven over the border in search of food. One day, a couple appeared at our door, carrying in their arms a dead child. They begged my mother for food, which she readily gave them. Then she pointed at their child and asked whether they wanted help to bury it. When they had caught her meaning, they shook their heads and made it clear that they intended to eat it. My mother was horrified and at once invited them in and emptied the entire contents of her larder before regretfully sending them on their way. Even if it meant giving away the family's own food so that we ourselves went hungry, she never let any beggar go away empty-handed.[23]

Over the village brooded the awesome Kyeri, the holy mountain where lived Kye, the area's protective deity. Mountains were important in Tibetan culture: their national flag carries at its centre the image of a snow mountain and a snow lion. In Taktser, as in many villages or towns, a heap of stones (known as a *labtse*) was dedicated to the mountain deity. Here the villagers 'offered up white quartz, coins, turquoises and corals, and prayed for rain, or for sun, or for a good harvest, or for protection from bad weather'. Monks from nearby monasteries would come and conduct the ceremonies, the sonorous beating of their gongs and the ringing of their bells heightening the solemnity of the occasion.

Two days in the year were specifically devoted to the mountain-god, and then the villagers would set off on a long trek to pay their respects, present their offerings and pray to the god for peace and prosperity.

> The ride to the foot of the mountain lasted three days and went through a completely uninhabited area, so the villagers had to take everything they needed along with them. When they arrived at the end of their journey we children would be left behind in tents whilst the adults went up to the ice limit, there solemnly to burn incense.[24]

When the ceremonial was over, it was time for a huge party, with large tents and awnings worked with traditional Tibetan designs erected on the meadows; singing, dancing, plenty to eat, fresh *chang* to drink, games of dominoes and dice; and of course, in the meadows, the horse-racing and sports for which the area was famous, lassoing and shooting at moving targets – first with a rifle and then with bow and arrow – from the backs of galloping horses. Contestants would gallop past each other trying to grab the opponent's scarf from round his neck, while the villagers urged on their favourites with shouts. The winner had to provide a bowl of *chang* for the loser to drink. Though these equestrian sports were traditionally a male preserve, Tsering Dolma, truly her father's daughter, revelled in them; she could 'do anything on a horse', her daughter said many years later, 'quite amazing things, like picking up a scarf from the ground without losing speed'.[25]

It was a typically Tibetan mix of religious devotion and uninhibited fun. 'We led a happy and contented life in our remote little village,' recalled Cho-la,

> and we found it strange when the occasional travellers who passed through sometimes felt it necessary to express their sympathy with us on account of what they conceived to be our hard lot. In fact we felt that we had everything we needed for life and enjoyment. We certainly would not have changed places with any of those travellers. We lived peaceably, and on feast days even gaily; and the Buddhas listened to our prayers.[26]

Buddhism gave the people their identity. 'Everybody, rich or poor (except a few misers),' wrote the Dalai Lama, 'spent all his spare income...in building religious monuments, contributing to temples, making offerings, giving alms to the poor, and saving the lives of animals by buying them from the butchers.' Prayer-flags festooned the roof of every house; the people spun prayer-wheels as they went about their daily tasks, and constantly on their lips was the *mani* prayer, *Om Mani Padme Hum* (Hail to the Jewel in the Lotus), an invocation of the eternal compassion lying deep in the heart of all sentient beings. 'Whenever I recall my home village,' Cho-la would write,

> I always see the forest of white, weather-worn prayer-flags fluttering in the constant breeze from the mountains. I shall never forget the eerie noise they used to make when they whipped and cracked against the flagpoles when a storm was approaching from Kyeri.[27]

Before that innocent way of life vanished for ever, there was an addition to the family. A second boy had been born a year or two after Cho-la's birth, but had died in infancy. 'My mother cried a little,' he remembers, 'but we try not to cry on such occasions, and if we do, then we try to hide it. I remember being very worried and giving my mother what comfort I could, telling her that we should take my young brother to a nice place and bury him properly.'[28] But things were about to change. One day he and Tsering Dolma were awakened by the sound of lusty yelling. During the night, their mother had given birth to another 'kicking, wriggling little bundle' in the cow byre. He was given the name of Gyalo Thondup.

NOTES

1. Samten G. Karmay, 'Amdo, One of the Three Traditional Provinces of Tibet', *Lungta* 8, Amnye Machin Institute, Dharamsala.

2. Fourteenth Dalai Lama, *My Land and My People.*

3. In old Tibet, no activity of any importance was undertaken without consulting the astrologers.

4. For details of the marriage of Choekyong Tsering and Sonam Tsomo, I am indebted to chapter 3 of Michael Harris Goodman's *The Last Dalai Lama*, Shambhala, 1987.

5. Goodman, *The Last Dalai Lama.*

6. A flour made from roasted barley, the staple of Tibetan diet.

7. Goodman.

8. Goodman.

9. Goodman.

10. Tibetans, unless they belong to the aristocracy, do not have surnames or family names. For the most part, the names are given to either sex and it is often hard to decide whether one is referring to a man or a woman.

11. Thubten Jigme Norbu (with Heinrich Harrer), *Tibet Is My Country*, Wisdom, 1960.

12. Amdo people drank a tea made from dried leaves pressed into bricks which were imported from China. It was coarse and sometimes contained whole leaves and even stalks.

13. The Tibetan yak is an unbelievably useful animal. It lives on grasses and lichens, yet is a powerful beast of burden. The male gives meat while the female gives milk for butter, cheese and yoghurt. In the old days in Tibet, the yak's hide was turned into boots, saddlebags and even coracles in some parts of Tibet; its hair was used in tent-making, for blankets, ropes and clothing; its bones for building houses, its dung for fuel and insulation. Even the backbone, when crushed to powder and mixed with gold dust was put to use as a female contraceptive.

14. Author interview with Gyalo Thondup, New Delhi, July 1995.

15. Norbu, *Tibet Is My Country*.

16. Thubten Jigme Norbu (with Colin Turnbull), *Tibet*, Chatto and Windus, 1968; Pelican Books, 1972; Penguin, 1976.

17. Pema Bhum, 'Amdo: the People and their Struggle', in *The Invincible Amdo Tibetans*, by Poulius Normantas, Finland, Biokustannus Oy, 1994.

18. *Tibet Is My Country*.

19. *Tibet*.

20. *Tibet Is My Country*.

21. *Tibet Is My Country*.

22. Kim Yeshi and Emily Phipps, 'Precious Jewels of Tibet', article in *Chö Yang: The Voice of Tibetan Religious Culture* 5.

23. Fourteenth Dalai Lama, *Freedom in Exile: The Autobiography of the Dalai Lama of Tibet*, Hodder & Stoughton, 1990.

24. *Tibet Is My Country*.

25. Author interview with Khando Chazotsang (known before her marriage as Khando Tsering), Utah, February 1996.

26. *Tibet Is My Country*.

27. *Tibet Is My Country*.

28. *Tibet*.

4

Kumbum

The mountain at whose foot Tsong-khapa was born had become a famous place of pilgrimage. Lamas came from all parts to build their cells there, and the flourishing lamasery whose fame spread to the furthest confines of Tartary gradually came into being. It was called Koumboum, from two Tibetan words which mean 'Ten Thousand Pictures'. The name refers to a tree which according to legend was born out of the hair of Tsong-khapa and which bears a Tibetan character on each of its leaves.

Régis-Evariste Huc, who visited Tibet in the
mid–nineteenth century

In 1930, when Cho-la was eight, a far-reaching change took place in his life. It is a strange story, bound up with his paternal grandmother's disappointment over the birth of Tsering Dolma. Shortly before that birth, the old woman's brother, the Twenty-third Taktser Rinpoche, had died. As the search for his reincarnation would soon be under way throughout the area around Kumbum Monastery, his sister became obsessed with the idea that the rebirth would take place in her own household. When the child turned out to be a girl she lost all interest in life, turned her face to the wall – and died.

The search had already begun; a list of boy candidates was drawn up and taken to Lhasa by a party led by the two Stewards of Taktser *labrang*,[1] the

junior of whom was farmer Choekyong Tsering's elder brother. Their journey, on horseback and in caravan, took over three months. In Lhasa, the
Thirteenth Dalai Lama received them very warmly: in 1904, after the
Younghusband Expedition to Tibet,² he had fled to Outer Mongolia and on
the way had spent a year in Kumbum Monastery and had come to know
Taktser Rinpoche well. (Taktser had been unpopular with his monks for
trying to introduce the Great Thirteenth's monastic reforms.) Dalai Lamas
were said to have the gift of knowing the identity of lesser reincarnations;
His Holiness scrutinized the list with interest – then handed it back saying that, alas, the right name was missing; they must return to Amdo and
come back again in the following year with a new list.

Dejectedly, they made the long trek back to Kumbum, and a year later
left for Lhasa with a fresh list. Same exhausting journey, same disappoint-
ing result. When the Dalai Lama again insisted that the right name was
still missing, they all but wept. So demoralized were they that, on the journey back, the Senior Steward fell ill and died shortly after reaching home.

Choekyong Tsering's brother, Ngawang Changchup, now became Senior
Steward and leader of the search party. Wearily, he set off yet again for
Lhasa, with a list which now included the name of Dekyi Tsering's first-
born son. Gyalo Thondup takes up the story, as told him by his mother:

> When he arrived in Lhasa, my uncle put on his finest brocades and went to the
> Jokhang Temple to light butter-lamps and make offerings and prayers. When
> he poured the butter into the lamps, it all spilled down his front, ruining his
> beautiful clothes. My uncle was a very bad-tempered man and the monks who
> were with him were terrified he'd blame them for the accident. But to their
> surprise, instead of exploding with anger, he actually seemed pleased, telling
> them that indeed this was a very good omen for their mission. In fact, he
> asked for his garments to be preserved in all their buttery splendour.
>
> Once again they were summoned to the Presence. This time, His Holiness
> told them to wait in Lhasa for two or three days while he prayed about the
> matter. On the third day, he handed my uncle a sealed letter with instructions
> to take it to the Abbot of Kumbum and tell him to open it in the presence of
> all the candidates' families.
>
> So, back in Kumbum, a large gathering was summoned to hear the an-
> nouncement. The Abbot duly opened the letter – and read out the name of my
> brother! My parents looked at each other and said what a pity it was my
> grandmother hadn't lived to see this day!³

The monks were soon riding off towards the Taktser farmhouse bearing gifts. As Cho-la – who was about to be given the new names of Thubten (one of the Dalai Lama's own names) Jigme Norbu – relates:

> I was six or seven years old, and I remember very well how I was playing in the fields at the time, down by a little stream. My sister came running out to tell me that some monks had come to visit our home, and that they wanted to see me. She took me to the house and there in the courtyard I saw a lot of fine big horses and inside the house were the monks.[4]

Cho-la watched them through the spy-hole he had made in the thick rice paper which served as a window; then, when the monks were taken into the kitchen, he tiptoed to the wooden partition near the food-hatch and listened. Somehow, he knew, even before he heard them speak, that they had come to take him away. He could see that the head of the party was his uncle, the Steward of Taktser *labrang*, the rich and splendid establishment within Kumbum monastery which Cho-la, as the new Incarnation, would now inherit. They told him that he was the latest reincarnation of the fifteenth-century monk Taktser, and that he must leave home within a few days, to begin his studies in the little Shartsong hermitage, where the great fourteenth-century Buddhist reformer Tsong-khapa[5] had been initiated as a monk.

The boy appeared delighted and wanted to leave straight away. One of his favourite fantasies – by no means unusual among Tibetan children – had involved running away to a monastery to become a monk! Once when he was about six, he had rolled up a few belongings into a bundle and escaped through a hole in the wall. But, getting hopelessly lost, he had to be ignominiously rescued by his mother.

His parents rejoiced at the honour done to their family; and the whole village was happy, since the monks stayed for several days, handing out presents as they spread the good news around. They had brought large chests of new clothing, of finer weave and cut than Cho-la's old worsted *chuba*, and boots of top-quality leather, their uppers elaborately embroidered. Cho-la was pleased and excited by the fuss and by the unaccustomed respect which the village children were showing him. It hadn't really sunk in that he was about to say goodbye for ever to his family and his childhood.

A few days later, Cho-la (whom we shall now for a short while call by the second of his new names, Jigme) was dressed in his new clothes and told to leave behind everything that belonged to his life in the village. He managed to stow away a small bag of treasured sheep's bones and pebbles in the fold of his robe before going outside to join the waiting caravan of nine horses. His parents and sister were going too, his father carrying the infant Gyalo Thondup on the saddle in front of him.

It was only a couple of hours' ride to the Shartsong hermitage which loomed high above them as they approached, surrounded by mountains and clinging improbably to the top of a sheer 500-feet-high cliff. A welcome party waited at the base, and Jigme (Cho-la) was delighted to be treated as an important personage. But his self-confidence plummeted during the terrifying climb up the almost perpendicular reddish-brown rockface, buffeted at every step by the wind. The view from the top, however, where four white-washed houses perched on the edge of the solid rock, down into the deep gorge, more than repaid the discomfort.

Years later, in exile, he would remember this place as the most beautiful he had ever known, and, long after Shartsong had been destroyed by the Chinese, would yearn for 'its red rocks, its trees filled with birds, the deer and other wild animals', for the stream, with its 'blue, blue water', and 'the infinite peace I knew then, and the cleanness of the scents of pine and juniper and wild rose'.[6]

Each of the twenty or so monks had a modestly-furnished room in one of the houses, the only decoration being a picture portraying scenes from the lives of Buddhist saints. The monks had no personal possessions; they lived on alms donated by pious pilgrims and fed on tsampa (barley-meal) and butter sent up by relatives from the surrounding villages. For water, they made the daunting climb down to the river below, with wooden barrels strapped to their backs.

As an Incarnation, the new incumbent of the wealthy Taktser *labrang*, Jigme would not share their poverty; a beautifully-furnished room awaited him. He was inducted into his new role through ceremonies lasting three days, attended by his whole family. Though still excited, the realization was dawning that when the ceremonies were over, he would be left alone, and he clutched his little bag of coloured stones for reassurance. The parting was even more painful than he had imagined:

When I saw my parents preparing to leave, a terrible regret invaded my heart and I wept bitterly, and not all the loving encouragement and persuasions of my parents and the monks could console me. I felt a stranger in the new surroundings, I wanted to go home with my parents, and I was moved by a deep longing for my playmates and for all the things I had left behind.[7]

In vain did the kindly monks try to console him with sweets and toys and stories. They made paper dragons for him and kneaded fantastic figures out of tsampa dough; but they could not make him smile. Even when the cook brought a dish of his favourite roast mutton, he was unconsoled and refused to eat. He stared out into the dusk, shaken by uncontrollable sobs.

The gentle monk, Puntso, who was assigned to Jigme as tutor and servant, slowly put him at his ease and introduced him to his new duties, first among which was learning to write. Kumbum was the monastery where the great Tsong-khapa was born, in a tent set up by his nomad parents near a convenient watering-place. There is a famous tree growing there which is said to have grown on the exact spot where he was born. Round that hallowed place the monastery had gradually come into being, as a lasting memorial to the wonder-child who grew up to establish Buddhist rule in Tibet. Here, at Shartsong, Tsong-khapa had begun his religious studies.

> The early part of my life was spent just exactly where Tsong-khapa spent his...I was taught to write probably much as he was, for we had no pens or pencils or paper even when I was there. I used a wooden slate that was covered with chalk so that the writing showed up dark when the surface was scratched with a sharpened wooden stick.[8]

Jigme's days were filled with lessons, games and instruction, leaving little time for tears. But, though he slowly settled into the daytime routine, when night fell he was overcome with homesickness. It was, therefore, with an incredulous delight that one summer's evening he heard the sound of a horse's hooves in the courtyard below and recognized his father:

> Tears of joy and happiness rolled down my cheeks and for a moment or two I was speechless. My normally so unemotional father had to pull himself together too, and with suspiciously bright eyes he handed me a basket of my favourite pastries mother had sent me. We kissed each other on forehead and cheeks, and I made no attempt to stop my tears, forgetting the well-meant exhortations of the Abbot and of Puntso that a Rinpoche must behave like a man and not cry like a child.[9]

After two days, his father left, promising to return soon with the rest of the family. This had a galvanizing effect on Jigme; having something to look forward to spurred him on. In any case, his early longing to join a monastery had been genuine and now that he had recovered from the first shock, he was eager for his parents to be proud of him. Under Puntso's guidance, he applied himself to his lessons and made good progress. When his parents came, with Tsering Dolma and Gyalo Thondup, his bright-eyed and mischievous younger brother, he proudly showed them round his new domain, taking them to see the wide variety of birds he had made friends with on his verandah; and the tame musk-deer scampering over the rocks. In this place, where no one had ever knowingly killed anything, all wild things seemed to know instinctively that they were safe.

The visit was short, but this time the pain of parting was less acute.

Jigme was beginning to enjoy Shartsong. So he felt sad when, after three months, he had to leave for the huge parent monastery of Kumbum, home to three thousand monks, many of whom came from far-distant Mongolia to study in this ancient monastic university.[10] He was given clothes of the finest silk and the embroidery on his new boots was even more sumptuous than before. In addition, he wore a shallow, broad-brimmed hat made of gilt papier-mâché, befitting his exalted rank of incarnate lama. His horse was decked out with a new harness, a head-dress of gilt and a bushy, scarlet yak-tail springing from its halter.

Taktser, his native village, lay *en route*, and there Jigme was received like the important dignitary he now was. New prayer-flags flew from all the roof-tops and freshly-laundered sunblinds covered the doors. The incense fumes of burning alpine rose petals filled the nostrils. The whole village had turned out to express their gratitude that this brand-new Rinpoche had been chosen from amongst them, and the first to pay homage was his old hero, the herdsman.

Jigme's mother greeted him at the door with a white scarf and a ceremonial bowl of sweet cream. Only when this ritual had been observed did they drop the formalities and hug and kiss each other. Jigme looked around him, surprised to see the unfamiliar new carpets and silken hangings which had been brought by the Kumbum monks to celebrate his arrival. Before long, a crowd had assembled in the courtyard and a party was under way.

Happy and elated, oblivious both of his new silk garments and the need to keep them clean, Jigme made his way to the cowshed to cuddle a new-born calf and hug the huge black mastiff, Kyimo. Too late, he saw that he was covered with spots and stains. But it seemed there was no limit to the patience of his tutor and servant Puntso, who, without comment, produced another silk outfit for him.

Once again, the whole family came too. Neighbours lined the caravan route as they set off; and the old village headman, Pasang, urged Jigme with tears in his eyes to be sure and be a credit to Taktser village. This journey took two days and led through Churkha, his mother's old home, where he received another ecstatic welcome. Half-way between Churkha and Kumbum, five monks on horseback rode out to meet them. A brief ceremony of welcome took place in a ceremonial tent erected by the wayside, and when Jigme's party again rode on, it was with an official escort. About an hour later, from the brow of a hill, they saw Kumbum lying far below, encircled by brown hills dotted with juniper bushes and cedars, while in the valley the lush fields were edged with poplar and willow. Overcome by the size and beauty of the place, Jigme reined in his horse and stood gazing down on it. As his gaze cleared and the vision below took shape, he noticed myriad red dots at the foot of the monastery, moving 'like corn in the wind':

> And then I could hear, at first softly, and afterwards more and more clearly, the sounds of oboes and trumpets, followed a little later by the sound of the monks chanting. Was this really all for me, the incarnation of Taktser? [11]

Spurring his horse forward, Jigme was soon amongst them. Then, an umbrella of yellow silk held high over his head in token of his rank, he rode slowly through the narrow streets of the vast monastery, past the serried ranks of praying, bowing monks. Exhausted though he was, he had to be greeted by every single inmate of the Taktser *labrang*, the monastic college which he had inherited. Most of them were old and dignified monks who smiled at him with great friendliness. Jigme did his tired best to smile back, to ignore his increasing desire to slump down in his seat and sleep. But the ordeal seemed to be endless.

At last it was over and his new servants came in bearing 'a large copper dish decorated with silver and containing almost a whole stewed sheep' – just for him.[12] Only when he had eaten his fill, did the monks at last retire, leaving him alone with his family.

A few days later, his parents went home and Jigme plunged into a rigorous regime of lessons and prayer. Fortunately, there were boys of his own age to share the lighter moments, one of them a boy from Taktser who had just been initiated as a monk. 'I had a wonderful time with them; they took me all around and showed me things I had never seen or heard of before, like cuckoo clocks and music boxes.'[13] It was a revelation. To see watches and clocks for the first time and no longer need to rely on cock-crow or the position of the sun in the heavens! To his great delight, he was the proud possessor of fifteen cuckoo clocks, most of which hung on the walls of his room. His predecessor had returned from his travels in Tsarist Russia with a caravan full of treasures, including the cuckoo clocks and a number of musical boxes which Jigme found intriguing:

> When one of them, perhaps the most beautiful of all, was played, the little fig-ure of a girl appeared, and that always moved me deeply. She pirouetted gaily round and round, and in her hands she carried a box from which, to my great delight, an even smaller figure emerged. I loved this particular toy and played it again and again, and I used to imagine that the tiny figure which came out of the box carried a still tinier box from which a still tinier figure emerged – and so on, and so on.[14]

It was, he realized some years later, his first illustration of the mysterious concept of eternity!

After breakfast each day, he was free to play with the other boys. 'We used to run about the monastery and hide from each other, or else we would make statues or build houses of mud. In the summertime we were free to go out and play on the mountainside, so long as five or six of us went together.'[15]

The Taktser *labrang* possessed many fields and farms leased to peasants and farmers who must then hand over an agreed percentage of their yield as an annual rent. Out of these revenues, the *labrang* paid its own annual taxes to Governor Ma Pu-feng in Siling.

After Jigme had been a few months at Kumbum, the astrologers decreed that it was time for him to receive the monk's habit. Another boy, a six-teen-year-old called Kesang, was to be initiated with him, and three days before the ceremony the two boys' heads were shaven, apart from a small lock left on the crown. Choekyong Tsering, who visited his son about once a month, hurried to Kumbum for the great event, but Jigme himself was seized by a sudden unaccountable desire to run away.[16]

> I was afraid of the monk's habit which was now lying ready on a small table. According to the strictly prescribed ritual I was now asked whether I wished to become a monk, and to the astonishment of everyone present I remained silent. Both Puntso and my father urged me to answer, but I found it impossible to get a word out. Even the tears which finally came did not relieve my tension.[17]

As Jigme was already a *tulku*, the ceremony went on regardless, with Ke-sang firmly answering all the questions. Then the last lock of hair – the last remaining link with the world – was cut away and after being symbolically washed from head to foot in holy water, the boys were given the simple maroon woollen clothing of a monk. Henceforth their lives were to be devoted exclusively to religion.

Jigme felt confused and anxious. On the one hand, he was proud that he, a nine-year-old boy, had been accepted as a monk in the Order founded by Tsong-khapa,[18] and was now entitled to wear the same garment that the founder had worn.

> But I was still not able to talk about the reasons which had caused my strange silence during the ceremony. My father and Puntso were both deeply disturbed, and they questioned me urgently. But I could only shake my head. I wasn't even prepared to admit how deeply ashamed of myself I was.[19]

But fears and regrets had to be set aside. The training of an Incarnation involves long years of study and is far more rigorous than that of ordinary monks. From now on, however reluctantly, he had to get up each morning at four o'clock to fulfil his religious duties. Lessons became more difficult, and the prayers he had to learn by rote each day grew longer. With his new tutor, Lhagsam, he embarked on a course of studies to prepare him for the important examination which would qualify him for admission to the General Assembly of the Kumbum monks.

Not that he became a model pupil overnight. On the contrary, he often abused Lhagsam's good nature:

> Every morning and in the afternoon from four o'clock until late in the evening, [Lhagsam] had to be present at the general assembly for prayers, and whilst he was gone he relied on me to do the work he had set me. But when he left me in the early morning I would go back to bed again and have some more sleep. By the time he returned, there I was, virtuously poring over my books, the very model of zeal and industry.

For a time, the old monk was taken in, but when the truth came out,

> In holy anger he put me across his knee, raised my robes and administered a thorough slapping with the palm of his hand. I burst into loud howls of pain, with the result that the worthy man was deeply shocked at his own outburst, suspended the punishment and rather clumsily took me in his arms and tried to console me. Taken completely by surprise at this sudden change of attitude,

49

and feeling deeply ashamed of myself, I pressed my head to his chest and sobbed as though my heart would break.[20]

Slowly Jigme was beginning to understand what it meant to be an Incarnation. While still at Shartsong, he hadn't really taken it in, he kept asking where Taktser was and when he would be coming back. Then, at Kumbum he was puzzled when the monks pointed out certain places and objects, saying, 'This was where you used to sit', or 'You used this in your previous life'. He vaguely realized that the Taktser *labrang* with all its wealth in some way belonged to him but only now did he begin to realize that 'it was all mine not because, in some strange way, it had all been given to me as a present, but because, in a far stranger way, it had been mine even before I was born, that I actually *was* Taktser'.[21] It bothered him that he remembered nothing of his previous life.

> Nothing stirred in me except a growing realization of the responsibility that had been bestowed on me. All these people were looking up to me, an uneducated child from a peasant family, for spiritual guidance, all of them hoping secretly for some miracle. And out in the countryside, on the lands owned by my monastery, peasant folk like my own family, were depending on me to help them and guide them, using my knowledge and power and wealth for their good. It would have helped me if I had been able to recall even one event from my previous life, but I, who can often not even remember what happened yesterday, what chance is there of my remembering back to another existence?

Gradually he was absorbed into the life of the monastery. One day he stood for some minutes idly observing a group of people who had ridden into the courtyard below his window, before realizing that they were his parents, brother and sister. Then recognizing them with a rush of emotion, he dashed down the stairs to welcome them.

Someone else was with them – Phuntsok Tashi, a youth to whom Tsering Dolma had recently become betrothed and was soon to marry. The two families had long had close ties with each other. Chungtsi, Phuntsok Tashi's village, was lower down the mountain than Taktser, and whenever the Taktser crops failed, Phuntsok Tashi's family came to the rescue. They lived near some famous hot springs, and Choekyong Tsering would sometimes go and stay with them to try and cure his chronic indigestion with the waters. When the time came to look for a husband for seventeen-year-old Tsering Dolma, Phuntsok Tashi, their friends' fifteen-year-old son, was an obvious choice. But Tsering Dolma would not be leaving home. The bridegroom's parents, being gentle, unassuming folk who fully understood that their neighbours could ill afford – and indeed would be unwilling – to part with their hard-working (and much-loved) daughter, had agreed that their son should marry into his bride's family. The young man would shortly be providing an extra pair of hands in the Taktser household. Gyalo Thondup had come to Kumbum too. From the start he had been – and would remain – the wildest of all Dekyi Tsering's children. Tsering Dolma reported that as a baby he 'cried and cried and cried', and as he was in her charge, she was always accused of making him cry. Almost five now, he was a handsome boy, with large, luminous eyes, who kept his family entertained by singing a number of Tibetan folk-songs he had learned by heart. 'Altogether an agreeable child,' decided Jigme, who scarcely knew him.

In the autumn of 1932, a third son, Lobsang Samten, was born, and it was in the following year, while Choekyong Tsering was visiting Jigme in Kumbum, that news came of the Thirteenth Dalai Lama's death. As tens of thousands of butter-lamps blazed on the monastery roofs, the monks plunged into mourning for a ruler who had been both spiritual leader and king. Jigme recalls being 'so carried away by my sorrow that I couldn't conceive that things could ever be the same again, and that in time our or-dinary everyday life would start up once more'.[22]

Amidst his tears, Jigme uttered a heartfelt prayer: that the Dalai Lama would soon return to live among his people. Some months later when he visited his old home in Taktser, *en route* once again for Shartsong, he found that his mother had given birth to another son, Lhamo Dhondup – 'the most delightful baby I had ever seen'. He did not know, of course, that his prayer had been answered; the Dalai Lama had returned.

It is said that one day, feeling particularly frustrated by his Ministers, the Great Thirteenth had sworn that when he was reborn it would be into a large family, with brothers and sisters who would help – not hinder – him in his work. It looked as though he had kept his word.

NOTES

1. Every large monastery in Tibet was divided into separate colleges, each of which had its own property and finances. The estate was known as a *labrang*. The amount of wealth, of course, varied. Thanks to the travels and skills of the recently deceased Taktser Rinpoche, his *labrang* was now an extremely wealthy one.

2. In 1904, the British in India feared that Tsarist Russia was about to obtain serious influence over Tibet and then might cause trouble on India's northern border. (This was the era of the Great Game, when Britain, China and Russia jockeyed for influence in Central Asia.) Accordingly, an expeditionary force was sent to Tibet under Colonel Francis Younghusband, who trounced the tiny and badly-equipped Tibetan Army. Later, however, good relations were restored between Britain and Tibet, and an Agreement was signed. The 1904 Convention with Britain, signed in the Potala Palace, made it clear that Britain was dealing with an independent Tibet over which China had no control. It arranged for British trading posts to be set up at Gyantse and Gartok in Western Tibet. (The British had since 1893 had a trading post at Dromo.)

3. Author interview, Gyalo Thondup, New Delhi, July 1995.

4. Norbu, *Tibet.*

5. See chapter 1.

6. *Tibet.*

7. Norbu, *Tibet Is My Country.*

8. *Tibet.*

9. *Tibet Is My Country.*

10. Tibetan monasteries were like complete townships, with streets, colleges, temples, etc.

11. *Tibet Is My Country.*

12. Most Westerners seem surprised to learn that Tibetan Buddhists eat meat. But vegetarianism was never a practical possibility in those parts of Tibet where few vegetables would grow. Yaks and sheep were the chief source of Tibetan food, and though some lamas and monks did refrain from meat-eating on principle, most people did not even try. However, they were never entirely easy in their minds about it and they did not lightly kill an animal. Whenever a herdsman found it necessary to slaughter for food, he would first pray for forgiveness from the animal itself and then perform rituals for its rebirth into a happier state of life. He would put holy water on the nose or mouth of the yak or sheep before killing it. In the towns, Muslims acted as butchers. Small animals and birds, which would feed only a small number of people, were taboo; and in only one area of Tibet, around the Yarlung Tsangpo river, was fishing allowed.

13. *Tibet.*
14. *Tibet Is My Country.*
15. *Tibet.*
16. Not all those who are discovered in childhood to be *tulkus* stay the course. They remain *tulkus* and are addressed as Rinpoche for the rest of their lives, but many meanwhile renounce the monastic state.
17. *Tibet Is My Country.*
18. The Buddhist Order to which most Tibetans adhere is the reformed Gelugpa Order. The others are: Nyingmapa (the old) which follows the teachings of Padmasambhava; Kagyupa (the sect of Marpa, the teacher of Milarepa); Sakyapa (the sect of Sakya Panchen, known as the Gracious Teacher). All four Orders owe their allegiance to the Dalai Lama.
19. *Tibet Is My Country.*
20. *Tibet Is My Country.*
12. *Tibet.*
22. *Tibet Is My Country.*

5

The Holy Child of Amdo

Those children wrested from their families, subjected to the strict supervision of elderly wardens...led through the endless maze of lamaistic liturgy and dogmatics and plunged forcibly into the ponderous works of their former embodiments, certainly do not know the blissful astonishment of childhood...Such strict discipline, such statue-like immobility as the dignity of that office imposes, the daily intercourse with gloomy, elderly people, look to me like a violent, ruthless suppression of childhood. That is why I actually believe there should be something exceptional in those boys, born as they are with the dreadful burden of a saintliness which must be reached and lived up to at all costs.

Giuseppe Tucci, To Lhasa and Beyond

In old Tibet, it was believed that when a high incarnate lama was about to be reborn, the place of his rebirth would first suffer a series of misfortunes. When for four successive years, the seventeen peasant families of Taktser (fifteen Tibetan, two Chinese) suffered severe crop failure, either through hailstorms when the corn was ripe or drought when it was still young, they muttered among themselves that something extraordinary must be about to happen in the village. But when disasters began to fall thick and fast on Choekyong Tsering and his wife in particular, they found a less charitable explanation: 'They were all speculating that our family had done something dreadful in a previous life and were now being punished for it,' says Gyalo Thondup.

First of all, two of the couple's babies had recently died in infancy. In spite of this, the local oracle, when consulted, told Choekyong Tsering not to worry. 'You will have many children,' he prophesied, 'and at least one of them will become famous. Through him, money will flow like water to your house.' The farmer was consoled, but, alas, his misfortunes were only just beginning, as Gyalo Thondup relates:

For example, we had seven beautiful horses. Our valley was located at the top of a steep cliff. One day we had taken the horses to the drinking trough when suddenly all seven of them leaped in the air, ran to the cliff and jumped off it. They were all killed. We also had six mules, and at this time they caught some disease and died, one after another...Then my father became seriously ill. He could no longer walk or even get out of bed, he had become just like a skeleton. I was so frightened by his appearance that every day when I came home from school, I used to bend double when I crossed the room where he was, eyes down to avoid seeing him. So the gossips were having a fine time; they were sure there was a curse on our house. First the children dying, then the horses, then the mules and now, presumably, my father. And my poor mother was pregnant again.

Before dawn on the morning of 6 July, there was a violent thunderstorm followed by torrential rain. That day, my sister, Tsering Dolma, who was not yet married, was supposed to be taking me to the market, to buy fruit and some sweets. We were both very excited at the prospect of our day out. But, during the thunderstorm, my mother went into labour and began to shout from the cow byre, calling to my sister to run and get one of our neighbours, an old lady, to come and help. I was a bit scared, my father was ill, my mother now seemed to be ill, and my sister was abandoning me. But my sister soon returned with the old lady, who was almost one of the family. She took charge of the situation and told my sister she couldn't go to market, she'd be needed at home to boil water and things like that. 'Let your brother go with the other people who are going,' she said. My sister was upset because she'd been looking forward to her treat, but the old lady told her to stop moaning and make herself useful. I was packed off.

That morning, after the baby was born, my father called out, using my mother's maiden name as he always did, 'Sonam Tsomo, Sonam Tsomo, is our baby born?' 'Yes, yes, it's a boy,' she answered. He didn't hear and repeated the question. Whereupon the old lady yelled impatiently, 'IT'S A BOY!' Suddenly, this man who'd seemed to be on the point of death got up and went to the altar-room, to light the butter-lamps in thanksgiving to our protector deities. Amazed at his sudden cure, he vowed, 'I shall make this boy a monk.''

Dekyi Tsering was understandably in two minds about her husband's miraculous recovery. 'My mother,' the Dalai Lama would write, 'remembers being annoyed...and accusing him of having stayed in bed through laziness, but he declared that he was cured.'

In Tibet, one in four boys – usually at least one in every family – was sent to a monastery, not only for pious reasons but because for poor families in a semi-feudal society it was the only way for their sons to be properly educated and have the chance of rising to the top. No farm could support too many men, whereas a monk, even from the poorest family, could aspire to very high office if he had the ability. So Choekyong Tsering's announcement would have been unremarkable, if he had not already offered two sons to the monastic life. Three-year-old Lobsang Samten was shortly to join his brother, Jigme, in Kumbum. 'I was the only layman in the family,' Gyalo Thondup says cheerfully, 'the only one who became a farmer. My father used to take me round with him, especially to the horse-fairs. He was a difficult man, with a very hot temper. When he was in a rage, he would sometimes kick me, although I must admit he didn't do so all that often. In any case, I know I was a difficult child, even my mother would get furious with me and pinch me hard. My mother could be very fierce indeed when roused, even fiercer than my father.'

Dekyi Tsering reported that she had had a number of extraordinary dreams before the birth. In one of these, two dragons came out of the ground, holding a bright jewel which they threw up into the air and watched as it fell to earth. The dragons, bowing low, picked up the jewel and presented it to her. In Tibet, dreams were important, and the fact that no one could offer an explanation of this one worried her. Still, she felt that the child she was carrying – the thirteenth to whom she would have given birth – must be someone special.

He came into the world by the light of a single mustard-oil lamp, at daybreak on the fifth day of the fifth month of Wood Hog Year (6 July 1935). Like his older siblings, he was born on a straw pallet in the cowshed amid the smell of the yak-cows and the sound of suckling calves. Neighbours told Dekyi Tsering that there was a rainbow just overhead at the time – a good omen. The baby was named Lhamo Dhondup, perhaps an odd name for a boy, since strictly speaking Lhamo was a female name, -mo being a feminine suffix. But the goddess, Palden Lhamo, was a protector deity in the Tibetan pantheon, and at times of emergency and insecurity her name was frequently given.

Though babies are usually born with their eyes closed, this child had one eye completely open. 'Maybe,' as the Dalai Lama once suggested, 'some slight indication of a clear state of mind in the womb.'[2] His sister, Tsering Dolma, however, thought that both eyes should be open and took immediate action. 'Without hesitation,' wrote the Dalai Lama, 'she put her thumb on the reluctant lid and forced it open, fortunately without ill effect.'[3]

Farming women took birth in their stride – and soon afterwards the 35-year-old mother was back at work in the barley fields with the other village women, carrying the baby on her back as she hoed and tilled the ground. She was surprised to find that whenever she paused to feed him, he would cry; but the other women reassured her:

'He is a special baby,' the women said. 'He doesn't like being fed in front of us. You must take him to a private place.' So after that I took him away from the field when I gave him my breast, and he was content.[4]

Then she would leave him to sleep on the ground under an umbrella tied to an upright stake. Later, when he started to walk, he would go with her when she went to milk the *dzomos*, carrying his wooden bowl for her to fill with fresh, warm milk. She sent him to the chicken coop each day to collect the eggs; one day he went missing for several hours, and was eventually found sitting in one of the nesting boxes, clucking like a contented hen.

As a baby, he slept on a bed with his mother, and later on in the kitchen with Tsering Dolma, by the stove. Once, when he was about a year old, his mother and Tsering Dolma left him asleep on the bed while they went to watch some horse-racing contest in the village. When Dekyi returned, she was relieved to find everything quiet; but relief turned to terror when the baby was nowhere to be found. She panicked, fearing the worst. Then Lhamo Dhondup crawled from underneath the bed, chortling merrily. She always felt he had been born with a fully-developed sense of humour.

He has vague memories of the family gathering in the altar-room to make offerings at the beginning of each day; and clearer ones of pulling his father's moustache 'and being hit hard for my pains'. His brother, Jigme, had already left home, and Gyalo Thondup went each day to school in a neighbouring village. Only three-year-old Lobsang Samten was still at home, the gentlest and least complicated of them all. While Gyalo Thondup, a mass of uncoordinated energy, went spinning round the room like an out-of-control top, Lobsang would pursue him anxiously, vainly trying to protect him from falling. He adored his mother and would hang on to her skirts, unwilling to lose sight of her. But at three, shortly after the arrival of Lhamo Dhondup, he was sent to Kumbum monastery.

Lhamo Dhondup, then, had to learn to play on his own. He was advanced for his years, bubbling with life, stubborn, independent and given to tantrums when he did not get his own way. To his father's disgust, he disliked horses and flatly refused to ride, but otherwise he showed little fear of anyone or anything. If he saw a group of children scrapping, he would go and join the losing side – using an imaginary rifle and shouting 'bang bang' – even if it meant getting a bloody nose. 'Even if I saw two insects fighting,' he laughs, 'I'd rush to help the one which was getting the worst of it. The desire to protect the weak seems to have been inborn in me – I suppose you could say my compassion was more than a bit partisan.'[5]

His mother observed that his play was different from that of other children. He seemed to have ideas above his station:

> He was always drawing houses in the earth. They were big houses, bigger than any in our village or any he could have seen at this time, yet he told me that soon we should live in such a house.
>
> Sometimes he touched my homespun robe, feeling the coarseness of the cloth and then pushing it away, saying it was not good and that I would soon be wearing pretty skirts which would be soft and smooth to touch. But he had never seen a silken robe in our humble dwelling.[6]

The gossip in the village had died away. It seemed clear to everyone who saw him that Lhamo Dhondup was extraordinary. A year later, Hugh Richardson of the British Mission in Lhasa would write to Basil Gould, the British Political Officer for Sikkim: 'As he grew up his parents realized that he was an exceptional child, but as they did not want to lose him, they did not bring him forward as a candidate when the party headed by [Kesang Rinpoche] came to search for the reincarnation of the Dalai Lama. It happened that while the late Panchen Lama Rinpoche was in Jyekundo he heard about the child and sent word to [Kesang Rinpoche] that he should go and see him.'[7]

By the time that letter was written, Lhamo Dhondup was already in Kumbum in the care of Jigme, now a serious young novice of fifteen who had passed his examinations and been accepted into the general monastic assembly. Earlier, he had witnessed the anguish of three-year-old Lobsang Samten's arrival at the monastery. Jigme, who was absent when his parents had left Lobsang Samten behind, had returned to find an inconsolable bundle of misery.

> On my couch sat little Lobsang Samten obviously feeling very sorry for himself. Big tears rolled down his chubby cheeks, and convulsed with sobs he was hardly able to utter a word. He just couldn't grasp the fact that his mother and father had left him behind alone in this strange place…Suddenly all the misery I had suffered when I was in his situation revived in my memory. And he was considerably younger than I had been at the time. When all my well-meant efforts to comfort him were of no avail I lost my head too and there we sat locked in each other's arms, sobbing, until in the end we were both so exhausted that we fell asleep.[8]

Jigme even sent a message to his maternal grandparents begging them to persuade his parents to take Lobsang Samten home. But the grandparents would not interfere, and Lobsang Samten settled to his new life faster than anyone had dared hope. Or at least, as he later, rather wistfully, noted, 'Time was a great healer. I adjusted to my new home and tried to make myself happy.'[9] This, in spite of the fact that he was no longer allowed to call his brother Cho-la, as he had always done. Cho-la, Jigme, as an Incarnate in training to become one of the most important lamas in the land, had another name now: he was Taktser Rinpoche, even to his family.

The nightmare was now repeating itself and the poor Rinpoche found himself with not one but two homesick little brothers to console. 'One bright and tingling winter morning' in 1938, his parents arrived at the monastery with Lhamo Dhondup; and a few days later set off again for home without him. His mother left first, telling the little boy she was going to visit her parents. When, soon afterwards, his father left too, Lhamo Dhondup was naturally upset. How could he have known – or cared – that he was to be the next Dalai Lama? All he knew was that his parents had abandoned him. As a tiny child, he had often been taken, propped up on his father's horse, to see Jigme, and had always been disappointed that Jigme could not come out and play with him. Now the positions were reversed: *he* was the one who couldn't go out to play. Jigme – Taktser Rinpoche – felt desperately sorry for him:

> Dissolved in tears he begged us to take him home. I was almost seventeen years old now, but I was still helpless in the face of such misery. Lobsang Samten was the first to join little Lhamo Dhondup in his sobs, but it was not long before I too dissolved into tears. A last attempt to distract my little brother by getting him to look at the dancing snowflakes outside the window naturally failed, and then we were all three in tears.

There were few consolations. Five-year-old Lobsang Samten, still so small that he had to be lifted over the lintels of schoolroom and assembly hall, was already attending scripture classes with other boys of his own age and was no longer available as a playmate. Lhamo Dhondup was lonely, miserable and bored. Years later he would remember 'waiting impatiently outside his classroom, and sometimes peering round the curtain in the doorway to try and attract his attention without letting his tutor see me. But the tutor was strict and Samten was helpless.'[10] Lobsang's tutor, though a strict disciplinarian who kept order with a bamboo rod, felt sorry for Lhamo Dhondup:

> Sometimes [he] used to put me on his lap and wrap me in his gown and give me dried fruits [apricots], and that is almost the only solace I remember.

Their uncle, Ngawang Changchup, was meant to be keeping an eye on the two younger boys, but they were scared of him. It was partly his appearance – pock-marked face, bristly black beard and fierce moustache – and partly his lack of patience with small boys. Once when Lhamo Dhondup, a mischievous child, had knocked over his uncle's book of loose-leaf scriptures, the latter picked him up and slapped him hard. When that sort of thing happened, the two brothers would run away and hide and though the matter usually ended with their uncle offering them sweets – 'which he never gave us when we behaved ourselves' – they never lost their fear of him. It was a wretched period of their lives.

While his own little personal tragedy was running its course, Lhamo Dhondup was the subject of some relentless power-bargaining in the world outside. Ma Pu-feng, convinced that the Taktser child was the genuine Dalai Lama, was unwilling to let the boy leave Amdo unless officially recognized as such. He was supported by the Kumbum monks, who wanted the prestige of having had the next Dalai Lama under their roof.[11] The

Tibetans wired Lhasa for the ransom money demanded – 100,000 Chinese dollars (the equivalent of 7,000 to 8,000 pounds sterling) – to be distributed partly to the authorities in Ch'inghai and partly to Kumbum. But, even when payment had been made, Ma asked for a further 300,000 Chinese dollars before he would allow the boy to leave. He would not budge, and the unfortunate search party had to spend the winter of 1938 in Kumbum monastery awaiting Lhasa's response. In the end, some sort of compromise was reached and the Tibetans agreed to pay the second instalment of the ransom. This they could only do with the help of the British Government of India.

Since 1936, the British had had a small Mission of their own in Lhasa. In the time of the Great Thirteenth, the Political Officer for Sikkim used to make fleeting visits to Lhasa if anything important had to be discussed with the Tibetan government. When a Chinese wireless station was set up in Lhasa after the funeral of the Great Thirteenth, the British, not unreasonably, were suspicious. 'We wanted to know what was going on,' says Hugh Richardson, at that time the British Trade Agent in Gyantse,[12] 'the Chinese had no treaty right to be there and we wanted to keep an eye on them.'[13] The British Mission consisted of one Officer with two clerical assistants; a Medical Officer with a small staff; and a wireless operator. 'The Tibetans were delighted to have us there, with our own radio transmitter, a much more powerful one than the Chinese had. The Chinese didn't like it. They went to the government and asked them to make us withdraw our radio transmitter. The Tibetans said they would do so if the Chinese withdrew theirs. And that was the end of that.' Within a year, the British Mission had become a semi-permanent arrangement under Basil Gould;[14] and when Gould left Lhasa in 1937, he left Hugh Richardson in charge – to keep an eye on the Chinese.

It was to Richardson that the Tibetans now turned. 'We didn't put the money up ourselves,' he says, 'but we arranged for them to have the silver without paying duty on it. The money itself was actually all raised by Muslims.' A group of rich Muslim traders going from Siling to Mecca by way of India, agreed to advance the required sum and allow the Tibetans to pay it back in Indian rupees. Thanks to the Tibetan exchange rate, the Muslim merchants would do well out of the deal, and they would also be the guarantee that Ma would not renege on the deal. Moreover, they would travel to Lhasa with the Tibetans – far more acceptable companions than the Chinese military escort that Ma was insisting on.

At last everyone was more or less satisfied and a binding document was signed by all sides, the Kumbum monks included.[15] The latter had demanded their own rake-off: a complete set of the Great Thirteenth's clothes, one of his thrones and decorations, and a 108-volume set of Buddhist Scriptures written in gold.[16] Ma Pu-feng insisted on one of the search party being left behind as a hostage – against the safe arrival of the goods from Lhasa![17]

When everything had been settled, Lhamo Dhondup was dressed in new robes and placed on a throne in Kesang Rinpoche's private quarters in Kumbum. In a brief installation ceremony, the lama uttered special ritual prayers. 'After receiving blessings from the boy, the group offered 100,000 butter-lamps at the Temple of the Golden Tree and spent the rest of the day making meritorious offerings to the monks and novices of the monastery, offering each of them a silver dollar. Then Lhamo Dhondup was taken to the Congregation Hall, where the Abbot of Kumbum offered him tea and rice followed by fruits.'[18] He dimly recalls a ceremony taking place one day at dawn. 'I remember this particularly as I was surprised to be woken and dressed before the sun had risen. I also remember being seated on a throne.'[19] He was three years old.

Lhamo Dhondup was delighted to learn that he was to go on a journey. Life seemed to be looking up. Best of all, his parents and two of his brothers, eleven-year-old Gyalo Thondup and six-year-old Lobsang Samten, were to go too. Taktser (Jigme), to his great disappointment, was to be left behind, like his sister, Tsering Dolma, now pregnant with her first child.[20]

On the first day of the sixth month of the Year of the Earth Hare (21 July 1939), two weeks after Lhamo Dhondup's fourth birthday, he and Lobsang Samten rejoined their parents and with a caravan of fifty people and three hundred and fifty horses and mules left Kumbum on a historic journey that had taken three weeks to prepare and would last for three months and thirteen days. As Lobsang Samten later recorded in a diary, 'From our village of Taktser in the region of Kokonor, from among our barley and potato fields, from our yaks and cows, from our simple peasant home, our family set out on a long, tedious journey across the endless expanse of the Tsaidam Marshes. Our destination was the Holy City of Lhasa, a city every Tibetan hopes to visit once in a lifetime to receive blessings from the seat of the Dalai Lamas.' Taktser (Jigme) has recorded his misery at the moment of departure:

The parting with my family...was very difficult. In my heart of hearts I was resentful at the decision which threatened to separate us not merely for the time being, but perhaps for ever. Together with many other monks I accompanied the great caravan for the first two hours of its journey, and my heart was heavy within me...On a little hill we all embraced each other for the last time. Secretly I still harboured the hope that at the last moment I should be asked to go with them, but nothing came of that, though my father did seem to guess my feelings and promised that he would do his best to see to it that later on I too should be called to Lhasa. Then the caravan moved off leaving me sadly staring after it.[1]

When Taktser returned to his *labrang*, it seemed empty and deserted, the children's toys still lying around as a mute reminder of the vanished past. For nights afterwards he would wake up suddenly 'with the feeling that Lobsang Samten had called out for me, or that Lhamo Dhondup had cried out in his sleep'. It was hard for him to realize he might never see either of them again.

Tsering Dolma felt equally bereft, though she was consoled by her parents' promise to send for her, should they be remaining in Lhasa. We do not know the feelings of Choekyong and Dekyi Tsering who, despite their nomadic Amdo blood, must have felt it a wrench to say goodbye to their homeland. They were leaving behind their two eldest children, their village, their house, their relations and friends, to embark on a perilous journey into the unknown. They knew that Lhamo Dhondup was in the running to be the next Dalai Lama; but although Dekyi Tsering said later that she had felt ninety per cent sure that he would be chosen, nothing had been officially decided.

As well as the family, there were the members of the search party, the Muslim pilgrims, the Chinese escort, several government officials and a large number of muleteers and scouts who, with their vast experience of the caravan routes and familiarity with the terrain, were indispensable to any long journey: only they knew where to ford the rivers and how to cross the formidable mountain passes. There were, of course, no cars, nor indeed any roads. The main party rode on horses and mules, Dekyi Tsering travelling in a separate conveyance, and Lhamo Dhondup in a specially made *treljam*: a wooden sedan-chair construction attached to two poles and fastened onto the backs of two mules. Over smooth ground he and Lobsang Samten would ride in this contraption, but when the going got rough, they had to be carried, with considerable difficulty, by the monks of the search party.

The party followed the well-worn caravan route from Amdo to the Holy City,

> through the forests of the Sandal Valley, amid scores of tiny lakes glimmering like sapphires and surrounded by lush, verdant pastures teeming with deer, antelope, wolves, bears, and large herds of *drongs* (wild yak) and *kyangs* (wild asses); on to the awesome Kokonor, its brilliant deep-blue waters reflecting the ring of snowcapped peaks along its shores...through vast steppe lands resplendent with yellow, brown, red and violet vegetation; over craggy, weather-beaten mountain passes above which eagles and vultures loomed; along the eastern edge of the marshy plains of Tsaidam, where a single mishap could cause pack animals to be swallowed up without trace; and across the eastern reaches of the windswept Chang Tang.[22]

The journey, recalled Dekyi Tsering,

> took us right across the bleak, uninhabited high plateau of Tibet. There were many dangerous rivers to cross, some with no bridges where the pack-animals had to swim across, drifting downwards with the strong current, until they could scramble ashore on the other side. We either rode our ponies and followed in their wake or were borne across in small, light coracles.[23]

Each day they travelled about ten miles, riding, as Tibetans on long journeys always did, from dawn till noon, resting in the afternoon before the winds got up, and camping in yak-hair tents at night, close to water and good grazing places, as the only dwellings on the route were a few nomad tents. In the evenings the men would sit around and chat and drink *chang*, while Dekyi Tsering busied herself with embroidery. Lobsang Samten remembers 'being wakened very early from sleep each morning and bundled into the palanquin. It was high summer and we could feel the cold wind in the air. Lhamo Dhondup and I played, teased each other and fought to the brink of tears in the palanquin.'[24]

The two boys were close, but like most small boys they wound each other up and spent much of their time sparring and punching each other. Lhamo Dhondup, the younger by two years, was usually the aggressor, and always came off best. Lobsang Samten was no weakling, but he was a peace-loving child, 'so good-natured he could not bring himself to use his superior strength against me'.[25] On this journey, the muleteers had a hard time of it, with the boys constantly scrapping in mid-palanquin. 'It was a marvellous play area,' chuckles the Dalai Lama, 'and we made the most of it.' The conveyance would lurch ominously from side to side, in danger of toppling over; and the driver would stop and summon the boys' mother. Running up to see what the matter was, she was invariably faced by a tearful Lobsang Samten, sobbing, 'The little bastard's been hitting me again.'[26] Lhamo Dhondup just sat there looking smug. 'When we'd finished fighting and had each retired to our allotted corners,' he chuckles, 'that must have been the best moment of the entire journey for the men carrying the palanquin. It was the only time it was evenly balanced. When we were quiet inside, everything was peaceful outside too. But when we started squabbling again, there was no more peace for anyone. Everyone was shouting at once. It was pandemonium.'[27]

They journeyed on, meeting no one along those vast open spaces but the occasional nomad arriving from afar to pay his respects. Even the two little boys in the *treljam* were awed by the majesty of their surroundings, the

gargantuan mountains flanking immense flat plains which we struggled over like insects. Occasionally, we came upon the icy rush of meltwater streams that we splashed noisily across...But mostly, it was just arid, empty space with only savage dust-laden winds and angry hailstorms as reminders of Nature's living forces.[28]

And now at last the news broke in Lhasa. As autumn approached, the inhabitants were overjoyed to hear that a young boy, about whom there could be no possible doubt, had been found near Kumbum and was expected to reach Nagchuka, ten days' march north-east of Lhasa, about 20 September.

As soon as the party was over the official border with Central Tibet – and thus beyond the reach of Ma Pu-feng – the Tibetan Government dropped all pretence of uncertainty. Summoning the National Assembly in Lhasa, they formally declared the boy from Taktser to be the Fourteenth Dalai Lama. The uncommon haste was probably in order to pre-empt the Chinese official who would be coming from Peking for the enthronement ceremony, to prevent him claiming, as he was sure to – and did – that the proclamation could not be made without him.

Several days later, the travellers crossed the last high pass to arrive at the village of Bumchen, where they encamped for the night.

As the sun began to rise next morning, the parents of Lhamo Dhondup saw a crowd of standard-bearers and officials and an elaborate camp laid out in the form of a square. Here at the 'Meadow of the Four Joys', one of the monks in the search party lifted the child onto his shoulders and carried him into a yellow tent which had belonged to the Thirteenth Dalai Lama. He was dressed in new robes and seated upon a throne hurriedly constructed out of dry clods of earth. In a brief service of welcome, the child was given an official document from the Regent acknowledging him as the Dalai Lama; and presented with gifts which may only be offered to the highest Incarnation present:

> ...the Offerings to All the Gods, in the form of a butter-cake with a number of turrets; an image of Tsepame, the god of endless life; a model of a chorten; and a miniature holy book...Also gold, silver, ceremonial garments, and rolls of silk and other materials.[39]

From now on Lhamo Dhondup would ride alone in the gilded palanquin of the Dalai Lamas. The secret was a secret no longer. The parents were officially told that their son was the new god-king; they were hailed as Great Mother (Gyayum) and Great Father (Gyayap) of Tibet and presented with ceremonial robes and jewellery. They then proceeded on their way to Nagchuka, the last staging-post on the caravan route to Lhasa.

In this huge gathering-place where the routes from all over Tibet converged, the camels were left behind and the caravans reassembled for the ten-mile journey to the Holy City. Here, seated on the throne of the Dalai Lamas in the monastery which is called 'the Palace of True Peace' the four-year-old held his first official reception.

Lobsang Samten felt only relief that the long journey was almost over; he was too young to understand that it was the end of more than a journey; that from this time forward his younger brother would no longer be Lhamo Dhondup to him. Such is the mystique surrounding a Dalai Lama that even the child's own family – even his mother – would henceforth refer to him as Kundun, meaning Presence of the Buddha. It was as Kundun that Lobsang Samten would address his brother for the rest of his life.

NOTES

1. Author interview with Gyalo Thondup, New Delhi, July 1995.

2. John Avedon, *An Interview with the Dalai Lama*, Littlebird Publications, 1980.

3. Fourteenth Dalai Lama, *Freedom in Exile*.

4. Conversation of Dekyi Tsering with Lady Gould, Isle of Wight, October 1960, as reported to the author.

5. Author interview with HH the Dalai Lama, June 1994.

6. Conversation with Lady Gould, 1960.

7. Letter dated 1/10/1939, Oriental and India Office Collections, L/P&S/12/4/178. Death of the XIIIth Dalai Lama and question of successor, December 1933 – October 1940.

8. Norbu, *Tibet Is My Country*.

9. Diary in the possession of Lobsang Samten's widow, Namlha Taklha.

10. Fourteenth Dalai Lama, *My Land and My People*.

11. Cf. Richardson, *Tibet and its History*.

12. Trade Agencies, established under treaty between Britain and Tibet after the Younghusband Expedition of 1904, were Vice-Consulates in all but name.

13. Author interview, 29 September 1993.

14. The British Political Officer based in Sikkim but responsible also for relations with Bhutan and Tibet.

15. Goldstein, *A History of Modern Tibet*.

16. 108 is a sacred figure to Tibetan Buddhists.

17. Goldstein, p. 322.

18. Goodman, *The Last Dalai Lama*, chapter 1.

19. Fourteenth Dalai Lama, *Freedom in Exile*.

20. Marriages in Tibet were secular occasions, though the couple did go to the temple afterwards to seek the Buddha's blessing.

21. *Tibet Is My Country*.

22. Goodman, chapter 5.

23. Conversation of Dekyi Tsering with Lady Gould, October 1960.

24. Diary of Lobsang Samten, in the possession of his widow, Namlha Taklha.

25. *Freedom in Exile*.

26. As reported by his mother to Tendzin Choegyal.

27. Author interview, June 1994.

28. *Freedom in Exile*.

29. Report by B. J. Gould.

6

Lord of the Lion Throne

He is supposed to be the temporary embodiment of a god...called upon to lead, comfort and improve sinful, suffering mankind, and to teach the way to release. It is throughout the same being who sits on the Lhasa throne in successive embodiments. The secret person, the spiritual reality of the Dalai Lama, is immutable and only his body changes, a perishable vessel employed to reach down to the lowly human level and to make the dazzling light of the truth he embodies accessible to our limited understanding.

Giuseppe Tucci, To Lhasa and Beyond

It was almost seven years since the Thirteenth Dalai Lama had died, leaving a great void at the heart of Tibet. Now at last, he had returned. The timing was auspicious: the new ruler must enter Lhasa before the end of the eighth month of the Tibetan Year, the ninth month of the current Year of the Earth Hare being considered unlucky.

Hugh Richardson, as the *Times* Special Correspondent, shared the excitement of the people as the child drew near to the Holy City: [1]

Boy God in Lhasa

The Dalai Lama's Return

TIBETAN HOMAGE

Rigya, over two miles east of Lhasa and within sight of the soaring Potala, was the scene the day before yesterday of the first ceremony on the return of the Dalai Lama to his capital in his fourteenth reincarnation. On a plain below rocky foothills a large encampment had been set out in square formation, three lines deep around a splendid reception tent standing in a yellow walled enclosure. Its outer cover was bright yellow – a colour used only for the tents of the Dalai Lama – and decorated with blue designs; its inner roof was richly embroidered with circular patterns in blue, red and yellow; and on the roof-pole were gilded figures, including peacocks, from which it gets its name of the Peacock Tent...

The Regent went in procession with the state sedan chair up to Rigya Monastery on the hill above the camp. Before long an excited murmur told that 'the Presence' was coming and the crowd on a spur hiding the road to the east stirred expectantly as the band of the Bodyguard was heard. Soon, above clouds of dust mingled with the smoke of incense and above the mass of the people, tall banners came into sight. Deep trumpets sounded from the monastery on the hill. A reverent, silent crowd of Tibetans pressed forward to see the four-year-old child from the distant Chinese province of Siling[1] in whom their compassionate ruler Chenrezi has again become incarnate. A small troop of Chinese soldiers in dusty, quilted clothes came a little in advance, followed by a body of mounted men in bright silks and tall Mongolian hats holding banners. Behind them rode officials in ascending importance wearing magnificent brocade robes and, preceding the centre of the cavalcade, a sedan chair covered in yellow silk through the glass windows of which the small Dalai Lama could be seen looking with calm interest at the crowd. Behind rode his father and mother and his two brothers.

HOMAGE

After a short rest the Dalai Lama was carried down in the large gilded palanquin over which waved an umbrella of peacocks' feathers and one of yellow silk, to receive homage in the Peacock Tent. There he was seated on the throne. After making three prostrations before him the officials, headed by the Regent, began to file past, offering white silk scarves and receiving his blessing. The stream, which included British, Nepalese and Chinese representatives and Lhasa Moslems, poured past the throne for almost an hour, while the Dalai Lama, wearing yellow brocade and a yellow peaked fur hat, sat solemnly and with dignity holding out his hands to touch the worshippers...

The dignity and self-possession of the child impressed everyone. He looked about calmly, seeming unmoved by the magnificence and as if he were in familiar surroundings. Although appearing to grow tired towards the end of the ceremony he did not lose his composure. He never smiled, but maintained a placid, equable gaze. Much of his attention was directed to a calm inspection of members of the British Mission, as though he were trying to recall where he had seen such people before.[3]

The travellers had reached Rigya on 6 October, and the whole of Lhasa turned out to greet them. The Dalai Lama's father was resplendent in the official robes of a Cabinet Minister, but the new Great Mother still wore her simple Amdo clothes. Everyone 'was very happy to see her, and at the same time amused by her costume'.[4]

The official party spent two nights in the encampment before setting out on the last leg of the journey to Lhasa. Lobsang Samten confided his wonderment to his diary:

> The closer we got to the Holy City, more and more parties came out of Lhasa to see His Holiness. Splendidly-robed members of the Cabinet came to us amid the music of horns, cymbals, drums and gongs. Juniper branches were lit along the route, the air was full of sights and smells. The officials were so splendid, the peasants by the roadside were dressed in their best chubas and wearing all the jewellery they owned. We were dazzled. It seemed as if the whole population not only of the city but of the surrounding villages had turned out to get a first glimpse of their precious Yeshi Norbu and get his blessing. The unforgettable crowd, the music and the joy was felt by everybody, not least by the four-year-old boy for whom this great performance was being laid on.[5]

The Dalai Lama remembers only 'a sense of homecoming and endless crowds of people. I had never thought there could be so many.' Hearing the people shout 'The day of our happiness has come', he felt he was living in a dream.

Hugh Richardson watched as the procession arrived in Lhasa:

> The procession enclosing the yellow palanquin rode through streets lined
> with monks holding banners and auspicious emblems. The villagers were
> dressed in bright colours as dancers and musicians. Every window was shut
> and curtained, for no one should look from above on the Dalai Lama...
>
> As the middle of the procession reached the south entrance of the cathedral
> it was met by the Oracle of Nechung in a state of possession. A god who acts
> as guardian of religion is said to enter into him, and when he is so possessed
> he dances with convulsive movements, bending his body fiercely to the
> ground, forwards and backwards. He wears a high head-dress of white plumes
> over a golden crown and brandishes a sword and a bow. This terrible figure
> rushed to the Dalai Lama's palanquin and thrust in his head so that the spirit
> in him could do reverence. There had been some apprehension that the sight
> would frighten the child, but it is said that he was quite unperturbed.[6]

The *Times* correspondent was full of admiration for Lhamo Dhondup. 'His
calm assurance during the exacting two days of his entry into Lhasa has
been a source of wonder and delight to the people of Tibet and has confirmed their trust in the reincarnation.'[7]

Shortly after his triumphal entry into the city, the new Dalai Lama was
taken to the Jokhang Temple where he and Lobsang Samten were initiated
as monks. His hair was symbolically shorn by Reting Rinpoche, the Regent; and he was given a string of imposing new names, among them two
of the Regent's own:

> In accordance with ancient custom, I forfeited my name, Lhamo Dhondup,
> and assumed his, Jamphel Yeshe, along with several others, so that my full
> name now became Jamphel Ngawang Lobsang Yeshe Tenzin Gyatso.[8]

His names meant: Holy One, Tender Glory, Mighty in Speech, Compassionate One, Learned Defender of the Faith, Ocean of Wisdom. He would
sign himself with the last two names: Tenzin Gyatso, the Fourteenth
Dalai Lama.

The boy was then escorted to the Norbulingka Palace. Though it was already winter (past the date when the Dalai Lamas traditionally transferred to the cold and draughty Potala Palace), he was to stay in the summer palace until after his formal enthronement at the Potala. The original Norbulingka, about five kilometres west of the Potala, had been built by the Seventh Dalai Lama in the eighteenth century and successive rulers had added their own two-storey palaces and pavilions and developed the park, filling it with tame musk-deer, peacocks, pheasant and many other birds and animals. Pet fish abounded in the ponds, and on its exceptionally fertile soil grew poplars, willows, junipers, fruit trees and myriads of flowers imported from India.

The two boys were in the three-storey Kelsang Palace, largest of the smaller palaces in the inner court of the park which was surrounded by a yellow wall. It had about twenty rooms and various chapels, storage rooms for clothing, books and the writings of past Dalai Lamas.

The new ruler was happy that winter. Too young to begin his studies, he had his brother to play with, and his parents and Gyalo Thondup were lodged close by in a farmhouse known as Gyatso, about fifteen minutes' walk on the other side of the yellow wall enclosure. Life had never been so good:

> Almost every day I used to steal over, with an attendant, to spend time with them. This was not really allowed, but the Regent, who was responsible for me, chose to ignore these excursions. I particularly liked going there at mealtimes. Boys destined for the monastery were not supposed to eat pork, eggs and fish as it was believed that these foods rotted the brain. So when my parents sat down to a meal of roast pork and crackling which I loved, I would sit between them like a hungry dog with its mouth open for scraps. My mother would give in first – she was soft-hearted and couldn't stand the strain of seeing me look so longingly at what was on her plate, so she kept passing me bits surreptitiously. My father would then slip me some pieces of crackling when he thought she wasn't looking.[9]

Once a senior official caught him eating an egg. 'He was very shocked. And so was I. I shouted "Go away" in the loudest voice I could manage.'

One curious incident had startled his mother. On arrival in Lhasa, the four-year-old had mysteriously insisted that his teeth were in a certain house within the Norbulingka park. When taken there, he pointed to a box, saying that was where he'd left them. When the box was opened, it was found to contain a set of dentures which had belonged to the Thirteenth Dalai Lama![10]

Young as he was, he was already giving official audiences at the Norbulingka. Everyone was struck by his firm gaze, his personality and the extraordinary concentration and ease with which he carried out the ceremonials, granting blessings, and knotting the silk scarves to be conferred on those deemed worthy of this special honour. All who saw him were convinced that he was truly the Dalai Lama reborn. His close attendants were pleased to note his obvious affection for those with whom his predecessor had been friendly, his kindness to the Great Thirteenth's former servants and the love of flowers which he had inherited from his former manifestation.[11]

New Year 1940 – Year of the Iron Dragon – a memorable time to be in Lhasa. New Year (Lhosar) was the greatest and happiest of the annual festivals, usually located between the end of February and the beginning of March. It lasted for several weeks, being also the main season of religious observance in Tibet, the time of the first new moon, when the evil of the past year was symbolically driven out. Basil Gould[12] was among the large crowds who that year gathered to celebrate the festival – and to catch a rare glimpse of the Regent with the parents of the new Dalai Lama and his two elder brothers, Gyalo Thondup and Lobsang Samten. The brothers were, reported Gould, in a telegram to the Foreign Office in New Delhi,[13] 'aged about 11 and 8, very strong, bright, intelligent boys'.

This New Year had been chosen by the Tibetan Government for the formal return of the Dalai Lama to his Lion Throne in the Potala Palace. For six years, food had regularly been placed beside the vacant throne, as if, wrote Gould (who was to represent the British Government and the Government of India at the enthronement), 'the Dalai Lama were merely absent on a journey and might return at any time; and always those who attended ceremonies had bowed to the throne and offered a silk scarf at it, as if the Dalai Lama had been present'.[14]

Before leaving Lhasa on 4 June, Gould would advise his colleagues in New Delhi that 'in finding its Dalai Lama Tibet has also found itself and has gained enormously in confidence and hope.'[15] He had felt privileged to be an eye-witness on 21 February when the young Amdo boy made a spectacular 'return' to his palace:

73

Entry of the Dalai Lama into the Potala

Almost everyone who was not on duty set out at dawn to line the route. Here were assembled many ladies of the chief families in Lhasa, gay in head-dresses set with seed-pearls, coral and turquoise, over which were looped the black coils of their long hair – eight-inch ear ornaments cut flat and set in gold gem-set charm boxes – silk robes of every colour, with silk shirt-sleeves of some contrasting colour turned back over the wrist – a cascade of pearls and gems over the right shoulder – and, in the case of married women or grown-up girls, an apron in rainbow stripes of green, red, purple, green, gold, green, purple, or whatever succession of bright colours the individual weaver had chosen...

Along the route were men and women tending incense crocks, set on walls or carried on arm or shoulder, fed with artemisia or other fragrant herbs; troupes of strolling dancers, some in head-dresses like red Indians, some in masks; mummers; bands and drummers; clean-featured shepherds dressed in sheepskin, their broad-browed and plump wives wearing their hair in an hundred closely-plaited ringlets; monks of every age from four upwards in maroon robes, often tattered; beggars, farmers – thousands turning prayer-wheels of every device and size.

THE PROCESSION

First came servants, on ponies and on foot, dressed in green tunics, blue breeches and broad, red-tasselled hats, carrying the Dalai Lama's food, kitchen-ware, garments and bed-clothes; grooms to be ready for their master at the Potala; attendants carrying tall banners to ward off evil spirits; some members of the Chinese delegation; high lamas followed by the State Oracle and the Chief Secretaries; the led ponies of the Dalai Lama in gorgeous silk trappings; the head monks of the Potala monastery in claret robes fringed with gold and silver embroidery; junior lay officials in their long mantles of many colours, black shirts and white boat-shaped hats set sideways on the head and tied down under the ears; lay officers in ascending order of rank, all stiff in heavy brocade. And then through the clouds of incense which were drifting across the route, and between lines of standard-bearers, came two long double lines of men in loose green uniforms and red hats with white plumes, holding draw-ropes – which would be needed for the climb up the Potala – and men in red with yellow hats, bearing, as they moved with short, shuffling steps, the yokes which supported the poles of the Dalai Lama's great golden palanquin.

The child was invisible behind gold curtains and bright bunches of paper flowers. To his right rear was carried the tall peacock umbrella which is the privilege of the Dalai Lamas. Next came the Regent, under a gold umbrella, dressed in robes of golden silk and a yellow conical hat trimmed with black fox-skin, his horse weighed down with trappings and led by two grooms; then the Dalai Lama's father, mother and brothers; then Abbots and Tulkus from monasteries throughout Tibet, in peaked hats and wrapped in coats of gold brocade worn over maroon robes. It was seen that some Incarnate Lamas, boys as young as the Dalai Lama himself, were firmly tied to their saddles. Towards the end of the procession came more civil officials, seniors leading; more monk-officials; and finally a giant monk door-keeper of the Potala monastery who with stentorian voice kept back the dense crowd of monks, citizens and villagers who, in the manner of spectators everywhere, were closing in from the sides of the route to accompany the Dalai Lama on his progress.

As dawn broke on the great day, long before the child was due to make his entrance, the huge audience hall dominated by the Lion Throne was already full. While the officials, guests and family waited, in an anteroom attendants were laying out the splendid gifts to be presented later in the day. Among them were two magnificent horses from the Maharajah of Sikkim, and, from the British Government, 'a brick of gold, fresh from the Calcutta Mint, ten bags of silver, three rifles, six rolls of broadcloth of different colours, a gold watch and chain, field glasses, an English saddle, a picnic case, three stoves, a musical box, two pairs of budgerigars and a garden hammock'.[16] More exotic gifts had arrived from the monastery of Tashilhunpo, seat of the Panchen Lamas: golden Buddhas wrapped in coloured silks; 'holy books, sets of golden silk clothes; sets of the eight lucky signs in gold and in silver; bags of gold dust; a six-foot elephant tusk; a rhinoceros horn set in silver; silver ingots; countless rolls of silk and fine cloth; and provisions of every kind'.[17]

On that day, the Tibetan love of spectacle surpassed itself:

The Dalai Lama rode in a great golden palanquin, the draw-ropes and rear-ropes of which were held by long lines of men wearing green uniforms and red hats with white plumes. The palanquin was mounted on four long poles, each having six bearers with red dresses and yellow hats who advanced with shuffling steps. It was flanked by two great ceremonial umbrellas, one of gold and the other of peacock green. The Dalai Lama sat invisible behind the gold curtains. The palanquin was preceded by the servants of the Dalai Lama, carrying his food and clothes; they wore red hats with broad tassels, green tunics and blue breeches. Next came the carriers of the banners which are supposed to ward off evil spirits, followed by the Dalai Lama's state oracle and his chief secretaries. The ponies of the Dalai Lama were led in the procession and after them came the monks of the Potala Monastery in claret-coloured robes, the lay officers of state in order of rank, and the Cabinet Ministers. Behind the Dalai Lama's palanquin came the Regent, in gold robes with a conical yellow hat trimmed with fur; he was followed by the father, mother and two brothers of the Dalai Lama, who excited the curiosity and interest of the onlookers. The father was dressed as a *Kung* (Duke), a title bestowed on him by the Tibetan authorities. Abbots and Incarnate Lamas from monasteries throughout the country brought up the rear, wrapped in cloaks of gold brocade.[18]

To the blare of Tibetan horns and trumpets, the Dalai Lama and his retinue entered the hall and the ceremony began. The child climbed the lower steps of the Throne and was lifted on to it, wrapped in warm coverings to keep out the cold. One at a time, the monks and officials approached, prostrating their length, offering good wishes, prayers and gifts. On and on and on, for well over five hours. That ceremony represented, said Gould, 'the public and definitive acknowledgement of his people by the Dalai Lama, and of the Dalai Lama by his people'. Particularly striking was:

> the extraordinary interest of the child in the proceedings, his presence, and his infallible skill in doing the right thing to the right person at the right time. He was perhaps the only person amongst many hundreds who never fidgeted and whose attention never wavered. It was very evident that the *sitringasol* was indeed the return, in response to prayer, of the Dalai Lama to a throne which by inherent authority was already his.[19]

On the following day, 23 February, members of the small British Mission in Lhasa attended at a repeat performance of the Installation Ceremony, with Gould representing His Majesty's Government and the Government of India. The little matter of the date almost caused an international incident. The British in New Delhi, having already ascertained that the Chinese delegate, Mr Wu Chang, was 'a person of considerable importance' in China,[20] were anxious lest he be given a significant role in the ceremony. Their anxiety increased when the Associated Press of India issued – in advance of the event – a report of what they had been assured (by the Chinese) would happen at the enthronement: namely that the Regent and Mr Wu would together escort the Dalai Lama to his throne and preside over the ceremony, during which Wu would read from a golden scroll the Chinese Government's formal acknowledgement of the installation. Though this scenario turned out to be no more than Chinese wishful thinking, the British were furious! And when they heard that Wu but not Gould had been present at the ceremony on the twenty-second, Gould had a lot of explaining to do.

Telegrams winged between him and his outraged masters in New Delhi. Had the British not been invited on the twenty-second? they cabled,[21] obviously fearful that they might have been relegated to the B List. And again, a few days later,[22] 'Was there, in your opinion, ever any expectation that you would be invited to attend the ceremony on Feb. 22? Do you attribute exclusion to religious prejudice or to Regent's desire to placate Chinese by thus emphasising the special position of China vis à vis Tibet?' Weary of this inquisition, Gould replied firmly that there was 'NO question of religious discrimination, no question of the ceremony on 22nd being more important than on 23rd or of our being excluded from it. The question I had to consider was whether we should be present on 22 Feb. and again on another date with gifts, or make a single appearance with our gifts. I decided on the latter alternative and chose 23 Feb.'[23] Wu, he explained in a second telegram that same day,[24] 'was originally allotted the 26th for the presentation of his gifts but (apparently at the last moment) decided to attend on 22 February also. Possibly this may have been done with a view to affording some sort of foundation of truth for his false account of proceedings'. The Chinese, Gould insisted, did nothing at the ceremony which was not also done by the British and other foreigners present – i.e. Wu had merely presented a silk ceremonial scarf. 'It did not, however, perhaps suit the Chinese book to admit this and on this as on other occasions they have published a deliberately false account of what took place.'[25]

It was not true, then, that the Chinese (as they would indeed claim) played a central role in the installation of the new Dalai Lama – or that the British had been slighted.[26] Far from feeling put down, Gould was clearly ecstatic. 'As I knelt before the child,' he said later,

A long white scarf which he had blessed was placed round my neck and I felt two small firm hands on my head. Through those small hands I felt an inner strength, as though some of the strength and wisdom of many Dalai Lamas was being imparted to me.[27]

The family were there, absorbing everything with unsophisticated delight, as Gould rather touchingly commented in a letter to his superiors in New Delhi:

> It was clear that the Dalai Lama is interested in us; and constantly, before and during the installation ceremony, the parents and brothers, who were only a little way to our right across an empty space, were as smiling, and as communicative by means of smiles, as it is possible to be. I am certain that they are really nice people and that they want to be friends...

The family were entranced by the gifts the British had presented, specially chosen by Gould himself, among them 'a gold clock with a nightingale that pops out and sings, a pedal motor car and a tricycle'. The child himself could not take his eyes off them. As the audience ended, he

> was lifted down from his throne and left the hall of audience, holding the hands of two Abbots who towered on either side of him, but looking back at the things which had gripped his attention. Within a minute, his six-year-old brother was on the spot, to find out how everything worked, and additionally keen and anxious because, as he said, if he did not at once find out all about everything, his four-year-old brother would certainly beat him up...The little monk was soon going round the smooth floor of the audience chamber in the pedal car.

There was an amusing sequel to this story, when Gould came up against an unsuspected streak of stubbornness in the young god-king. As he wrote to Olaf Caroe in New Delhi:

> I have had my first tussle with the Dalai Lama...With the presents we had to submit a formal list, to be entered in the records of the Potala, and this list made mention of two pairs of budgerigars. The Lord Chamberlain had already told me that the Dalai Lama loved birds and loved his nightingale [clock], but we had wanted to keep the budgerigars with us for a time, to become acclimatized after their trying journey, and to breed. But it was no good. Messenger after messenger, each a degree more important than the last, came down from the Potala to demand the delivery of the birds, and by the time Norbhu's clerk, Pemba, was approaching the Dalai Lama's apartments with the birds, a high dignitary of the church was there to receive them.
> Pemba, considerably overcome, handed over the birds and tried to make himself scarce; but he was sent for by the Dalai Lama who, talking Tibetan clearly and easily, discussed the birds' food and how to keep them safe. Pemba

then noticed that the watch, nightingale clock and musical box were all on the Dalai Lama's private table, and was told that the Dalai Lama, when off duty, will hardly let them out of his sight...[28]

Before leaving Lhasa, in June, Gould would write with some satisfaction that it was 'common knowledge that the Dalai Lama refers to us [i.e. the British] as the people who gave him the presents which he likes best'.[29] He also noted that 'His Holiness has a strong will and is already learning to exercise the privileges of his position'.

'It seems clear,' scribbled the Under-Secretary in the margins of Gould's report, 'that the new Dalai Lama must be a very remarkable little boy'.[30]

Behind the glitz of public ceremonial, all was far from well in Tibet. Though Regent Reting had played a prominent role in the installation – shaving the Dalai Lama's head and bestowing his names on him – there were many who believed that he was unworthy of such honour. During his Regency, the Great Thirteenth's warnings were coming true: corruption was rife at every level of the Tibetan administration, and the social and ethical standards of the previous reign had virtually collapsed. Reting's own reputation was more than a little tarnished: his dissolute lifestyle was notorious, his greed a byword – the trading company he had set up in his *labrang* at Reting had grown into the third largest trading outfit in the whole of Tibet. The British Representative in Lhasa, Hugh Richardson, expressed the opinion that 'The Regent is governed by self-interest. He has no fixed policy and his actions are dictated by monetary considerations.'[31] Since coming to power in 1933, Reting had promoted his cronies and eliminated his critics, becoming by April 1939 effectively the sole ruler of Tibet. Opposition to him began to build up. A Lhasa street song complained that:

Yesterday's Tibetan Government
Had Tigers and Lions facing each other.
Today the wolves and the jackals
Have blown the Government to the winds.[32]

The growing public unease was heightened by the fact that in 1942 the Dalai Lama was to take his first set of monastic vows, including one of permanent celibacy. These were traditionally administered by the Regent, his Senior Tutor, a man naturally assumed to be of blameless habits. This

Reting palpably was not. Yet 'if the vows are given by someone who has broken the vows, then the vows he has given are meaningless, and the young monk has in effect taken no vows at all'.[33] The dilemma was as acute as it was unusual.

Even as the young Dalai Lama prepared to return to the Potala after his enthronement, wall-posters appeared all over Lhasa, attacking the Regent and even naming a particular Lhasa woman with whom he was said to be associated. Many declared that it was crucial for the young Dalai Lama to be tutored by a lama who was true to his own vows. For Regent Reting, the writing was quite literally on the wall.

NOTES

1. *The Times*, 4 November 1939.
2. Siling, the capital of the province of Amdo (known to the Chinese as Ching'hai).
3. *The Times*, 8 October 1939.
4. Rinchen Dolma Taring, *Daughter of Tibet*, John Murray, 1970.
5. Diary of Lobsang Samten, courtesy of his widow, Namlha Taklha. 'Yeshi Norbu' (Precious Protector) is another of the Dalai Lama's official titles.
6. *The Times*, 10 October 1939.
7. *The Times*, 8 October 1939.
8. Fourteenth Dalai Lama, *Freedom in Exile*, chapter 2.
9. Author interview with HH the Dalai Lama, Dharamsala, July 1995.
10. John Avedon, *An Interview with the Dalai Lama*.
11. Gould, *The Jewel in the Lotus*.
12. The Political Officer for Sikkim, with a 'vaguely diplomatic role' in Tibet.
13. 8 February 1940.
14. Sir Basil Gould, C.M.G., C.I.E., 'The Discovery of the Fourteenth Dalai Lama', article in the *Geographical Magazine*, October 1946.
15. Oriental and India Office Collections of the British Library, L/P&S/12/4178, File 15 (1).
16. Report by B. J. Gould.
17. Goodman, *The Last Dalai Lama*.
18. *The Times*, 23 April 1940.
19. Report by B. J. Gould.

20. Confidential letter to External Affairs Department, New Delhi, from Gould, 2 December 1939. 'The status of Mr Wu...corresponds roughly to that of a junior Minister of non-Cabinet rank. This means that in China he is a person of considerable importance and the Chinese Consul-General when writing about him refers to him as His Excellency.' Oriental and India Office Collections of the British Library, L/P&S/12/4178, File 15 (2).

21. Telegram No. 670, from External Affairs Department, New Delhi to Gould, 2 March 1940.

22. Telegram XX No. 751, 11 March 1940, External Affairs, New Delhi, to Gould.

23. Telegram XX No. 40, 14 March.

24. Telegram XX No. 39, 14 March.

25. Telegram XX No. 39 from Gould, as above, 14 March 1940.

26. Gould eventually issued a printed pamphlet on the Enthronement, 'to counter false Chinese propaganda by giving an authentic account of what actually happened'. This was later summarized for an article in the *Geographical Magazine*, October 1946.

27. Letter from Basil Gould in Lhasa to Olaf Caroe, C.I.E., Secretary to the Government of India in the External Affairs Department, New Delhi, 1 March 1940. Oriental and India Office Collections of the British Library, L/P&S/12/4178, File 15(1).

28. Letter to Olaf Caroe, Oriental and India Office Collections, as above.

29. Letter, 4 June 1940, as above.

30. L/P&S/12/4179, File 15 (2) Oriental and India Office Collections of the British Library.

31. Report of the British Mission in Lhasa, October 1938–September 1939. Quoted by Goldstein, *A History of Modern Tibet*, chapter 9.

32. K. Dhondup, *The Water Bird and Other Years*, New Delhi, Rangwang, 1986.

33. Goldstein, chapter 9.

7

City of the Gods

Lhasa is by no means the only city or town in Tibet, yet in Tibet, as in the world outside, to hear people talk you would think that Lhasa *was* Tibet. It is the one place that every Tibetan yearns to see at least once before he dies. Many walk over a thousand miles across snow-covered mountains and wind-swept plateaux to fulfil their desire, and many die in the attempt.

Thubten Jigme Norbu with Colin Turnbull, Tibet

Lhasa, whose name means 'abode of the gods', is twelve thousand feet above sea-level, and on roughly the same latitude as Delhi, Cairo and New Orleans. It is situated on the right bank of the Kyi Chu river, thirty miles east of where it meets the great Tsang Po, known outside Tibet as the Brahmaputra. The city was said to have been founded fourteen centuries earlier in the reign of King Songtsen Gampo (617–650) when Buddhism first flourished in Tibet. The social and commercial heart of the city which grew up around the sacred Jokhang temple was Barkhor Street, at once a pilgrimage circuit and a market-place. It was alive with people and life there had changed little over the centuries.

Apart from the numerous pilgrims swarming in and out of the city – seekers after spiritual truth used to come to this 'Mecca of High Asia' from as far away as Siberia and the southern borderlands of China – Lhasa had a resident population of forty to sixty thousand, living for the most

82

part along narrow streets in white-washed stone houses with flat roofs and inward-sloping walls. No house was permitted to be more than two storeys high, since it was considered blasphemous to appear to compete with the Jokhang Temple or the gold-roofed Potala which crowned one of the two hills on which the city was built. The rule about height was strictly observed and applied not only to the sacred buildings but also to the person of the Dalai Lama, and by extension to the Regent.

Lhasa was to be the home of the new Royal Family. From the day the Dalai Lama arrived in Lhasa, 6 October 1939, the Tibetan Government made itself responsible for them. Although traditionally a Dalai Lama's family had no political role to play in Tibet, the change in their social position must have been unnerving to say the least. A rags-to-riches fairy-tale with elements of nightmare. Simple, untutored peasant-farmers from a remote mountainous province, where everybody knew everybody else and spoke the same dialect, suddenly Choekyong and Dekyi Tsering were transformed into royalty and required to live in a city which was the hub of the Tibetan universe. Like all previous Dalai Lamas' families (and almost all of them had come from similar peasant backgrounds) they were given the royal rank of Yapshi. The parents became the Gyayum and the Gyayap Chenmo, Great (Holy) Mother and Great (Holy) Father. Choekyong Tsering as head of the family became a Kung, roughly the equivalent of Royal Duke. Their male children were Sey Kusho or Prince, the females Semo Kusho, Princess. When they married, the men would also have the title Kung, while the girls would be called Lhacham Kusho, Your Ladyship. Nor was the Yapshi name restricted to mere titles; it carried with it a house in Lhasa and one or more manorial estates with attached servants.[1] As Giuseppe Tucci wrote, 'whether such families were rich or poor, as soon as they were blessed with so happy an event, they were granted an estate to be held in fee, which would secure their welfare ever after'.[2]

As landowners they needed a family name. (Only landowning families had one.) The couple first thought of adopting the name of their village, Taktser, but as it meant 'Roaring Tiger', it was felt to be unsuitable for the family of a Dalai Lama. So they chose Taklha, 'the House that Seeks Happiness', and from then on were known as the Yapshi Taklha family.

While the Kashag looked out for a suitable home for them, they were temporarily accommodated in Gyatso, an old two-storey farmhouse (four rooms down, three up) near the Norbulingka Park, about fifteen minutes walk from the enclosure where the Dalai Lama and Lobsang Samten were living. It was surrounded by fields and plentifully endowed with springs of pure, sparkling water.

Despite the rural setting, the couple missed the easy camaraderie of Amdo where every neighbour and tradesman was a relation or friend; in Lhasa their new acquaintances were aristocrats. 'They had to get by as best they could,' comments one of their sons. 'They were refugees, having to learn everything from scratch, mixing with families who had six hundred years of tradition behind them.'[3] They were understandably disoriented, ignorant of the language, bemused by the strict etiquette which had pitchforked them to the lonely pinnacle of society. Dekyi Tsering was still her old, simple self, but she found the aristocratic ladies were in awe of her status as Great Mother. 'Some of the great ladies would go and call on her, but they wouldn't socialize with her,' remembers Hugh Richardson. 'It had nothing to do with snobbery. It was just that as soon as they became The Family, they were automatically treated with the deference due to royalty.'

In adapting to her new situation, Dekyi Tsering was helped by her own strength of character. She may have been raised to a dizzy social height, but she did not intend to let it turn her head. One of her future daughters-in-law said that 'when extraordinary things happened to her, she never let them make any difference. She never felt she was special.'[4] Dekyi Tsering remained unaffected by the dazzling changes, she was and would remain a housewife, referring to herself without affectation as 'the Farmer's Wife'. She would scold her husband when he shouted at the servants; she herself treating them with the camaraderie and innate kindness which she had bestowed on the hired help or travelling artisans in Amdo, expecting them to eat with the family, for example – which they found quite shocking. When the Kashag showered her with fine silken clothes, splendid necklaces and ear-rings, she stowed them away carefully and – except on ceremonial occasions – continued to wear only the homespun clothes and traditional jewellery of Amdo. At first the city sophisticates found this hilarious; but gradually they came to understand that Dekyi Tsering was that rare phenomenon, a completely natural human being. She was as she was, and felt neither need nor desire to emulate the fine ladies of Lhasa. Always generous, welcoming and kind, Dekyi Tsering was soon as much loved in the capital as she had been in Amdo.

Her husband, the Kung, was another matter. It is not really surprising that Choekyong Tsering was thrown off-balance. Confused by the language barrier, ill-at-ease with the nobility, he let his new wealth and status go to his head. His wife might go on being the Farmer's Wife, but he had no intention of continuing to be the Farmer.

It seems that the Kashag's problems with the Kung began almost at once, when he demanded large amounts of cash for his own use. When, in June 1940, the Kashag offered him two estates – one of them the Gyatso farmhouse, the other Chayul, site of an abandoned tea plantation in southern Tibet – he accepted both, then demanded more! A confidential letter from a Tibetan official in the Government of India service dated January 1942 is quite specific about the Kung's greed.[5] (The official includes both the Dalai Lama's parents in his censure, but, in the light of all that is known of Dekyi Tsering, it seems likely that this was merely blame by association):

> As soon as the Dalai Lama's parents took over these two estates, they again demanded more fertile estates and a good living house. The Tibetan Government convened a meeting of the National Assembly and informed the parents of the decision of the meeting, that the Government cannot grant any more estates as [their] financial position is poor and they have to spend a considerable amount of money in worshipping and burning of butter-lamps. The Tibetan Government offered a living house belonging to an official...who was dismissed from service and banished on 6 June. The parents refused the offer of the house on the grounds that they [would] not feel at home in a house which the Tibetan Government had confiscated.
>
> The Dalai Lama's parents again complained that they [could] not maintain and support themselves with the two estates and they demanded three more estates, viz. Dongtse, 12 miles west of Gyantse, Seshing, about 40 miles west of Lhasa, and Jora in Lhoka (southern Tibet). They said that before they left their country with the Dalai Lama, the Tibetan Government had promised to give them everything they required and now they must get what they require. The Kashag and the National Assembly had to grant these estates and the Dalai Lama's father took charge [of them] in August 1941. [IIc] selected a building site in Changs[h]ep Shar in Lhasa, which is about 800 yards in length and about 500 yds in breadth. Building materials are being hurriedly collected by the Tibetan Government.[6]

All of which must have made the Kashag reflect that their new Great Father was something of a mixed blessing.

Meanwhile, the family had to settle into their new surroundings. Lhasa was no modern city; conditions were primitive. Throughout winters that were bitterly cold, houses were unheated. There was no running water for drinking, but it could be fetched from Lhasa's numerous wells.[7] Since water for washing had to be heated over yak-dung fires, washing was not a popular winter pastime. But, at a height of twelve thousand feet, washing was not of prime importance anyway, since there was little decay, and no foul smells polluted the cold, dry air. Spring was the time for washing clothes, and when the warmer weather came, women could be seen on the banks of the Kyi Chu, stamping garments with their feet or beating them against stones. The women 'would pour wet sand on the fur side of the skins; when the sand dried they would beat it out with sticks, singing all the while. The garment turned fluffy and fresh again.'[8]

Dr Regolo Moise, an Italian doctor who visited Lhasa in 1948, described sanitary conditions there as 'low but not absolutely disastrous, nor any worse than those of several better-known countries', and reported the absence of diseases such as pneumonia and pulmonary tuberculosis. 'Cold helps the Tibetans in the defence against infective illnesses, by rendering garbage innocuous and making life hard for bacteria and parasites at large.' At the same time, he points out that:

> Indoor air is usually polluted by the smell of the stables below and made sometimes unbreathable by yak-dung smoke. Acute or chronic irritation of the mucoses of the breathing channels and of the conjunctiva are the usual result.[9]

It was indoor pollution that made Tibetans particularly prone to catarrh, sinusitis, arthritis, neuritis, rheumatism and cataracts. Tibetan medicine – herbal and based on an assessment of the various humours of the body – was a mixture of the medieval and what in modern terms might be described as holistic.

With no cars, radios, theatres, cinemas, organized sports, newspapers, magazines, nor even any books apart from ancient Buddhist Scriptures, people were forced to make their own entertainments. The Tibetan historian W. D. Shakabpa, a native of Lhasa, paints an attractive portrait of life in those far-off days:

> All the residents of Lhasa, rich and poor, high and low, are peaceful. In the evenings many people walk about the Barkhor singing and playing musical instruments. Even the beggars of Lhasa have only to ply their trade for some time in the morning to get enough food for the day. In the evening they are all

nicely drunk. The people of Lhasa are physically relaxed, mentally contented and happy. The food of the city is also nutritious. No one has to strive unduly hard to make a living. Life takes care of itself, as a matter of course. Everything is splendid.[10]

With the easy-going Reting as Regent, life, at least for the nobility, was indeed pleasant. Parties were a way of life in Lhasa, particularly in the summer and early autumn when in the meadows and open spaces around the city, elaborate picnics were held in beautifully decorated tents and pavilions. 'They loved parties,' recalls Hugh Richardson:

And their parties lasted all day...people drifted into little groups and played mahjong or bridge and then almost always you'd go for a walk with someone and have a discussion with them. In fact we got quite a lot of work done while the party was going on. If you wanted to go and write a letter, you could do that. Even if you wanted a sleep. You could idle through the whole day if you wished. A lot of Tibetan tea was served and there was a fairly prolonged lunch with those little dishes of various Chinese foods, sea-slugs, sharks' fins, fish stomachs and mushrooms of various sorts. And then bowls of excellent *thukpa* (soup). If you stayed on to dinner, you had bowls of rice and sat around the table.[11]

Spencer Chapman, who had accompanied the British Mission when it first arrived in 1936, remarked that most of these succulent delicacies seemed designed to elude the unpractised wielder of chop-sticks, 'but if one of the Shappés [Cabinet Ministers] saw us struggling with a particularly slippery slug or an intractable slice of stomach he would deftly catch the morsel with his own chop-sticks and convey it to our plates'.[12] And Basil Gould recalled the *chang* girls at the Tibetans' parties:

Beautiful girls come round and urge each guest in turn to drink. They are said to have the right to run a long pin into a guest who hesitates.[13]

The new royal couple had to adapt as best they could to this Lhasa-style *dolce vita*. No longer were their days filled with back-breaking toil and do-it-yourself, make-do-and-mend economies. Like all the other nobles, says Richardson, 'they idled about'. Yet, says her youngest son, his mother did not actually like parties very much: 'Parties were for those who liked gambling; they were for merry-making, eating, drinking, exchanging stories and gossip. And my mother was never keen on either gambling or gossip.'[14]

In March 1940, a few days after the Dalai Lama's installation, Basil Gould wrote from the British Mission to Olaf Caroe in New Delhi,

> If, about the time when this letter is likely to reach you, I manage to get the Dalai Lama's family to a children's party with a Christmas Tree and cinema – at which the King and Queen, Charlie Chaplin and Mickey Mouse are certain to be a popular favourite – it will be because all the best children in Lhasa are anxious to come.[15]

The party did take place and over a hundred children came to it. It was a huge success:

> There was nothing wanting in the spirit in which the parents and their children [the unfortunate Dalai Lama was excluded] entered into the spirit of the party. At lunch, served on low tables in front of broad, flat cushions, all present tackled strange English foods with strange implements and good appetites and without hesitation. Then downstairs for a cinema show, at which the King and Queen's tour in Canada and the United States, and some shots of Balmoral Castle and the Gardens, were favourites, followed, in close competition, by Charlie Chaplin, Mickey Mouse, *Do You Like Monkeys?* and Kodachrome scenes of Sikkim, Tibet and Bhutan. Then tea with more strange foods faithfully dealt with, crackers and balloons – and finally a Christmas tree, presided over by two Father Christmases whose native language proved to be Tibetan, and who knew all the children. But all the time the Dalai Lama's brothers and sister, and especially the monk-brother, were wanting to save up crackers and balloons and toys for the Dalai Lama, and they went off happy with a parcel of things in the uses of which they soon instructed him when they had returned to the Potala.[16]

However popular the films about the British Royal Family, Rin Tin Tin (a weepie about a dog which had all the women sobbing with emotion) and Charlie Chaplin (who made them weep with laughter) were the undoubted favourites.

In Amdo, Taktser waited avidly for news, for the assurance that his parents had not forgotten him:

> The first news of the caravan was brought to me by a traveller who had met it crossing the high Tibetan plateaux, and he now brought me greetings from my family, together with an envelope containing ten *gormo*, and a beautiful cream-coloured pony as a riding horse.[17]

This amazing largess on the part of his father was symptomatic: the Kung was being exceedingly liberal with his new wealth. He had handed over his old farm to a cousin, Chandzo Jampa, who, leaving his wife and children in charge, had promptly set out for the installation in Lhasa.[18] Crossing the snow-covered plateaux by camel caravan, the cousin had now returned home, and arrived in Kumbum with four splendid Tibetan hounds as a present for Taktser from his father. He was also charged with buying a large number of fine horses at the Siling horse-fair – and with escorting Tsering Dolma and Phuntsok Tashi to Lhasa. (The young couple's first child had unfortunately lived for only a few months.)

When Chandzo Jampa's caravan was ready for this second journey to Lhasa, he came to say goodbye to a very disconsolate Taktser. The latter begged him to get him invited to Lhasa too, and almost wept with self-pity when, in the early summer of 1940, the caravan escorting his sister set off from Kumbum

> with thirty horses and over a hundred mules and draught animals, leaving me looking sadly after him. Apart from myself, the whole family would soon be assembled in Lhasa. How long should I still have to wait before my turn came?[19]

Taktser's longing rapidly became an obsession. He had managed to scrape through his mid-course examinations and saw no reason why he shouldn't go to Lhasa to pursue his studies at Kumbum's parent-monastery, Drepung. The argument that he had an obligation to stay in his own Taktser *labrang* cut no ice at all, and he began to work out ways of achieving his dream. In the end, his superiors, seeing that he was determined to have his own way, bowed to the inevitable and gave him permission to go to Lhasa, if and when an invitation should come. When Chandzo Jampa arrived back in Kumbum some months later with the longed-for invitation, Taktser instantly began his preparations for departure.

Most of the provisions for the journey had to be taken along, packed so as to be waterproof during river-crossings. Tsampa, stone-hard wheaten rolls, butter, dried vegetables, diced turnips, beetroots, pickled radishes, herbs and tea were all part of the necessary iron rations. Meat could be obtained along the way either by hunting or by bartering with passing nomads.

In the wild north-east, bandits were an ever-present threat and no man dared travel alone; it was always advisable to join with a larger group of travellers. In the event, Taktser found himself arranging for twenty-two people with their horses, yaks and mules. His party included an uncle, and

Chandzo Jampa, who was making the journey to Lhasa for the third time in two years. Again commissioned by the Kung to bring back some fine horses from Siling, he had taken the opportunity to buy some for himself – about one hundred and fifty horses, in fact – to sell at a handsome profit to the nobles and officials in Lhasa.

Taktser rode out of Kumbum as slowly and ceremonially as he had first entered it, 'followed by a monk carrying a large yellow umbrella behind me as the symbol of my rank, passing through long lines of monks silent and praying'. But he was no longer an impressionable boy:

> The lugubrious sound of the oboes and those four-sleeved trumpets...got on my nerves now, and I breathed with relief when we finally reached the tent where I was solemnly offered the last bowl of tea.[20]

Taktser and Chandzo Jampa left Siling in the summer of 1941, together with a group of Muslim officials and a few smaller groups of monks and nomad families who were going to the Holy City on pilgrimage. For three weeks, they wound along the shores of Lake Kokonor (the Blue Lake), that vast inland sea surrounded on three sides by craggy, snow-capped peaks. Then they pushed through uninhabited steppes and wild, mountainous terrain to the swampy plains of Tsaidam and the great nomad camp which was the last caravan assembly point. It was buzzing with activity:

> Innumerable fires were burning, and the cooks were busy preparing solid meals for their parties, something which was made easier because the nomads willingly sold us butter, meat and milk. Along the shores of the nearby salt lake some of the men were breaking up the thick salt crust and putting the pieces into sacks for the long journey. I bought a dozen sheep from the nomads for my group; they were to trot along with the yak caravan and be slaughtered for food at need.[21]

By the time the whole caravan was assembled, it included about twenty thousand animals. And though that may have improved the travellers' chances of safety, it did little for their speed.

The swamps stretching ahead for hundreds of miles would claim many victims among the pack animals. Each morning at about two, the first groups set off over the frozen ground, battling with an icy wind. After a day's march – about five or six hours in the saddle – they would pitch camp at sites where caravans had stopped since time immemorial. Hot drinks were prepared, the animals let loose to graze, fuel collected for fires.

Then, with a brief pause for enough food to dull the edge of appetite, the equipment had to be examined (and possibly repaired), the animals fed and watered. Only after all this would they take their evening meal of meat, tsampa and tea. Then the horses were covered up with saddle cloths, and the entire camp would settle to sleep and silence.

Struggling through high passes in a cold so intense that it took their breath away; crossing rivers, sometimes on horseback, sometimes walking naked into the ice-cold water, their clothes strapped to their backs in bundles, they came at last to the River Drichu, the upper reaches of that great Yangtse River which seemed to stretch ahead into infinity. It was the last great river before Lhasa and the sight of it filled Taktser with despair: how would he ever cross it? However, by dint of desperately clinging to his horse's mane, he arrived safely on the far bank and sank to the ground in exhausted relief.

Summer was already giving way to autumn and it was becoming noticeably colder in the valleys as the caravan drew near to the area which was under the political jurisdiction of the Dalai Lama. Almost immediately Taktser was made aware of his new exalted status as brother of the god-king, for the officer in charge of the frontier-post had been instructed to provide him with a military escort over the last high pass.

They began the climb in the afternoon amid a flurry of snow:

An icy wind swept down on us from the snow and ice-covered mountain peaks ahead, but we rode on and up without pausing until by midnight we had reached the highest point of the pass, a stony desert under a glacier over which a veritable storm howled.[22]

Shivering with cold and exhaustion, they started the descent without pausing to rest; and when they reached the valley floor next morning the weather had cleared. Taktser was about to collapse into his tent when a messenger arrived from his father, bearing affectionate greetings from all the family.

Four days later they reached a nomad settlement and a safe haven at last. Giving thanks to the gods for having spared them from death by bandits, wild animals, flood, freezing or thirst, the huge caravan now split up, each group going its separate way. Two days later, almost within sight of the town of Nagchuka, Taktser and his party saw a magnificent cavalcade coming towards them. In amazement, he recognized his father at its head:[23]

He had obviously spotted me too for he now urged on his horse to greater speed. What a great change had come over the simple peasant Choekyong Tsering since I had last seen him! His upright bearing and his natural air of authority had always impressed me even from early childhood. But now, seated on a fine horse and clothed in splendid silk garments, he bore himself with the dignity of a king.[24]

They rode on together and at the last stop before Lhasa, Gyalo Thondup and Phuntsok Tashi also came out to meet them, both of them so splendidly attired that at first he hardly recognized them. They had brought sumptuous garments for him too and, best of all, a box of his mother's freshly-made pastries.

His first glimpse of the Potala, its golden roofs glowing as though aflame with the afternoon sun, filled Taktser with awe. Everything else dissolved in a haze of impressions: the crowds lining the route to greet him; the great park where the new family house was being built; and finally the Norbulingka with its stone lions guarding the gate, its sentries in British-style uniforms presenting arms as he and his father dismounted. But everything was forgotten when he caught sight of his mother – and realized that she hadn't changed at all. 'She had always been the dominant personality in the family and now even as Great Mother of the King, Dekyi Tsering behaved in a simple but modest fashion while at the same time radiating a quite impressive grandeur.'[25]

Wordlessly, the mother handed her eldest son a bowl of curdled milk and stroked his hair. In that moment the loneliness of the past was wiped out, as first Lobsang Samten ran into the room, then Tsering Dolma, holding two babies in her arms – her own son, Tenzin Ngawang, born after her arrival in Lhasa, and her nine-month-old sister, Jetsun Pema.[26]

In the afternoon, Taktser was taken to see the Dalai Lama in the Norbulingka. He prostrated himself three times before his six-year-old sibling and their conversation was at first formal and stilted. But when the ceremonial was done with,

he took me by the hand and led me out into the garden where wonderful flowers were blossoming in the shade of magnificent trees. He introduced me to all the wonders of this small paradise: the flowers, the pond, the tame animals – and the nuts, which were just ripe. Gleefully, he showed me the best way to crack them.[27]

That first evening, the whole family assembled at the Gyatso farmhouse for the last meal of the day. It was like old times: father and mother; Gyalo Thondup and Lobsang Samten; Tsering Dolma and Phuntsok Tashi. Only one was missing, the one to whom they owed their presence in this beautiful place. Would he come?

> It was already dark [wrote Taktser] when the door opened and the Dalai Lama came in and greeted us all cheerfully. We all asked him to take the seat at the head of the table, but this he refused to do, saying that it was due to his father or to me as the eldest. Finally, he sat down on a silk cushion and we all squatted on woollen cushions. After our meal the time went very rapidly with happy family chatter, and all too soon our young brother was taken away from us again.[28]

After that, the Dalai Lama managed a brief visit to Gyatso every evening.

Taktser's days were filled with visits and receptions and sightseeing, with the excitement of discovering that everything in Lhasa was so much grander than in Kumbum. Streams of visitors arrived to pay homage to him as Taktser Rinpoche and as the Dalai Lama's eldest brother. But as an Incarnate he could not remain indefinitely at home. He was destined for Drepung, the monastery which, with its ten thousand monks, was the most influential in Tibet and said to be the largest in the world. Allotted a three-room apartment on the top floor of a five-storeyed house within the monastic university, he was able to plunge at last into the studies he had so long neglected. And he did so with a zeal and enthusiasm which surprised him.

Before leaving for Drepung, he watched, a star-struck provincial, the solemn procession in which his young brother was carried in state to his winter residence, the Potala Palace. Lobsang Samten accompanied his brother. Both boys had already mastered the Lhasa dialect and used it with ease, while the rest of the family continued to speak in the patois of Amdo, able only with difficulty to make themselves understood.

NOTES

1. All land in Tibet was owned by the State, but most of it was portioned out to monasteries and to nobles in exchange for services and taxes. Except in the case of the monasteries, all land ownership involved some form of unpaid government service.

2. Tucci, *To Lhasa and Beyond*.

3. Author interview with Tendzin Choegyal, Dharamsala, 1993.

4. Author interview with Rinchen Khando, Dharamsala, June 1994.

5. Cf. also Goldstein, *A History of Modern Tibet*, chapter 10.

6. Letter from Rai Bahadur Norbhu, CBE, British Trade Agent in Dromo and assistant to the Political Officer in Sikkim, to whom the letter was addressed. The Political Officer sent it to the Foreign Secretary of the Government of India. Letter No.4 (2)–8/41 dated January 1942.

7. Today, in Chinese-occupied Lhasa, the wells have been polluted and the water is unsafe to drink.

8. *Lost Lhasa: Heinrich Harrer's Tibet*, New York, Harry N. Abrams, and Hood River, Summit Publications, 1992.

9. From Dr Regolo Moise's remarks on Medicine and the State of Health in Tibet, included in Giuseppe Tucci's *To Lhasa and Beyond*.

10. Shakabpa, *Tibet: A Political History*.

11. Author interview with Hugh Richardson, September 1993.

12. F. Spencer Chapman, *Lhasa, the Holy City*, London, 1940.

13. B. J. Gould, *The Jewel in the Lotus*, Chatto & Windus, 1957, first published in India by Oxford University Press in 1943.

14. Author interview with Tendzin Choegyal, October 1993.

15. Letter from Basil Gould in Lhasa to Olaf Caroe C.I.E., 1 March 1940, Oriental and India Office Collections of the British Library, L/P&S/12/4178, File 15 (1).

16. Report by B J. Gould.

17. Norbu, *Tibet Is My Country*.

18. This was common throughout Tibet, where the women were considered to be very much more efficient than the men.

19. *Tibet Is My Country*.

20. *Tibet Is My Country*.

21. *Tibet Is My Country*.

22. *Tibet Is My Country*.

23. Tibetans were in the habit of going two days' distance to greet their friends and family (with *chang*, tea and other refreshment) if they had come from afar.

24. *Tibet Is My Country*.

25. *Tibet Is My Country.*
26. A baby girl born in Amdo after the birth of the Dalai Lama had not lived.
27. *Tibet Is My Country.*
28. *Tibet Is My Country.*

8

Inside the Potala

And then there is the Potala Palace which must date from
Tibet's days of greatness. No one today would think of erect-
ing such a building. I once asked a stonemason why such
buildings were no longer put up. He answered indignantly
that the Potala was the handiwork of the gods. Men could
never have achieved anything like it.

Heinrich Harrer, Seven Years in Tibet

The amazing Potala Palace would surely have been listed as one of the
Wonders of the World if the Tibetans had ever admitted more than a handful of foreigners into their country to wonder at it. It is named after a
mountain at the southern tip of the Indian continent, believed to be the
abode of Chenrezig, the compassionate god who is embodied in the Dalai
Lamas. A place of meditation built in the seventh century by King Songtsen Gampo on a hill slightly outside the city, it was enlarged a thousand
years later by the Fifth Dalai Lama – the Great Fifth – at about the same
time as the Taj Mahal and the Palace of Versailles were being constructed.
(The Great Fifth died in 1682, but to ensure continuing popular support for
the colossal building project, the Regent managed to conceal the fact for
twelve years until the palace was completed.) The Potala is virtually a city
in itself, a quarter of a mile long, thirteen storeys high, and entirely covering the summit of Lhasa's Red Hill.

Here were the tombs of seven Dalai Lamas, the grandest being those of the Fifth and Thirteenth, covered with gold, encrusted heavily with precious jewels, their interiors filled with gemstones, artefacts of gold and the finest porcelain. In the western wing of the palace was the monastery, home to one hundred and seventy-five monks whose exclusive duty was to assist the Dalai Lama in his spiritual practices. There were libraries, repositories of religion and culture, containing massive, heavy volumes, many of them illuminated in inks made of powdered gold, silver, iron, copper, turquoise, coral and conch shell. The eastern wing housed government offices, a school – the Tsedrung – for training monastic officials,¹ and the meeting halls of the National Assembly. Climbing ever more steeply towards the summit, past numerous chapels, audience halls and meeting rooms, one came finally to the lofty apartments of the Dalai Lamas and their attendants.

For centuries, the Dalai Lamas had come to the Potala at the start of winter – the seasons being immutably fixed, as Sir Charles Bell explained:

> On the anniversary of Tsong-khapa's death [on the twenty-fifth day of the tenth Tibetan month] winter begins; on the eighth day of the third Tibetan month it ends. This fixes winter between a date in the first half of December and another in the last half of April. Between these two dates all officials...must wear fur hats and cloaks strictly in accordance with the patterns prescribed for each grade. Outside these dates, however cold the day, they must appear only in their summer silks, gorgeous indeed in their yellow and blue, but affording cold comfort where the land is raised 12,000 feet above the ocean.²

Installed on the top floor of this mausoleum, the two boys were cut off from normal society. Though commanding a superb view over Lhasa and the Kyi Chu River, their quarters lacked home comforts. Lobsang Samten had a room of his own, vast, gloomy, high-ceilinged. A nervous and insecure child, he was terrified of the huge shadows; and when he asked if one of the monks could sleep in there with him, he was told to pull himself together and behave like the brother of a Dalai Lama. His brother was luckier, the only way into his room being through an ante-chamber in which an attendant always slept. In any case, he was not a nervous child, though the Potala, he admitted, was 'not a nice place to live'. As Sir Charles Bell had written:

> It is cold, this vast palace, in winter-time. I found the water in the large bowls that find place in the steps of the tombs to be frozen from top to bottom even at midday.

The bedroom allotted to the new Dalai Lama had once belonged to the Great Fifth. At one end of the room was an altar, in front of which were butter-lamps and little dishes of food and water placed in offering to the Buddhas. Every day, mice would come in search of the grain and, once he grew accustomed to their scurrying over his bed, he was glad of their lively company.

As befitted his exalted rank, he was given three other rooms, a small chapel, a room for his scriptures and commentaries, and a private bathroom, the only one in the entire palace. The bathroom, with a toilet-seat covered with fur, was reserved for the sacred personage alone: Lobsang Samten had to go outside like everyone else, down the hundreds of stone steps, even in the freezing winter weather!

The six-year-old Dalai Lama, whom we shall henceforth call Kundun – 'Presence' – knew nothing of the political dust-storm swirling around his head. He was too young to understand that his Government was corrupt; that, under Reting and his cronies, the welfare of Tibet took second place to personal greed and ambition. Kundun was fond of Reting, noting in his childish way that his Senior Tutor's 'most striking feature was a constantly blocked nose'.³ Reting rightly regarded the discovery of the Fourteenth Dalai Lama as his finest achievement, and it was natural that he should form close ties with the boy's family. Easy-going, sociable, keen on horses, Reting had much in common with the Kung, and the two had become friends. But his moment of glory had passed. Young as he was, Kundun thinks he must have heard the rumours of misconduct, since he remembers primly telling his parents that they should not be so friendly with the Regent.⁴

In January 1941, Reting suddenly resigned both as Regent and Senior Tutor, explaining that in a dream he had been told that his life was at risk if he did not resign and pay more attention to his spiritual life! He nominated as his successor the Junior Tutor, Taktra Rinpoche, an elderly man with the reputation for moral probity that he himself so conspicuously lacked. The appointment of the austere, ultra-conservative Taktra reversed the slide into moral collapse and restored a high level of discipline and ethical standards to the Government. But it soon became apparent that Reting's withdrawal was merely tactical: he seems to have considered Taktra as a caretaker, to hold the fort until he was ready to make a comeback.

Taktra now became the Senior Tutor, his own Junior Tutor role being taken by Ling Rinpoche, a stern, rather reserved man who at first struck fear into Kundun's heart, but who came to be one of his most trusted friends. The unofficial third tutor was Kesang Rinpoche, who had led the search party into Amdo and of whom the boy was very fond. 'He was so kind that I could never take him seriously. During our lessons, instead of reciting what I was supposed to, I used to hang round his neck and say, "You read it."'[5]

In addition to his tutors, Kundun had three personal monk-attendants, the Master of the Ritual, Master of the Kitchen and Master of the Robes. For both brothers, these three were surrogate fathers. 'They looked after us as though we were their own children,' said Lobsang. The undoubted favourite was the Master of the Kitchen, Lobsang Jinpa, known as Ponpo ('the Boss') – 'a very kind and simple man, almost completely bald'. Ponpo was no good at telling stories or thinking up games, but Kundun loved him devotedly and for a long time couldn't bear to let him out of his sight. Kundun's affection for this simple monk was perhaps the deepest emotional tie of his life. 'Ponpo came into my life,' he recalls, 'when we were still a few days' journey from Lhasa on the way from Amdo. From then on, he was always there for me, he took care of me, fed me, played with me. He was my father, my mother, my whole family. I remember that he had a large brown nipple-shaped mole on his face and at the age of four, separated from my mother, I would suck at it for comfort.'[6] To the end of his days, Ponpo loved to relate how as a young boy Kundun had longed for a pair of trousers like those worn by the Westerners he had seen in magazines. Trousers being unknown in Lhasa, Ponpo solved the problem by inserting the child's legs into the arms of a voluminous Tibetan shirt and tying it round his waist with string. Kundun was delighted.

Once the boys' formal education had begun, the days were strictly mapped out. Just before sunrise large buckets of water, heated in the kitchens for Kundun, icy-cold for Lobsang, were carted up from down below for washing. After dressing, they spent an hour in meditation and prayer, while the water on the altars was changed and the butter-lamps were lit. At seven, in the middle of this prayer time, breakfast was brought in,

Tibetan butter-tea, tsampa kneaded into balls in specially-made leather bags. Sometimes a cheesecake was served, dried cheese, sugar and butter mixed into a cake and added to the tsampa.[7]

The boys would often save some of the tsampa and 'go up on the Potala roof to feed the crows; or make fantastic shapes out of the dough'.

At nine, all the monk-officials – 175 of them – gathered for soup, rice and yogurt. This was the hour for public and official audiences and, when his presence was required, the Dalai Lama would be brought in to preside in solemn state.

Then came a two-hour lesson period in the schoolroom, for which neither of the brothers felt much enthusiasm. They were kept in line, however, by the sight of two whips hanging on opposite walls, one of yellow silk, the other of leather:

> The former, we were told, was reserved for the Dalai Lama and the latter for the Dalai Lama's brother. These instruments of torture terrified us both. It took only a glance from our teacher at one or other of these whips to make me shiver with fear. Happily, the yellow one was never used, though, the leather one came off the wall once or twice.[8]

'We bullied you terribly when you were small,' Ling Rinpoche admitted to Lobsang many years later, in Dharamsala. Reluctant to take a whip to the backside of the god-king, the tutors had vented their frustration on his long-suffering brother.

The first lesson – learning four difficult Tibetan scripts on chalk-covered boards – was followed by the memorizing of texts from scripture. Religious training was the entire purpose of this education; reading, writing and grammar were no more than a means to that end.

After reciting to the Junior Tutor the passage they had memorized earlier that morning, the latter would read and explain the next one. This went on till noon when a bell sounded, a conch was blown, and the magic hour of playtime arrived. For one who was 'a very reluctant pupil' and 'disliked all subjects equally', this was the most precious time of the day.

The boys were free to roam as they pleased. With their bodyguards scurrying after them,[9] they wandered through the maze of corridors and explored the vast subterranean store-rooms of the palace, excitedly opening cupboards, chests and drawers. Dashing from one room to another, they were constantly making fresh discoveries: chests containing a large number of old wooden animals – camels, elephants, yaks, snow leopards, for example. They were fascinated by the armoury with its suits of armour, flintlock guns and antique swords; and they particularly loved rummaging among the possessions of the Great Thirteenth. In the huge cavernous store-rooms, they found an old air-rifle, complete with targets and ammunition; a telescope; and a pile of illustrated books in English about the First World War. Following the Chinese incursion into Lhasa in 1910 the Great Thirteenth had gone into exile in British India, in the hill-station of Darjeeling, where he was looked after by the Tibetan-speaking Political Officer for Sikkim, Sir Charles Bell. A deep and lasting friendship sprang up between the two men, both of whom loved Tibet and firmly believed in its right to independence. The books and maps that the brothers now stumbled on had been gifts from Bell to his friend.

Apart from the store-room treasures, there was no shortage of new toys to play with. Some (presents from abroad) were sent up from the Indian border; and visiting foreign officials would come to Lhasa laden with gifts. The Chinese tended to bring adult gifts like bolts of silk, but others understood that the intended recipient was only a child. Captain Ilia Tolstoy and Lieutenant Brooke Dolan, two American officers who came to Lhasa on a goodwill mission in 1942 presented a pair of singing birds, a model sailing ship made of silver and a gold pocket watch.[10] Favourite toys were the red pedal-car given to Kundun by the British, a wind-up clockwork train set and a large collection of lead soldiers with which the boys played at armies. Much loved too was the Meccano set presented by Sir Basil Gould at the time of the installation – and added to over the years. Kundun built cranes and railway wagons long before he had ever seen the real things. Perhaps it was his early discovery of Meccano which gave him a passion for all things mechanical. Not content with just playing, he wanted to know how everything worked. And as there was no one on hand to explain, he had to work things out for himself. He caught on quickly and soon became expert at opening up old clocks and taking them to pieces, sending the bodyguards frantic with anxiety:

> They tried to dissuade him from doing so but he was quite stubborn. If they succeeded in stopping him one day, he was certain to resume these activities the next. I don't know how he did it, nor did anyone else, but somehow he made all these things work.[11]

Lunch, the main meal of the day, brought playtime to an end at one. By two, the brief sunlight which had flooded the room at midday had already begun to fade and the Potala returned to its habitual gloom. Kundun hated this moment, feeling a shadow fall on his heart as the room sank back into shade. Afternoon lessons probably did little to lift his spirits.

At seven, he usually ate supper with his three monk-attendants – tea, broth, maybe a little meat, yoghurt and different kinds of bread sent in by his mother. Afterwards he would go down the seven flights of steps to the courtyard below, ostensibly praying and reciting scriptures as he walked, but more often making up stories in his head and anticipating the ones that his attendants might tell him before bedtime. He loved ghost stories, but they scared him and made him dread creeping back into his dark, mouse-infested bedroom at nine. 'One of the most frightening tales concerned giant owls which were supposed to snatch small boys after dark...It made me very particular about being inside by nightfall.' There were a great many night-owls around the Potala.

Few apart from the family and his personal officials and attendants were allowed to speak to Kundun directly; and even his family's access was restricted. The Great Mother had permission to visit whenever she wanted, but was not allowed to sleep at the Potala. For her, the visits to her youngest son must have been bittersweet, her relationship with him being now irrevocably changed. Now, even to her, he was Kundun. Visits to him were ceremonial occasions for which she wore her finest clothes and jewellery; and when she left she bowed before him, and he laid his hand on her in blessing. Nevertheless, she preserved some kind of normality by smuggling in some of his favourite food. Not only the bread but also little packages of chicken, eggs and sometimes even pork. She had to be careful, as these foods were frowned on. Even milk was forbidden, since its high fat content was considered bad for the liver. (The only time Kundun managed to drink any was during certain ceremonies in the Potala which called for offerings of milk. He would hide some of it to drink later.)

With the official end of winter came the annual departure to the Norbulingka, his sole excursion into the outside world. He looked forward eagerly to this escape from his gilded prison. Beginning with a two-hour ceremony which seemed like an eternity, it was followed by a formal procession. A gala day for everybody – the Regent and Cabinet Ministers marching in procession through the streets lined by crowds whose good behaviour was ensured by burly monk-police wielding clubs.

To the people's delight, the young ruler's nightingales and parrots called out from their cages while his brilliantly caparisoned horses, decked in yellow saddles, bridles and bits of gold, pranced behind their grooms; monks blew shrill, high-pitched *gyalings* or short horns and the regimental bands played 'It's a Long Way to Tipperary'. From behind the palanquin's silk-fringed windows, though, it was the sight of nature that pleased the young Dalai Lama most. 'The season was most beautiful,' he remembered. 'All the lawns were turning green, the apricot trees flowering and the birds singing. I used to love that day going from the Potala to the Norbulingka.'[12] Yet he would have given much to be allowed to walk and enjoy the natural beauties of the countryside for himself.

At the Norbulingka he could share a room with Lobsang; indeed the boys could stay in any of the smaller palaces they chose. They spent many happy hours walking through the gardens, watching the animals and birds:

> Amongst these were, at one time or another, a herd of tame musk-deer; at least six…enormous Tibetan mastiffs which acted as guard dogs; a Pekinese sent from Kumbum; a few mountain goats; a monkey; a handful of camels brought from Mongolia; two leopards and a very old and rather sad tiger…several parrots; half a dozen peacocks; some cranes; a pair of golden geese; and about thirty, very unhappy Canada geese whose wings had been clipped so that they could not fly. I felt very sorry for them.[13]

Seeing one of the parrots eating out of his Master of the Robes' hand, he eagerly held out some nuts to the bird himself. But when the parrot ignored his outstretched hand, he indignantly threatened it with a stick. 'Of course, thereafter it fled at the sight of me. This was a very good lesson in how to make friends; not by force but by compassion.'[14] He had better luck with the fish in the well-stocked lake, though even here he was not above a show of petulance:

> I used to stand at the edge and call them. If they responded, I rewarded them with small pieces of bread…However, they had a tendency to disobedience and sometimes would ignore me. If this happened, I got very angry and, rather than throw them food, I would open up with an artillery barrage of rocks and stones. But when they did come over, I was very careful to see to it that the small ones got their fair share. If necessary, I would use a stick to prod the larger ones out of the way.[15]

Once, playing at the edge, he spotted a lump of wood and tried to sink it with his stick. Unfortunately, he fell in and might have drowned had he not been rescued by one of the Norbulingka sweepers, an ex-soldier from western Tibet. The 'sweepers', whom to this day he remembers as – apart from Lobsang and Ponpo – the only real friends of his childhood, were middle-aged men, both monks and laymen, who tidied the rooms and swept and polished the floors at the Potala and the Norbulingka. (He thought they did this for his benefit, so that he could skate round the gleaming floors.) A child among grown-up children, he spent much of his leisure time with them; he loved them and they loved him.

But even in the Norbulingka, the many restrictions placed on him by Regent Taktra irked him. In the early days, he would walk with an attendant as far as a stream of the Kyi Chu river just beyond the outer wall of the Park. But in the sacred name of protocol this practice came to be forbidden and he was 'compelled to remain hidden away like an owl'.

He hated the meaningless rituals and rules by which his life was governed, and escaped whenever he could to relax with the servants at Gyatso. Most of them had come from Amdo and loved telling him stories about his native village of Taktser. They treated him just as they would any other (naughty) little boy, and sometimes joined in his pranks:

> I enjoyed their company when we went and raided my parents' food stores…The best time for these forays was in late autumn when there would always be fresh supplies of delicious dried meat, which we dipped in chilli sauce. I liked this so much that, on one occasion, I ate far too much and soon afterwards was violently sick.[16]

Every year, for the Monlam or Great Prayer Festival which immediately follows the New Year celebrations, Kundun took up temporary residence in the Jokhang Temple. He dreaded the central ceremony of Monlam more than anything else in the year. In the first place, his rooms at the Jokhang were even gloomier and colder than those at the Potala, and he almost invariably caught flu. In the second place, the ceremony lasted over four hours and at the end of it he had to recite a long passage of scripture from memory. It was an agonizing ordeal, especially as he sat high up on a throne and no one could prompt him.

> But remembering my lines was only half the problem. Because the proceedings went on for so long, I had an additional dread: I feared that my bladder might not hold out…I remember being apoplectic with fear.[17]

His worst fears were never realized, but neither did time diminish them. When the ceremony was over, his relief knew no bounds:

> Not only was the whole dreadful business over for another twelve months, but there now followed one of the best moments in the Dalai Lama's year. After the ceremony I was allowed outside to walk round the streets so that I

could see the *thorma*, the huge, gaily coloured butter sculptures traditionally offered to the Buddhas on this day. There were also puppet shows and music played by military bands and an atmosphere of tremendous happiness amongst the people.[18]

Accustomed as he was to the gloomy silence of the Potala, he was fascinated when, watching from the east window at the Jokhang, he saw little novice monks of about his own age fooling about in the courtyard below.

> Quite a lot of them…spent their whole time playing. Every so often a scuffle would break out. Then they would take out their wooden bowls and crack each other over the head. The scene provoked a curious reaction in me. On the one hand, I told myself that these monks were extremely stupid. On the other, I could not help envying them. They seemed not to have a care in the world.[19]

His favourite view was from the west window, looking down on to the market place. He could only peer through a curtain, for if the people down below had spotted him, they would have rushed over to prostrate before him. On his first visit, however, his innate mischievousness got the better of him:

> The sight of all those people down there was too much for me. I boldly poked my head through the curtain. But, as if this were not bad enough, I remember blowing bubbles of spit which fell on several people's heads as they threw themselves down to the ground far below.[20]

Here too there were sweepers, whose company he could enjoy. When he left the Jokhang, he missed them sorely. But one New Year, he found that all but one had been sacked after his departure. 'After I had gone last time, they let themselves into my apartment by climbing down through the ceiling skylight and made off with various items – gold butter-lamps and the like.'[21] So much for his taste in friends, he shrugs ruefully!

In Amdo, he had scarcely known his father, but circumstances now brought them together more often. The Kung frequently attended the brief morning tea-ceremony, at the Potala (in winter) or the Norbulingka (in summer). Kundun did not fail to notice that his father came more often to the Norbulingka, where the royal horses were stabled. Nor that his first visit was to the horses!

The Kung was in his element, going to the stables to feed his fine horses every day before breakfast. He rode out alone each morning towards Sera Monastery and surrounded himself with men who knew and cared about horses as he did.

But, as his son Gyalo Thondup freely acknowledges, the Kung had grown arrogant and greedy. 'People in Lhasa had shown a great deal of respect to our family because we were the Dalai Lama's family,' says GT. 'They treated us with great kindness – and my father often took advantage of them. If he saw a horse he fancied in the street, he would make the owner sell it to him then and there. He would bargain and force the price right down. The people he treated like this naturally got very upset and began to have second thoughts about the Dalai Lama's father.'[22]

The Kung refused to pay taxes on his estates; and unlawfully requisitioned free transport and labour from other people's feudal subjects without prior consultation. Yet, as Hugh Richardson points out, 'the power of landlords was not arbitrary and the subjects could appeal to the District Officer or directly to the Kashag or to the judges in Lhasa'.[23] In his letter to the Political Officer in Sikkim (see Chapter 6), Rai Bahadur Norbhu comments acidly: 'The Dalai Lama's father is interfering too much with the affairs of the Government and is taking the law into his own hands.' The Kung, he went on, was interfering in individual debt cases between creditors and debtors, and, in cases of assault, re-trying the cases himself – without acquainting himself with the true facts – and threatening the magistrates who had originally tried the case. He was making a handsome profit for himself, charging exorbitant fees, accepting bribes and even demanding protection money. His arrogance was breathtaking:

> When [the Kung] is going out to the city or returning to the Norbulingka, all mounted persons crossing [his path] must dismount and pay their respects to him regardless of their own rank. Persons who do not dismount and salute him are beaten severely in public by [his] servants.[24]

On one occasion, the scandalized Norbhu reports:

> A sick man coming to the Mission hospital for treatment came across the Dalai Lama's father as he was going out to the City. The sick man could not dismount and salute him, with the result that the [Kung] confiscated his pony.[25]

Mules and ponies were at the heart of the matter, he continues:

The Dalai Lama's father trades in ponies and mules. He calls [to the] Norbul-ingka Tibetan officials who like ambling ponies and mules, and makes them purchase his mules saying, 'Don't worry about the price, it will be alright even if you pay me after a year.' Some officials purchased ponies and mules from [him] without even asking the price. He called them after four or five days and made them pay [anything from] Rs 500/- to Rs 1000/- for a mule or pony. Some of the officials tried to return the animals, but the [Kung] would not take them back.

Often the victims would turn to Dekyi Tsering for help. 'The women-folk of the victim would come to her and she would try and sort things out. She exerted a really calming influence,' said an official. But very often even she was helpless.

On another occasion, in the autumn of 1942, when several farmers from Bet-sang village near Lhasa went to the Tsona area in southeast Tibet to barter salt for rice, they were met...by the headman of one of the Dalai Lama's father's estates who wanted to buy salt. The Betsang villagers, suspecting that they would be forced to accept an unfavourable exchange rate, refused to do busi-ness with him. The headman complained to the Yapshi Kung in Lhasa, who summoned the Betsang headman and then imprisoned him.

Because Betsang village was an estate of Drepung monastery's Loseling col-lege and under its protection, the Loseling Abbot went to the house where the headman was being held and personally released him, sending him to Drepung for safety. The Abbot then called on the Yapshi Kung, told him what he had done, and asked him why the headman had been imprisoned. The fa-ther cursed the Abbot and threatened to shoot him with his pistol. At this point, it is said, the Abbot coolly invited him to shoot, but he did not do so. The Abbot filed a complaint demanding that the Yigtsang Office examine the issue, and the Dalai Lama's father filed a counter-suit with the Kashag.[26]

Fortunately, the Kung's friends persuaded him to withdraw his complaint, and the Abbot did likewise.

Having read Norbhu's letter, the Foreign Secretary in New Delhi won-dered if Basil Gould's glowing admiration for the new royal family had not been somewhat naïve. 'It seems to me extraordinary that the Tibetan Gov-ernment should allow the Dalai Lama's family to behave in this outra-geous fashion,' he commented. In a secret memo,[27] the Under-Secretary in the Department of External Affairs referred to 'the ambition and greed of the Dalai Lama's parents' [sic], whose position seemed 'to be not unlike that of parents who produce child "movie-stars" and expect to bask in the fame'. Commenting on the Kung's unorthodox ways of 'getting rich quick', he added, with massive understatement: 'He may prove an annoying influence in the State'.

Indeed he would. Far from 'allowing' such behaviour, the Tibetan Government was thoroughly exasperated by it. The Kung had become an embarrassment to the new Regent – not least because he was a friend of Reting. Taktra summoned the National Assembly to discuss the situation.

In late November 1942, the Assembly recommended that any servant of the Kung who abused his position and exacted tribute either in cash or in kind from Tibetan subjects should be arrested. Regent Taktra approved the edict and, being prepared to do everything in his power to clean up the mess of the Reting years, ordered a proclamation to be exhibited on the streets of Lhasa and throughout Tibet. It revealed that ever since the arrival of the Dalai Lama's father, the Treasury had paid out a small fortune for him, over and above the cost of feeding and clothing the family and the grain-bearing estates they had bestowed on him. Yet

> The Dalai Lama's father requisitions grass, grain, butter, salt, firewood and yak-dung from poor dealers and does not pay the full cost of such articles. Moreover, he fines people heavily for minor offences without any reference to the Tibetan Government...Further, he had instructed his tenants not to obey the demands of the Tibetan Government for forced labour. Be it known to the public that henceforth the Dalai Lama's father has been ordered to behave himself in a manner similar to the other Yapshis. If any of his servants commits an offence, and if the Kashag takes no steps to try the case against the Dalai Lama's father, then the National Assembly will straightway judge the matter.
>
> The above proclamation has been passed by the National Assembly and bears the seal of the Kashag.[18]

It was clear that a line had to be drawn somewhere. Taktra would not allow anyone – not even the Dalai Lama's father – to believe himself above the law. Reting was furious at this attack on a personal friend. Perhaps it was now, when he realized the extent of Taktra's animosity towards him, that he began to regret his decision to hand over power.

In the winter of 1944–5, Reting returned to Lhasa in great pomp and style. A number of his supporters, including the Kung, rode out the traditional two days' distance to welcome him. He had come to ask Taktra to hand the Regency back to him, and it was plain that he could still count on a bedrock of support. Taktra, however, never having seen himself as a caretaker, refused to play ball and Reting retired, angry and humiliated, to his monastery. From there, as Taktra began a relentless purge of the ex-Regent's remaining supporters in the Government, Reting would plot his revenge.

Sometimes, the Kung took Lobsang Samten away with him for two or three days. They would ride on fine horses from the Norbulingka's stables into the wilderness around Lhasa, where they would pitch camp by the banks of a lake or river and make long excursions into the hills. On Lobsang's return, Kundun always wanted to know every detail of the trip. He was quite envious of his brother's freedom, although in fact neither of them liked horses and Lobsang would have preferred to stay at home. When he was a small boy in Amdo, his father had insisted on teaching him and Gyalo Thondup to ride bareback over the grasslands. Gyalo Thondup had loved every minute but poor Lobsang had fallen from his horse and been seriously concussed.

History was about to repeat itself. On one of their expeditions, the Kung, exasperated by his son's lack-lustre horsemanship, 'whacked Lobsang's mount across the hindquarters with a stick. The startled animal took off like a shot and in trying to clear an obstacle that lay in its path pitched the boy onto the ground, where he lay unconscious from a severe concussion.'[29]

The unassertive Lobsang was much put-upon, and not only by his father. Life in the Potala was very demanding, and despite their closeness the relationship with his younger brother was not an easy one. They scrapped constantly, Kundun usually being the instigator. Matters came to a head one day in the summer of 1946, as Kundun was chasing his brother with an ivory-topped swagger-stick which he had discovered in the storerooms: 'Somehow I must have whirled it round my head and it hit Lobsang Samten who fell down, with blood gushing from his head. For a few terrible moments I thought I'd killed him...Then to my relief he stood up – in floods of tears and with a huge gash over his right eyebrow.'[30]

The wound healed, but Lobsang would retain the scar for the rest of his life. For those in charge of the two boys, however, it was the last straw. Kundun's tutors had always been nervous that Lobsang, with freer access to the outside world, might introduce his brother to dangerous modern ideas. But this latest incident made them realize that the two simply could not be left alone together. It was time for a change, time for twelve-year-old Lobsang to attend school in Lhasa. Without delay, he was enrolled in the Tharkhang school for young trainee-officials.[31]

When the moment came to say goodbye, eight-year-old Kundun knew that he was losing his last link with normal family life. He gave his brother a wooden board for writing on and a few other small parting gifts, then 'went on to the roof and watched and watched until he disappeared inside the door of the Yapshi House, my parents' house.'[32]

From now on, his daily companions would be a handful of elderly monks – and, of course, the sweepers.

But what companions they were! Despite the difference in age, these men played just like small boys themselves, with no holds barred. With them he played at war-games, running competitions to see who could mould the best tiny tanks and aeroplanes from tsampa dough, allowing them about half an hour in which to build an army and judging the results himself. He excelled at that sort of thing, using as models the pictures of actual Second World War tanks and planes he'd found in a Tibetan newspaper published in India. At this stage, he almost always won. But when actual battle was joined, it was a different story:

> Up until now, I had had everything my own way, so this was when I generally lost. For my sweepers never gave quarter in any sort of competition. I often tried to use my position as Dalai Lama to my advantage, but it was no use. I played very forcefully. Quite often I lost my temper and used my fists, but they still did not give in. Sometimes they even made me cry.[33]

Years later, in his memoirs, Kundun would recall Norbu Thondup, his favourite sweeper, 'a devoted friend and constant source of fun':

> We often came to blows during my mock battles and I remember being quite vicious towards him at times...But he gave as good as he got and never for a moment lost his great sense of humour.[34]

But there were times when he avoided even the sweepers. Once, when his mother brought him a Taktser delicacy, sausages made of minced meat and rice, he scoffed the lot, rather than share them with his friends. He paid for his greed by vomiting throughout the night. The Regent blamed the Master of the Kitchen, and poor Ponpo might have lost his job in disgrace had the illustrious culprit not owned up. Yet another lesson in the realities of life, he ruefully conceded.

Though they would not have suspected it, the sweepers were invaluable teachers for the young Dalai Lama. They groused about the difficulties of their own lives, about the injustices meted out by certain officials and high lamas; and they kept him up to date with the latest gossip on the street. His debt to them, then and later, was incalculable.

NOTES

1. Each Dalai Lama had a civil service to help him run the country. There was one branch of 175 specially-trained monk-officials (recruited from all classes of society); and another of 175 trained lay noblemen.

2. Sir Charles Bell, *The Religion of Tibet*, Oxford, 1931.

3. Fourteenth Dalai Lama, *Freedom in Exile*.

4. Author interview with HH the Dalai Lama, June 1994.

5. *Freedom in Exile*.

6. Author interview, HH the Dalai Lama, Dharamsala, July 1995.

7. From notes written by Lobsang Samten and now in the possession of his widow, Namlha Taklha.

8. *Freedom in Exile*.

9. The Dalai Lama's personal bodyguards were on average six feet tall and wore heavily-padded clothes to make them appear even larger.

10. Goodman, *The Last Dalai Lama*, chapter 7. The mission was partly a social one, to establish contact between the American and Tibetan Governments. But there was a more urgent reason. The Second World War was raging and the Americans came with a message from President Roosevelt, asking the Tibetans to allow them a land-route over which supplies might be sent from the Western Allies to China. The Tibetans, however, would not relinquish their strict neutrality.

11. Quoted by Goodman, chapter 8.

12. Avedon, *In Exile from the Land of Snows*, chapter 1.

13. *Freedom in Exile*, chapter 2.

14. *Freedom in Exile*.

15. *Freedom in Exile*.

16. *Freedom in Exile*.

17. *Freedom in Exile*, chapter 2.

18. *Freedom in Exile*, chapter 2.

19. *Freedom in Exile*, chapter 2.

20. *Freedom in Exile*, chapter 2.

21. *Freedom in Exile*, chapter 2.

22. Author interview with Gyalo Thondup, New Delhi, July 1995.

23. In a letter to the author, 12 December 1993.

24. Letter sent by Rai Bahadur Norbhu CBE, British Trade Agent in Dromo, to the Political Officer in Sikkim, and by him to the Foreign Secretary of the Government of India. Letter No.4(2)-P/41, dated January 1942.

25. See previous note.

26. Goldstein, *A History of Modern Tibet*.

27. Dated 11 April 1942.

28. Goldstein.

29. Goodman.

30. Author interview with HH the Dalai Lama, June 1994.

31. According to Rinchen Dolma Taring's *Daughter of Tibet* (John Murray, 1970), there were no public schools in Lhasa. There were just two official schools, the Tse, in the Potala itself, and the Tsikhang in Lhasa, where young monks and laymen were trained for government service.

32. Author interview with HH the Dalai Lama, June 1994.

33. *Freedom in Exile*.

34. *Freedom in Exile*.

9

A Window on to the World

> When the Dalai Lama passed by me in his sedan chair and found me filming he gave me a smile. My private thought was that he was congratulating himself on his little cinema, but I am sure that no one else thought as I did; though what could be more natural for a lonely fourteen-year-old boy? Then a look at the humble and rapturous face of my attendant reminded me that for everyone else except myself, he was not a lonely boy but a god.
>
> *Heinrich Harrer, Seven Years in Tibet*

1945 – Year of the Wood Bird. The Kung's grand new house in the parkland of Changseshar (Eastern Garden) was ready at last. Lying just east of the Potala, it was popularly called the Yapshi Taklha House. When Taktser first saw it, he marvelled at the strangeness of fate:

> There it stood in a large garden amidst fine old poplars and willow trees, a big two-storeyed house surrounded by a high brick wall. The first time I entered it I could not help thinking of our modest old farmstead in T[akt]ser. What a difference there was![1]

The royal couple had recently suffered the loss of another son – a devout two-year-old who loved to go into the family altar-room and pay reverence to the statues. In March 1945, he had caught a fever – perhaps the smallpox which was raging in Lhasa and against which Kundun was vaccinated that year.

When it was clear that the child's death was imminent, the parents asked the Gadung Oracle to come, but he died just as the medium arrived. Gadung told the distressed parents to embalm the tiny corpse in salt, first marking it in an easily recognizable way, so that the boy could be reborn into the same house. So the servants put a smear of butter on the dead child's left buttock, before the tiny body was embalmed and taken down to the cellars.[2]

Tsering Dolma had just given birth to a daughter, Khando Tsering, in the absence of her husband, Phuntsok Tashi, who was away in Amdo at the time. The Kung had borrowed money from monasteries and from certain prominent Lhasa traders to provide loans for some of his Amdo friends; and when the latter showed no inclination to pay him back, had despatched his son-in-law to expedite the repayment. (A fruitless mission since the money had all been spent.)

Tsering Dolma was six months pregnant when Phuntsok Tashi left Lhasa. When he reached Kumbum three months later, he received a cable announcing Khando's birth. For Tsering Dolma (known to her siblings as Achala, older sister), these were fairy-tale years. She had exchanged a life of dawn-to-dusk drudgery for that of a princess in a palace; and she was revelling in her new status and freedom. Despite her Amdo accent, the older Lhasa ladies made rather a fuss of her. It was refreshing for them to meet this simple young countrywoman, frank and brave and without a streak of deviousness. She was innately artistic, and before long had become a fashion trendsetter, creating different new designs and colour-mixes for the ladies' aprons. 'For those first few years,' says Khando Tsering, Tsering Dolma's daughter, 'my mother was carried away by it all, the attention, the glamour, the comfort, the luxury. It was all new, exciting and fun, and she was happy. She joined in everything, loved the parties and became an avid mah-jong player. However, no matter what she saw, enjoyed and learnt in high society, she always remained a farmer's daughter.'[3]

It seemed to Tsering Dolma that her five-year-old sister Pema had been born with a silver spoon in her mouth. The younger girl was growing up, knowing nothing of hardship. Pema recalls an idyllic childhood at Changseshar with Khando and Tenzin and with the servants' children – playing hide-and-seek, climbing trees, swinging on homemade swings and playing at make-believe in improvised tree-houses...The boys looked for birds' nests and threw stones at them. The girls, disapproving of such wanton destruction, would go and rescue the baby birds and the eggs that were still intact. 'As there was no mother around, we used to take the fledglings to my poor aunt to look after.⁴ As if she hadn't got enough to do!'⁵

Khando's memories of Changseshar consist of isolated flashes.⁶ The huge house, a little lake, the garden surrounded by walls; four gates, each with a road leading up to the entrance; a large open roof-top where the children could play; the big staircase down which her mother once fell and ripped open her leg; her great-grandmother, a very tiny lady lost in the shadows;⁷ bone-crushing hugs from her grandfather, the Kung – 'He was very warm and loving and used to nearly smother us' – the death of Lobsang's favourite Alsatian. Having inherited her mother's (and grandfather's) passion for horses, Khando recalls insisting on having her pony in the bedroom when she had measles. As for the Kung, he had even had a special staircase built in the new house, leading down to the stables.

About two or three times a month, Amala (Dekyi Tsering, the Great Mother) and Tsering Dolma took the younger children to visit Kundun – their only forays outside the estate: 'My mother was always bustling around the kitchen,' says Pema. 'When we were going to see Kundun, she would be especially active, preparing his special foods, baking his special bread. Whenever we saw her with that bread, we knew we were going to the Potala or to the Summer Palace and we got quite excited.'⁸ Sometimes they rode but mostly they walked, and there were hundreds of steps to climb to the top of the Potala before they were ushered into the dark room where Kundun waited impatiently for them. Amala would give him the goodies she had brought, and the two of them would then be lost in conversation for a while. 'I realized later,' said Pema, 'that for my mother these moments were uniquely precious.'

Most thrilling of all was the New Year festival, Lhosar, 'when we were got out of our beds at about two in the morning and dressed in our new clothes. At that hour, all we wanted was to be back in bed again. But it was exciting too. At about four-thirty or five we went to the Potala to receive His Holiness's blessing and attend a religious ceremony.' Khando was luckier: she was so small that someone dressed her and carried her, still half-asleep, up to the Potala. After that early morning audience, they were free to enjoy themselves. 'On leaving the Potala,' remembers Khando, 'we would go and wish my grandparents Happy Lhosar and they would give us candies and money. In the evening, there would be a huge party in the courtyard, with lots of *chang* and all the servants there, singing and dancing.' Then there would be the Great Prayer (Monlam) Festival two weeks later. 'We were dressed in our new clothes again and we all had to keep very quiet,' recalls Pema. 'We didn't understand what was going on but it was fascinating. We couldn't take our eyes off all the people prostrating, lighting lamps, making offerings.'

Pema was six when Lobsang Samten left the Potala to come and live at home and go to the Tharkhang school with Gyalo Thondup and Phuntsok Tashi. She and the other little ones went to a small private school nearby. 'My mother,' she says, 'had had no formal education herself – I don't think she'd ever set foot in a school – but she was very keen that we should all be educated. At about seven or eight, we were packed off to school to learn Tibetan in a special school run by a Tibetan Government official – Khando, Tenzin, myself and four of the servants' children. We all went off each day on our ponies – a twenty-minute ride.'⁹ There were about fifty private schools in Lhasa, attended by children from all walks of life and run by Buddhists who charged no fees but taught in order to gain merit. (None of the Lhasa schools was exclusively for the children of aristocrats.) By modern secular standards, the education was very limited. 'The Tibetan child,' wrote Spencer Chapman, 'is taught to read and write, to recite prayers and long passages of the Buddhist Scriptures and the elements of arithmetic, which are taught with such elementary paraphernalia as the rosary and small pebbles or fruit-stones.'¹⁰ Religious teaching was paramount.

In his spare time, Gyalo Thondup, the only son brought up as a potential farmer, enjoyed gardening, producing 'turnips eighteen inches long, large tomatoes and fine cabbages'. He grew flowers from seeds obtained from the Norbulingka gardens and was advised and encouraged in his hobby by George Sheriff, the British representative in Lhasa, and his wife.¹¹ But his most consuming interest was in the history of the relationship between China and Tibet: he discussed the subject endlessly with his brother-in-law, Phuntsok Tashi, and with his new friends at the Chinese Mission in Lhasa. (His mother disapproved of these friendships, feeling that he was getting into bad company.) Gyalo Thondup now desperately wanted to go and study in China.

The Kung at first objected, but his friend, ex-Regent Reting, talked him round, urging that as Chinese-speaking officials were scarce in Central Tibet and those who understood the Chinese mind even scarcer, if Gyalo Thondup could learn to understand both language and people, he would be immeasurably useful to his country. Gyalo Thondup – and Phuntsok Tashi – began taking private lessons in Chinese.

Amala, meanwhile, was about to give birth again – exactly a year after the death of her last child. When another son was born, with the tell-tale butter-smear clearly visible on his left buttock, it seemed that the oracle was vindicated: everyone was satisfied that the dead child had returned.

Once again Tsering Dolma acted as midwife. There would always be a special bond between her and this her youngest brother; twenty-seven years older, she was a second mother to him. The baby was given the names Tendzin[12] (Defender of the Faith) and Choegyal (Religious King) by his brother, the Dalai Lama.

Three days after the birth, an official celebration was held. Among the guests at Changseshar was Heinrich Harrer, an Austrian mountaineer who had been interned by the British in a POW camp in northern India at the outset of the Second World War. He and another member of the mountaineering team, Peter Aufschnaiter, had made a dramatic escape from the camp, and after enduring blizzards, bandits and near-starvation, had recently arrived in Lhasa.

The two Austrians were both destined to play a key role in the life of the Dalai Lama and his family. They brought with them a breath of the outside world; and were the subject of much excited gossip and speculation. Although they had not yet received official permission to stay in Tibet, they spoke fluent Tibetan and had been adopted by Lhasa society. Harrer was already working as a gardener and Aufschnaiter as an engineer. Before long they were invited to the home of the Dalai Lama's parents. Bearing the white silk scarves which were *de rigueur* when paying social calls in Tibet, they hastened to the audience:

> We soon found ourselves standing before a great gate, near which the gate-keeper was already on the look-out for us. We were led through a large garden full of vegetable plots and clusters of splendid willows till we came to the palace. We were taken up to the first floor; a door was opened and we found ourselves in the presence of the mother of the God-King, to whom we bowed in reverence. She was sitting on a small throne in a large, bright room surrounded by servants. She looked the picture of aristocratic dignity. The humble awe which the Tibetans feel for the 'Holy Mother' is something strange to us, but we found the moment a solemn one.
>
> The 'Holy Mother' smiled at us and was visibly pleased when we handed her the scarves...Then with a beaming countenance she shook our hands, contrary to Tibetan custom. At that moment, in came the father of the Dalai

Lama, a dignified elderly man. We bowed low again and handed him scarves with due ceremony, after which he shook our hands most unaffectedly.[13]

Having thus broken the ice, they sat down to drink tea Amdo style, with milk and salt, not as the Tibetans usually make it, with butter. (The family had even learned, through visiting the British Mission, to take it the English way, with sugar!) Lobsang Samten translated from the Amdo patois into Tibetan. He was fascinated by the strangers and deluged them with questions. For their part, they were delighted to learn that his brother, the Dalai Lama, had charged him to report every detail of his meeting with them.

When they stood up to go,

> a line of servants marched up with sacks of meal and tsampa, a load of butter and some beautiful soft woollen blankets. 'By the personal desire of the Kundun,' said the "Holy Mother", smiling, and pressed into our hands a hundred-sang note. This was done so naturally and as if it was a matter of course that we felt no shame about accepting.
>
> As a final proof of friendliness, Lobsang, on behalf of his parents, laid the scarves on our necks as we bowed to him.

Next day, an excited Lobsang Samten returned the visit. For him, Harrer's arrival was miraculous. Being the Dalai Lama's brother and a monk – he was now training to be a monk-official – meant that his life was very circumscribed. Harrer, the stranger from another world, would become a lifelong friend. As the Austrian wrote,

> I was soon on terms of cordial friendship with Lobsang Samten. This attractive youth was just entering upon his career as a monk. As the brother of the Dalai Lama he had brilliant prospects. One day he was to play a great part as the intermediary between his brother and the Government. But the burden of a great position was already beginning to weigh him down. He could not choose his acquaintances freely. Whatever he did and wherever he went, all sorts of inferences were drawn. When he called on a high functionary on some official occasion, his entry into the room caused an awestruck silence and everyone, even Cabinet Ministers, rose from their seats to show respect to the brother of the God-King. All this might have turned a young man's head, but Lobsang Samten never lost his modest demeanour.[14]

For Lobsang, Harrer was opening a window on to the world outside and he was hungry to know more of it.[15] One day he would introduce Harrer to his brother, the Dalai Lama, but that time was not yet.

On the eve of Gyalo Thondup's departure for China, Kesang Rinpoche invited him and Lobsang Samten to lunch. 'We went and Rinpoche was very happy to see us,' says Thondup. 'He knew I was going to China and was very encouraging. Then when lunch was over, he confessed his real motive in inviting us. "If I die suddenly," he said, "will you two conduct the search for my rebirth?" We were shocked, he looked very healthy to us and we couldn't think why he was talking like that. I don't really remember what we said, but the conversation returned to normal and we spent a pleasant afternoon with him before riding home. Three days later we heard that he had died. Lobsang and I rushed over to his *labrang* and were told, no, he hadn't been ill, just a slight headache, that was all. It was very very strange. And it remains a mystery to this day.'[16]

On 2 March 1946, Gyalo Thondup and Phuntsok Tashi[17] left Lhasa with a Tibetan delegation going to India and China, bearing congratulations to the former on the Allied victory in the Second World War, and to the latter on the successful outcome of the Sino-Japanese War. How could they guess that the end of the foreign war which had preoccupied China from 1937 to 1945 would spell disaster for Tibet? The Chinese Communists, a spent force before the Japanese invasion of Manchuria in 1931 had precipitated the war with Japan, had covered themselves in glory in that struggle. Under their new leader, Mao Tse-tung (elected in January 1935), they had steadily increased their popular support and, after the Japanese defeat, had renewed the Civil War with Chiang Kai-shek's Kuomintang Government.

The two young men spent a year visiting Indian cities while arrangements were made for their journey to China. It was not until April 1947 that they flew with the Tibetan delegation to Nanking, the capital of Kuomintang China, where they were formally received by Generalissimo Chiang Kai-shek. When Tsering Dolma also arrived in Nanking (*en route* for Kumbum to escort her grandmother, uncle and aunt, to Lhasa), the Generalissimo invited all three Tibetan royals to a meal. It was Gyalo Thondup's first meeting with the man who would become a second father to him. Meanwhile, as her husband and brother were to enter the Minorities College to study Chinese, the ever-practical Tsering Dolma asked

Lhamo Tsering, a cousin from Amdo who was already at the College, to keep a watchful eye over them.

Just before the New Year of 1947, the Kung suffered an agonizing colic and took to his bed. The family took it in turns to keep vigil by his bedside, watching helplessly as he writhed in pain. Everything was done that could be done, doctors and astrologers were called in, medicines prescribed, prayers said; but the Kung's condition grew rapidly worse. The family sent a messenger to Kundun, asking to be excused from the official New Year visit. The patient then seemed to rally, recovering sufficiently to drink a bowl of tea. Taktser, who had been staying at Changseshar, left to offer New Year's greetings to various friends. But at his very first port of call, a messenger arrived to say that his father had had a relapse:

> Of course I hurried back to the house immediately, but my father was dead when I arrived. My mother, her face a mask of sorrow, sat beside his death-bed with my youngest brother on her lap. Crouched by her side were Lobsang Samten and Jetsun Pema. It appeared that in the end my father had died a quick and painless death.[18]

A question mark hung over the 47-year-old Kung's untimely death. Some said it was food-poisoning – over-indulgence in roast pork, perhaps. Others suggested a stomach ulcer, others cancer. Inevitably, there were darker rumours: in those days it was not unusual for awkward *prominenti* to be disposed of by poison. The Kung was close to ex-Regent Reting – and to the recently-deceased Kesang Rinpoche. Could this have been a political assassination? Gyalo Thondup, for one, is in no doubt of it:

> I'm quite certain my father was murdered. He was a simple farmer who knew nothing about politics, especially about the complicated saga of the two Regencies. We were close as a family to Reting, who was especially close to my father. I was told that the Taktra clique wanted to depose His Holiness because he had been brought to Lhasa by Reting. They had plans to dispose of Reting, and they feared that if His Holiness took over the political power later he might punish them. So they wanted to remove him while there was still time and replace him with a candidate of their own, a young lama called Ditru Rinpoche. Then there was my father. If he remained alive, he would get in the way of their plans for Reting. So they poisoned him.

GT claims to have seen a document which proves his father's murder, though he admits the evidence was circumstantial. 'The crime was admitted to the Chinese after the 1959 rebellion, by the person who actually did the poisoning. *They probably interrogated him to extort a confession.* He said he had administered a Tibetan herb known as Mad Elephant to my father. I think my mother always suspected the truth, that he had been poisoned.'[19]

But as there were no post-mortem facilities in Tibetan medicine, for the time being it remained mere speculation. Before sunrise on the third day after his death, the Kung's body was carried up into the mountains and ceremonially cremated. A prescribed mourning period of forty-nine days of praying and fasting followed.[20] At the end of it, Amala, sorely in need of change and rest, went off to the family property near Gyantse, which lay on the caravan route to India. The family's finances were by now so chaotic that the Kashag appointed two senior officials to take control of them – a decision which infuriated Gyalo Thondup.

Long before the end of the mourning period, Lhasa was in the grip of a shoddy little civil war, arising from the feud between the two Regents. In early 1947, a small group of Reting's more unprincipled followers tried to assassinate Taktra by means of a hand grenade packed in a parcel. The bomb exploded before reaching its intended victim. Nobody was killed, but the near-miss convinced Taktra that he must act. Then, on 14 April, a coded telegram sent to Lhasa from the Tibetan Bureau in Nanking revealed that Reting had asked for Chinese troops, weapons, military equipment and even planes to help him overthrow Taktra; in return for accepting the Chinese claim that Tibet was part of China. The Kashag needed no further proof of Reting's treachery.[21] A small army was despatched to arrest him and bring him to Lhasa. Whereupon the monks of his college, Sera Je, rose in revolt, killed their abbot, a Taktra supporter, and stormed towards Lhasa, intent on rescuing the ex-Regent. Lhasa was in a ferment, its citizens terrified that thousands of enraged monks were about to descend on the town with murderous intent.

By the time Reting and his escort reached the confines of Sera Monastery *en route* for the Potala, the Government was ready for them. When several hundred monks swooped down from the monastery to rescue the ex-Regent, they were met with a burst of artillery fire which forced them to retreat. Reting was taken secretly to the Potala dungeons; and the Sera monks were threatened with dire consequences if they persisted in their rebellion. Ignoring the ultimatum, they declared they would fight to the last man, even if their monastery should be reduced to the condition of 'a collapsed tent'. In the fierce fighting that ensued, about two hundred monks died. Only on 26 April when Government troops surrounded the monastery and bombarded it with a few howitzers, did the rebels finally surrender.

Meanwhile, Reting and his associates were being interrogated in the Potala. It was still winter and thirteen-year-old Kundun was in the Potala when the ex-Regent was brought there:

> Some kind of committee of the National Assembly conducted the interrogations in the main hall of the Potala. Each day they brought Reting from his cell and he had to cross a big open courtyard. Once, as he passed, I was in the kitchens and some of the cooks were watching from the window. I squeezed myself in between them and watched too. I could only see him from a distance and he couldn't see me at all. I heard afterwards that he had asked to see me. I hadn't known that, but even if I had been able to see him, what could I have done? I had no official power then. He'd probably have asked for clemency, but I'd not have been in a position to grant it. I felt very sad, two Regents fighting like that and involving a whole monastery in their quarrel.[22]

Reting and his associates admitted their guilt to the National Assembly, but before sentence could be passed, Reting, suddenly and inexplicably, died in the Potala dungeons. Once again the rumour machine was busy. Heart attack or political murder? If the latter, was it poison? There are many who believe, as needless to say Gyalo Thondup does, that he too was murdered. Hugh Richardson does not rule out the possibility but is understandably cautious: 'I don't think he was physically murdered. It is certainly not true that his eyes were put out, as some have said. He may have been given the wrong medicine, perhaps deliberately, but we shall never know.'[23] When he visited the Kashag to inquire about the death, Richardson was suavely assured that 'the Regent had been so overcome by shame and remorse that he voluntarily departed this life'.[24]

The property of the rebels was confiscated and sold at public auction. Reting's houses and pavilions were demolished, his beautiful fruit trees transplanted into other gardens. Most of the Sera monks implicated in the revolt had already fled to China. As Harrer said, 'It usually happened that when there was a rising in Tibet, the Chinese had a finger in the pie.'[25] (This most recent Chinese interference was particularly disturbing since

in this year (1947) the Tibetans' traditional allies, the British, were handing over power in India to a National Government; thus severing their official links with Tibet.)

The conspirators were flogged and sentenced to life imprisonment, a
sentence which, together with Reting's mysterious death and the earlier
public humiliation of his own father, is said to have caused Kundun to distance himself from Taktra and his advisers. He contrived to send one of
his personal attendants down with food, bedding and other comforts to the
victims.[26] Despite Reting's misbehaviour, he grieved for him. But the ex-
Regent's names, Jamphel and Yeshe, which Kundun had assumed at his
enthronement, were quietly dropped.

Taktra had won, but it was a hollow victory. The rift between his supporters and Reting's was now unbridgeable, their struggle being, as one
commentator later put it, 'not between the good and the bad but between
the bad and the ugly'.[27] A present-day official in India remembers his father
talking about the situation:

> Rivalry, in-fighting, corruption, nepotism, it was decadent and horrible.
> Everything was a matter of show, ceremonial, jockeying for position. There
> were far too few people in governing circles who had any sense of service to
> the people of Tibet. And yet there *were* many people in Lhasa who saw the sit-
> uation clearly and knew the desperate need for reform and change.[28]

Tibet was falling apart just as its moment of greatest danger approached.
Few doubted that in the struggle against Mao Tse-tung's Communists, Chiang Kai-shek would win. But whichever side emerged victorious, it seemed
likely that China would soon be looking to consolidate – and extend – its
western borders. And that would inevitably mean trouble for Tibet.

When Kundun was twelve, Taktra decided that he should no longer make
visits home; the family's visits to him were also curtailed. He embarked
on an arduous course of education, which was, he later admitted, more
suited to the training of a medieval prince-prelate than that of a late-twen-
tieth-century ruler. Although he attended the meetings of the Government at ten each morning, he knew nothing of international events or of
the revolutionary discoveries of science and technology in the world outside Tibet. His education was in the realm of Buddhist philosophy, logic,
rhetoric and dialectics (debating), subjects in which one day he would be

expected to gain a doctorate. As that time seemed far-off, 'mostly I just worked hard enough to keep out of trouble'. Once, to jolt him out of his laziness, his tutors trapped him into a mock debating contest with the sweeper, Norbu Thondup. The latter being briefed with the answers in advance, Kundun lost. He was mortified. 'For a time I worked very hard out of sheer anger. But in the end my good intentions wore off and I slipped back into my old ways.'[29]

Secretly his tutors were pleased with his progress. Ling Rinpoche remarked that although he had 'occasionally to prod the boy with a finger or gaze thoughtfully at the whips hanging on the wall to encourage him to work more diligently, once Kundun was taught something, he never forgot it.'[30] On his first introduction to metaphysics and logic, he felt 'dazed, as though I were hit on the head by a stone', but he recovered quickly and, as other subjects were added to the curriculum, found it easier and easier to assimilate them.[31] Indeed he began to bombard his tutors with more questions than they had answers for.

Yet he hungered for knowledge of the secular world too. Eagerly he turned to a little newspaper called *Tibet Mirror*, written, edited and published by a Tibetan Christian in West Bengal; the only newspaper of any kind written in Tibetan, available in Tibet, and touching on international affairs. It appeared erratically, and its news was several weeks out of date by the time it arrived, but no matter. The Thirteenth Dalai Lama had been a subscriber, and the Regents had kept up the payments. Kundun was fascinated by this publication and devoured its contents eagerly. He was particularly keen to follow the progress of the Second World War, and loved the pictures of tanks, trucks, jeeps and aeroplanes. Learning of his enthusiasm, the British Mission sent him copies of the *Illustrated London News* and *Life*, and he had their captions translated into Tibetan by the few Lhasa nobles who had been educated in India and knew English. These men were well-travelled and well-informed, but, because of protocol, he could not speak to them directly, nor they to him, and any questions had to be put in writing and delivered by an intermediary. Kundun decided to learn English for himself and pored doggedly over crate-loads of musty text-books which he found in the Potala store-rooms.

His thirst for knowledge was not limited to books; he had always been intrigued by machines; and those magazine pictures gave him further incentive. Finding a broken generator at the Norbulingka, he became obsessed with making it work, even when it meant missing meals. (His guardians were terrified he would electrocute himself.) Then he thought about the old cars rusting away at the Norbulingka. Enlisting the help of a young Tibetan who had learned to drive in India, together they plundered one of two 1927 Baby Austins (presents to his predecessor) for spare parts and got the second one going, along with a 1931 Dodge. He was forbidden to go near the cars on his own, but one evening he crept to the shed and, having gingerly backed the Baby Austin out, drove it at speed around the garden, finally crashing it into a tree. When he saw that he'd smashed a headlight, he was apprehensive that his nocturnal joy-riding would be discovered. Managing somehow to get the car back into its shed, he fashioned a piece of replacement glass for the headlight, inexpertly fogging it with repeated applications of sugar syrup! Next day, to his undying gratitude, his driver pretended to have noticed nothing. Years earlier, he and Lobsang had discovered an old hand-cranked film projector and thirty or forty reels of film. With an old Chinese monk who knew how to operate the machine, the boys spent many fascinated hours watching Tarzan; films about the Boer War or the Jubilee of George V; one based on trick photography, showing girl dancers being hatched out of eggs; and a documentary on gold mining. By the time the Chinese monk died, Kundun had learned to work the machine himself. But when one day the projector broke down, neither he nor anyone else knew how to repair it. Determinedly, he took it to pieces and put it together again, a dozen times and more, before he found a way to make it go – only to discover there were no bulbs:

> It was my fault. When it seemed the projector would never work again, I took out the bulbs and dropped them like bombs from the upper windows of the Potala. They made a lovely explosion when they landed.[32]

It was Kundun's passionate interest in watching films that finally brought Heinrich Harrer into his life. After two years in Lhasa, Harrer was translating foreign news and articles and photographing special events for the Tibetan government. One day, towards the end of 1948, Lobsang Samten brought a request from Kundun for him to build a cinema-room at the Norbulingka. Harrer chose a suitable site and, long before the spring exodus to the Norbulingka, had completed his task. Then the Dalai Lama sent for him. Overwhelmed by this unique honour, Harrer made his way to the cinema-room to meet the legendary ruler. The abbots with Kundun looked on disapprovingly. The young ruler, on the other hand, beamed all over his face and poured out a flood of questions. He seemed to me like a person who had for years brooded in solitude over different problems, and now that he had at last someone to talk to, wanted to know all the answers at once.[33]

Asking Harrer to put on a film about the surrender of Japan, he soon impatiently pushed him aside and began operating the machine himself. Before long, he and Harrer were engaged in animated, bantering conversation, to the shocked horror of the abbots who deplored the foreigner's disregard for protocol.

Kundun was delighted with his new acquaintance, and nicknamed the fair-haired Austrian *Gopse*, or 'yellow head'. For the next year and a half, despite the unrelenting hostility of Kundun's advisers, Harrer paid regular weekly visits to the palace, talking to Kundun about international politics, about the recent war in Europe, about the discoveries of science. In addition, he helped him with his study of English and of Western-style arithmetic.

Harrer was uniquely privileged. Other foreigners, like Hugh Richardson at the British Mission, were often received in audience but protocol did not allow them to speak to the ruler directly. Kundun, through Harrer, now tried to bridge that gap: 'We used to exchange messages through Heinrich,' says Richardson, 'exchange books, packets of seeds and so on. And we got him films. He would send us messages asking for certain ones. Most Tibetans liked the Charlie Chaplin films and an edited version of *Henry V*...The Dalai Lama borrowed *Henry V* and liked it. But he didn't want any of the comic films. He wanted films of factories and modern events. He wanted to know what was going on in the world. So we sent him the newsreels. Then he asked us to get him the book of *Henry V*, so I bought him a paperback edition in India. He was learning English then, listening to the BBC at dictation speed.'[34]

Lobsang Samten, who visited his brother twice a month, reported that 'he never complained of being either lonely or unhappy'.[35] But he *was* lonely and must often have yearned for normality. When the working day ended at five-thirty, he would climb up on to the flat roof of the Potala with his treasured telescope, looking down at the scenes below: the stall-holders in the market, pilgrims prostrating; women shopping; children playing, caravans of yaks, ponies and camels arriving with brick-tea from China or cotton goods and sugar from India. He grieved in autumn when the herdsmen brought large numbers of yaks and sheep to be sold to the slaughterers: 'When I saw those poor animals, several thousand of them, on their way to be slaughtered, I felt an intolerable pain in my heart. I had to do something. I had some money, so I was able to send someone out to buy the animals for me. I could not bear to think of all those poor creatures going to their deaths.'[36]

And when he watched the prisoners walking in the yard of the Shol prison at the foot of the Potala, he could not help identifying with their plight, knowing what it was like to be deprived of freedom.

Did anyone really care about this young boy, this Presence, Wish-Fulfilling Jewel, Precious Protector, except in his role as national icon? Richardson was told by Harrer of the long hours the boy spent alone: 'He did all these ceremonials in the morning, everyone bowing and scraping in front of him. But in the afternoons he was left to himself in a dark room. That's when he virtually lost his eyesight. If he wanted anything from the market, there was nobody to get it for him. There were some idle soldiers supposed to be guarding him and he'd ask one of them or maybe the gardener. I went in one day – I'd gone to see one of his household – and I found a scruffy guard asleep on duty. I spoke to the Government about it, warned them that the Dalai Lama's life might be in danger if he wasn't looked after properly. But they didn't take kindly to criticism, they didn't like anyone interfering in their affairs.'[37]

As he left the years of his childhood behind, Kundun's religious faith gradually matured. He came to understand the importance of *dharma* – the Buddhist teachings – to his life, and felt a growing gratitude to the Buddha and to those past teachers who had brought knowledge of his teachings to Tibet. With the gratitude came a burgeoning sense of responsibility to his own high calling. Though still a high-spirited young boy, he had 'begun to realize what a destructive thing anger was and I was making a big effort to control my terrible temper'.[38] His spiritual life was awakening. Whereas in the past, during long periods of enforced mantra meditation he had waited for his tutor to fall asleep so that he could fool around, he now began to meditate seriously, at first for quite short periods, then gradually for much longer. As he made his annual spiritual retreat at the Potala, he meditated on the *dharma* and expressed his silent gratitude. And though sometimes, as he sat at his high window in the Potala, watching the boys and girls of his own age bring their animals home from pasture, he found himself wondering 'what it would be like to be happy like them', it was without any trace of self-pity.

NOTES

1. Norbu, *Tibet Is My Country*, chapter 15.

2. According to a letter sent from the British Mission in Lhasa to the Foreign Secretary in New Delhi (dated 16 April 1945, O and IO Collection, etc. File 15(2)), the boy had been treated by the Chinese doctor in Lhasa. When Pema also became ill, the parents called in Dr Terry from the British Mission. Pema thankfully recovered.

3. Author interview with Khando Chazotsang, Salt Lake City, Utah, February 1996.

4. Amala's mother and brother, together with the Kung's sister, came from Amdo in 1947 to live at Changseshar.

5. Jetsun Pema, *Tibet, Mon Histoire*, Paris, Éditions Ramsay, 1996.

6. Author interview with Khando Chazotsang, Salt Lake City, Utah, February 1996.

7. Amala's mother, brought to Lhasa in 1947 by Tsering Dolma (see 4 above).

8. Author interview with Jetsun Pema, Dharamsala, June 1994.

9. Author interview with Jetsun Pema, Dharamsala, June 1994.

10. F. Spencer Chapman, *Lhasa: The Holy City*, London, 1940; New Delhi, 1992.

11. George Sheriff died of a heart attack in 1944 and Hugh Richardson returned to Lhasa temporarily to replace him.

12. Although this name is usually spelt without a 'd', Tendzin Choegyal has always preferred to use the 'd' – the more traditional and older spelling.

13. Harrer, *Seven Years in Tibet*.

14. *Seven Years in Tibet*.

15. Interview with Namlha Taklha, October 1993.

16. Author interview with Gyalo Thondup, New Delhi, July 1995.

17. Tsering Dolma stayed at home. It was and is quite normal for Tibetan couples to be separated for longish periods.

18. *Tibet Is My Country*, chapter 15.

19. Author interview with Gyalo Thondup, New Delhi, July 1995.

20. Strict procedures were followed after a death. For seven weeks thereafter, food was served as usual in the living-room of the deceased, and prayers were offered by whichever lama was present at the death. Prayers were offered every seventh day (for a man) or every sixth day (for a woman). After forty-nine days, it was believed that reincarnation would already have taken place, and the official period of mourning came to an end.

21. See Goldstein, *A History of Modern Tibet*, chapter 14.

22. Author interview with HH the Dalai Lama, Dharamsala, July 1995.

23. Author interview with Hugh Richardson, September 1993.

24. Letter from Hugh Richardson, June 1993.

25. *Seven Years in Tibet.*

26. Goldstein, interview with Kundeling Dzasa, note at the end of chapter 14.

27. K. Dhondup, 'The Regents Reting and Tagdra', *Lungta 7.*

28. Author interview with Tenzin Geyche Tethong, Dharamsala, 1994.

29. Fourteenth Dalai Lama, *Freedom in Exile.*

30. Goodman, *The Last Dalai Lama*, chapter 8.

31. Goodman.

32. Goodman.

33. *Seven Years in Tibet.*

34. Author interview with Hugh Richardson, September 1993.

35. Goodman.

36. Author interview with HH the Dalai Lama, Dharamsala, July 1995.

37. Author interview with Hugh Richardson, September 1993.

38. Author interview with HH the Dalai Lama, October 1993.

10

Twilight of the Gods 1947–50

The Chinese People's Liberation Army must enter Tibet, liberate the Tibetan people, and defend the frontiers of China.
From the Chinese Government's letters of 30 October and 16 November 1950, addressed to the Government of India

Liberate from whom?
Jawaharlal Nehru's reply

Having passed his exams with distinction, Taktser Rinpoche was about to set off on a long pilgrimage to the Buddhist shrines of India and China, when his father's death and the Reting riots intervened. In the event, he set out on a very different pilgrimage, to take his father's ashes back to the mountains of Amdo. Phuntsok Tashi, who had rushed home from Nanking on hearing of the Kung's death, was to escort him as far as Calcutta.

Seven years had passed since Taktser had made that first perilous journey from Kumbum to Lhasa. This time the journey was easier and full of wonders and marvels, from Hugh Richardson's farewell gift of a pair of sunglasses to the astonishing revelations that awaited him in India – 'things I had never seen in my life before – things I should not have believed possible'. In Calcutta, he was startled to hear a train letting off steam, 'with a tremendous hissing, stamping sound'; and later gazed in complete disbelief at 'the monstrous silver birds' on the tarmac of the International Airport.

Fear soon gave way to pleasure when he flew in a 'silver bird' from Calcutta to Hong Kong and Shanghai. At Shanghai he was met by Gyalo Thondup and Lhamo Tsering, and taken to Nanking where the two cousins were studying Political Science at the Central University. Though the Civil War had moved into its final stages and the Communists were sighting victory, the capital, Nanking, was still unscathed. Gyalo Thondup was enjoying life. As the Dalai Lama's brother, he had been taken up by Chiang Kai-shek and his wife:

> They couldn't have been kinder. They paid all my expenses, invited me to their home for weekends and holidays, and altogether I was very close to them. The Generalissimo was always encouraging me, telling me I must study hard to understand China. He promised that when I had finished my five years' study in China he would send me to the USA and England for more study, and only then would I return to Tibet. He said I would be very useful to the Dalai Lama and the Tibetan Government, and he himself would feel more comfortable about Tibet if I was there in a position of responsibility. He was worried about Tibet, because it was China's back door, and he didn't want the Tibetans to fall prey to foreign manipulation. But, he said repeatedly, 'If you return to work in Tibet, then I will support the idea of independence for your country.'[1]

After a few days, Taktser flew on alone to Peking. But the accelerating crisis soon forced him to cut short his visit. The Communists were coming close, he could hear their artillery, and the railway lines had already been cut.[2] Returning to Nanking, he made his slow and difficult way westwards to Amdo. At Kumbum monastery, he received a warm welcome from the monks, but found depressingly few familiar faces among them.

His first task was to take his father's ashes to the mountains above Taktser and as he said his final goodbye, he felt indescribably sad. Seven years earlier, Choekyong Tsering had left his native Amdo for power and riches beyond the imagining. Inevitably perhaps he had lost his bearings. But now he was back where he truly belonged, lying just above the village in which he and his forbears had lived for countless generations. Taktser's eyes glistened with tears as he looked down from the mountain top:

> That small village with its neat and spotless houses perched on its gentle hill looked more beautiful to me than anything I had seen on my long journey abroad; and with gratitude in my heart I turned towards Kyeri, whose snow-clad peak shone above me in the sun.[3]

In the village he greeted his old companions and Pasang, the village head-man, now stooped and white-haired. He was invited by every family in the village in turn, all of them bombarding him with questions about the Dalai Lama, the Potala, and what it was like to live in Lhasa. They were tremendously proud of having given Tibet its Dalai Lama, and proud too of this other famous son, Taktser Rinpoche, who had returned to them.

They would soon have even greater reason for pride, for at this time the Abbot of Kumbum resigned and Taktser was chosen to succeed him. Though doubting his fitness for the task (and knowing very well that he had been chosen because he was the brother of the Dalai Lama), Taktser accepted and was formally inducted just as Chiang Kai-shek's Kuomintang were facing up to the fact that they had lost the Civil War.

By the end of April 1949, the People's Liberation Army (PLA) was with-in a few days' march of Nanking. Gyalo Thondup (now twenty-one) had recently married a Chinese fellow-student, Zhu Dan, daughter of one of Chiang Kai-shek's Generals, Chu Shi-kuei.[4] 'Until then, we hadn't had any disturbances in Nanking itself, except for the student revolutionary move-ments,' he says. 'The Communists were mobilizing leftist groups among the students. But not in the school where I was, the Central Political Uni-versity. None of us took part in those demos and riots. But we were hear-ing more and more about the terrible fighting and killings in other parts of China. Then in 1949, everything changed, the Generalissimo acknowl-edged defeat, resigned and fled with his troops to the island of Taiwan.'[5]

Panic-stricken Kuomintang officials abandoned Nanking in droves. Some of them tried to persuade Gyalo Thondup to go with them to Taiwan – as the Dalai Lama's brother he would have considerable propaganda value. But, reasoning that he had gone to China solely to study Chinese, he decided to head for home.

With his wife, Lhamo Tsering, two Amdo friends and the Tibetan Gov-ernment representative and his staff, he left on a crowded train for Shang-hai, which the Communists still had not reached. From there they sailed to Hong Kong. It was a close-run thing; a few days later Shanghai was sur-rounded by the PLA and panic set in. There was a frantic run on the banks, with many people trampled underfoot in the rush; then the banks were shut down, their windows boarded up. The only way out of the city was by sea; but there were no longer any ships.

There is confusion over Gyalo Thondup's movements after this, and ac-counts vary. His own version (as told to myself)[6] is as follows:

When I finally arrived in India, I stayed first in Kalimpong with friends. Mr Nehru contacted me there and invited me to Delhi as his personal guest. He even sent his private plane for me. Nehru questioned me about China and about my own plans – was I intending to continue my studies in India or return to Tibet? He wanted me to stay in India, but I told him I hadn't decided yet. After staying as Nehru's guest for a week, I returned to Kalimpong and from there went to Calcutta in October 1949. I stayed there for seven months.

The next move came from the Communist Marshal Chu-deh who asked me to contact the Tibetan Government with a view to establishing better relations with them. Otherwise, he said, the People's Liberation Army would invade Tibet. I asked Thubten Sangbo, a Tibetan official in Kalimpong who was in telegraphic communication with the Tibetan Government, to convey this information to Lhasa as a matter of urgency. Then Nehru sent the Indian Ambassador to Peking, Mr Sardat Panikkar, to warn me that the Chinese Communists meant business and that the Tibetan Government should put itself on a war footing, start mobilizing the people immediately...He asked me to inform the Kashag, through Thubten Sangbo, that the Indian Government would help in any way it could, would even provide arms. Even the American Ambassador, Mr Anderson, asked me what help Tibet needed.

I replied that I couldn't speak for the Tibetan Government, but would pass on the messages. I passed everything to Thubten Sangbo, but months went by and there was still no response from the Tibetan Government. Nehru kept on asking if any word had come and said that the situation was growing more grave by the minute and that total mobilization by Tibet was now absolutely vital. 'Even if China invades Tibet,' he told me, 'the Tibetan Government must stand firm. If they overrun Amdo and Kham, you must move all the valuable paintings, sacred texts, statues to Central Tibet and from there to India.' India, he kept on assuring me, would provide the Tibetans with arms and ammunition and would stand four-square behind them. If necessary, they would build an airstrip outside Lhasa and send an aircraft to rescue the Dalai Lama from Lhasa.

Three times both the American Ambassador and the Indian Ambassador to Peking contacted me. But no reply ever came from Lhasa!

Why did the Tibetan Government not respond to these overtures? Gyalo Thondup puts forward several suggestions:

Well, for a start, the Tibetans had been isolated for too long, living in a world apart. They didn't know China, they didn't know India. They were far too busy quarrelling among themselves to understand the danger they were in. And no one had any control over those powerful lamas. They made an awful mess of everything. If they'd shown some political sense, things might have turned out very differently.

For another thing, they didn't trust me. In 1946, after they murdered Reting, the Tibetan Government issued a proclamation about his 'treason'. At the end of this document, they wrote that Gyalo Thondup, a protégé of his, *was now in China*! The implication was obvious. My mother knew or suspected the truth about my father's and Reting's deaths and in 1949 she wrote to me in India, advising me not to go back home. It would be too dangerous, she said. Dangerous for His Holiness too! My mother told me that His Holiness's safety depended on my not returning to Tibet where they suspected me of working for the Chinese.[7]

In those days the Tibetan Government did not keep written records, so the allegations cannot be checked. But there can be no doubt that they were suspicious of Gyalo Thondup, not only as a Reting protégé but because he had gone of his own free will to study in China. What guarantee was there that he was not a Chinese spy? They were not unaware of the danger they were in: they knew very well that Lhasa was full of Chinese agents – both Communist and Nationalist – disguised as traders or even monks. In fact, when Gyalo Thondup sent his first warnings – in 1949 – they had already taken what they thought was effective enough action. Fearing a rapid Communist take-over of the small Chinese Mission in Lhasa (the Communists had already taken over the Bank of China in Calcutta), the Kashag closed it down and expelled all Chinese officials from Tibet. When the People's Republic of China was inaugurated by Chairman Mao in Peking on 1 October 1949, the Tibetan Government believed they had asserted their independence in the nick of time. Their action, however, was interpreted as a slap in the face by Communists and Nationalists alike, and its main effect was to exacerbate the ancient quarrel between Tibet and China.

Nothing now stood between the Communists and the heartlands of Tibet but the Tibetan-populated borderlands which the Kuomintang had nominally controlled. The fate of Tibet hinged on the amount of resistance put up by those two vital frontier regions, Eastern Kham and Amdo. In the event, there was almost none. The various Kuomintang garrisons in Eastern Tibet were scattered and demoralized, lacking the revolutionary fervour of their opponents. Some of them simply went over to the Communists, some put up a token fight before quietly surrendering. In Amdo, the warlord, Ma Pu-feng, on whom the Kuomintang had pinned their hopes, commandeered two Dakota aircraft and fled with his wives and treasure before hostilities so much as began. The Communists entered Amdo unopposed.

Fugitives from the Communist onslaught and former Kuomintang soldiers with nowhere to go straggled in to Kumbum monastery, bringing reports of Communist outrages against civilian populations. 'We already knew,' wrote Taktser, 'how badly they had behaved towards our co-religionists in Mongolia and China, and we were well aware that our high dignitaries and wealthy monks in particular had every cause to fear them. Many Tibetan Buddhists in Mongolia and China had lost their lives on account of their religion, and we were sorely afraid that the Communists would persecute us and forbid us to practise our religion.'[8] In these circumstances, it was hardly surprising that many monks quietly left the monastery and went to ground in the neighbouring villages, while others joined bands of wandering nomads, in the forlorn hope that the Communists would not think of looking for them on the steppes.

With the red flag of the Chinese People's Republic hoisted over Siling, compulsory meetings aimed at the political re-education and indoctrination of the people began immediately. Taktser and a few of his senior monks went to see their new masters to find out where they stood. The PLA Commander assured them they had come as liberators, driving out the Nationalist criminals who had long persecuted the Tibetan people, and assuring a better and fairer future for all. The empty sloganizing only increased the forebodings of Taktser and his monks, who returned home in dismay.

Alarming reports began filtering through: of monasteries burned to the ground, of Communist-led mobs incited to plunder and desecrate their sacred treasures. The beautiful little cliff-top monastery of Shartsong where Taktser had begun his studies had been utterly destroyed. Fearing for Kumbum itself, Taktser went to Siling to protest to the new Governor. Once again, bland assurances were given, the Governor promising to investigate any 'irregularities' that might have taken place. Then, nothing. Instead, Taktser was formally interrogated in the offices of the new Tibet Commission in Siling:

I had to provide them with a meticulous account of my life and my career, and submit a detailed list of all the properties of the monastery and of the nobles. I was also asked searching questions about the rank, property and activities of everyone I knew.[9]

On his return, the monks heard him out with mounting anxiety. They knew by now that they were dealing with an enemy who would stop at nothing, and that among the asylum-seekers in Kumbum were many Communist spies and informers out to trap them into political discussion. Eavesdroppers were everywhere, night and day.

Villages such as Taktser, which were within the orbit of Kumbum, were already suffering not only hunger and neglect but the destruction of their centuries-old lifestyle. Taktser Rinpoche's protests fell on deaf ears, the new Governor retorting that everything was the fault of the monks and the outdated economic structure of the country. The monasteries, he said, must redistribute their lands and return their monks to the labour force. In vain did Taktser point out that there had been no hunger until the Communists arrived; that Amdo had lived in peace and harmony with its monasteries for hundreds of years; that many of the monks were skilled artisans who had learned their craft in the monasteries.

The confrontation did Taktser no good; from then on he was given two minders, with orders to 're-educate' him and never leave his side. A prisoner within his own monastery, he dared not communicate even with his closest friends. The minders argued with him round the clock, relentlessly attacking his religious beliefs, mocking his obsolete views, setting political traps for him:

If they came upon me in prayer they would ask sarcastically whether prayer had ever filled anyone's belly. At first I tried to make them understand that prayer gave me serenity and confidence, and that a life without it was just unthinkable for me. But they mocked at our beliefs and our gods, and they insisted that it was men like Stalin and Mao Tse-tung who had put food into the bellies of the starving millions, not our Buddhas. I quickly realized that it was pointless to try and make them understand what life meant to us, and what Tibet had owed to its monasteries and its monks for many hundreds of years. Again and again they reproached me with standing in the light of progress, and declared that the monks exploited the people and wasted the national patrimony.[10]

The minders searched Taktser's possessions and censored his correspondence. Their merciless attentions brought him to the edge of breakdown; he began to wonder how much longer he could carry the responsibility for Kumbum and its monks on his shoulders. He knew, of course, that the cat-and-mouse game the Chinese were playing with him owed everything to his being the Dalai Lama's brother. Before the Communists came, this had made his appointment as Abbot eminently desirable. But he was now a terrible liability to everyone concerned.

After a number of sleepless nights, he reached a decision. During a ceremony to commemorate his first anniversary as Abbot, Taktser offered his resignation to the assembled monks and implored them to accept it. The monks listened in appalled silence. They knew what it cost him to take this step; but they knew also that he was right: they *would* be better off without him. A few weeks later, a new Abbot was installed and Taktser retired to his own *labrang*, hoping to be left in peace.

But the bulldogs stayed. In fact, now that he no longer had any official duties, it became harder than ever to shake them off. 'It was quite clear to me now that I owed their special attention to the fact that I was brother of the Dalai Lama.'" Taktser refused to be drawn as they constantly extolled the totalitarian State as the only way to human equality and happiness. But his depression deepened:

> Although by this time I had already heard this sort of thing often enough before, the thought of such a State never ceased to horrify me anew. It was a conception in crass opposition to everything we held dear; and as they described their paradise it sounded like hell on earth to me: a life of grey, uniform dullness, without warmth, without individual love and affection, a life not worth living, and a world not worth living in."

Everything that Taktser held dear was falling apart. A ruinous system of taxation had come into force. In the days of Ma Pu-feng (which seemed in retrospect a Golden Age), the peasants had paid a fixed annual sum to the local monastery, which had then paid the required taxes to the authorities. But now payment was to be made directly to the authorities in Siling, whose demands became ever more extortionate. When the peasants protested, there were threats, increased demands and punishments, with the People's Liberation Army always on hand to back up the threats with force. Anarchy threatened:

Robbery and murder had become common in a once peaceable countryside. Dissatisfied elements banded together, and the once-feared robber bands became a reality again...and such were the topsy-turvy conditions brought about by the new rulers that the oppressed masses regarded them as heroes.[13]

About a month after Taktser had resigned, the Chairman of the Tibet Commission proposed that he should go to Lhasa to present a list of Chinese demands to the Dalai Lama. If he did this, his 'previous obstinacy and former relations with the Kuomintang and the Western Powers in Lhasa' (!) would be overlooked. If, however, he were to accept the commission, but use the opportunity to escape over the border to India, he would 'never be allowed to set foot on Tibetan soil again'. Taktser rejected the proposal outright, assuring the Chairman that, other objections apart, he would be assassinated as a traitor if he turned up in Lhasa as a messenger boy for the Communists.

They did not give up. The secretary of the Governor tried; then the Governor himself; and finally the Commanding Officer of the PLA. All without success. But, even as Taktser continued to stall, he was aware of the appalling danger he faced. If he continued to refuse, he might well be held as a hostage, a pawn with which to blackmail Lhasa. Indeed, the opportunity the Communists were offering was probably his last chance of escape. Wearily, he agreed to their suggestion, stipulating that if he was to have any credibility in Lhasa, he would need to travel with an entourage of at least twenty senior lamas. But his hopes of thus saving the lives of twenty of his colleagues were stillborn: he was allowed only two. Moreover, he was to have a Chinese escort of three: a married couple and a wireless operator with a portable transmitter. Obviously his masters were taking no chances.

Before he left, they proposed a bribe so outrageous that it winded him:

It was nothing less than a promise to make me Governor-General of Tibet if on my arrival in Lhasa I managed to persuade the Tibetan Government to welcome the entry of Chinese communist troops into Tibet as liberators, and to accept the Chinese People's Republic as an ally. As Governor-General, they pointed out, I should be in a position to assist and guide the great work of Socialist reconstruction in my country and to help replace antiquated religious beliefs with the new communist ideology. Should the Dalai Lama resist the march of progress, they indicated, ways and means would have to be found to get rid of him. At this point they even let me see quite clearly that if necessary they would regard fratricide as justifiable in the circumstances if there remained no other way of advancing the cause of Communism.[14]

Taktser could barely restrain his disgust: 'What sort of a man did they think I was, for heaven's sake? Did they really suppose that I was capable of such abominations in return for the privilege of becoming their puppet?'[15]

Once again, but with a heavy heart, Taktser prepared for the journey to Lhasa. He was given 'a large-calibre pistol and twenty-five rounds of ammunition, three old Japanese rifles, three horses and three thousand gormos', and told that he and his two companions should make their way to the caravan rendezvous at Tsaidam, where their Chinese escort would join them.

At last the bulldogs were called off, and Taktser could move around freely. As he said goodbye to his friends, he knew it was unlikely that he would ever see any of them again and he was in little doubt as to their probable fate. It was with considerable mental anguish that he left the monastery.

Not even the majestic panoramas of the Tibetan plateau could raise his spirits, their austere immensity serving only to plunge him into deeper gloom. He sank into a state of nervous irritation, particularly as the Chinese couple seemed set on delaying the caravan as often and for as long as possible. As time after time they insisted on stopping for rest-days, the tensions inside Taktser threatened to boil over.

But when the party crossed the border into the Dalai Lama's territory and the Governor of the Northern Provinces turned out to meet him, it was the turn of the Chinese to be enraged. The Chinese writ did not run here, and they were refused permission to enter. When the leader of the Chinese group realized that the Tibetans were not going to let them in, he 'completely lost his head and shouted that he had just heard over his radio that Red Chinese troops had already marched into Chamdo, the capital of western Kham'. In spite – or perhaps because – of this horrifying announcement, the Governor confiscated the wireless transmitter and had the three Chinese arrested and taken away under escort.

But the news was all too true. It was the twenty-third day of the ninth month of the Year of the Iron Tiger (7 October 1950) – a year in which the astrologers had long foretold that 'evil forces would enter Tibet'. Thirty thousand Chinese troops had just invaded Tibet from six different directions at once. The 'peaceful liberation' had begun.

The old Imperial idea of 'barbarians' being happy to kowtow to the Son of Heaven (whether called Emperor, Generalissimo or Chairman) was ingrained in the Chinese psyche; and it implied that 'the spread of Chinese civilization into a universe of barbarian darkness was a natural process'.[16] On this matter the majority Han Chinese, whether Kuomintang or Communist, were of one mind: the national aspirations – and rights – of the minority races on their borders were completely irrelevant.

Early in 1950, the South-West China Military District was charged with invading and conquering the Kham area of Tibet. (One of the two Communist leaders who distributed instructions about the conduct of this operation was Deng Xiao-ping.) Throughout the year, the Chinese propaganda machine continued to threaten Tibet, and make wild allegations that foreign powers were arming the Tibetans for an attack on China.

It would have been laughable if it hadn't been so tragic. On 1 January 1950, Robert Ford, a Briton employed by the Tibetan Government as a radio officer in Kham's capital, Chamdo, was shocked by an announcement on Radio Peking. 'The tasks for the People's Liberation Army for 1950,' intoned the voice, 'are to liberate Formosa [Taiwan], Hainan[17] and Tibet from American and British Imperialism.'[18] Ford did a mental count: there were no Americans in Tibet, and the only Britons were Richardson (soon due to leave and hand over to his Indian counterpart), Reginald Fox, another radio operator, in Lhasa (crippled with rheumatoid arthritis), and Ford himself in Chamdo. Four 'foreign imperialists' in all, unless one included the Austrians, Harrer and Aufschnaiter. Listening to news broadcasts in both English and Tibetan, Ford regularly heard the same unvarying message. 'There was no criticism of Tibet's feudal system, no promise of land reform, no appeal to the workers to rise up and throw off their chains. It was simply a matter of getting rid of American and British Imperialism.'[19]

When the border regions succumbed to the Communists in 1949, apprehension in Lhasa turned to panic. Military training, deliberately run down since the Great Thirteenth's death because of opposition by the powerful Abbots – they had accepted supplies of arms from the Indian Government, but had declined all offers of training in their use[20] – was belatedly started. Kundun was called upon to consecrate the Army's new colours – when Chiang Kai-shek's armies were already fleeing to Taiwan. In any case, the Army amounted to only ten thousand men, and what chance would they have against the battle-hardened Communists?

Too late, the Tibetan Government realized the folly of the isolationism long imposed on it by the monks. ('The monks,' says Hugh Richardson, 'far more than the nobles, were responsible for the fall of Tibet, by failing to see that foreign contacts could have been used to safeguard their religion rather than undermine it.'[21]) Belatedly, they began broadcasting their own claims to independence – in Tibetan, Chinese and English – through Radio Lhasa, the station Robert Ford had built and opened for them. In addition, they prepared to send four separate 'goodwill missions': to India, Nepal, the United Kingdom and the USA, to try and counter the Chinese propaganda and ask for help. But Peking intervened, stating that Tibet was not an independent state but an integral part of the Chinese People's Republic, and any talks that might take place must be in Peking. They warned – with India and Nepal in their sights – that any country receiving one of these proposed 'goodwill missions' would be considered as an enemy of the Chinese People's Republic. Thus was Tibet doomed from the outset. Though ministers fired off telegrams beseeching these formerly friendly nations to receive them, the replies were, as the Dalai Lama recalls, 'terribly disheartening'.

> The British Government expressed their deepest sympathy for the people of Tibet, and regretted that owing to Tibet's geographical position, since India had been granted independence they could not offer help. The Government of the United States replied in the same sense and declined to receive our delegation. The Indian Government also made clear that they would not give us military help and advised us not to offer any armed resistance.[22]

The only remaining possibility lay in talks with the Chinese.[23] Hoping against hope for a peaceful solution, the Tibetans were prepared to hold talks – on some neutral ground, not in Peking. The go-between was Gyalo Thondup's father-in-law, Chu Shi-kuei, now a member of Communist Peking's Mongolia and Tibet Commission Office.

Chu Shi-kuei asked the new Chinese Government to arrange a meeting with a Tibetan delegation in Hong Kong. When the British authorities refused to issue visas, he suggested New Delhi as a venue, perhaps in September after the arrival of the Chinese Ambassador, General Yuan. (Jawaharlal Nehru, Prime Minister of a newly-independent India, had lost no time in recognizing the new Chinese Communist Government.)

In Lhasa, the Government was doing what came naturally to it:

All the monks in Tibet were ordered to attend public services at which the Tibetan Bible was to be read aloud. New prayer-flags and prayer-wheels were set up everywhere. Rare and powerful amulets were brought out of old chests. Offerings were doubled and on all the mountains incense-fires burned, while the winds, turning the prayer-wheels, carried supplications to the protecting deities in all the corners of heaven. The people believed with rock-like faith that the power of religion would suffice to protect their independence.[24]

When the official State Oracle[25] was consulted, he proclaimed somewhat obviously, 'A powerful force threatens our sacred land from the north and east' and 'Our religion is in danger'. Lhasa was alive with rumours, people looked to the omens for comfort. But the omens were all bad. The previous year, a comet had been seen at night and around dawn in the direction of the hills south of Lhasa. It was regarded by the Tibetans as an omen of war; the last comet having been followed by the Chinese invasion of 1910. Other fearful signs were to follow: a gilded dragon on the roof of the Jokhang Temple began dripping water, though the season was dry and no rain had fallen; freak births among domestic animals were reported; and one night the capital of an ancient stone pillar, erected at the foot of the Potala Palace to seal the peace between China and Tibet, came crashing to the ground. Fear and uncertainty crept into even the stoutest hearts.

Then on 15 August came a devastating earthquake, the fifth largest in recorded history. In the late evening, Kundun was emerging from his outside washroom at the Norbulingka when the earth shook beneath his feet. When he went back inside,

> I noticed that several pictures hanging on the wall were out of alignment. Just then, there was a terrific crash in the distance. I rushed back outside, followed by several sweepers. As we looked up into the sky, there was another crash, and another. It was like an artillery barrage.[26]

A huge red glow suffused the cloudless dark sky. Next day, the inhabitants of Lhasa learned from All-India Radio that a massive earthquake had struck in the Himalaya of south-eastern Tibet and that tremors had been felt all over Tibet and India. The destruction was colossal; the face of the earth had quite literally been changed. Mountains had become valleys, valleys raised up into mountains; and the Yarlung Tsang Po (Brahmaputra) River, its course diverted by an enormous landslide, flooded hundreds of villages and claimed thousands of victims.

How could a people as superstitious as the Tibetans not see this as heralding some unspeakable disaster? Even the Dalai Lama, who set little store by popular superstition, was unconvinced by Heinrich Harrer's assurance that there must be a purely scientific explanation. This, he felt, was 'beyond science, something truly mysterious'. Whatever the cause, the citizens of Lhasa were terrified. 'People began to whisper about "Lha-mak", a Tibetan *Götterdämmerung*. The gods of Tibet were doing battle with the demons of China and the frightened Lhasa folk dared not speculate on the result.'[27]

At the beginning of October 1950, as the Tibetan delegates still waited hopefully in New Delhi, the People's Liberation Army swarmed across the Upper Yangtse River and attacked the Tibetan positions in Chamdo. The Twilight of the Gods had descended.

The Tibetan Eastern Command in Chamdo was hopelessly ill-equipped to defend a 200-mile border along the west bank of the Yangtse River. Poorly-trained and outnumbered ten to one, what hope did the Tibetans have against an army equipped with the latest automatic machines and weapons – and fresh from their victory in the Civil War? The Lhasa Government, still obsessed with its own feuds, tried to gather itself together but, with conflicting reports coming out of Kham, was unable to provide any coherent leadership. Eleven days after it began, the battle for eastern Tibet was over. The Tibetan army surrendered – and the way to Lhasa lay open. Radio Peking told the Chinese people that People's Army units had been sent into Tibet 'to free three million Tibetans from imperialist oppression and to consolidate national defences on the western borders of China'.

Regent Taktra, contemptuously known as 'the old man', was widely seen as a divisive force and in this overwhelming crisis had no option but to resign.[28] The people, sick to death of all Regents, were clamouring, through street-songs and wall-posters, for the young Dalai Lama to be made Head of State, even though at fifteen he was still three years short of his majority. At such a time the country needed to unite behind its rightful ruler. A decision of such magnitude, of course, had to be referred to the State Oracle. The latter, wrote Kundun, 'tottering under the weight of his huge, ceremonial head-dress, came over to where I sat and laid a *kata*, a white silk offering-scarf, on my lap with the words *Thu-la bap* – "His time has come".'[29]

Kundun protested at first, aware of his youth and inexperience. But, in the face of the looming catastrophe, how could he not accept? The prospect was daunting but

> I could no longer refuse to take up my responsibilities. I had to shoulder them, put my boyhood behind me, and immediately prepare myself to lead my country, as well as I was able, against the vast power of Communist China.[30]

The seventeenth of November 1950 was fixed for his investiture. Before it could take place, one more shock lay in store. At the beginning of November, Taktser arrived 'in a terrible state', to stammer out the Chinese ultimatum.

Kundun was stunned. 'My brother was supposed to trick me into submission and if he didn't succeed he was to kill me. We knew that Communists committed atrocities, of course; we had heard what happened in Mongolia and we had been warned by my predecessor's Last Testament. But this was the first time it had been brought home to me, the first time it had touched me personally. And it was my own brother, someone I knew well and trusted, who was telling me these things. I was very frightened.'[31]

To this boy king, largely ignorant of the outside world with its cruel ideologies, Taktser spelled out the realities of life under Chinese Communism, urging that the only hope for Tibet was to secure foreign support and to take up arms against the Chinese. Taktser's own mind had been made up during the long journey: he would renounce his monastic vows and go abroad, to become a spokesman for Tibet. He urged his brother to leave Lhasa with all speed before the Chinese cut off the escape routes to India.

Kundun was reluctant; there was so much to be done. He had begun his reign by announcing a general amnesty for prisoners and had many other reforms in mind. Now, when he looked down with his telescope from the Potala roof, he could see nothing and no one in the prison courtyard below, 'save for a few dogs scavenging for scraps'. His isolation was complete.

During the enthronement ceremony which took place at dawn on 17 November, he was handed the Golden Wheel which symbolized his assumption of supreme secular power. His heart sank. Though the people celebrated, he knew only too well that the situation was hopeless. He was just fifteen, head of a Government that had lost all credibility, undisputed leader of a people faced with a confrontation that they did not want, that they were certain to lose, but which they could not possibly avoid.

NOTES

1. Author interview with Gyalo Thondup, New Delhi, July 1995.

2. Peking fell to the Communists on 31 January 1949.

3. Norbu, *Tibet Is My Country*, chapter 16.

4. One of the original supporters of Dr Sun Yat-sen, the revolutionary leader who had overthrown the Manchu Empire in 1912.

5. Author interview with Gyalo Thondup, New Delhi, July 1995.

6. Author interview with Gyalo Thondup, New Delhi, July 1995.

7. Author interview with Gyalo Thondup, New Delhi, July 1995.

8. *Tibet Is My Country*, chapter 17.

9. *Tibet Is My Country*, chapter 17.

10. *Tibet Is My Country*, chapter 17.

11. *Tibet Is My Country*, chapter 18.

12. *Tibet Is My Country*, chapter 18.

13. *Tibet Is My Country*, chapter 18.

14. *Tibet Is My Country*, chapter 18.

15. *Tibet Is My Country*, chapter 18.

16. Warren W. Smith, 'The Nationalities Policy of the Chinese Communist Party and the Socialist Transformation of Tibet', Robert Barnett and Shirin Akiner, eds., *Resistance and Reform in Tibet*, C. Hurst and Co., 1994.

17. On 16 April 1950, the Communists invaded Hainan and had taken it a week later.

18. Robert Ford, *Captured in Tibet*, Harrap, 1957, reissued OUP, 1990.

19. Ford, *Captured in Tibet*.

20. Letter from Hugh Richardson to the author, 12 December 1993.

21. Letter from Hugh Richardson to the author, 12 December 1993.

22. Fourteenth Dalai Lama, *My Land and My People*.

23. For a full account, see Goldstein, *A History of Modern Tibet*, chapter 18.

24. Harrer, *Seven Years in Tibet*.

25. Tibetan oracles are not soothsayers or foretellers of the future, but men and women who act as mediums between the natural and the spiritual worlds.

26. Fourteenth Dalai Lama, *Freedom in Exile*, chapter 3.

27. From an unpublished manuscript shown to the author by Jamyang Norbu.

28. He remained as Senior Tutor but died a year later.

29. *Freedom in Exile*, chapter 3.

30. *My Land and My People*.

31. Author interview with the Dalai Lama, Dharamsala, June 1994.

11

A Flight and a Return

The Chinese have...a profound regard for history. But history, for them, was not simply a scientific study. It had the features of a cult, akin to ancestor worship, with the ritual object of presenting the past, favourably emended and touched up, as a model for current political action. It had to conform also to the mystical view of China as the Centre of the World, the Universal Empire in which every other country had a natural urge to become a part...The Communists...were the first Chinese to have the power to convert their atavistic theories into fact. They saw their opportunity, calculated that no one was likely to oppose them, and acted.

Hugh Richardson, Tibet and its History

People in the West often wonder why the Han Chinese were so keen to annex Tibet. The answer is four-pronged: land, mineral resources, strategic position and naked power. The vast emptiness of Tibet could provide living-room for China's surplus millions; her untapped resources of mineral wealth beckoned; and, once in possession of the land which was the highest point on the planet, China would have strategic mastery over the rest of Asia.

Whatever its reasons, China was determined to claim Tibet for itself. Taktser reported in detail to the Kashag on Peking's plans to swallow up the entire country. Learning that the UN had recently mounted a rescue operation for a South Korea attacked by the Communist North, the National Assembly appealed to that Organization, pleading that the Chinese invasion of Tibet was an equally flagrant 'violation of the weak by the strong'. Tibet begged India to present its appeal to the UN, warning that the destruction of Tibet as a buffer state would imperil India's own security. But since gaining Independence in 1947, Prime Minister Nehru had rejected the old concept of Tibet as a buffer against China and the Soviet Union, in favour of a friendship with China which would bring peace and stability to Asia. Nehru would say or do nothing to displease China.

In the UN, only El Salvador sponsored a move to condemn the Chinese onslaught on Tibet. The British delegate – cravenly turning his back on Britain's long friendship with Tibet and tacit acceptance of Tibetan independence – commented weakly that Tibet's legal status was 'confusing'. Both Britain and India voted to do nothing. (To the Tibetans, Britain's betrayal was the unkindest cut of all.) The US, sympathetic but already committed to an expensive war in Korea, agreed that the question of Tibet should be shelved. 'Our friends would not even help us to present our plea for justice,' lamented the Dalai Lama. 'We felt abandoned to the hordes of the Chinese Army.' And in that grim November of 1950, that is precisely what they were.

The atmosphere in Lhasa was tense, with many of the nobles already fleeing the country. The National Assembly begged the Dalai Lama to leave immediately for Dromo, a village in the Chumbi Valley, less than three hundred miles away, just six miles from the border with India. From there he could plead his country's cause, and, if necessary, escape into India. The departure had to be a close-kept secret, because if the people came to hear of it, they might panic and try to prevent him leaving. Kundun was reluctant, but the argument that it was not he himself but the sacred person of the Dalai Lama – the very soul and essence of Tibet – which must be protected at all costs could not be denied. (The Chinese knew well that the key to a peaceful take-over of Tibet lay in their being able to take control of the Dalai Lama's person.) So Kundun resigned himself to the inevitable – 'I had to allow my people to take far more care of me than I would have thought of taking for myself.'

Lobsang Samten, now a Government official, had been ill with what the doctors had diagnosed as a heart condition – but later turned out to be a nervous breakdown. 'He was so ill,' recounts his future wife, Namlha, 'that for a time people thought he was actually dead. He wouldn't speak,

147

couldn't eat, simply stayed in bed. If Lobsang was to go with his brother – and he desperately wanted to – he would have to be carried on a stretcher as far as Dromo.'²

Taktser's problems were of a different kind. He knew it would not be long before the Chinese discovered he had double-crossed them, and therefore it was imperative for him to leave Tibet without delay. He persuaded his mother to go at once with the younger children to the family estate at Gyantse and wait for him there. Bidding farewell to the monastery of Drepung, he exchanged his monk's robes for ordinary layman's clothes and began the journey which would take him out of Tibet – and the monastic life – for ever.

Distressed though she was by this fresh upheaval, Amala knew there was no alternative if Kundun were not to fall into Chinese hands. Later, she remembered little of the journey to Dromo, except the exhaustion of long hours in the saddle. As Great Mother, she was entitled to travel in a palanquin, but she always refused the privileges of rank and elected to ride like everyone else. And as they journeyed by night and early morning to avoid the stinging sandstorms which blew by day across the open plateau, riding – often in fifty degrees of frost – was a nightmare.

Leaving Lhasa is Tendzin Choegyal's earliest memory: 'I remember the morning we left. Lobsang Samten was too ill to travel and was coming on later with His Holiness. But he had come out to the courtyard to say goodbye to Amala. It was very early in the morning, before daybreak. I could see the outline of my brother and my mother against the background of a starry sky. They were embracing, saying goodbye.'³ The five-year-old was carried on horseback by a servant, so small that the man simply tucked him in the pouch of his *chuba* – 'like a kangaroo...except that I was facing the wrong way'. He remembers that 'it was bitterly cold and my feet never warmed up'.

The Tibetan Government had already begun despatching over a thousand pack-animals, each laden with treasure, towards the border. Forty mules carried gold dust, six hundred carried bars of silver and the rest sacks of old coins⁴ – all to be concealed somewhere on the estates of the Maharajah of Sikkim.

Late in the evening of 18 December, Kundun and his officials drank a symbolic last cup of butter-tea in the Potala. That done, they refilled their cups and left them standing there, in token of their hope of a speedy return. At about 2 a.m., the young ruler, wearing layman's clothing: 'a rich coat of dark red silk lined with fur, a fur hat and woollen muffler',[5] left Lhasa with an entourage of 40 nobles, a 200-strong bodyguard and about 1500 pack animals. There was a hold-up on the outskirts of Lhasa when thousands of monks streamed onto the road to try and prevent his departure. Only with difficulty were they persuaded to let the caravan proceed. Even then, the monks threw themselves down on the track and begged Kundun to return as soon as possible.

The caravan went on its way, crossing three high passes, one of them 17,000 feet above sea level. Heinrich Harrer met them at Gyantse, horrified to see his friend, Lobsang Samten, being carried on a litter and to find that 'the doctors had used the same rough methods on him as they do on a sick horse. On the day the convoy was to leave he had lain in a swoon for several hours, so the Dalai Lama's physician recalled him to life by applying a branding-iron to his flesh.'[6]

Then on to Phari (the highest town in Tibet), before dropping down into the deep and narrow Chumbi Valley, the main channel of trade between Tibet and India, just inside Sikkim on the southern slopes of the Himalaya.[7] At the far end of the valley, squeezed in between vertical cliffs, stood Dromo, with its 'four rows of half-timbered cottages roofed with shingles, flanking two longitudinal streets of which the bigger, with its little shops, constitutes the market'.[8] The huge caravan arrived there – weary and half-frozen – on 2 January 1951, after a journey of sixteen days.

Accommodation was hard to find. For the first month, Kundun stayed in the house of the district Governor (renamed Heavenly Palace of Universal Light and Peace in his honour). Then, since hardly any light reached that house and it was piercingly cold, he moved to the small hillside monastery of Dungkhar, where Taktser was also staying. From there he could keep in touch by courier with those members of the Government who had remained in Lhasa. The rest of his family, the nobles, officials and Heinrich Harrer (who was leaving for India), were quartered in small cottages or scattered farmsteads. Some of the officials' families went directly to the Tibetan enclaves of Kalimpong or Darjeeling across the border, and, as soon as sufficient military checkpoints had been set up, the bodyguard was sent back to Lhasa.

The Chinese, meanwhile, wanting to show the world that they favoured diplomacy over force (and waiting to see how the UN would respond to Tibet's appeal), had halted their military advance about one hundred miles to the north-east of Lhasa and were offering peace talks – in Peking. The

Kashag, being in no position to argue, authorized the group of five officials still on standby in New Delhi to go to Peking and salvage whatever they could for Tibet. (The group's interpreter was Phuntsok Tashi, now an official in the Department of Foreign Affairs.)

With the Government of Tibet completely paralysed, Kundun's rigorous schedule was relaxed. When spring came, he and the now convalescent Lobsang were free to make long treks into the hills, getting rid of their pent-up energies by striding ahead of their largely overweight attendants. 'They fell behind constantly,' said Lobsang, 'but we could always tell where they were by the sound of their panting.'⁹ The brothers visited 'every monastery, shrine and temple in the entire area'.

Tendzin Choegyal was staying with his mother, Tsering Dolma, Pema, Tenzin Ngawang and Khando, in a small wooden house, so tiny that the younger children were packed off outdoors each day with a picnic lunch. 'We used to chase small birds from one bush to another. I remember the ice-cold water, crystal clear, and the masses of wild flowers. We played with pebbles. And Mr Harrer used to come. He brought us chocolate, and that was the first time I had ever tasted it. My sister, Pema, was at school in India, so she was learning English. At first I was allowed to sit in on the lessons. But I was too naughty, and they kicked me out.'¹⁰

Pema, with Tenzin Ngawang and Khando, had been sent to India a year previously. They had travelled with Tsering Dolma who was ill and had to be carried in a palanquin placed on the backs of two mules. While Tsering Dolma sought medical treatment in Calcutta, the children were sent to St Joseph's Convent in Kalimpong, transplanted suddenly into a world of school uniforms, huge dormitories and the unfamiliar English language. The change was traumatic, especially for five-year-old Khando who had never been left alone at night before. 'From the very first evening,' wrote Pema, 'the nuns decided to put her near me. I was suddenly wakened from a deep sleep by the sound of stifled sobs. My niece had just fallen out of bed. I took her in with me, consoled her, and I believe she fell asleep in my arms.'¹¹ When one day, the children heard that the family were coming to Dromo and that they were to pass the winter of 1950/1 together, they were 'mad with joy'. 'I must admit,' says Pema, 'that we did not understand the real reasons that had brought His Holiness to Dromo.'

The idyll was soon to be shattered. In Peking, the Tibetan delegation, under orders not to sign anything without reference to Lhasa, discovered that the Chinese did not intend to discuss peace terms so much as dictate them. They were insulted, abused, threatened and coerced into signing (on 23 May 1951) a Seventeen-Point Agreement, the only choice being between 'peaceful liberation' and the annihilation that would follow a renewal of the fighting. The Agreement was sealed with a replica of the Dalai Lama's personal seal, newly forged in Peking. This, the first treaty concluded between China and Tibet since AD 821, was a vaguely-worded document which promised to leave intact the Dalai Lama's authority and the political system of Tibet; and to respect the religion, language and customs of the Tibetans. No question, however, of genuine autonomy or independence, since it declared that Tibet was part of China and that henceforth all policy-making, both domestic and foreign, would be taken over by Peking. Clause One stipulated that:

> The Tibetan people shall unite and drive out imperialist aggressive forces from Tibet. The Tibetan people shall return to the big family of the Motherland – the People's Republic of China.

Kundun heard the news three days later from a Tibetan language broadcast on Peking Radio. Tuning in to a crackly old Bush radio receiver, he heard a strident voice announce the signing of a Seventeen-Point 'Agreement for the Peaceful Liberation of Tibet' by representatives of People's China and the 'local government' of Tibet. Kundun sat transfixed:

> The speaker described how 'over the last hundred years or more', aggressive imperialist forces had penetrated into Tibet and carried out 'all kinds of deceptions and provocation'. It added that 'under such conditions, the Tibetan nationality and people were plunged into the depths of enslavement and suffering'. I felt physically ill as I listened to this unbelievable mixture of lies and fanciful clichés.[12]

But, being both helpless and alone, the Tibetans had no choice but to accept their fate and hope that China would keep its side of 'this forced, one-sided bargain'.[13] Even now, they did not realize how cleverly the Chinese had played their cards. As Goldstein observes, 'This "peaceful" liberation avoided the very negative international criticism that renewed military liberation would probably have produced, and it precluded the possibility of interference from anti-Communist countries such as the United States if fighting was renewed.'[14]

Now that Tibet had been abandoned to its fate, there was a heated debate about whether or not the Dalai Lama should accept the Agreement and return to Lhasa, or 'denounce it, go into exile, and launch a political and military struggle against the Communists'.[15] The majority of his monastic advisers wanted him to return home. (It would not have crossed their minds that the Chinese would actually try to destroy Buddhism; but they foresaw trouble for themselves if Kundun did not return.) Others, including Harrer (who was already in Kalimpong), urged him to go to India and look for allies in the fight against the Chinese. Peking was putting pressure on Taktser to dissuade his brother from leaving the country. But Taktser, convinced, not least because of his own experience, that his brother was surrounded by Chinese Communist spies, begged him to go to India and from there to the United States. In this he was supported by Amala.

Taktser was now determined 'to seek that freedom abroad which I already knew from bitter experience was impossible under Communist rule'.[16] Enlisting the help of a friend who was already in the United States, he received an encouraging response. He then sought Kundun's permission to take his mother and the younger children on a pilgrimage to India, where he would arrange for a medical check-up. Kundun had been notified that the newly-appointed Commissioner and Administrator of Civil and Military Affairs in Tibet, General Chiang Chin-wu, was travelling to Lhasa via the Chumbi Valley – and was to escort him back to the capital. Taktser, knowing he must be gone when the General arrived, hastened, with much sadness, to say goodbye to his brothers.

> They knew nothing of my ultimate plans, and I could not bring myself to add to their sorrow and distress by revealing them. Would I ever see either of them again? And if so, under what circumstances?[17]

The younger children were excited at the prospect of the pilgrimage. But Taktser's heart was heavy:

> I knew that in all probability I should never again set foot on Tibetan soil, that I should never again return to my home. Voluntarily, I was now turning my back on my country for ever.'[18]

When General Chiang arrived in Dromo, Kundun was peering out of a window at Dungkar Monastery to catch a glimpse of him, half-convinced that all the Chinese would have horns and tails:

I don't know exactly what I expected, but what I saw was three men in grey suits and peaked caps who looked extremely drab and insignificant among the splendid figures of my officials in their red and golden robes. Had I but known, the drabness was the state to which China was to reduce us all before the end, and the insignificance was certainly an illusion.[19]

He left Dromo on 21 July with Lobsang Samten on horseback, though he was no lover of horses. For once, though, he was glad of the freedom of riding across the open plains and continually urged his mount forwards. (It was actually only a mule called Grey Wheels, and the Head Groom was disgusted that the Dalai Lama had been given such an inferior mount.) He arrived back in Lhasa in mid-August, after a nine-month absence. The people turned out *en masse* to welcome him. But, amid the demonstrations of public joy, he detected an undertow of hysteria. Reports had begun reaching the capital of atrocities in the eastern areas of Kham and Amdo. Fear and foreboding were in the air. Yet, quite irrationally, there was also a conviction that with Kundun's return, all would surely be well.

Hope died on 9 September when 3,000 troops of the Chinese 18th Route Army entered Lhasa, 'tubas and drums blaring, portraits of Mao and Chou En-lai held aloft, between phalanxes of China's red flag, one of whose four small orbs, circling the great yellow star at its centre, was now Tibet'.[20] Within three months two more contingents had arrived – about 20,000 soldiers, backed up by 30,000 camels and horses which they had commandeered along the way. On 24 October, after a meeting of the National Assembly, the Dalai Lama reluctantly approved the Seventeen-Point Agreement, and Tibet officially became part of the People's Republic of China. The bell had tolled for the Tibetan way of life. But as *Life* magazine mused, one crucial question hung in the air: now that the Dalai Lama had returned home, would he become merely 'one more in the succession of Moscow-pulled puppets'?[21]

NOTES

1. Quoted by Goodman, *The Last Dalai Lama*.

2. Author interview, Namlha Taklha, Dharamsala, October 1993.

3. Author interview with Tendzin Choegyal, Dharamsala, November 1993.

4. Avedon, *In Exile from the Land of Snows*, p. 91.

5. 'Flight of the Dalai Lama', *Life* magazine, 23 April 1951.

6. Harrer, *Seven Years in Tibet*.

7. Sikkim was originally an independent Buddhist Himalayan kingdom strongly linked to Tibet. In 1861, however, the British had annexed some of its southern territory, including Darjeeling. Although theoretically still a sovereign state, in practice the British administered Sikkim in much the same way as any other Himalayan state with whom they had an agreement. When they left India in 1947 the Indian Government took over the administration of these northern states, and in 1975 Indira Gandhi sent Indian troops into Sikkim to depose its ruling king and incorporate Sikkim into India proper. The issue is still a running sore in Indian politics.

8. Fosco Maraini, *Secret Tibet*, Hutchinson/Readers Union, 1954.

9. Goodman.

10. Author interview with Tendzin Choegyal, Dharamsala, November 1993.

11. Jetsun Pema, *Tibet, Mon Histoire*.

12. Fourteenth Dalai Lama, *Freedom in Exile*.

13. Fourteenth Dalai Lama, *My Land and My People*, p. 88.

14. Goldstein, *A History of Modern Tibet*, p. 772.

15. Goldstein, p. 773.

16. *Tibet Is My Country*.

17. *Tibet Is My Country*.

18. *Tibet Is My Country*.

19. *My Land and My People*.

20. *In Exile from the Land of Snows*.

21. 'Flight of the Dalai Lama', *Life* magazine, 23 April 1951.

12

The Brothers

By November 1951 it was clear that, to effect their aim of political domination, the Chinese intended to use the old form of government as their instrument and mouthpiece to control every aspect of Tibetan domestic affairs. The presence of the Dalai Lama at Lhasa was an essential part of that design; but an equally important part was the reduction of his absolute power and divine prestige. Inroads on his authority and on that of the monasteries, from which much of his support was derived, began almost at once.

Hugh Richardson, Tibet and its History

Three-year-old Tendzin Choegyal had been recognized as the sixteenth reincarnation of the former illustrious teacher, Ngari Rinpoche. 'My immediate predecessor,' he says today, 'was a fairly worldly person, interested in building houses, planting small saplings, digging springs. He was also a skilled administrator, and with his interest in small mechanical gadgets, you could say that, like the Thirteenth Dalai Lama, he was a man before his time. I'm told that when he and the Great Thirteenth were studying with the same teacher, they became good friends. And when the Fourteenth Dalai Lama arrived from Amdo, Ngari Rinpoche was among the crowds outside Lhasa to welcome him.'[1]

When the Fifteenth Ngari Rinpoche died, the Gadung Oracle prophesied that he would be reborn in the house of the Yapshi Taklha;[2] and so he was.

(As Hugh Richardson comments, 'the Ngari Rinpoche was not *per se* very high, but added lustre was conferred on the role by a brother of the Dalai Lama.'[3]) Tendzin Choegyal, already recognized as being the reincarnation of his own older brother, was now proclaimed to be the reborn Ngari Rinpoche as well. (Nobody seems to have noticed anything bizarre in this double achievement!) The fact that three of Amala's sons were now recognized *tulkus* set the seal on her reputation as the greatest of all Great Mothers: her achievement was unique in the Tibetan Buddhist tradition. Many in Lhasa believed her to be the goddess Tara reincarnated; and no one wondered that the Dalai Lama had been born to such a mother. As her friend, Rinchen Dolma Taring, recalls: 'She was unique, a truly great woman; she had no anger, no hatred, no greed, no jealousy towards anyone. She was a luminous person.'[4]

To be recognized as a *tulku* was the highest of honours. But it placed a heavy load of responsibility on young shoulders which were often ill-equipped to carry it. Tendzin Choegyal was a high-spirited child who would always find monastic discipline stifling. Now in his early fifties, he voices serious doubts about choosing young children as *tulkus*:

> I don't discount the possibility of reincarnation. We do have a past and will
> have a future. But choosing a particular person as a particular reincarnation of
> another particular person, I think that's very dicey. After all, this system de-
> veloped nowhere but in Tibet and then only at quite a late stage. So, on all
> sorts of grounds, I have very mixed feelings.[5]

His brother, Taktser Rinpoche, who renounced the monastic state on leaving Tibet and adopted his other name, Thubten Jigme Norbu,[6] had long had similar doubts. After all, the system was not guaranteed infallible; mistakes could be – and presumably were – made. 'I suppose it would be strange,' he wrote, 'if I did not wonder, as I do, if I really *am* Taktser's reincarnation. The Gyalwa Rinpoche [Dalai Lama] believed it; everyone else believes it; but I myself, I just do not know.'[7]

As the years passed, his attitude remained ambivalent and today the question seems to bore him: 'Well, I certainly could never remember anything about a previous life,' he says. 'But then I can't remember what I did yesterday, let alone in a previous existence. All I can say is that it's our Tibetan custom, so I go along with it. If the Tibetans think I'm a reincarnation, all right. I don't care one way or the other. Everyone still calls me Rinpoche but they could say I was a reincarnated donkey for all I'd care.'[8]

Not all *tulkus* lived up to the high ideals expected of them. In the early eighteenth century, the Sixth Dalai Lama turned out to be a libertine given to the pursuit of girls rather than sanctity.[9] But Tibetans believe that everyone is entitled to work through each of his lives in his own way, and anyway once a Rinpoche, always a Rinpoche. The monk's robes may be discarded, but one's acknowledgement as the reincarnation of a great teacher cannot be set aside. Probably neither Norbu nor Tendzin Choegyal was suited to the position assigned to them in childhood, but for many years both of them accepted it. And though both have long since renounced their vows and married, they will continue to be addressed as Rinpoche by their fellow Tibetans for as long as they live.

The Dalai Lama, saddened by their defection, believes that if history hadn't intervened his brothers would still be in their monasteries. Not surprisingly, he defends the *tulku* tradition, though with less force than one might have expected. 'There's good and bad in it, as in most traditions,' he explains. 'In our practice of choosing boys as a rebirth of some important teacher there is something positive and something negative. They do receive very special nurturing, and if that goes well it's a very positive thing. Sometimes they themselves become very special teachers. But, in cases where the young boy becomes arrogant and uses his position as a social status, manipulating other people to his own ends, then that's very bad. And yes, it does happen.'[10]

There was no sudden dramatic change in Tendzin Choegyal's life. He was not instantly taken away to the monastery but continued to live at home with his mother, with a monk from Drepung as tutor. 'I was a *tulku* but I still had to do as I was told and got into trouble if I didn't. Nevertheless, as the youngest, I suppose I *was* a bit spoilt.'[11] To Pema and Khando that is an understatement: 'He was manifestly treated in a very special way and everyone, servants, monks, friends, visitors, danced attendance on him...When we played together, we always had to obey his every whim.'[12] For instance, as Pema recounts,

My sister had a beautiful black mare which had borne a magnificent foal. As the foal got bigger, my brother decided he wanted to ride it...on the roof of our house. The servants were packed off to find the foal. Then they had to get it up the stairs...When they got the foal up to the top, the spectacle was impressive. Never before in the memory of any Tibetan had a horse been seen on a roof. On the way down, when my brother's caprice was satisfied, the servants had to hold the foal by the tail to prevent him falling.[13]

But at least Tendzin Choegyal shared the life of the family and to some extent at least was treated as an ordinary human being. It was not so with Kundun. He addressed his mother as Amala and his younger siblings by their names, but to them he was always the Dalai Lama and their attitude towards him was one of the deepest respect.

When Tendzin Choegyal was four (in 1950), his mother took him to the monastery built by the first Ngari Rinpoche at Kumulung outside Lhasa; and there he was solemnly enthroned as the latest Incarnation of the ancient lineage. He remembers nothing about the ceremony, and he and his mother returned home together a week later. It cannot be said, however, that life then returned to normal, for the time exactly coincided with the Chinese invasion and the family's flight from Lhasa.

When Amala and the younger children left Dromo with Norbu, they followed the ancient caravan route over the main range of the Himalaya by the Nathu la Pass (14,800 feet) into Gangtok, the capital of mountainous, jungly Sikkim, 'a toy capital, with a toy bazaar, toy gardens and toy houses, set among tree-ferns and wild orchids on a hillside among the clouds...It is connected with the rest of the world by telegraph...it has a post-office, a hospital and the Maharajah's palace. All the same you feel out of the world. The whole thing is a fairy-tale.'[14]

Tendzin Choegyal has two vivid memories of this journey into fairy-tale. The first is of being in disgrace for breaking a teapot in one of the bungalows established by the British trade missions. 'The keeper of the bungalow was terribly upset because he didn't know how he could account for the breakage. So my mother bought a new one when we went to India, and we gave it him on the return journey. It was a dark brown pot, mass-produced, probably in Stoke-on-Trent, or somewhere.'[15] The second memory is of his first introduction to one of his abiding later passions, the motor car. He was scared nearly out of his wits on first sighting the old English Austin which had been sent to take them into the town:

I was so frightened, it looked like a huge insect with two bright eyes. And the noise of the horn terrified me. I refused to ride in it so was allowed to continue on horseback till we stopped for the night. Next day we were to go to Gangtok, and the driver, a Nepalese, persuaded me very gently to approach the car and got me to touch it and stroke it and smell the leather seats. He was such a sensitive, understanding man. I loved it when he made the indicators flick in and out. Later that evening, I agreed to go in the car with my mother. I was in for another shock when it got dark and they put the car lights on. The dashboard was a marvellous sight. That was the moment I fell in love with cars, and I've loved them ever since.'[16]

From Gangtok they crossed the southern ridge of the Himalaya down to Kalimpong in the far north of Bengal, the traditional centre for trade (particularly in wool, musk and yak-tails) between Tibet and India, where many Tibetans had come to live. Here Norbu heard that the American Committee for Free Asia – the CIA under another name – had invited him to the USA for a year as their guest. With his immediate future thus assured, he was able at last to tell Amala and Tsering Dolma of his plans. Though naturally upset at the prospect of his departure, they understood his reasons and gave him their blessing.

Norbu left for Calcutta, to make arrangements for the journey; and from there wrote to tell Kundun that he was on his way to America. 'He wrote me this long letter,' recalls Kundun, 'saying that he saw no alternative and that therefore we might not meet again for a very long time. "Whether or not we meet again in this life, till Buddha-hood do not forget me," he wrote, using the words of our Buddhist farewell. It was a very sad moment for me.'[17]

In Calcutta, Norbu ran into the Tibetan delegates on their way back from signing the Agreement in Peking. They were all (including Phuntsok Tashi) firmly lodged in the Chinese Embassy, under the watchful eye of General Chiang Chin-wu who was on his way to Dromo to escort Kundun back to Lhasa. Norbu was urged (rather too warmly for his peace of mind) to join the party, and had to pretend to be considering the matter. At the first opportunity, however, he took his brother-in-law on one side and told him he was flying to New York that very night. Phuntsok Tashi, though alarmed, promised not to betray him.

In the USA, news that the Dalai Lama's brother was shortly to arrive had somehow leaked out, and at Idlewild Airport Norbu was greeted by 'a barrage of exploding flashlights' and surrounded by excited journalists. His host was Robert Ekvall, the son of Christian missionaries who had worked for many years in Amdo and spoke the dialect fluently. From now on it was plain sailing. As Norbu soon realized, 'Everyone's door was open to the Dalai Lama's brother.'

When at last he received the much-needed medical check-up and was found to have congestion of the lungs, Ekvall arranged treatment for him and placed a small farmstead in Fairfax, West Virginia, at his disposal. Hardly had Norbu arrived there than a telegram came from Gyalo Thondup announcing the imminent arrival of himself and family.

Before the Chinese actually invaded Tibet, Gyalo Thondup had hoped to go to Peking to resume his studies and find some way of helping his country. His decision was, he admits, irrational and naïve, but he had to do something. 'I tried to get a visa to travel via Hong Kong but the British wouldn't give me one. Then I thought, maybe I could go by way of Macao, or perhaps via the Philippines. I decided on the latter. It was an unlucky choice. There I was contacted by former Kuomintang friends who persuaded me to go to Taiwan instead.'[18] He was in Taiwan for sixteen months.

He was a welcome guest on this island where Chiang Kai-shek had re-established his Nationalist Chinese Government: 'The Generalissimo and Madame Chiang Kai-shek were very pleased to see me and tried to persuade me to settle in Taiwan, to take a job in the Tibetan Affairs section of the Government Service. But I was becoming increasingly anxious. The Communists had now begun their invasion of Tibet and I wanted to help my brother somehow. After all, I'd surely have been useful to the Tibetan Government as an interpreter. So, despite the danger, I felt I ought to go back.'

Unfortunately for Gyalo Thondup, the Kuomintang Security Department had discovered the letter which the Communist Marshal Chu-deh had written him in 1949. Naturally enough, they were suspicious.

I suppose they had begun to think I might be a Communist spy, or at least was ripe for exploitation by the Communists...Government officials, some of whom had been my teachers at the University in Nanking, began inviting me to their houses and getting at me. They would say things like, 'Gyalo, the Chinese Communist Party is like a beautiful girl, but her beauty is skin-deep, she is riddled with disease.' Since I didn't know my letter from Marshal Chu-deh had fallen into the hands of Chinese Intelligence, I didn't know what on earth they were talking about. But I soon realized I was under virtual house-arrest. I can't claim it was uncomfortable – my wife, baby daughter and I were lodged in the Grand Hotel – but there was no doubt I was under surveillance.

The only other people staying in the hotel were American military advisers. Gyalo Thondup became friendly with one of these and used to go fishing with him. One day the American suggested that if he cared to write to President Truman, or to the Secretary of State, Dean Acheson, asking for permission to study in the USA, he would deliver the letter personally. 'My wife and I sat down and composed a letter and gave it to him, just as he was leaving for a visit to the US. Not long after, a friend of mine in the Kuomintang came rushing into the hotel, saying, 'Mr Thondup, Mr Thondup, we've had a letter from the American Secretary of State, asking us to let you go to the USA, so you're free to go.'[19]

The Generalissimo and his wife accepted defeat with a good grace, giving GT a sumptuous farewell dinner and $50,000 towards his education. But the British still would not give him a transit visa for Hong Kong. His wife, Zhu Dan, had no difficulty – since her mother was currently in Hong Kong, but Gyalo Thondup was forced to go via Japan. Zhu Dan joined him in Tokyo with their baby daughter, and they travelled together to the USA and the farmhouse where Norbu was staying.

Hardly had he arrived – in September 1951 – than he announced his intention of returning to Tibet. His new acquaintances in the State Department offered him a Scholarship to Stanford University and did their best to dissuade him from such suicidal folly. He appreciated their concern, and was indeed tempted by their offer. 'But, as I kept telling my friends, my obligation was to serve Tibet in her hour of need. My conscience wouldn't let me stay. I knew how ignorant most Tibetans were about China and Chinese Communists. Well, I didn't know the Communists, but I did know the Chinese and the way their minds worked.' His mind was made up.

His brother was furious.

Norbu said he knew what the Communists were like better than I did and I would be crazy to go back. But I knew I had to go. I told them all, 'Tibet is a huge country, the Chinese won't be able to control everybody there. In any case, if I can't handle it, then I'll escape to India.' Crazy talk, but I was young and young people are like that. They said it would be impossible to escape from Tibet, but I laughed at them. I knew the terrain well and there was a 2,000-mile border between India and Tibet. The Chinese couldn't have eyes everywhere.[20]

So in February 1952, Gyalo Thondup returned to India via Darjeeling, where he left Zhu Dan, now pregnant with their second child. Pema, Tenzin Ngawang and Khando would join her there and go to school. He had alerted his mother to wait for him in Kalimpong.

Amala, Tsering Dolma and the children had been on pilgrimage to the sacred Buddhist places of India and Nepal. But the sweltering heat of the Bengali plains had driven them to cut short the pilgrimage and return to the relative coolness of Kalimpong, where friends had been loaned them a house.

The family were in Kalimpong in October 1951 when the People's Liberation Army entered Lhasa and Tibet was swallowed up by China. Amala feared for her other two sons and for her widowed mother who had been brought from Amdo to live with the family in Lhasa. She could neither sleep nor eat and lost weight alarmingly. Since no local doctor was able to suggest a remedy, a Tibetan doctor travelled from Lhasa with a supply of herbal medicines. By early 1952 she was pronounced fit enough to travel, and as soon as Gyalo Thondup arrived, the family set out on the return journey.

Whatever their apprehension about the future, they were going home. When Amala caught sight of the Potala's golden turrets gleaming in the sunlight, she felt as though a weight had been lifted from her shoulders.[21]

NOTES

1. Author interview with Tendzin Choegyal, July 1995.
2. Families of Dalai Lamas were known as Yapshi families.
3. Letter to the author, 12 December 1993.
4. Letter to the author, 6 November 1993.
5. Author interview with Tendzin Choegyal, Dharamsala, November 1993.
6. Since this time, he has been usually known as Norbu.
7. Norbu, *Tibet*.
8. Author interview with Thubten Jigme Norbu, Dharamsala, July 1995.
9. He was also a fine lyrical poet.
10. Author interview with HH the Dalai Lama, Dharamsala, June 1994.
11. Author interview with Tendzin Choegyal, Dharamsala, June 1994.
12. Jetsun Pema, *Tibet, Mon Histoire*, my translation.
13. Jetsun Pema, *Tibet, Mon Histoire*, my translation..
14. Fosco Maraini, *Secret Tibet* 162.
15. Author interview with Tendzin Choegyal, Dharamsala, June 1994.
16. Author interview with Tendzin Choegyal, Dharamsala, June 1994.
17. Author interview with HH the Dalai Lama, Dharamsala, June 1994.

18. Video recording made by Gyalo Thondup for the monks of Namgyal Monastery, Dharamsala in 1991.

19. Author interview with Gyalo Thondup, New Delhi, July 1995.

20. Author interview with Gyalo Thondup, New Delhi, July 1995.

21. Goodman, *The Last Dalai Lama*.

13

Gyalo Thondup in Lhasa 1952

How can there be laughter, how can there be pleasure, when
the whole world is burning? When you are in deep darkness,
will you not ask for a lamp?

The Dhammapada

When the Chinese 18th Army first marched into Lhasa, the inhabitants
had clapped their hands, not in applause but in the time-honoured way for
driving out evil. Children threw rocks and stones and many of the monks
were observed 'knotting the ends of their shawls and hitting the Chinese
who were riding by'.[1]

This first phase of the occupation of Lhasa was puzzling. The soldiers
were orderly and made considerable efforts to be friendly and co-operative.
Loudspeakers assured the populace that the Chinese had come in a spirit
of brotherhood to liberate the Tibetans and bring them back to the Great
Motherland; they would respect the Tibetan way of life and honour the
Seventeen-Point Agreement. But to ordinary Tibetans they were not liberators, they were the *Tenda Gyamar*, the Red Chinese Enemies of Religion.

The United Front policy – which operated until Chinese Communist
power could be properly established – required that the leaders of society
should be wooed and encouraged with new titles and fat salaries. Far from
persecuting the upper and middle classes, the Chinese openly courted them,
promising that if they studied Marxism and sent their children to the new
Chinese schools, their status in the new society would be assured.[2] There

was no talk of 'class-enemies', nor so much as a whisper of 'democratic re-forms'. The Chinese even gave money to the monasteries – and the word 'barbarians', their habitual description of the Tibetans, was firmly taboo.

Many of the nobles and Government officials seemed happy enough to accept the Chinese occupation, not all of them for self-serving reasons. Some of the more progressive and socially aware among them recognized their country's need of economic and social reform and genuinely believed that the new, radical ideas coming out of China would be Tibet's salva-tion. When the PLA marched into Lhasa, many of these progressives joined the Chinese and set to work translating Marxist texts into Tibetan. 'The Seventeen-Point Agreement was in force,' explains Phuntsok Tashi, 'and we had to make the best of it.'³ Hugh Richardson conjectures that 'Ti-betan officialdom, both monk and noble, did as they had done at those times when the Manchu emperors sought to assert authority in Tibet – they ostensibly acquiesced in the new arrangements while constantly try-ing to obstruct and delay changes and to blunt the edge of Chinese zeal.'⁴

That wasn't the way Gyalo Thondup saw it when he returned to Lhasa in February 1952, afire with youthful zeal and intolerance. He was in-censed at the sight of 'most of the Tibetan officials busy chasing after Chi-nese silver dollars, collaborating with the Chinese, getting a few hundred silver dollars a month for very little work. They all seemed to be on the Chinese payroll, my own sister and her husband among them.'⁵ Khando comes to the defence of her parents: 'I think they had a very difficult tightrope act to perform. It wasn't that they were collaborating, they really liked some of the Chinese as friends and tried to work with them, believ-ing that that was the best course. They didn't see what else they could do, and they just hoped it would work out right for Tibet.'⁶

Gyalo Thondup's own behaviour must have seemed ambivalent, to say the least. The Chinese top brass treated him as the prodigal son returned, a high-profile, Chinese-speaking fellow traveller. 'General Chiang Chin-wu, the Military Commander, General Tan Kuan-sen, the Political Commis-sar, all the senior officers and officials, were very happy that I'd decided to come back. They gave parties for me, banquets, we exchanged visits about once a week, sometimes I went to them, sometimes they visited me.'⁷

Whatever the Tibetans may have thought about these shenanigans, Gyalo Thondup claims he was playing a double game. However much the officials were cosying up to the Chinese to preserve their jobs and positions, he knew that the ordinary people of Lhasa detested them unreservedly.

The latter were almost at breaking-point, not least because there were too many Chinese mouths to feed in Lhasa and the food was running out.

The twenty thousand Chinese troops required food, lodging and transport, all, under the terms of the Agreement, to be provided by the Tibetans. (In the absence of motorable roads or airfields, there was no way of bringing in provisions or equipment from China.) At first, the Chinese had paid their way, requisitioning, renting or even buying houses from the nobles, while building a large military camp in the pleasant picnic-meadows beyond the Norbulingka. But before long they began demanding free food and lodging as of right. Their demand for two thousand tons of barley was more than the state granaries could cope with and reserves had to be called in from the monasteries and private estates. As food got scarcer, prices first doubled, then shot sky high. When a new General with another thousand troops arrived, the fragile economy collapsed completely. For the first time in living memory, the people of Lhasa were faced with starvation. Fuel was so scarce that people were burning horns and bones, filling the city with a terrible stench.[7]

It was too much. Although new laws made any opposition to China treasonable, the people began putting up CHINESE – GO HOME posters and handing round leaflets, shouting slogans, singing ribald street-songs, spitting, throwing stones. A popular resistance movement (the *Mimang Tsongdu*) came into being, and, as tension mounted in the streets, five men presented a six-point list of grievances to the Chinese. But instead of acknowledging the people's genuine distress, General Chiang reacted angrily with talk of 'imperialists' and 'conspiracy', blaming the crisis on the Dalai Lama's two Prime Ministers, the layman, Lukhangwa, and the monk, Lobsang Tashi. Lukhangwa, who had taken no Chinese money nor deigned to collaborate in any way, had dared to point out to General Chiang that the people were hungry and the Chinese demands exorbitant. For this the General hated him: Lukhangwa, he accused, was an imperialist reactionary who did not want to improve relations between China and Tibet. He would not accept that Lukhangwa was simply an honest patriot who was not for sale.

Shortly after his arrival, Gyalo Thondup had gone to see the two Prime Ministers with a plan of his own concerning land reform: 'I knew about the terrible atrocities that had taken place in China during the land reforms. I wanted to advise His Holiness that it was imperative for them to take the decision now to redistribute Tibetan lands, and not leave it to the

Chinese. The old system of land ownership was rotten and needed reform, but if the Kashag didn't take action themselves soon, the Chinese would eventually do it much more brutally. I told them I was ready to give up all the Yapshi Taklha properties, and I painted the picture for them of what had happened in China. They must not let the same thing happen in Tibet, I said.'[8]

The two Prime Ministers, being sensible men, warned Gyalo Thondup to keep his opinions to himself. Talk to nobody, they insisted, not even to Kashag Ministers; Lhasa was full of informers. Gyalo Thondup heeded their advice. 'I had to call on those senior Ministers, but I was careful. I just told them I was glad to be home after so many years, and that it was good to see my mother and His Holiness again.' He was beginning to realize he had dropped into a hornet's nest.

Promising to keep the two Prime Ministers informed, he set about cultivating the Chinese military. He talked to the ordinary soldiers who confided that they hated Lhasa. They couldn't sleep because of the high altitude; they had no appetite and were plagued by headaches; the children threw stones at them, adults sang songs which they couldn't understand but which were obviously rude; they spat at them and hurled abuse.

> Perhaps it was because they were behaving like conquerors, I suggested. They seemed surprised when I told them that was why the Tibetans disliked them. It hadn't occurred to them before. Yet every time I invited General Tan to dinner at my house, I could see soldiers posted on the roof with their rifles.

Like General Chiang, Lhasa's Political Commissar, Tan Kuan-sen, cultivated Gyalo Thondup:

> They were always assuring me that the *Mimang* (People's Movement) was being masterminded by Lukhangwa and Lobsang Tashi, both of whom were reactionaries and American spies. I laughed and said they were wrong, the two Prime Ministers were good men, but so ignorant that they wouldn't even know where America was! I told them to be patient, to move slowly, otherwise they would destroy a thousand years' relationship between the Chinese and the Tibetans. We had for the most part lived in harmony all that time. I told them that to arrest – or, even worse, execute – the two Prime Ministers, would be a terrible mistake. 'You say Tibetans and Chinese are brothers. Well, Tibetans are the younger, you the elder brother. If Younger Brother is behaving badly, you must try to persuade him patiently to stop. You have the power, you have the weapons, but what you are doing will in the long run be against

the true interests of China.' I said that the situation was getting worse only because of the growing Chinese presence in the city, that the Tibetans were protesting because they were afraid the Chinese were going to take away the power of the Dalai Lama and that this fear had nothing to do with the two Prime Ministers. But Tan didn't listen, he was striding furiously up and down the room, banging the table at intervals and threatening to have the two men executed straight away. Of course they were American spies, he shouted: one of the Kashag Ministers had told him so the previous night![9]

The Chinese did not execute the two Prime Ministers, but in the early spring of 1952 they 'asked' Kundun to remove them from office. As the 'request' was backed by the assurance that if he refused the army would be brought in, and as the Kashag begged him not to make things even worse than they already were, Kundun knew he must sacrifice his Prime Ministers to avoid a blood-bath. For the sake of appearances, they were allowed to resign. As there was no question of their being replaced, there was no longer anyone whom Kundun could whole-heartedly trust. To underline his powerlessness still further, he was made to imprison the five men who had presented the initial petition to the Chinese.

Kundun was no less keen than GT to bring about reforms and modernize Tibet. As a young boy, his sweepers had told him of the great injustices in his country, the imbalance in the distribution of wealth, and he knew that such inequality was out of line with Buddhist teachings. A radical reformer by instinct, he longed to be able to improve the lives of his people, but so far he had been given no chance.

Taking advantage of the brief truce which followed the removal of his Prime Ministers, Kundun set up the Reform Committee which he had had in mind ever since, on the way to the Chumbi Valley in 1950, he had seen for himself the state of deprivation in which so many of his people lived. He wanted to establish an independent judiciary, build some much-needed roads, and provide the Tibetans with decent schooling. He had no very clear idea of what constituted modern education, but he knew his country needed it.

In the short term, he agreed with Gyalo Thondup, the land-tenure system must be reformed. The large private estates ought to revert to the State, and when compensation had been paid to the owners, be redistributed among the peasants who actually worked the land. After that, he would abolish the principle of hereditary debt owed by a tenant to his landlord. His sweepers had told him how unbearably the peasants suffered from this burden:

> It meant that the debt owing to a landlord by his tenants, perhaps acquired as a result of bad harvests, could be transferred from one generation to the next. As a result, many families were not able to make a decent living for themselves, let alone hope one day to be free.[10]

Given time, and if fate had been on his side, Kundun might have gone down into history as a great social reformer. But in the present context, he could not hope to succeed. In the first place, the landowners themselves stubbornly resisted reform. Even more significantly, the Chinese would never allow him to upstage them. *They* were the liberators of Tibet, the ones to whom the masses must be indebted; the Dalai Lama and his Government were cast in the class-war role of 'enemies of the people'. The Chinese were already showing their contempt for the Tibetan political system, bypassing the Kashag and dealing direct with the Dalai Lama, at once isolating and increasing their control over him.

Time was running out for Gyalo Thondup and he knew it. His insane mission to save Tibet single-handed had failed miserably:

> I had wanted to help the people of Tibet and my brother, but such a situation made it difficult for me to do anything at all...I kept urging the Tibetan Government to go along with His Holiness's land reforms, but all they could say was, 'Mr Thondup, *you* may not care about owning land, but what about your children?' I said, 'For heaven's sake, long before my children or yours are old enough to care, the land will have been taken anyway. If you don't act now, you'll be giving the Chinese a sword with which to divide us.'[11]

He resolved at least to set an example. 'I had two estates near the Indian border...The Chinese knew what I was intending to do: I had sworn to give away every inch of my land to the people who worked on it, and to set fire to generations of debts.'

Fate intervened when General Tan was directed, in a cable from Chairman Mao, to appoint GT to lead a Tibetan Youth Delegation to Peking. There he was to join the Chinese Youth Delegation going to the World Peace Conference in Vienna. In 1952, as part of a public campaign of indoctrination designed to soften up the Tibetans for Socialism, the Chinese were setting up 'patriotic' and 'cultural' groups, among the first of which was the Patriotic Youth Association (PYA). Gyalo Thondup, as the Dalai

Lama's brother, was scheduled for a starring role, like his sister, Tsering Dolma, who was to be Chairwoman of the Patriotic Association of Women (PWA). (She and Phuntsok Tashi were also destined for Peking and Vienna.) Gyalo Thondup, feigning rapturous delight, said that first he must carry out his projected land reforms. General Tan agreed to wait.

It was make or break time:

> I talked the situation over with my mother and Lobsang Samten. The Tibetans at that time seemed to have no friends anywhere, but we all felt that if I went to India, I could use the good offices of the Indian Government to persuade the Chinese to go easy on Tibet. I could also tell the outside world what was happening. My mother said I must go and see Nehru. So I contacted the Indian Representative in Lhasa and told him I wanted to escape to India, preferably to Darjeeling – to get outside help for Tibet. Next day, I was informed that Nehru had agreed to grant me asylum. So the only question now was how to get out of Tibet? [12]

The Chinese Generals gave him a farewell lunch and told him to hurry back.

Gyalo Thondup did not return. Taking with him only 700 rupees, to avoid suspicion, he hurried to his estates, divided the property among the workers, tore up the debts as promised, then, with seven companions slipped over the border into what was then still known by its British name, the North East Frontier Agency area of India (NEFA). 'We had good weapons, maps, a compass and above all good horses. As a family we were excellent judges of horse-flesh and I chose some of the finest horses from our stables, so swift that even if the Chinese had chased us, they wouldn't have caught us.' The journey, however, was not without its terrors: there were five hundred Chinese troops patrolling the area. 'It was very worrying, but fortunately we knew the terrain well and how to avoid the troops. We lay low during daylight hours and travelled only by night.'

By an irony of fate, their real troubles began when they reached Assam. After descending the Se la Pass they encountered a posse of Indian military police, who, seeing them to be armed and possessed of maps and compasses, arrested them as Chinese spies. Gyalo Thondup, confident that by now the Indian authorities must have alerted the border security forces to his expected arrival, handed over his weapons and maps and asked to be taken to HQ. Under guard, they walked for about a day and a night from the border to the town of Tawang, only to find that the CO was on leave and the Political Officer was visiting the nearby Buddhist monastery.

Above: The search for a new Dalai Lama. Original woodcuts depicting the cavalcade looking for Tibet's new spiritual leader in Amdo in 1937 and their triumphant return to Lhasa with the four-year-old Lhamo Dhondup almost two years later. (These woodcuts were presented to Sir Basil Gould by the Tibetans following the installation of the Dalai Lama in 1941, and are now in the possession of his widow, Lady Gould.)

Left: The Fourteenth Dalai Lama of Tibet as a young monk. One of his many titles is Kundun, meaning the Presence (of the Buddha).

Top: Dekyi Tsering with her husband Choekyong Tsering, the parents of the Fourteenth Dalai Lama, in the early 1940s. The children are (left to right): their granddaughter Khando Tsering, younger daughter Jetsun Pema and third son Lobsang Samten.

Above: Lobsang Samten with Professor Heinrich Harrer in 1966.

Left: The children of Tsering Dolma, Kundun's elder sister, in Cambridge, 1961 – Khando and her brother Tenzin Ngawang, on his graduation day.

Above: Tibet's capital, Lhasa. In the foreground is Changseshar, the residence of the family of the Dalai Lama (Photo: Noji).

Below: Dekyi Tsering, also known as the Great Mother and also informally as Amala, with her youngest son Tendzin Choegyal (Photo: Noji).

Right: Family gathering in Dharamsala, 1979. (Left to right) Amala, eldest son Thubten Jigme Norbu, Lobsang Samten, the Dalai Lama, Jetsun Pema, Tendzin Choegyal.

Below: Second son Gyalo Thondup (right) and his family, 1960.

Below middle: Dharamsala, the northern Indian home of the exiled Tibetans.

Top right: Amala enjoys a trip to the circus in the 1970s.

Below right: Lobsang Samten, with a nomad girl, during the first fact-finding visit to Tibet, 1979.

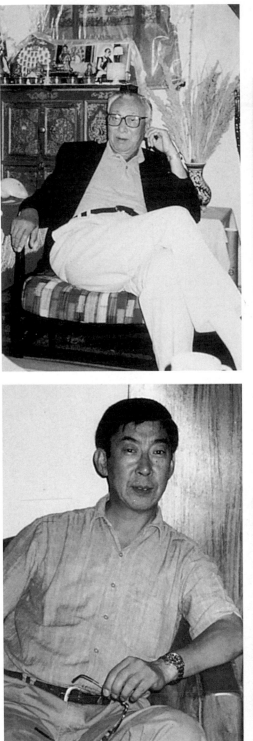

Clockwise from top left: The four surviving siblings of the Dalai Lama pictured in 1995, Thubten Jigme Norbu, Gyalo Thondup, Jetsun Pema, Tendzin Choegyal (Photos: Anne Jennings Brown).

Above:
A family portrait for the Dalai Lama's 60th birthday celebrations in Dharamsala in 1995.

Left: With the author in 1994.

His Holiness Tenzin Gyatso, the Fourteenth Dalai Lama of Tibet (Photo: Vijay Kranti).

They kept us in their military compound. I was very tired as I hadn't slept for four days and nights. So I asked the Indian official to leave me alone and just let me sleep, but to tell me when the Political Officer returned. At midnight, the Political Officer came back, half-drunk. He rushed into where I was sleeping, shook me awake and accused me of being a Chinese spy. I told him who I was and asked him to check his files. I wrote out my name for him. He was very angry and extremely rude. I insisted that he should go and check and he stormed off, returning within minutes to say there was nothing at all on file about me. I asked him to try again, to look further back in his files. At 2 a.m. he came back, shaking with fright. He had found the instructions, which in fact had come about a month earlier. Well, then he wanted to transfer me instantly to the best room in their guest-house, but I was too exhausted to care. I told him I'd move in the morning, but right then all I wanted was to go back to sleep. Would you believe it, next morning he brought me my breakfast in bed on a tray, still apologizing profusely?

Gyalo Thondup stayed for about a week in Tawang. News of the arrival of the Dalai Lama's brother spread, and people from neighbouring villages came to see him. 'Hundreds of them came. They brought me chickens, eggs, butter. It turned out they thought I had come to settle their future. In 1950, three years after the British had left, the Indian Government had sent troops to occupy their area, but the people were Tibetans and felt that they had really always belonged to Tibet. Had I come to solve their problem? I told them I was very sorry, but I was actually a refugee myself. I couldn't help them but I went to see them quite often – I've never eaten so many eggs in my life.'

As there was no road between Tawang and the railway terminus at Tezpur, Gyalo Thondup and his companions covered the distance on foot, walking for seven days. From Tezpur he returned at last to Darjeeling to find his pregnant wife, their daughter Yangzom and baby son, Tenzin Khedup. (A second son, Ngawang Tenpa, was born shortly after his return.) Pema was in the house and remembers the shock of his arrival. 'One morning, at dawn, Gyalo Thondup arrived in a pitiable state, gaunt, haggard and suffering from malaria. Two servants supported him, one on each side.'[13]

From Darjeeling he set about organizing help for Tibet. Making contact with the Indian Government he described the state of affairs in Lhasa, begging them to persuade the Chinese to relax the pressure on the Tibetans. 'At the same time I wrote to the President of the United States and to Chiang Kai-shek. Nehru didn't like that. In August he sent his

Political Officer, Mr B. K. Kapoor, to see me, asking me to stop writing to international leaders, and asking for copies of the letters I'd already sent. Mr Kapoor came to Darjeeling with this message and I was very angry. I said, "Before I left Tibet I informed Nehru that I was coming for this one particular purpose, to get help for Tibet. He agreed. Is he now changing his mind?" I refused to give him copies of my letters.'

Mr Kapoor 'went away and told the police superintendent in Darjeeling to keep me under surveillance. I went on writing letters to anybody I thought might help. In October I received a telephone call in Darjeeling from a Mr Kumar in the Police Security Office in Calcutta. He had been Second Secretary at the Chinese Embassy in Nanking in 1947 when I was there, so I knew him quite well. Kumar told me a high official wanted to meet me. He said he didn't know any details, but this man had travelled from Delhi to Darjeeling and wanted me to have lunch with him in a certain restaurant. I went to the restaurant – and the mystery man turned out to be the Director of Indian Intelligence. He brought an apology from Nehru, and a promise that I was free to do whatever I wanted. So from October 1952 onwards I was in constant contact with Indian Intelligence and Nehru simply turned a blind eye.'[14]

The letters abroad bore fruit. From Taiwan, the Kuomintang offered material and financial support, but as their publicly expressed view was that America and India were behind the trouble in Tibet, and that Tibet's real desire was to 'rejoin' the Chinese Motherland represented by Taiwan, GT refused to have anything to do with them. It was different with the Americans. They had been watching events in Tibet with great interest and considerable anxiety, and needed someone to monitor the situation for them. Who better than a well-informed, articulate Tibetan who, by an incredible stroke of luck, was also the Dalai Lama's brother? To the CIA, Gyalo Thondup must have seemed heaven-sent. From now on, he would play a crucial role in the accelerating saga of Tibet.

For the next two years, he lived quietly in Darjeeling, on the lower slopes of the towering Kangchenjunga, the third highest mountain in the world. They were halcyon days, in which he recovered his health and learned to relax with his family. The town had once belonged to the kingdom of Sikkim, but in 1861 the British, by agreement with the Maharajah, had annexed the heavily-forested southern Darjeeling district, turning it into a hill-station, a fashionable summer resort away from the humid heat of the plains. When the British left India in 1947, the new Indian

Government quietly took over all the Himalayan northern border states. But Darjeeling kept its special links with Tibet, based on religious allegiance, trade and ethnic affinity – after all, its very name is Tibetan, being a corruption of Dorje Ling, Place of the Thunderbolt. In the 1950s when the first Tibetan refugees from Communist China began crossing the border into India, it was natural that they should choose to settle either here or in Kalimpong.[15]

It was in Darjeeling that Gyalo Thondup would plan and scheme for the Tibetan cause. There in 1954, with two fellow exiles, he set up the Committee for Tibetan Social Welfare, which, despite its innocuous-sounding name, was in reality an intelligence-gathering organization and was destined to become the nerve-centre of the Tibetan Resistance.

NOTES

1. Rinchen Dolma Taring, *Daughter of Tibet*.
2. The Chinese were indeed building schools, but these were little more than centres for political indoctrination.
3. Author interview with Phuntsok Tashi Taklha, London, 1993.
4. Richardson, *Tibet and its History*, chapter 12.
5. Author interview with GT, New Delhi, July 1995.
6. Author interview with Khando Chazotsang, Utah, February 1996.
7. Rinchen Dolma Taring.
8. Author interview with GT, New Delhi, July 1995.
9. Author interview with GT, New Delhi, July 1995.
10. Fourteenth Dalai Lama, *Freedom in Exile*, chapter 3.
11. Author interview with GT, New Delhi, July 1995.
12. Video recording made by Gyalo Thondup for the monks of Namgyal Monastery, Dharamsala in 1991.
13. Jetsun Pema, *Tibet, Mon Histoire*.
14. Author interview with GT, New Delhi, July 1995.
15. By an agreement with Bhutan, Kalimpong also had been attached to British India in 1861.

14

In China 1954–5

Integration of the nationalities into the PRC political system
was a prerequisite for their socialist transformation. The socialist transition process itself was a method to increase central control over minorities...Autonomy for nationalities was
to be confined to such superficial aspects of nationality culture as song and dance which were in any case, according to
Marxist ideology, the only meaning of nationality.

Warren W. Smith, 'The Nationalities Policy of the CCP'[1]

Though Kundun had been deliberately kept in the dark about Gyalo
Thondup's flight, the Chinese suspected him of being involved. 'I think
they wondered what my game was,' he says. 'After all, a few years earlier
they had sent my eldest brother, Taktser, on a mission to me, and from
their point of view he had betrayed them. Then Gyalo Thondup came and
went – and they had had high hopes of him too. So I suppose it's not surprising that at this stage they were very suspicious of me.'[2]

The Chinese were disappointed in the Tibetans: instead of the gratitude
and admiration which they had expected, they were treated as unwelcome
aliens and shown active hostility in the streets. And they had signally
failed to win over the Dalai Lama. If they were to have any hope of con-
trolling Tibet through him, a change of strategy was called for.

As a first step, they invited him to China, ostensibly to lead a Tibetan
delegation to the first National Assembly of People's China in Peking

where a new Constitution was about to be adopted; but in reality to step up the brainwashing process. They were fairly certain that a visit to the Motherland would do the trick. Apart from his historic journey from Amdo to Lhasa, he was untravelled, had been nowhere. At nineteen he was still an impressionable boy – and his interest in the modern world and modern technology were well known. Surely, when he saw the political, economic and cultural marvels of Mao's China, he would be eager for Tibet to share in them.

Kundun was no fool. He knew that he was being manipulated, that the Chinese intended to use his presence in Peking as proof to the world that he agreed to Tibet's being part of China, but there was not much he could do about it. Besides, as a Buddhist, he genuinely believed that patient co-existence with the enemy was better than confrontation. He accepted the invitation.

His decision caused anguish and wringing of hands among Tibetans, who were convinced that their beloved ruler would disappear forever if once he set foot in China. Delegations came from all corners of Tibet, begging him to change his mind. From Darjeeling, Gyalo Thondup's Committee for Tibetan Social Welfare 'forwarded several letters to the Dalai Lama and to Chairman Mao Tse-tung, all to the effect that the absence of His Holiness from Tibet was contrary to the wishes of the Tibetan people'.[3] Though Kundun assured them all that he was going to China of his own free will, and Tibetan officials borrowed loud-hailers to promise that he would return within a year, the people simply did not believe that he was acting as a free agent.

In the high summer of 1954, Kundun and about five hundred of his officials set off on the two thousand mile journey from Lhasa to Peking. Despite their forebodings, the citizens put on their best clothes and came in their thousands to say goodbye. There was a farewell reception in a huge tent by the river – with music played by military bands from both Tibetan and Chinese regiments. Then, as monks waved banners and the people burned incense and hoisted flags to wish him a safe journey and speedy return, Kundun walked down a white carpet to the river's edge and crossed the little Kyi Chu river in two yak-hide coracles lashed together. Attendants held a red umbrella over his sacred person. As he turned to wave goodbye to his people,

I could see that they were in an emotional state. Many were crying and it looked as if some were on the point of throwing themselves into the water, convinced that they were seeing me for the last time.[4]

Hundreds of Chinese and Tibetan troops lined the bank to discourage any such extravagant reaction; and the crowds watched mournfully as their leader disappeared from view. But, as he began his journey, riding with Lobsang Samten in the old 1931 Dodge car which had belonged to his predecessor, Kundun could not resist a feeling of exhilaration. He was, after all, setting out on a rare adventure.

Tendzin Choegyal was in the party. Two years earlier, aged six, he had been taken to the monastery of Kumulung to begin his formal education and training as a *tulku*. From then on, he had to wear a monk's garb, and though life in Kumulung was relatively easy-going, and his holidays were spent at home, he was very homesick: 'I missed my mother terribly. She used to send me homemade cookies, lollipops, chewing gum (in small quantities in case I made myself sick) all wrapped up in a scarf. I would sniff the scarf, desperately trying to recapture the smell of her.'[5] When he heard that the Dalai Lama was going to China and that his mother, Tsering Dolma (as Chair of the Patriotic Women's Association) and Lobsang Samten (as Youth Association Chairman) were to accompany him, he determined not to be left behind. He pestered his mother until she agreed to take him along.

One of the two old Austins had been repaired and he, Amala and Tsering Dolma travelled in it. Phuntsok Tashi, recently appointed Commander of Kundun's Bodyguard, rode a motorcycle: Kundun recalls that when he removed his dust mask and protective goggles some hours later his nose was bright red with sunburn![6]

After about ninety miles, they exchanged their wheeled transport for mules; and twelve days out of Lhasa, the going became extremely rough. Though the Tibetans had wanted to follow their old caravan route to Kham, the Chinese had insisted on using the new Lhasa–Chengdu road which was still under construction. Unfortunately, heavy rains had washed away whole sections of it, there was flooding from mountain streams, bridges had collapsed, and as rocks and heavy boulders crashed down, the way was frequently blocked by landslides. Three people were killed and several mules fell over precipices onto the rocks below. The rest trudged on painfully, up to the knees in mud, wretched in the rain and fog. 'I had never in my life seen so much fog,' remembers Tendzin Choegyal.

Even more distressing to him was the sight of large numbers of Chinese workers, 'literally hewing out the road from rocks. I discovered later that they were either prisoners of war or people who had been arrested during the land reforms in China. They had been "liquidated".'

General Chiang, the Military Commander escorting Kundun, gloomily predicted that conditions would soon get even worse and they would have to proceed on foot:

> Therefore, in his capacity as representative of the Central People's Republic, he would personally link arms and escort me along the way...It occurred to me that the General was under the impression that not only could he exert his power over my two Prime Ministers, but he could also bully Nature!'

A month after leaving Lhasa they reached a motorable road and piled into Russian jeeps and trucks for the journey to Chamdo, which had been under Chinese occupation since 1950. The further they travelled from Lhasa, the more obvious were the signs of Chinese domination: loud-speakers blaring forth canned Chinese music, and at every stopping-place a welcome committee, a formal banquet and a guard of honour. But nothing could have prevented the Tibetans from turning out in force to greet their beloved Kundun. He gave them his blessing before crossing the ancient border between Tibet and China and proceeding to Chengdu, the first town in China proper.

From there a short plane ride (his first ever) took Kundun to Xian where a special train waited to carry him on the twelve-hour journey to Peking. At the railway station, the clapping and cheering of the rent-a-crowd students and youth groups disturbed him; he knew they would just as readily have booed and jeered, if so ordered. Yet, by and large, he was enjoying the lack of formality in China – enamel mugs instead of jade cups, friendly waves and handshakes in place of prostrations and reverently lowered eyes. It was refreshing to be treated like an ordinary human being rather than a god-king. And the brand-new spotlessly clean train waiting in the station could not fail to excite one who had never so much as seen a train before. 'The train really stunned us both,' recalls Tendzin Choegyal. 'It was purpose-built, a show-piece, ordinary people didn't travel in that sort of style. There were sleeping cars, dining cars, proper sitting-rooms. Marvellous food in the dining-car.'⁸

The Panchen Lama had been brought along. The Chinese lost no opportunity of showing that the two most important Lamas of Tibet were equal in status. Throughout history, they had always tried to play off one against the other and although the Panchen Lamas had no claim to political power at all, the Chinese chose to disregard that fact. The Ninth Panchen had died in Amdo in 1937, still waiting to return home to his monastery in Shigatse. Within the next few years, two boys were discovered as possible reincarnations, one in Amdo, the other in Kham. Though neither had been submitted to the religious tests, in 1944, the Chinese Kuomintang Government declared the eight-year-old Amdo boy to be the true reincarnation and enthroned him forthwith, thus acquiring a convenient figurehead for their own purposes. When the Communists won the Civil War in 1949, it did not take them long to see what a prize had fallen into their laps – and without delay (or any inconvenient sense of irony) they pronounced the boy to be spiritual and temporal leader of Tibet. Making him Chairman of a 'Provisional Government of Tibet', they proclaimed on Peking Radio that the Panchen Lama had invited Mao to 'liberate Tibet'. Mao graciously replied that 'The People's Liberation Army can surely satisfy the yearnings of the Tibetan people.' To the Tibetans, the Amdo boy was merely one of two candidates – but as part of the Seventeen-Point Agreement in 1951 they were forced to acknowledge him. Ever since, the Chinese had been building up their man as a counterweight to the Dalai Lama, conferring powers on him which the Panchen Lamas had never traditionally enjoyed. Now, in Peking, the two young men were equals; where one went, the other went too.

Kundun fell under the spell of Mao Tse-tung. When he first shook hands with him, he felt himself to be 'in the presence of a strong magnetic force'. Mao 'did not have the aura of a particularly intelligent man', but he had an air of dignity and decisiveness that was impressive. He was shabby and down-at-heel, but 'his mere presence commanded respect'.

In the course of their first meeting, Mao expressed disappointment that the Tibetans were so ungrateful to their Chinese benefactors. The Dalai Lama explained that patience was needed; social reforms could not be imposed instantly or by force. Mao said he had abandoned his original intention of governing Tibet directly from Peking, in favour of a degree of self-government. A Preparatory Committee for the Autonomous Region of Tibet (PCART), consisting mainly of Tibetans, would prepare Tibet – by which he meant only that area which had been under the Dalai Lama's direct authority at the time of the invasion in 1950 – to take its place as a constituent part of the People's Republic of China.

Kundun was relieved to hear that Tibet would retain at least some control over its internal affairs. Mao's proposal seemed reasonable, particularly as the Chairman assured him that the pace of reform would be dictated by the wishes of the Tibetan people themselves.

With Mao assuring his guest that China's whole purpose was to help Tibet, Kundun began to relish the idea of co-operating with such a man. His hosts' efforts were already paying off, he was finding Marxism attractive:

A senior official at the Minorities Office was appointed to indoctrinate me. He was a very nice man, he used to come to my room and lecture me on the history of the Chinese Revolution and on Marxist philosophy...Here was a system based, like Buddhism, on equality and justice for everyone. I couldn't accept its materialistic view of human existence, but I felt sure that it ought to be possible to work out a synthesis between Marxism and Buddhist doctrine. I still believe that some of those original Marxist ideas were excellent.

Then I had many meetings with the veterans of the Long March – and with a few good Tibetan Communists. They seemed selfless in their service to others, I admired them and they had a big influence on me. At that time I really had faith in Chairman Mao and I had a genuine respect and admiration for the Communist Party. I even expressed a wish to become a Party member![9]

After ten weeks of official meetings, interminable rambling speeches and endless banquets, Kundun and his officials were taken on an orchestrated tour of northern China to see the marvels of industrial progress at first hand: factories, co-operative farms, workers' organizations, schools, universities and museums. Unlike his officials, most of whom were bored rigid, Kundun was awed by the new technology and dazzled by the Communist achievements. He longed for some of that efficiency and progress to rub off on Tibet.

But Communism's darker side did not escape him. He was disappointed, for example, that he was not allowed to speak to the ordinary people and was given no chance to step outside of his official programme or visit unscheduled places. The excuse was always that they dared not put his safety at risk. 'Yet it was not only I who was kept isolated from the common people, so were all the Chinese from Peking. They too were forbidden to do anything independently.'[10]

As time went by, he saw that the Chinese people were like programmed robots. Oppressed by 'a grey fog of humourless uniformity', remorselessly organized and processed, they had lost all trace of spontaneity and

individuality. The human cost of all this progress, he concluded regretful-
ly, was too high. Attractive though Marxism might be as a theory, Kundun
could only pray that his own people would never be subjected to this fa-
natical interpretation of it. He knew now what he was up against.

Amala and Tsering Dolma had been busy in Peking. Apart from the
mandatory political lectures, there was sightseeing, shopping, official banquets and receptions, even a visit to the zoo. As Chair of the PWA, Tsering
Dolma had meetings to attend; she was also learning Chinese and continuing the study of Tibetan begun when she had first arrived in Lhasa. Then
there was Tendzin Choegyal to supervise. This *enfant terrible* was in his
element. Always a sociable child, he found the Chinese friendly and kind.
'They kept enthusing, "Look how good things are in today's China, so
much better than under the Kuomintang. Isn't everything splendid?" I
knew they were just trying to impress us but I didn't in the least mind playing along with them, paying them all the compliments they wanted. In any
case, I meant many of them. For example, I thought the Chinese soldiers,
their weapons, their drill, everything about them, *were* wonderful.'

The child learned to speak fluent Mandarin in a matter of months, a
skill of which the official party made good use when they returned to
Peking in January 1955. 'I was easier to deal with than the official interpreters,' he says, 'so after a bit I became the translator for the whole entourage, particularly if anyone wanted to see a doctor. I loved it, I was glad
to have something to do – and they gave me cookies and sweets.'

But, as Kundun noted, his brother's linguistic prowess had its drawbacks:

> If ever my mother or anyone made a disparaging remark about one of our
> hosts, my little brother would pass it on without hesitation. We all had to be
> very careful of what we said in front of him. Even then, he could always sense
> when someone was being vague or evasive.

Tendzin Choegyal was 'a constant source of delight and terror to everyone,
including the Chinese', remarks Kundun. Affectionately regarded as a
kind of mascot, in the guest-house where the family stayed he spent his
time 'mainly fooling around', sometimes with calamitous results. Once he
threw cold water over the head of a steward who was snoozing just outside
the kitchen. 'He woke up with a start and banged his head on the shelf
above his head. I saw the blood flowing and ran for my life.'

Kundun alone, it seems, was prepared to discipline his wilful young
brother. As Tendzin Choegyal ruefully recalls, 'There was an ornamental

pond full of goldfish in the garden where we were staying. I was very taken with it. I once took a badminton racquet and scooped the fish out onto the grass. They were leaping around. I put them back after a time, but someone told His Holiness what I'd done and he came down, gave me a ticking off and boxed my ears hard.'[11]

Just before Kundun's return to Lhasa, Mao summoned him to a last meeting. After a spate of fatherly suggestions about their future co-operation, he said abruptly:

> Your attitude is good, you know. Religion is poison. Firstly, it reduces the population, because monks and nuns stay celibate, and secondly it neglects material progress.[12]

'Religion is poison!' The words fell on Kundun like hammer-blows, but he had the self-control not to betray his shock: 'How could he have misjudged me so? How could he have thought that I was not religious to the core of my being?'[13] He could only suppose that Mao, aware of his new enthusiasm for Marxism, had presumed 'that my religious practices were nothing more to me than a prop or a convention'. Kundun's faith in Mao was shattered. He would continue to believe that Mao was a great leader, a sincere person even, without guile or deceit; but never again would he allow admiration to cloud his judgement.

The new road was now finished,[14] so when they left the train at Chengdu, Kundun's party was able to proceed by jeep and truck. Not that the return journey was without peril. There were still a number of landslides and at one river crossing where 'the terrible waters [looked] absolutely black, [and] one could not hear anything else above the terrific noise of water falling down and pushing boulder against boulder',[15] a bridge collapsed and was washed away moments after Kundun's jeep had crossed it.

Kundun's reservations about Maoism were reinforced on the three-month journey back to Lhasa. The good intentions professed by Mao did not seem to have filtered down to his provincial subordinates. Wherever Kundun stopped in eastern Tibet, he sensed 'a heavy air of foreboding', a mounting hatred and resentment of the Chinese. For the first few years of occupation, while the new roads linking eastern Tibet with Lhasa were still under construction, the Chinese had soft-pedalled on social change. But by the end of 1954 when the roads were finally completed, the need for conciliation passed and the mask of tolerance could be dropped. Marxism was to replace Buddhism, anti-religious propaganda was to be stepped up and the 'democratic reforms' implemented. By which was meant the forcible introduction of collective farming in which the people would be relieved of their meagre possessions without any regard for their customs, wishes or needs. Worse, Tibetan children were being forcibly abducted for education in China.

That the Chinese were now the masters in Kham and Amdo was brought home to Kundun during a visit with his mother to Kumbum and their native Taktser. (He had received invitations to towns and monasteries all over Kham, but was allowed to visit only those which actually lay on his route.) At Kumbum, only eight hundred monks remained, living in a state of wretched poverty. The longed-for visit to Taktser was not a happy one. For one thing, many of their friends had been deported or had died in unexplained circumstances. 'The visit to my old home was terribly upsetting for my mother,' recalls Kundun. 'Whenever she inquired about their living conditions, our relatives always answered like parrots, "Oh, thanks to Chairman Mao Tse-tung and the People's Republic of China, we are very happy." But they were crying as they said the words.'[16]

In this place, where he was surrounded by relatives and old friends, the Chinese paranoia about his security descended into absurdity and caused great distress, especially to his mother:

My mother was deeply disturbed. I remember her crying because there in my own birthplace I was not allowed to eat food prepared for me by the villagers, not even when they were members of my own family. The Chinese forbade me to eat anything that had not been prepared by themselves. My mother simply did not know how to explain this to her Taktser friends...There was another thing that my mother pointed out with real regret: even the bread they put on the table was smaller than it used to be. They used to bake these enormous round loaves, so big that a mule could carry only two of them. When you had that bread with mutton, it was so delicious. Or with tea, with some cream. Wonderful![17]

At a monastery in Kham, thousands of people had turned out to pay their respects; but, as Kundun later discovered, the Chinese authorities had spread the disinformation that his visit would take place the following week. 'They lied about the date in order to prevent people from seeing me. As a result, thousands turned up after I had left.'

In the crowd was an eight-year-old Khampa girl, Rinchen Khando Tasot-sang, from a village near the monastery. Many years later, in another country, she would become the wife of Tendzin Choegyal. This was her first sight of him:

> We went to a public audience, and one of our servants hoisted me onto his back so that I could see. There were many many people, a huge crush. I remember there was this little boy of my own age, and people kept telling me that he was His Holiness's brother and a Rinpoche. I also remember that I lost one of my shoes in the crush. When we'd all left the monastery, I discovered my left shoe had gone. I had to be carried all the way back to our tent because I couldn't walk.[18]

Kundun's visit was a small oasis of joy in the desert to which life in this once happy land was rapidly being reduced. The local lamas and chieftains to whom Kundun spoke were all fearful; they reported that the peasants were bitter over the growing threat to their way of life and to their religion; tensions were mounting and all the signs suggested that the Chinese would stop at nothing to enforce their will. A spiral of violence was in the making. The Khampas[19] presented a petition to Kundun begging him to persuade the Chinese to reverse their policies in these rural areas before it was too late.

Their belief in his power to change the course of history was touching; to them he was the Dalai Lama, the all-powerful god-king. But, as Kundun followed the road back to Lhasa in that summer of 1955, he must have reflected sadly that he was every bit as powerless as they were.

His arrival back in Lhasa in May 1955 was greeted with relief, and a huge gathering of Government officials, incarnate lamas, monks and ordinary citizens turned out to welcome him. Prayers of thanksgiving for his safe return were offered at the Norbulingka Palace.

But, with the opening of the two new roads from China (from Siling in the north and Chengdu in the east), Lhasa itself had undergone a sea change, its narrow streets suddenly choked with the noise and stench of Chinese cars and military trucks. The Chinese were still practising a degree of restraint, still trying to be liked. But with their lines of communication and supply assured, they were now free to consolidate their power. They had already stepped up their anti-religious propaganda and taken political indoctrination into the schools.

Nevertheless, for a time, Kundun remained optimistic. Now that he had openly shown his admiration for the Communist achievement in China, the authorities in Lhasa were more inclined to trust him. 'They thought,' he laughs, 'that I had the makings of a good Marxist after all.'[20]

Lobsang Samten had been appointed Lord Chamberlain – the head of the Dalai Lama's household and treasury, and his official personal representative on the Kashag. Lobsang was an honest, decent, but somewhat naïve young man. The Chinese, among whom he had many friends, used him as a liaison between themselves and the Dalai Lama; and many Tibetans, noting his frequent visits to the Chinese Office, accused him of fraternizing rather too freely with the enemy. 'But they were wrong,' protests Kundun. 'It was just in Lobsang's nature to like everyone. He was very uncomplicated, but he was also steadfast and loyal.'[21] 'The thing was,' adds Namgyal Lhamo (Namlha), his future wife:

> Lobsang was one of those in favour of radical change. He had come from a peasant home where there was a lot of freedom. He was open, frank, down-to-earth, not at all rigid or formal. He hated any kind of restriction. He wanted change for Tibet, to get away from the old rigid conservatism. So, yes, he was friendly with the Chinese, because he thought at first that that was what they wanted too. They knew what he was like and how idealistic he was; and they set out to exploit him.[22]

When Gyalo Thondup had escaped them in 1952, the Chinese had made Lobsang the Chairman of the Youth Association – one Dalai Lama's brother presumably being interchangeable with another. Like the Patriotic Women's Association, the Youth Association was a key part of the Chinese Communist system and all Tibetan children were at first encouraged – later on, ordered – to join. 'Under the age of fourteen we were called Pioneers and wore red scarves,' recalls Namlha (herself a fourteen-year-old schoolgirl at the time):

> When we passed fourteen we became members of the Youth Organization. Actually, although our parents were not very keen, many of us were really enthusiastic for this new order of things...In fact, we did do a lot of good work, social work, planting trees, cleaning the main street outside our (Chinese) school. It was fun too, there were lots of social gatherings and dances. We enjoyed the

freedom of going to dances and parties, a freedom we'd never had before the Chinese came. But there were also meetings where they quizzed us about our families, what property or land they had. They were busy collecting information for future use. They also used us to talk to people at certain events – if there was a big occasion, they would get us to explain to the Tibetans what it was about. We were well and truly brain-washed. Behind all their planning was the idea that we young people would become sympathetic to Communism and then we would be useful tools for them. But they were quite subtle about it and we didn't realize then that they were merely moulding us to their requirements.[23]

Namlha belonged to the important Tsarong family. In 1951 when many of the old noble families were sending their children away to be educated in British schools, she and her younger sister had been sent to school in India, but in 1954 many parents bowed to Chinese pressure to bring their children back to Tibet. Namlha returned to Lhasa in 1954, entered a Chinese school and became a flag-waving Pioneer. Lobsang Samten was then a remote figure, seen from afar on the occasion of important meetings.

By autumn of 1955 rumours of increasing Chinese brutality in the East began to reach Lhasa. Traders from places like Siling brought alarming stories of persecution. Far from relaxing their pressure, as the Dalai Lama had asked, the Chinese were ruthlessly implementing the democratic reforms, imposing huge taxes, confiscating estates, arraigning and executing landowners for 'crimes against the people', even rounding up thousands of the nomad farmers who roamed the steppes of Amdo and Kham. They were forcibly indoctrinating the people against religion, harassing, beating and publicly humiliating lamas, monks and nuns. In every village, the Khampas responded with active resistance, for which the Chinese were exacting a terrible revenge. They were forcing children to abuse or even execute their own parents, were seizing and deporting others to China, and had introduced the infamous practice of *thamzing* (class struggle sessions), in which men and women were shamefully humiliated, spat on, beaten, kicked, in order to make them confess to reactionary thoughts or behaviour. Attendance at these sessions was compulsory; participation had to be enthusiastic and positive, on pain of imprisonment or death.

As the first refugees arrived in Lhasa with their tales of indescribable horror, hostility to the Chinese rose to fever pitch. Leaflets were distributed on the streets and public meetings were held. When the Chinese arrested three men for 'inciting anti-democratic crimes', the people's rage merely intensified.

Would the establishment of the new Preparatory Committee for the Autonomous Region of Tibet solve anything? It was being hyped by the Chinese as a great step forward for Tibet, and in April 1956 was launched with a huge fanfare in a purpose-built municipal hall in Lhasa. Marshal Chen-yi, China's Foreign Minister, came from Peking for the occasion. Military bands played, rousing Communist ballads such as 'The East is Red' were sung, and scarlet flags and banners depicting Chairman Mao and his colleagues fluttered triumphantly in the breeze. Congratulatory speeches praising Socialism, the Party and even the Chinese activities in Tibet, were made. ('I even had to make one myself,' admits the Dalai Lama in embarrassment, '[I said hopefully] I was sure that the Chinese would honour all their undertakings to introduce reform at the pace the people wanted and to permit freedom of worship.'[24]) There were banquets and all sorts of lavish entertainments. (It was at a committee meeting to plan the Youth Organization dinner that Namlha first met Lobsang Samten: 'People were coming from all over China. We were told that the Dalai Lama's older brother would be coming to the dinner and they wanted a couple of Tibetan girls to sit on his table. I was one of the two chosen. I was about fourteen, we were generations apart, he was a monk and an important official; and we had nothing whatever to say to each other.'[25])

The new Committee was, Kundun knew, 'the last hope for the peaceful evolution of our country'. On the surface, his optimism seemed justified; the Committee must surely be preferable to direct military rule. After all, the word 'autonomous' was in the title, and it included representatives of all parts of Tibet under a single administration. Kundun was to be Chairman, the Panchen Lama Vice-Chairman, and out of fifty-six members, fifty-one were to be Tibetan.

In reality it was a shameless confidence trick, intended to propagate the lie that Tibet had chosen the Socialist path. Amdo and Eastern Kham, despite their largely Tibetan populations, had been integrated into China proper, and were no longer considered part of Tibet; and of the fifty-one Tibetan delegates on the Committee, not one was elected and all but fifteen (one of these being Kundun himself) had been hand-picked by the Chinese. 'Allowed,' said Kundun with some bitterness, 'to keep their power and property so long as they did not voice any opposition.'[26] And though the Kashag and the National Assembly continued to exist, they no longer had any power; they could be outvoted by a two-thirds majority on any and every issue. In any case, all real power lay with the Committee of the Chinese Communist Party of Tibet and no Tibetan was eligible to belong to that. The Dalai Lama's authority had vanished. He understood now that the Chinese needed him only as a figure-head, as a name to lend their schemes a spurious appearance of Tibetan approval.

Lobsang Samten found himself appointed to the newly-created Security Department. If Kundun was taken aback at the news, Lobsang himself was aghast:

> Being such a kind and gentle person, there can have been no one less suited to the job than he. I shall never forget the look on his face when he returned from a meeting with his Chinese opposite number. All had gone well until the man turned to Lobsang Samten (who spoke some Chinese) and asked him what was the Tibetan for 'Kill him'. Up to that moment my brother had thought this new official to be quite pleasant and straightforward, but this question left him dumbfounded. The idea of killing even an insect was so far from his mind that he was lost for words. When he arrived at the Norbulingka that same evening, his face was full of bewilderment. 'What *am* I to do,' he asked.[27]

To Lobsang his appointment must have seemed like a sick joke calculated to undermine still further his shaky reputation among ordinary Tibetans. It undoubtedly increased the stress and tension from which he was suffering. Yet, whatever the pressures on him, he remained, Kundun insists, 'remarkably serene. Lobsang was never in any doubt as to where his loyalties lay.'[28]

The Chinese had what they wanted now: all power was securely in their hands. So much for the Seventeen-Point Agreement, which had guaranteed to leave Tibet's political system intact and the status, functions and powers of the Dalai Lama unchanged.

NOTES

1. Barnett & Akiner, eds., *Resistance and Reform in Tibet*, p. 57.
2. Author interview with HH the Dalai Lama, Dharamsala, June 1994.
3. Shakabpa, *Tibet: a Political History*, chapter 18.
4. Fourteenth Dalai Lama, *Freedom in Exile*.
5. Author interview with Tendzin Choegyal, July 1995.
6. Goodman, *The Last Dalai Lama*.

7. *Freedom in Exile.*
8. Author interview with Tendzin Choegyal, Dharamsala, October 1993.
9. Author interview with HH the Dalai Lama, Dharamsala, June 1994.
10. *Freedom in Exile.*
11. Author interview with Tendzin Choegyal, Dharamsala, October 1993.
12. *Freedom in Exile.*
13. *Freedom in Exile.*
14. The much-vaunted building of this road and that from Siling to Lhasa benefited only the Chinese who were now able to move their armoured vehicles and military equipment into Tibet and secure their occupation of the country. Moreover, once the roads linking Tibet with China were completed, the Chinese moved to alter the age-old trading patterns of the Tibetans, ordering them to cease trading with India and to trade with China instead. Gradually Tibet's outdoor markets were closed down.
15. Rinchen Dolma Taring, *Daughter of Tibet.*
16. Author interview with HH the Dalai Lama, Dharamsala, June 1994.
17. Author interview with HH the Dalai Lama, Dharamsala, June 1994.
18. Author interview with Rinchen Khando, Dharamsala, October 1993.
19. People of Kham are called Khampas – those of Amdo are Amdowas.
20. Author interview with HH the Dalai Lama, Dharamsala, June 1994.
21. Author interview with HH the Dalai Lama, Dharamsala, June 1994.
22. Author interview with Namlha Taklha, Dharamsala, October 1993.
23. Author interview with Namlha Taklha, Dharamsala, October 1993.
24. *Freedom in Exile.*
25. Author interview with Namlha Taklha, Dharamsala, October 1993.
26. *Freedom in Exile.*
27. *Freedom in Exile.*
28. Author interview with HH the Dalai Lama, Dharamsala, June 1994.

15

The Storm Comes Closer

[In the summer of 1956] I was given a copy of a newspaper published by the Chinese authorities at Karze in Kham. In disbelief, I saw that it contained a photograph of a row of severed heads. The caption said something to the effect that they had belonged to 'reactionary criminals'. This was the first concrete evidence of Chinese atrocity that I had seen. Thereafter, I knew that every terrible thing I heard about our new masters' behaviour was true...I began to wonder if there could be any hope for the future. My predecessor's prophecy was beginning to be proved entirely accurate.

The Fourteenth Dalai Lama, Freedom in Exile

After six months of treatment, the American doctors declared Norbu cured of his lung congestion. He took a crash course in English at Berkeley University in California, then set off for the 1952 World Buddhist Congress in Tokyo.

Unfortunately, during his stay in Japan, his Indian identity papers lapsed, so he was unable either to visit India or return to the United States. He had to stay in Japan for almost three years, making the most of his time by learning Japanese and making many Japanese friends. It was a pleasant life, marred only by 'the bitterness, the frustrated hopes and the nagging anxieties of the emigrant who has to wage a seemingly hopeless nerve-racking struggle with a vast anonymous bureaucracy'.[1]

When his documents arrived (early in 1955), he returned to the USA via India and Europe, in order to meet Gyalo Thondup in Calcutta.

In his house in residential upper Darjeeling, Gyalo Thondup was father to a fairly rumbustious extended family. In addition to three children of his own – his daughter Yangzom, and two sons (Tenzin) Khedup and (Ngawang) Tenpa – during holidays and every fourth weekend, Pema, Tenzin (Ngawang) and Khando joined the family. With some help from the Indian Government, GT sent the boys to St Joseph's College, North Point, a celebrated boarding school run by Canadian Jesuits for about three hundred boys from Burma, Thailand, Sikkim, Bhutan, Nepal, as well as European children whose parents were working in India. The girls were at a Convent run by Loreto nuns from Ireland.

'It was a wonderful life with the Thondups,' says Khando. 'We weren't short of money, we belonged to the Gymkhana Club, we went skating and riding, Uncle and Auntie used to play tennis – in fact, they were the local champions. Auntie was a very kind person. We never thought of her as Chinese, we just loved her. She cooked our favourite dishes for us and looked after us well.' Though Gyalo Thondup was kind also, he was a strict disciplinarian of whom the children were very much in awe. 'At meal-times, we had to be in our places on time, with faces washed and hands and finger-nails scrubbed. And we weren't allowed to leave the table until everyone had finished. I was so small that I used to fall asleep at the table, and then would have to be carried up to bed. Pema and I shared a room. Uncle Thondup would come to say goodnight to us, then he would turn off the light and we didn't dare put it back on again when he'd gone.'

Khando was a bright, intelligent child who spent all her monthly pocket-money on books (sometimes, she admits, comics) and, having learned English almost from infancy, was completely bilingual and would read everything she could lay hands on. This passion for reading used to get her in trouble at school, where she was often found reading after lights-out. 'The nuns would confiscate the books, and, even worse, bring them down to show Uncle Thondup when he and Auntie brought us tuck at weekends. My heart used to sink, I knew I'd get a spanking when I went home at the end of the month.' Uncle Thondup would scold Pema for a different reason. She had always found study difficult, especially in English. While Tenzin Ngawang, a brilliant student, was winning almost every prize on offer and Khando the ones for the subjects which interested her, Pema was usually awarded the application or needlework prize. Uncle Thondup was mortified!

In that spring of 1955 when Norbu came from Japan to see his brother, they heard that their elder sister was due to arrive in India, on her way back from China. Tsering Dolma was to attend a Trade Show in Calcutta and then go on to New Delhi for a meeting of the Tibetan Women's Delegation. Phuntsok Tashi was also coming, so Tenzin Ngawang and Khando would be reunited with their parents.

Khando has good reason to remember that time. The thrill of a trip to Calcutta and then to the Chinese Embassy in New Delhi – where she watched the Chinese staff doing their morning exercises to music over the tannoy – was overshadowed by an unpleasant incident which marked the end of her political innocence.

> Wherever our group went we were escorted by a Tibetan-speaking Chinese officer. I couldn't stand the man – he was arrogant and never left us alone. One morning we were in our sitting-room, and he just walked in without knocking. He strolled over to the table where there was a big bowl of assorted fruits and picked one up. 'May I?' he asked casually. I saw red. 'NO, YOU CAN'T,' I shouted furiously. There was a dead silence. Then after a while, someone rather nervously broke the silence and relaxed the tension. My mother signalled me to follow her into the bedroom: and never before or later did she whack me as hard as she did that morning. 'Don't you understand anything?' she asked, angrily. 'Don't you realize the danger you are putting us all in?' Well, of course I didn't, it would never have occurred to me to think that a ten year old's hostility could be taken as a political statement. But I never forgot the lesson. I suddenly realized the seriousness of the situation for my parents and indeed for our whole family. From then on I was aware of fear.

She had more reason than she knew to be afraid, for her parents were under considerable pressure to bring the children back to Tibet. 'Uncle Thondup told us that the Chinese wanted to send all of us children to be educated in the Soviet Union.' He told us not to go, that it would ruin our lives. We didn't really understand what it was all about, but, at Uncle Thondup's prompting, every time our parents brought up the subject, we would shout, "WE DON'T WANT TO GO, WE DON'T WANT TO GO."' The brothers too were under pressure, and their joy at seeing their sister again was blended with irritation, since they knew she was under orders to bring them back with her. From her own point of view, there was nothing Tsering Dolma would have liked better. Besides, as she angrily assured her brothers, if they went on refusing to return, the Chinese would take it out on Kundun.

Neither Norbu nor Gyalo Thondup had any illusions about what going back would mean; and neither of them had the least intention of doing so. But they knew their sister was apprehensive about returning to Lhasa empty-handed: 'We both made it clear to her that so long as the Chinese Communists were in power in Tibet there could be no return for us, much as we longed to see our native land again. But because she urged us so persistently we did go to see the Chinese consul in Calcutta, and he too did his utmost to persuade us to go back to Lhasa. But we remained firm and gave him a number of ostensibly good reasons which would prevent our return to Tibet for an indefinite period.'[3]

Norbu flew back to New York to resume his studies, while Tsering Dolma and Phuntsok Tashi prepared to return to Tibet. 'We could tell they were afraid, and it made us anxious,' says Khando. The parting was difficult for all of them. 'We drove by car to Gangtok, and stayed there for a day or two with the Sikkimese royal family before going by jeep to the Nathu la Pass, where about twenty horses and mules stood waiting. We had a picnic meal and then it was time to say goodbye. I remember my mother getting on to her horse and we watched from the top as they rode down the side of the Nathu la towards Dromo. We felt so sad watching them go down the hill and out of sight.'[4] But Tsering Dolma had no choice but to return to Lhasa, where she would blame her failure on the stubbornness of her two brothers.

She continued to study Tibetan with Rinchen Dolma Taring. (Tendzin Choegyal remembers her working at it far into the night.) But it was an uphill struggle and her heart was never quite in it. She had begun to chafe at the role the Chinese had imposed on her as the Dalai Lama's sister. 'She was a patriot, devoted to the cause of Tibet,' says Tendzin Choegyal. 'The work she did for the Chinese made her very uneasy.'[5]

At nine, Tendzin Choegyal was still too young to be aware of the political situation and remembers carefree summer holidays at Gyatso, riding, learning to fish in the pond in front of the house, wearing ordinary clothes like a normal little boy, playing with friends:

We experimented a lot, we had to make our own toys and games and were fairly inventive. We'd make bows from the bamboo which was meant for making pens – we had better uses for it. For arrows, we'd wade knee-deep in mud to get reeds and then dry them. To make a sharp tip, we'd cut biscuit tins and shape them into arrowheads with a stone, then fix them to the reed. Then we'd add a feather to stabilize the arrow in flight. We used to take the feathers from the roosters' tails. Soon the poor roosters' tails were completely bald. My mother kept wondering why and we looked innocent and said we'd no idea. We confessed eventually and I don't suppose she was surprised.

The adults often joined in the fun: 'We used to jump from the upper storey into the place where the hay was stored. Some of the grown-ups would jump so vigorously they almost dislocated their shoulders...There were a few accidents, but nothing really serious.'

Tendzin Choegyal was at the monastery of Drepung, though with all his heart he would have preferred being at home. 'I was never cut out to be a monk,' he admits. On returning from China in the summer of 1955, he had lived at home for a while, before being formally inducted into Drepung monastery the following winter. Drepung, the biggest and richest of Lhasa's monasteries, had been founded at the beginning of the fifteenth century by a poor herdsman from Eastern Tibet, a disciple of the great Tsong-khapa. It owed its name (which means 'Rice Heap') to its tiers of white-washed buildings, one behind the other on a sloping site at the edge of a wedge-shaped valley. It was said to be the largest monastery in the world; and from a distance looked just like a fortified city. Its sheer immensity came as a shock to Tendzin Choegyal:[6] 'I think that going to Drepung for the first time I lost a lot of freedom. For a start, it was so big. I had to grow up when I went there. I found it extremely difficult to get used to the robe: the shape was the same, the style was the same, but it had to be made of coarse wool cloth rather than the cotton I was used to. It was rough and scratchy, I used to itch all over. I had a high fever when I first went to Drepung, yet I couldn't escape all the endless induction ceremonies. I felt terribly lonely.'[7]

It was the start of what, had history not intervened so dramatically, would have been an eleven-year course of arduous study. Despite his obvious lack of vocation, he would probably have survived somehow. Apart from the all-important rituals, there are no dogmatic rules in Buddhist monasteries. As Spencer Chapman wrote, 'As long as [the Tibetan monk] attends the service in the monastery temple and is subject to the lay discipline of the proctors, he can pursue any spiritual goal and can endeavour to reach it by whatever means he chooses.'[8] Tendzin Choegyal's memories of those years are those of any mischievous ten-year-old, characterized more by horseplay than piety.

I used always to carry a needle and thread in my shirt. When we sat down in Assembly, sometimes I would sew together the robes of the two people in front of me. My friends and I were *tulkus*, so we occupied important seats among the grown-ups. While those solemn monks were chanting or meditating, I used to stitch them together down the whole length of their cloaks. When the session was over and they stood up, it was quite a sight – both pulling in different directions and discovering they were joined together. I used to make myself scarce and watch the fun from a distance. Sometimes, for a change, I'd sew the monk's cloak to the cushion he was sitting on. Novice-monks always got up to tricks of that sort, it was traditional; we thought it was great fun and the older monks didn't seem to mind. We must have sorely tried their patience, though.

The boys cut the ropes that were used in dark places as handrails; and put homemade catapults to unorthodox uses: 'In the evenings there'd be long, dreary sessions of prayer and debating. During the prayer session, we would be sitting on some raised ground near a pavilion surrounded by butter-lamps. I used to organize my friends to use their catapults to knock off the butter-lamps when it got dark. I directed the fire and it sounded like an artillery barrage – they were actually quite good shots.'

Later on, he managed to smuggle air pistols into the monastery. He had a passion for guns and knew how to handle them – having been given his first air rifle at the age of six by a Tibetan trader, he had persuaded the Royal Bodyguard to teach him to use it. He later acquired a Webley air pistol which he took to Drepung with him and which afforded him plenty of scope for mischief: 'There were some bells in front of the hostel where I lived, and when the wind blew they used to make a terrible din. So whenever the wind got up, it was a marvellous opportunity to use the bells as target practice. Everyone was very puzzled, but nobody ever found me out.'

Despite Buddhist teaching about the sanctity of all sentient life, he enjoyed taking pot shots at birds. Until, that is, one day he shot a sparrow and watched in horror as it died, blood oozing from its wounds. Full of remorse, he vowed never again to take a life. From then on, he restricted his targets to inanimate objects.

He would organize the making of bows and arrows from the reeds that were used for making the monastery's sweeping-brooms and his ingenuity devised ever more dangerous games: 'I had seen the film of *Henry V* and noticed that in the battle scenes, the English longbow was shot very high into the air, with the French cavalry at the receiving end. I thought that was marvellous, arrows coming down from the sky like rain. So when we got out the bows and arrows, I would tell my gang to split into two groups and fire the arrows in the air at each other. Then we'd all dodge the arrows as they fell...It was very exciting.'

If only Kundun's existence could have been as carefree! Though, superficially, life pursued its even course – he prayed and meditated with growing seriousness, studied, gave and received teachings as usual – the background to these daily activities was growing ever more threatening. Public unrest in Lhasa was reaching danger level and, as the Chinese would tolerate no opposition, they made him issue a proclamation banning public gatherings and asking his people 'to refrain from anything that would impair the good relations between Tibet and China'.⁹

The full horror of the tragedy in Eastern Tibet had not yet come to light in Lhasa. Armed resistance had broken out in Kham and Amdo at the end of 1955 and became an organized guerrilla movement in the summer of 1956 after most of the nomad chiefs and village headmen had taken to the hills in protest at the punitive 'democratic reforms'. These Khampa warriors successfully attacked the new roads and bridges, army posts, military camps and supply columns but Chinese retaliation with superior firepower was devastatingly swift and merciless.

With the aerial bombardment of Lithang Monastery in Kham in June 1956, the struggle entered a new phase. The Chinese knew that the monastery had given refuge to resistance fighters from the local village and had ordered the monks to hand the rebels over or face being bombed. As most of the monks had never even seen an aeroplane let alone a bomb, they did not understand the significance of the threat. Until, that is, the bombs actually fell, killing the majority of those inside the monastery. 'When I heard of it, I cried,' said Kundun. 'I could not believe that human beings were capable of such cruelty to each other.' But even worse was to follow. The bombardment was followed by most sadistic reprisals: sexual abuse of celibate monks and nuns; and the torture and execution of the women and children whose husbands had dared to join the resistance.

Details of the Chinese atrocities in Kham were later supplied to the International Commission of Jurists and were published in August 1960. Eye-witnesses described how monks and laymen were tortured and many killed, often in barbarous ways; women raped and others publicly humiliated; venerated Lamas subjected to brutal and disgusting degradations; other monks and Lamas compelled to break their religious vows; men and boys deported or put to forced labour in harsh conditions; boys and girls taken from their homes, ostensibly for education in China; children incited to abuse and beat their parents; private property seized; monasteries damaged by gunfire; and sacred images, books and relics carried off or publicly destroyed.[10]

In vain did Kundun protest to General Chiang. The latter replied unblinkingly that any Tibetan who opposed the necessary reform of his country must expect to be punished![11] Still believing that these horrors were being perpetrated by over-zealous local functionaries out of step with the Chinese leadership, Kundun wrote to Mao. He received no reply, either to that letter or the next, or the one after that. It was difficult to go on believing in the Chairman's good faith.

Despite all his efforts, a peaceful resolution of Tibet's problems seemed further away than ever; the Preparatory Committee was an empty sham within which he and his ministers had been deprived of power; the standoff between the guerrillas and the Chinese looked set to continue indefinitely, with neither side victorious, and women, children and the elderly being made to suffer the consequences. He felt he was losing the moral control of his people in Lhasa: how much longer could he hold out against their understandable desire to retaliate? He longed to be able to renounce the political leadership; yet he could only do that if he left the country. And that he was still unwilling to do.

NOTES

1. Norbu, *Tibet Is My Country*.
2. This was, of course, before the break in relations between China and the USSR.
3. *Tibet Is My Country*.
4. Author interview, Khando Chazotsang, Utah, February 1996.
5. Author interview with Tendzin Choegyal, Dharamsala, June 1994.
6. Drepung was divided into four colleges, each housing monks from a different locality. As Ngari Rinpoche, Tendzin Choegyal was a member of Gomang College.

7. Author interview with Tendzin Choegyal, Dharamsala, June 1994.

8. F. Spencer Chapman, *Lhasa, the Holy City.*

9. Gompo Tashi Andrugtsang, *Four Rivers, Six Ranges: A True Account of Khampa Resistance to the Chinese in Tibet,* Dharamsala, 1973.

10. Hugh Richardson, *Tibet and its History,* chapter 12.

11. This was an article of faith with the Chinese. Since the Han Chinese were the spearhead of the socialist revolution, the national minorities should strive to learn from them and emulate them. Any attempt to thwart the plans of the Han Chinese was a crime and must be vigorously opposed. See *Resistance and Reform in Tibet,* p. 57.

16

Buddha Jayanti 1956

Though all we see may seem to be eternal
It will soon fall to pieces and disappear.
Yesterday perhaps one had enough or more:
All today is gone and nothing left.
Milarepa, eleventh-century Tibetan poet and saint

Towards the end of 1956, the 2,500th anniversary of the Buddha's birth –
the Buddha Jayanti – was to be celebrated in India. As Nehru was eager
for the Dalai Lama to attend, he consulted Gyalo Thondup and W. D.
Shakabpa, co-founders of the Committee for Tibetan Social Welfare. 'Mr
Shakabpa and I,' says GT,

> told Mr Nehru and the Indian Government that it would be tragic for His
> Holiness to come and then have to return to Tibet. The Indian Government
> said that if they found a way of persuading the Chinese and if we could per-
> suade His Holiness to accept, they would offer him asylum in India. They
> said he could live in any of the Maharajahs' Palaces in India, and that then
> they would help him negotiate with the Chinese. We were pleased with the
> offer. So in the spring of 1956 Nehru sent the Maharajah of Sikkim who was
> President of the Mahabodhi Association of India with an invitation to His
> Holiness to attend the Buddha Jayanti. Through different channels we con-
> tacted His Holiness and urged him to accept their invitation, whatever the
> Chinese said.'

Kundun says of the secret discussions that followed: 'Even Lobsang Samten was kept in the dark. Mr Phala who was now my Lord Chancellor had felt compelled to distance himself from him because he was thought to be too close to the Chinese. Mr Phala was in secret communication with the Indian Mission in Lhasa, trying to decide whether or not I should take part. From time to time he would tell me what was going on, but he said nothing whatever to Lobsang Samten.'²

Kundun had made it clear he wished to attend the celebrations, but the Chinese insisted that his presence was necessary in Lhasa, what with all the Preparatory Committee work, the trouble in the East and so on. Everybody else in Lhasa felt he should go to India, and Nehru even hinted that Sino-Indian relations might suffer if the Dalai Lama were prevented from attending the Jayanti.

The Chinese continued to stall – until an eleventh hour telegram from Nehru persuaded them to relent – on condition that the Panchen Lama went too! When told the good news, Kundun rushed off, 'smiling as if my mouth would reach my ears', to tell his two tutors and three council ministers to prepare for the journey. The Chinese controlled their anger, but with hindsight, Kundun came to understand that it was this decision in 1956 to go to India against their wishes that turned their latent mistrust of him into outright hostility.³

Kundun left Lhasa in late November with his speeches pre-prepared by the Chinese – and to the tune of a solemn lecture from General Chiang about what he was to say and not say whilst in India. 'Of course, the Chinese suspected him,' admits Tendzin Choegyal. 'After all, my mother already had two sons out of the country, both of them well known for their anti-Chinese sentiments.'

Amala and Tsering Dolma, believing there was little chance of Kundun being allowed to attend the Jayanti, had already left for India. Many Tibetans were doing likewise, some of them seizing the opportunity to get out for good. (Among the latter were the Tsarongs. 'My parents were very unhappy with the Chinese occupation of our country,' says Namlha, 'and they foresaw worse problems ahead. So my mother insisted on our going back to India, especially as they were coming under increasing pressure to send my sister and me to China for our studies. She just took us away for the Buddha Jayanti pilgrimage and we never went back.') Norbu also made his way to India, hoping against hope that Kundun would be allowed to come. When Gyalo Thondup's wife met him at Calcutta airport with the news that his mother and sister had already reached Kalimpong, he hastened there to meet them. They told him about the massacres in Eastern Tibet and about the growing tension in Lhasa, where the refugees were multiplying rapidly.

When news came that Kundun was actually on his way to India, both brothers set off for the border without delay.

Lobsang Samten was to join the party and once again Tendzin Choegyal was determined not be left out:

> I heard that all the family was going to India. So early next morning, I walked all the way from Drepung to the Norbulingka to find Lobsang Samten. He was in the middle of washing. I told him I didn't want to be left behind, and he suggested that I should talk to His Holiness. I did so straight away. Kundun sighed and said, 'Don't you think you should stay behind and study?' I started to cry and after a bit he relented, as I knew he would.⁴

For Tendzin Choegyal, going to India was a great jaunt, combining the pleasures of being with his mother, taking part in a special pilgrimage, seeing Pema, Tenzin Ngawang and Khando again, and escaping from the monastery. But for Lobsang Samten, it was a different matter. He was under enormous pressure from the Chinese, and his official job as a liaison between them and what remained of the Tibetan Government meant that he was trusted by neither side. He was very depressed.

The travellers followed almost the same route as in 1951, when they had fled to the Chumbi Valley, but this time, the new road allowed them to go as far as Dromo by car, the journey taking two days instead of twenty-one. At the last settlement before the border, they mounted ponies, and with Chinese exhortations ringing in their ears – to beware of foreign imperialists and spies and to remember the glorious benefits the Chinese had brought to Tibet – the Dalai Lama's caravan began the long trek upwards into the mists and cold of the Nathu la Pass which marked the frontier with India. At the top of the pass stood a large mound of stones festooned with the prayer-flags which the Tibetans called *lung ta* – 'wind-horses' – which carry the prayers of the people into the unseen spiritual realm. In accordance with time-honoured practice, each of them added a stone to

the mound and shouted out, *Lha Gyal Lo* (Victory to the Gods) before beginning the descent to the wooded, snow-encrusted gorges of Sikkim and
the steaming plains of India beyond.

In a bungalow just beneath the pass, Norbu and Gyalo Thondup were
waiting impatiently. 'At last, late one evening, we heard the bells of a large
caravan coming down from the pass, and despite the heavy falls of snow
we hurried up to meet it.'[5]

Tendzin Choegyal rode ahead of the main party, his horse descending
the hill at speed. 'I have a vivid memory of suddenly catching sight of Taktser Rinpoche and Gyalo Thondup, and they both started laughing and
running towards me. We hugged each other, we were so happy.'

Kundun rode forward to exchange more formal greetings, then gave the
signal for the caravan to proceed towards the bungalow. He recalls the
breathless urgency with which his two older brothers greeted him:

> I really hadn't made up my mind about whether I would be returning to Tibet.
> But as soon as I reached the Sikkim border I was met by my brothers and the
> very first words they said, before even hello, how are you, nice to see you, were
> '*You must not go back.*' Their urgency really shook me. I knew that the situa-
> tion in Lhasa had deteriorated beyond recall, and I knew there was good reason
> for me to stay in India. But it was a very difficult decision to make. I couldn't
> be a hundred per cent certain that I would be doing the right thing if I stayed.[6]

That night, 'for the first time in our lives, we five brothers were assembled
round the same table. It was a solemn moment', wrote Norbu. The discussions went on until well past midnight. Norbu reported to Kundun that
the outside world was showing an interest in the fate of Tibet and that
help might be forthcoming. (A guarded reference, perhaps, to the fact that
he – and, through him, Gyalo Thondup – had already approached the CIA
for help, but if so, it was lost on his brother. The unworldly Kundun had
no suspicion that his brothers might be up to something.) Tendzin Choegyal was unaware of the political undercurrents, 'but I knew the conversation was about very serious matters. Some Tibetans who'd lived in India
for years had come along and they were very agitated.'

Norbu and Gyalo Thondup, sharing a tent on that bitterly cold night,
found sleep elusive. Next day, the brothers went their separate ways. Kundun was taken to Bagdogra on the Indian plain, where he boarded a specially chartered plane for New Delhi. His three brothers made their own way
there via Calcutta, where they found their mother and Tsering Dolma at

the airport. Pema, Tenzin Ngawang and Khando, on holiday from school, also joined them.

Kundun was welcomed by Prime Minister Nehru and by a huge crowd of Tibetans, spinning prayer wheels, offering khatas, prostrating, showing their love and respect in every way they knew. Journalists present were baffled by so spontaneous an outpouring of love. One of them described the scene as 'strange and different, a blend of reverence, esteem and affection...This is something no reporter can demonstrate quantitatively, or even prove at all, but can only report as something he knew existed.'[7]

Next morning Kundun made a special pilgrimage to the Rajghat, to venerate the ashes of his hero, Mahatma Gandhi:

> I was deeply moved as I prayed there on the green lawns which slope down to the Jamuna River. I felt I was in the presence of a noble soul...a true disciple of Lord Buddha and a true believer in peace and harmony among all men. As I stood there, I wondered what wise counsel the Mahatma would have given me if he had been alive. I felt sure he would have thrown all his strength of will and character into a peaceful campaign for the freedom of the people of Tibet...I made up my mind...to follow his lead whatever difficulties might confront me. I determined more strongly than ever that I could never associate myself with acts of violence.[8]

At a UNESCO meeting in Delhi, held to coincide with the Buddha Jayanti, Kundun threw away the prepared speeches given him by the Chinese and, though careful not to abandon caution altogether, told his audience that while all the world was preaching peace, vulnerable small nations were being swallowed up by large powerful ones. This, he said simply, should not pass unnoticed.[9]

As the Indian Government had placed a train at Kundun's disposal, the whole family travelled with him across India, visiting the sacred Buddhist sites. Amala immediately made friends with the Indian cooks on the train and they sometimes allowed her to prepare Tibetan meals for them all. The only irritant was the inescapable presence of Chinese functionaries, most of whom understood Tibetan. When Pema showed her displeasure, one of them commented to Amala, 'Your daughter obviously doesn't like us.' Fortunately he took no action.

Sixteen now, Pema felt that it was on this journey that she began to know Kundun for the first time. While the younger children were running all over the train, she had the opportunity of long, serious talks with her brother. He showed an interest in her life in India and seemed to approve of the education she was receiving from the nuns. (Nevertheless, she longed to return to Tibet, and asked Amala if it might be possible. Aware of the ever-listening Chinese, Amala replied quietly that perhaps it might be better for her to remain in Darjeeling.)

Whenever Kundun had to stay several days in the same place, a house was put at the family's disposal. For Pema it was a dream come true. 'We all took our meals together. For the first time I saw His Holiness as an ordinary human being. Even though I continued to respect him enormously as the Dalai Lama, I realized at that time that he was also a wonderful man. There was no longer that distance between us symbolized by all those steps at the Potala.'[10]

In Calcutta the family were lodged at the Grand Hotel. 'It was an eye-opener,' recalls Pema. 'For the first time I was learning the true story of what was going on in Tibet. It brought it all so much closer and made me long to be able to do something positive for my country.'[11] In this close family atmosphere, Norbu was swept by a wave of nostalgia for the past:

> When my mother made tea for her assembled brood in the old familiar way, it seemed to me almost that the dull and typical hotel room began to look like our old kitchen in Taktser. We older ones reminisced, and told the younger ones...of the happy days we had spent in the uplands of Amdo as children. And later on in the evenings, when they had gone to bed, we talked with the Dalai Lama and my mother of the future outlook, and I did not conceal my opinion that their days in Tibet were numbered too.[12]

Throughout, Amala preserved a calm common sense. Her principal concerns were Pema and Tendzin Choegyal. As the latter hurtled about the train playing with the Indian servants, she wondered about his future. He was the last of her children: Norbu was settled in the States, GT in India, and Lobsang Samten (who had undergone an appendectomy and tonsillectomy in Nangal in mid-journey) had decided against returning to Tibet. Should she perhaps arrange for Tendzin Choegyal to stay behind in India for his education? She consulted her older sons, they advised against it. As an Incarnate, they said, his place was in Tibet – for as long as it remained possible.

In the three months he spent travelling around India, Kundun found the freedom exhilarating – so different from his experience of China two years earlier. It was wonderful to be able to talk about the teachings of Buddha to scholars from many countries, and he tried to imagine what it would be like to be free, as they were, to proclaim and discuss Buddhist ideas! When he thought about how his hands were tied, how powerless he was to help his people, he wondered about staying in India, from where he could tell the world what was happening in Tibet. Abruptly he made up his mind to ask Nehru for political asylum.

The illusion that the choice was down to him was understandable but it ignored the political realities. Whatever Nehru might have assured Gyalo Thondup, he still held passionately to his belief that the peace of Asia depended on the friendship between India and China. (Regardless of the fact that the only danger to the peace of Asia was posed by China itself.) Much as he revered and sympathized with the Dalai Lama, Nehru would not permit him to endanger his dream. When the Tibetan leader broached the subject of political asylum, Nehru urged him to return to Tibet and work with the Chinese within the Seventeen-Point Agreement. In vain did Kundun protest that he had tried for seven years to do just that, while the Chinese had broken every single term of the Agreement. 'You must realize,' Nehru retorted, 'India cannot support you.' The most he would promise was to speak to the Chinese Prime Minister, Chou En-lai, due to arrive in Delhi next day.

In the event, Kundun saw Chou En-lai (Chew and Lie, as one Indian newspaper called him) before Nehru did, and voiced his concern over what was happening in Tibet. Chou lived up to his reputation as a silken-tongued charmer, but his words held an undertow of menace. 'He said that he had heard a rumour that I was considering staying in India. It would be a mistake, he warned. My country needed me.'[13] Chou was well aware that the situation all over Tibet was getting out of hand and, while professing sympathy for the Tibetans, he made it quite clear that the Chinese would use force in the event of trouble.

Kundun understood that he had no option but to return to Tibet. He went first to Calcutta to rejoin the family for a few days. Norbu and Gyalo Thondup had also met with Chou En-lai. They had resisted his blandishments to return to Tibet, Taktser telling Chou that everything he had heard about Chinese behaviour in Lhasa, coupled with his own experiences as Abbot of Kumbum, convinced him that 'the Chinese Communists were deliberately out to destroy everything that was holy and dear to us'.[14] Chou oozed charm to both brothers, but when he realized he was getting nowhere with them, insisted that at least they should persuade the

Dalai Lama to return home with all speed. Norbu and Gyalo Thondup replied that though they themselves preferred to live in freedom they had no authority over their brother.

In fact they, especially Gyalo Thondup, were furious at the way Nehru, under pressure from Chou En-lai, had reneged on his promises. 'Nehru betrayed us,' says GT angrily. 'I told the Indian Government officials at the time, "You are murdering His Holiness, you are murdering the people of Tibet. Look at how he has exposed his real feelings while he has been in India, and now you're pushing him back into the jaws of death." I was absolutely livid and even today [1995] I still feel we were betrayed.'[15]

Both brothers were still doing their utmost to persuade Kundun not to go back, to seek asylum elsewhere, if not in India. 'We felt there would be some terrible, unthinkable disaster if he returned.' They were baffled by his obstinacy:

> When I explained that, although I could see the logic of their arguments, I could not accept them, Gyalo Thondup began to show signs of agitation. He was – and still is – the most fiercely patriotic of my brothers. He has a very strong character and a tendency to be single-minded to the point of stubbornness...Taktser Rinpoche is milder-mannered than Gyalo Thondup...but on this occasion he too showed signs of exasperation.[16]

When Amala urged Kundun to stay, he replied gently, 'What good would remaining here in safety be, while all the people of Tibet are left at the mercy of the Chinese?'[17]

Bad weather delayed his departure for almost a month, but towards the end of March 1957, when the snow began to clear from the Nathu la, he began the depressing journey back to Lhasa. First came the parting with Lobsang Samten. 'It was a very sad goodbye,' he recalls. 'Lobsang Samten was weeping, despite the fact that his cheeks had so often borne the mark of my nails when we were children together.'[18] Amala understood that from his own point of view Lobsang's decision not to go back was a wise one; but she was anxious for Kundun who would be losing his best friend and most loyal supporter. Moreover, the Chinese would probably hold him responsible for the defection of yet another of his brothers!

Gloomily, Norbu (who was returning to the USA) and Gyalo Thondup accompanied Kundun to the frontier where his caravan waited. The last snows of winter were still falling, as they joined the weeping crowds of Tibetans and Indians at the top of the Nathu la. Kundun must have shuddered when he saw, overpowering the Tibetan *lung ta* fluttering prayerfully over the pass, the blood-red banners of the People's Republic of China.

The Lhasa to which he returned on 1 April 1957 was in turmoil. Chou Enlai had indeed ordered a few cosmetic changes: the Chinese had removed some troops and some of the blue-uniformed political officers responsible for introducing the more unwelcome reforms; work had been stopped on a new army barracks and on a controversial hydro-electric plant; and there was much ostentatious breast-beating in the local papers about the excessive zeal shown by the Han Chinese, their lamentable failure to respect local customs, etc. But by and large, this belated sensitivity to Tibetan feelings was the usual hogwash, for in reality the situation was deteriorating fast. That the invaders were settling in for the duration was obvious – a whole new district had sprung up in Lhasa to accommodate the Chinese officials and their families. (It was the beginning of a ruthless take-over, which within a few years would transform Lhasa into a featureless concrete jungle indistinguishable from any other Chinese city.) The Provisional Committee continued to discuss meaningless policies, while relentlessly whittling down Kundun's authority and stifling any voice of protest.

The spiralling violence in eastern Tibet – attack followed by brutal military reprisals – had turned the region into a wasteland. Throughout the preceding year the proud and independent Khampa chieftains had overcome their ancient tribal animosities – and the vast distances that separated them from each other – to form a loose-knit alliance to protect their traditional Buddhist values. Called first 'The Volunteer Army to Defend Buddhism', it became known as Chushi Gangdrug ('Four Rivers, Six Ranges'), the old name for Eastern Tibet.

The rebels made contact with Gyalo Thondup in India, asking him for help with weapons and training. From now on, GT's Committee for Tibetan Social Welfare would become the power-house of the Tibetan Resistance. He had all the right connections. With the help of his Chinese-born wife, he enlisted the aid of the Nationalists in Taiwan in parachuting a limited number of arms and supplies to the guerrillas. And as these requests were always filtered through the CIA, the Americans suggested that perhaps he should deal directly with them.

In Darjeeling, Pema, Tenzin Ngawang and Khando had at least a glimmering of their Uncle Thondup's other life. 'He was always very political, very wrapped up in the Tibetan cause,' says Pema. 'He encouraged us to be patriots like himself, told us how important freedom was for a nation.'[19] He was 'always in and out, we were never quite sure where he was,' echoes Khando. 'He often used to come home and ask us to cyclostyle leaflets. We would spend the whole weekend doing them. Much later, he told us that they were being dropped over Tibet.'

When the CIA offered to train a number of Tibetans in guerrilla warfare, Gyalo Thondup did not hesitate. 'We chose a small group of Khampas and in 1956 we started a border crossing,' he says. 'I used to take the men from the Tibetan border to Darjeeling and Kalimpong, then to the Pakistan border where the Americans were waiting to collect them.' They were flown to an unidentified island in the North Pacific (possibly Guam) to be taught about modern weaponry and commando techniques. One of them was Gyalo Thondup's cousin, Lhamo Tsering.

A year later they were parachuted into Tibet, to help organize the Resistance more efficiently. Each of them carried 'a pistol, a small machine-gun, an old Japanese radio, $132 in Tibetan currency, and a bracelet containing vials of poison to be taken in the event of capture.'[20] There was also, and this later became a very contentious issue, a 'yellow parachute', allegedly containing gold, dollars, Tibetan and Indian money.

But, even with CIA help, the Tibetan freedom fighters were still hopelessly ill-equipped. Air-drops of weapons made by the Americans often did more harm to the Tibetans than to the Chinese. The Americans were anxious that their assistance should not be attributable, the Dalai Lama later wrote, so 'they dropped only a few badly made bazookas and some ancient British rifles which had once been in general service throughout India and Pakistan and thus could not be traced to source in the event of capture. But the mishandling they received whilst being air-dropped rendered them almost useless.'[21] Occasionally the CIA would delay too long and by the time help arrived it was already too late.

The Chinese response was savage. They not only shelled the villages which were giving support to the guerrillas, but let loose a campaign of atrocities against the people of eastern Tibet:

The obliteration of entire villages was compounded by hundreds of public executions, carried out to intimidate the surviving population. The methods employed included crucifixion, dismemberment, vivisection, beheading,

burying, burning and scalding alive, dragging the victims to death behind galloping horses and pushing them from air-planes; children were forced to shoot
their parents, disciples their religious teachers. Everywhere monasteries were
prime targets. Monks were compelled to publicly copulate with nuns and desecrate sacred images before being sent to a growing string of labour camps.[22]

Survivors, monks and laypeople from the villages, began a long and arduous trek towards Lhasa and by 1958 almost ten thousand were camped all
around the city. The people of Lhasa grew more and more inflamed by the
refugees' stories. As the Resistance Movement acquired a new headquarters in Lhoka, a region to the south-east of Lhasa, and thousands of angry
volunteers rushed to join it, it was suddenly clear that the focus of revolt
had shifted from the East to Central Tibet. Co-operation with the Chinese
was at an end. Hatred of the invaders was – temporarily, at least – uniting
all Tibetans. Under the leadership of a trader from Lithang, Gompo Tashi
Andrugtsang, the guerrilla force was reorganized and became the National
Volunteer Defence Army. As the rebels edged ever closer to Lhasa, notch-
ing up an impressive number of successes, the Chinese military commander, General Chiang, began pressuring the Dalai Lama to bring in the
Tibetan Army against them.

Kundun was in a Catch-22 situation. On the one hand, the rebels believed that he and his Kashag were in league with the Chinese since they
would not countenance the use of violence against them. On the other,
the Political Commissar, General Tan, made his life a misery, coming
every day to the Norbulingka, 'to urge, cajole and abuse me', until eventually the mere sight of the audience room in the palace began to fill him
with dread. Furious at Kundun's refusal to bring in his troops (on the
grounds that the Tibetan Army was too small, too ill-trained, and in any
case likely to defect and join the rebels), General Tan changed tack, denouncing Norbu, Gyalo Thondup and the Committee for Tibetan Social
Welfare as traitors and demanding that they be stripped of their Tibetan
citizenship. Kundun, reckoning his brothers were safely out of harm's
way, agreed to excommunicate them. His main concern was how to prevent the fighting from reaching Lhasa itself – which would make catastrophe certain.

'My classmates in Drepung were all talking about resisting the Chinese.
We knew there was going to be a fight, and we were sure we'd win.'[23]
Tendzin Choegyal at twelve was aware at last of the political realities.

Like all the monks at Drepung, he had gradually been drawn into the Chinese net: 'The Chinese used everyone, even me. I was paid a salary of thirteen Chinese dollars a year, with which I could buy toys. I was made a member of the Department of Religious Affairs while I was in Drepung. All the high lamas were paid a salary and given a job description. You hadn't got to do anything; just attend meetings whenever you were told to. Actually, they thought I was a good Communist. I was quite good at deceiving them.'[24]

As the Chinese began arming their own civilians and setting up barricades, tension escalated. 'No one dared speak openly because someone might be listening,' Amala later told a friend:

> Many people, especially those known to hold anti-Chinese views, disappeared never to be seen again...I visited His Holiness every week and brought him a loaf of the Amdo bread he liked so much. He kept reassuring me that everything would be all right and that I should not worry. I asked him why I shouldn't worry. 'What could happen?' he asked me. 'They will kill you,' I replied. 'What good would *that* do them?' he said, laughing. 'And if they try to take me to China against my will, I won't go.'[25]

With the family, the Chinese were still playing cat-and-mouse. 'On the surface,' says Phuntsok Tashi, 'things were all right, but in a subtle way we knew everything had changed.' The officials were still friendly, dropping in regularly to see Amala or Tsering Dolma. 'But when they came, they were really trying to feel the pulse of the family, trying to discover what they felt about things.'[26] Amala, suspected of engineering the escape of her three sons, was under strict surveillance; and it did not help that Pema, Tenzin Ngawang and Khando were still at school in India. As Pema later explained, the Chinese had forbidden the family to leave Tibet and contact with them had almost dried up:

> My mother and sister couldn't write to us, because the Chinese were always breathing down their necks, asking why their children were in India. They didn't even dare have our pictures in the house. They had to hide them away, because the Chinese kept insisting that we should be brought back to Lhasa and sent to Peking for our education. So they had to keep a low profile and we didn't hear from them very often. It was hard for us children to understand that.[27]

One day, a distant relative of Kundun's late father who worked in the Chinese Security Service let slip a warning while drunk. 'The Chinese mean you no good,' he blurted out after attending a meeting where plans to 'make sure of catching the old woman' had been discussed. And at an official Patriotic Women's meeting, Tsering Dolma was horrified to hear General Tan say that where you had a piece of fly-blown meat, you had to destroy the meat before you could get rid of the flies. His audience was left in no doubt that the polluted meat was the Dalai Lama and his Kashag. But, frightened though she was, Amala hid her fear and did her best to rally the spirits of her family. 'It doesn't matter what happens to any of us individually,' she told her youngest son firmly. 'Our whole country is being persecuted. Why should we bother about our family being singled out?'[28]

The long, cold winter months of 1958–9 passed with agonizing slowness. Amid daily reports of Chinese outrages against civilians in the East, Kundun forced himself to study in preparation for his final examinations scheduled for March. It was hard not to hate the Chinese, yet Buddhist faith forbade hatred: 'I reminded myself constantly of the Buddha's teaching that our enemy is in a sense our greatest teacher. And if this was sometimes hard to do, I never really doubted that it was so.'[29]

As tension rose, Kundun heard of a memo sent by the PLA to Mao. The prisons were all full of rebellious Tibetans, it said. What did Mao advise? Mao replied that Tibetan discontent was immaterial and if necessary they could gaol the whole population. Kundun thought of the old days when he had recognized and empathized with every prisoner in the Potala. He often wondered what his hero, Gandhi, would have done in this present situation. Would he have continued to advocate non-violence?

Time was running out. Even before the New Year of 1959 – Earth Hog Year – had dawned, Kundun had 'definite information that the Chinese were fully prepared to attack us. It was only a question of the day and the hour.'[30]

NOTES

1. Author interview with Gyalo Thondup, New Delhi, July 1995.
2. Author interview with HH the Dalai Lama, Dharamsala, June 1994.
3. Author interview with HH the Dalai Lama, Dharamsala, June 1994.
4. Author interview with Tendzin Choegyal, Dharamsala, October 1993.
5. Norbu, *Tibet Is My Country*.
6. Author interview with HH the Dalai Lama, Dharamsala, June 1994.

7. Goodman, *The Last Dalai Lama*.

8. Fourteenth Dalai Lama, *My Land and My People*, chapter 8.

9. Shakabpa, *Tibet: A Political History*, chapter 18.

10. Pema, *Tibet, Mon Histoire*.

11. Author interview with Jetsun Pema, Dharamsala, June 1994.

12. *Tibet Is My Country*.

13. Fourteenth Dalai Lama, *Freedom in Exile*.

14. *Tibet Is My Country*.

15. Author interview with Gyalo Thondup, New Delhi, July 1995.

16. Fourteenth Dalai Lama, *Freedom in Exile*.

17. Goodman, interview with the Gyayum Chenmo (Amala), Dharamsala, May 1980, quoted in *The Last Dalai Lama*.

18. Author interview with HH the Dalai Lama, Dharamsala, June 1994.

19. Author interview with Jetsun Pema, Dharamsala, June 1994.

20. Goodman.

21. *Freedom in Exile*.

22. Avedon, *In Exile from the Land of Snows*.

23. Author interview with Tendzin Choegyal, Dharamsala, June 1994.

24. Author interview with Tendzin Choegyal, June 1994.

25. Goodman, interview with the Gyayum Chenmo (Amala), Dharamsala, May 1980, quoted in *The Last Dalai Lama*.

26. Author interview with Phuntsok Tashi Taklha, London 1993.

27. Author interview with Jetsun Pema, Dharamsala, June 1994.

28. Author interview with Tendzin Choegyal, October 1994.

29. *Freedom in Exile*.

30. Avedon, *An Interview with the Dalai Lama*.

17

Uprising and Escape 1959

> The only published figure we have for Tibetans killed in the Lhasa uprising and its aftermath is from official sources. A booklet marked 'secret' and published in Lhasa on October 1, 1960 by the political department of the Tibetan Military District, says...'From last March up to now we have already wiped out over 87,000 of the enemy.'
>
> *Jamyang Norbu, 'The Tibetan Resistance Movement'*[1]

Yet Earth Hog Year started like any other, with festivities in the streets followed by a three-week prayer festival. The tragedy began in quite a low key with an invitation to the Dalai Lama and his family to attend a performance by a new dance troupe from China at the military HQ in Lhasa early in March; and with a statement on Radio Peking that the Tibetan ruler would be attending the National People's Congress in Peking in April.

Kundun had accepted neither invitation, being entirely preoccupied with thoughts of the looming final examinations for his Doctorate in Metaphysics, the goal towards which his many years of study had been leading him. It involved intensive debating on a wide range of subjects in which he must pit his wits against the finest minds in Tibet. The course usually took twenty years to complete, yet he had taken only half that time. For the last two years he had been studying hard and had already passed the preliminary bouts – dialectical debates in front of the combined colleges of all Three Seats: Drepung, Sera and Ganden. The all-important final would take place in the Jokhang temple, and now that the time had come he was nervous. 'The field of study was so vast, there were so many texts and commentaries, you simply had no idea from which area the debaters would choose their questions.'[2]

The Chinese had their own agenda and no mere religious examination would be allowed to interfere with it. On the evening before the examination, when Kundun had already taken up residence in the Jokhang, the Political Commissar, General Tang, despatched two junior officials to his quarters to insist on his fixing a date for the entertainment. Nothing could have been further from Kundun's thoughts at that moment and he managed to persuade the officials to wait at least until next day's examination was over. But however much he tried to concentrate on the work in hand, he could not fail to notice the signs of mounting tension outside. 'The examination hall was just opposite a house which the Chinese had bought from a noble family. It was sandbagged on the top of the roofs and round all the windows like all the other houses the Chinese occupied in Lhasa.'[3]

Next day, 2 March, he performed brilliantly and achieved a distinguished doctorate. Three days later he returned to the Norbulingka in the traditional glittering procession. It would, in fact, be the last parade, the swansong of Old Tibet. And from it, for the first time since the occupation, the Chinese were notably absent.

Having no excuse for further stalling, Kundun agreed on a date – 10 March – for the dance-troupe performance. On the ninth, his brother-in-law, Commander of the Bodyguard, Phuntsok Tashi, was summoned from his breakfast to discuss the arrangements. He was stunned to be handed a list of impossible conditions: that the visit should be kept secret (as if Kundun's movements could ever be kept secret from the Lhasa populace!); that Kundun was to go to Chinese headquarters unaccompanied by either ministers or bodyguard; and that no Tibetan troops were to be stationed beyond the bridge which marked the boundaries of the military camp.

With his customary cool, Kundun found the provisos merely 'a little strange and unusual', whereas to his ministers they seemed utterly bizarre. As for what the Tibetans would say when the news leaked out – as it assuredly would – of that there was absolutely no doubt. They would conclude that the Chinese intended to abduct the Dalai Lama to Peking and they simply would not allow it.

The news did leak out and Lhasa, overflowing with New Year revellers, monks attending the Great Prayer Festival, and refugees from the East –

reacted with predictable passion. Whatever scenario the Chinese had in mind, they had almost certainly underestimated the devotion of the Tibetans to their leader, their determination to protect him from harm at all costs. From now on, it would be the people who dictated the course of events. By sunset on 9 March, thousands of them had streamed out of Lhasa to camp – with cooking pots, knives and blankets – outside the Norbulingka gates, ready to defend Kundun to the death. Rinchen Dolma Taring recalls a young man running into her office with the news that everybody in Lhasa was off to the Norbulingka:

> Everybody knew that the Chinese had already invited some lamas in eastern Tibet to their theatres and then kidnapped them, so now thousands were around the Norbulingka, begging His Holiness not to go into such danger. The young man said he was on his way to join the crowd...[4]

By dawn on the tenth, their numbers were swollen to about fifteen thousand; the mood was ugly and uncompromising. When a junior official suspected of being a Chinese spy put in an appearance he was dragged from his bicycle and stoned to death. The people were serving notice on the Chinese that they had had enough.

Alarmed by this turn of events, Kundun cancelled his attendance at the entertainment. The crowds were told but they had already passed the point of no return – they had made themselves the guardians of his safety and would do whatever the situation demanded. For Kundun, it was like being trapped between two erupting volcanoes.

> On the one hand there was the vehement, unequivocal, unanimous protest of my people against the Chinese regime; on the other, there was the armed might of an aggressive occupation force. If there was a clash between the two, the result was a foregone conclusion. The Lhasan people would be ruthlessly massacred in their thousands; and Lhasa – and the rest of Tibet – would see a full-scale military rule with all its persecutions and tyranny.[5]

Until that day, Kundun had felt little anxiety on his own behalf. But now, he realized, everything had suddenly changed, the situation had assumed a relentless momentum of its own. Though perhaps neither side would in cold blood have chosen this particular place and time for a showdown, long-repressed resentments were rising to the surface, and could no longer be contained. He sensed that this 10 March 1959 was a date he would remember for ever:

I remember it with vivid clearness. I was upstairs with my Lord Chamberlain, Mr Phala, who was trying to explain what was happening and what we ought or ought not to do next. It was about ten in the morning. The sky was unusually blue, the sun very bright. I remember saying very slowly to Mr Phala that perhaps this day, 10 March, would be a landmark in Tibetan history. I didn't know then how right I was![6]

At roughly the same moment, his younger brother, Tendzin Choegyal, was being collected from Drepung in a Soviet-made car for the three-mile trip to the Chinese camp. With no sense that history was about to be made, the boy was looking forward to an interesting day out, away from the restrictions of Drepung. But on arriving at the camp he knew instantly that something was wrong:

> For a start, they were all armed, all the Chinese and all the pro-Chinese Tibetans. An old friend of my brother Lobsang Samten came up to me. I made to embrace him and could feel the pistol inside his gown. They knew something was about to happen all right, and they knew how they were going to respond...General Tan was furious that His Holiness wasn't coming. His face was crimson and he kept thumping the table with his fist, saying it was all the fault of a bunch of reactionaries. He would liquidate them, he shouted, if they didn't come to heel. I had never seen him so angry. They went ahead with the performance, though, or at least a shortened form of it.[7]

With hindsight, Tendzin Choegyal recognizes he was lucky to escape with his life that day. His mother certainly feared the worst. A former Amdo neighbour had burst in on her early that morning, with the news that everyone was heading for the Norbulingka. The Great Mother did not rush to the palace, but neither did she go to the theatrical performance. When the Chinese drivers came to collect her, her servants told them she was unwell – and after a brief scuffle threw them off the premises. From behind a curtain in her bedroom she watched them drive away in a fury. All that day she had feared for the life of her youngest son; even imagining she could hear his terrified cries. Without much hope, she posted a servant at the crossroads where the road from the camp forked off towards Drepung. When the man saw a car approaching with Tendzin Choegyal inside, he beckoned the Chinese driver to stop, telling him that the young man's mother was ill and he was to go home rather than to the monastery. 'I got out of the car and walked the remaining distance. The gate was – most unusually – closed, but when the gatekeeper saw it was me he opened it. My mother was watching from an upstairs window and when she saw me she was so relieved she clapped her hands, then burst into tears.'[8]

It was as though her son had returned from the dead.

Before going to bed that night, the boy looked out his old .22 rifle. Disappointed to find only one bullet left, he nevertheless loaded the rifle and slept with it by his side. All over Lhasa, people were doing likewise, determined to fight with what few resources they had, naïvely convinced that they would win.

Next morning, Tendzin Choegyal and his mother breakfasted on butter-tea and tsampa, talking of everyday matters, as though nothing untoward had happened. The charade ended at 7.30 when a driver arrived in one of Kundun's personal jeeps to take them to the Norbulingka. 'The Great Mother was quite calm,' Phuntsok Tashi recalls. 'She kept telling us not to worry. She was mainly concerned with making the proper arrangements for her seventy-year-old mother to be looked after.'[9] In fact, contingency plans for a possible escape had already been carefully drawn up, but all involved in the planning were sworn to the utmost secrecy. Phuntsok Tashi had made Tsering Dolma swear on oath that she would give no hint, not even to her closest friends, of what was afoot. She was to pack a few things, but discreetly, so that nobody might suspect that an escape was in the offing.

The pace of events began to accelerate. The Tibetan National Assembly in emergency session unanimously declared the 1951 Seventeen-Point Agreement to be null and void – the Chinese having breached almost every one of its clauses. Tibetan Army units which had been incorporated into the People's Liberation Army exchanged their Chinese uniforms for the old Tibetan khaki and distributed their surplus weapons to the crowds outside the Norbulingka.

Nervous householders were building stockades, covering their flat roofs with barbed wire, barricading themselves in with sandbags and sacks of salt; and though Kundun continued to plead for calm, everyone knew that the showdown was at hand. That evening, 'loudspeakers appeared on the roofs of buildings controlled by the Chinese. They announced that everyone should understand that all resistance to the Chinese occupation of Lhasa was futile. "You are like ants scratching at the elephant's feet," they said, "China is as mighty as the sun and wherever there is sun, there the Chinese are also."'[10] Over one hundred Chinese trucks converged on Lhasa from the west and east.

Next day, Kundun consulted the State Oracle:

To my astonishment, he shouted, 'Go! Go! Tonight!' The medium, still in his trance, then staggered forward and, snatching up some paper and a pen, wrote down, quite clearly and explicitly, the route that I should take out of the Norbulingka, down to the last Tibetan town on the Indian border...That done, the medium, a young monk named Lobsang Jigme, collapsed in a faint, signifying that [the god] had left his body. Just then, as if to reinforce the oracle's instructions, two mortar shells exploded...outside.[11]

'Until that morning, we had been in two minds about leaving,' recalls Phuntsok Tashi, 'but after the bombs exploded, we had no choice. I sent some people ahead to alert the guerrillas south of the river Kyi Chu.[12] 'I think the final decision to go was taken only hours before we left,' says Tendzin Choegyal. 'It was very hush-hush, and only a very few crucial people were in the secret. There were spies in the crowd who would have informed the Chinese about anything suspicious. In any case, if the Tibetans had known His Holiness was leaving, they'd all have tried to follow him and then there'd have been a bloodbath.'[13]

The sun was still shining, and they knew that if they were to have any hope of success, they must wait for darkness. That evening, one of the monk-officials on guard over the weapons store in the Norbulingka, noticed a man waiting beside an open-topped truck. 'This was very unusual. I asked what he was doing and he said vaguely he was just waiting for someone. I went back to the Norbulingka to collect some weapons and when I returned, the vehicle was no longer there. Then suddenly it re-appeared, with the cover down. I gaped as I saw His Holiness's tutors, the Gadung Oracle and various Kashag officials getting inside. They were leaving Lhasa, in a truck, hidden underneath a tarpaulin. I decided then and there it was time for me to go too.'[14]

It had been agreed that the party should split into small groups of three or four which would join up only after they had crossed the river Kyi Chu. Amala, Tsering Dolma and Tendzin Choegyal followed close behind, Amala wearing the green, fur-lined *chuba* of a Khampa man and a maroon hat with gold stitching. Tendzin Choegyal, who had found an old Luger pistol and managed to collect several bullets for it, had changed out of his monk's robes into a simple *chuba* and covered his shorn head with a woollen cap. When he saw his mother and sister dressed as Khampas, he burst out laughing.

The soldiers came, giving them the all-clear. It was, he remembers, about nine o'clock in the evening:

We went out into the cold March air and started to walk towards one of the gates which faced south. We just prayed that we wouldn't be seen as we crossed the courtyard. I have to say, we were very, very lucky. My mother, who had an arthritic knee, was offered a mule to ride on, but the rest of us walked until we came to the south bank of the river Kyi Chu. It was dark, with just a sliver of moon. When our eyes got used to the darkness, we could see the lights of the Chinese camp ahead of us. Fortunately, there was a wind blowing from the direction of the camp and I hoped it would muffle whatever noise we might be making.[15]

The 'wind' was one of those sandstorms by which Lhasa was habitually plagued. That night it probably saved their lives. The blinding sandstorm, wrote the usually sceptical Heinrich Harrer in *Life* magazine,[16] was 'so providentially timed that I found myself believing in a miraculous divine intervention'. Harrer, to whom Kundun told his story later, wrote that 'these sandstorms in Lhasa obliterate everything. You must close your eyes to avoid being blinded. You close your lips tight shut, yet still the sand gets into your teeth. When you are caught in such a storm you must just wrap your mantle right round you, covering your face and head and wait for it to pass.' This, suggests Harrer, is what the Chinese soldiers, in their garrison a mere two hundred yards to the south of the Norbulingka, must have done that night 'as the god-king moved invisibly through them'.

Small units of his personal bodyguard guarded the way to the river, with orders to draw off the Chinese fire in the event of an attack. 'It seemed like an eternity,' says Phuntsok Tashi. 'We kept mistaking the branches of trees for men. Fortunately the moon was not very bright and we had cloud cover. But we were so frightened, every time the clouds cleared we simply prayed for them to return.'[17] But the Chinese noticed nothing, as one after another, the small groups of Tibetans arrived at the far side of the river Kyi Chu. 'There was a stretch of sand and our feet sank into it as we walked, making progress terribly difficult,' remembers Tendzin Choegyal.

When we reached the river, we crossed it by the wooden ferry. You couldn't see anybody's face, but you could make out a lot of silhouettes moving up and down – and lots of horses. I walked by myself along the river bank until I could see the outline of my monastery, Drepung, in the distance, towards the north-west...I prostrated three times and prayed that I would see Drepung again before I died. Then I turned round and went back. A group of about thirty Khampa guerrilla fighters were waiting there with ponies for us all. Before we rode off, there was a tremendous commotion. I could hear voices shouting, 'He's come, here he is.' Then a figure rode up on horseback, wishing us all *Tashi Delek*, the greeting we generally reserve for New Year. I recognized the voice as that of Mr Phala, His Holiness's Chamberlain; and I knew then that His Holiness was safe and had gone ahead of us.[18]

Kundun was in an agony of spirit. Once the decision to go had been taken, he went to his chapel to pray before returning to his room and replacing his monk's robes with a soldier's uniform and fur cap. Exhausted and drained, he slung a rifle over his shoulder and removed his glasses to complete the disguise. Then, going out into the dark garden, he passed unnoticed through the Norbulingka gate. Throughout the ferry crossing he feared 'that every splash of the oars would draw machine-gun fire down on us', but he arrived safely on the opposite shore. The escape from Lhasa, one of the great epic stories of the twentieth century, was under way.

There are still those who argue that it should never have taken place, that the Dalai Lama was deserting his people in their hour of need. That argument, forceful enough to the Western mind, is meaningless to a Tibetan: it misunderstands the Dalai Lama's role, the fact that to Tibetans he is not just the ruler of Tibet but *is* Tibet; that if harm comes to him Tibet itself is finished. Given a choice, Kundun might well have chosen to stay and share his people's fate, but he too was reared in that tradition and had to bow to its logic. 'If I'd stayed in Lhasa, I don't suppose I'd have been left alive,' he says, 'the Chinese would have considered me expendable. But even if they had kept me alive, Tibet would have been finished.'[19]

The frequent criticisms infuriate Tendzin Choegyal: 'Those who say – or even think – such things have no idea what they're talking about. His Holiness could have done nothing for Tibet by staying. The Chinese would have increased their stranglehold just the same, all Tibetans would have been subjected to their power; we'd all have been slaves. They would have used His Holiness just as the Japanese used poor Pu Yi. That's what he would have become, another Pu Yi[20].'[21]

All that night and most of the next day, they rode towards the Brahmaputra River, which in Tibet is called the Tsang Po. Avoiding the well-worn south-westerly routes to India for fear of Chinese patrols, they headed south-east, to a vast area of pathless mountains, beyond which lay the main Himalayan range and India. By daybreak on the next morning they had reached the foot of the Che la, a 16,000-feet high Himalayan pass, which lay between them and the river. Ten hours after leaving the Norbu-lingka, they stopped for a first cup of steaming hot butter-tea before tack-ling the rigours of the high pass.

The climb to 16,000 feet over rocks and on horseback was exhausting and perilous. At the top, they dismounted and stood in the snow and ice to take a last sad farewell of Lhasa, before descending the steep sandy slopes on the other side. There is a saying in Tibet that if your horse will not carry you uphill, it is no horse, while if a man will not walk downhill to rest his horse he is no man.[22] Struggling through soft sand dunes blown up by storms from the river was particularly hard for Amala, says Tendzin Choegyal:

> Our horses would take one step up and slide back four. My mother was the worst sufferer. Her arthritic leg was hurting and she wasn't dressed very warmly. It wasn't too bad on the way up, but coming down at daybreak – on slippery, sandy slopes – we all had to dismount and walk, which was awful for her, with her arthritic knees. Two of our escort supported her between them one holding her left arm, the other her right, half lifting her off the ground, half dragging her along.

But however hard the going, his mother never lost her sense of humour and never complained:

> When we were negotiating those sandy slopes, for example, the going was very slippery. One of the members of our party was very fat and his saddle was almost sliding off his horse's back. He was hanging on to the mane for dear life, and my mother was convulsed with laughter.[23]

When finally they reached the level ground of the valley, another violent dust-storm blew up and almost blinded them.

Ten miles to the east was the Pentsha ferry, the only means of crossing the river – they could but pray the Chinese had not reached it first. Luck was with them and early in the morning on the second day they were rowed across in yak-hide coracles. Despite their exhaustion, they rode on, and the sun was already setting when for the first time in twenty-four hours they were able to stop and eat the tsampa, dried meat and dried cheese they had brought with them. There on the far side of the Tsang Po,

they were at last in the territory held by the Chushi Gangdrug, the Tibetan guerrillas. Phase One of the escape had been well handled by the
Palace party,[24] but from here on, the guerrillas would take charge. Rein-
forcements were waiting; the party swelled to one hundred, with an escort
of three hundred and fifty Tibetan soldiers and at least fifty guerrillas. 'We
had a radio link with our people in Lhasa, so we knew what was happening,' says Gyalo Thondup. 'At that time, the Resistance had more or less
stitched up the southern part of the country; no Chinese troops dared go
there. So as soon as His Holiness had crossed the river, our people were
there to meet him. I was the first to be informed that they had linked up. I
was very relieved when the message came through.'[25]

At the monastery of Rame, the travellers had their first night's rest.
Kundun had already been there for several hours when the rest of the family arrived. 'We went in,' says Tendzin Choegyal, 'and saw Kundun watching from a window facing the courtyard. I went straight up to see him. At
first he just stood there, wearing those unfamiliar layman's clothes, staring silently out of the window. Then he turned round and looked at me
and asked if I was tired. I said no. He turned to the window again and said
slowly, "Tendzin, do you realize we're free now?"'[26]

Breaking into separate groups to avoid detection from the air, and
watched over by relays of devoted guerrillas, they left Rame next morning
to cross the Sabo Pass. Kundun took Tendzin Choegyal under his wing, believing that his mother and sister would make better speed without him.
The boy was proud to be travelling with his brother; his Luger pistol was
pressing painfully into his hip-bone, but he would not remove it from its
place of honour on his belt. Thus armed – with a dagger in his belt for good
measure – he believed himself a match for any would-be attacker. Unfortunately for his romantic self-image, the aspiring hero was given Kundun's
umbrella to carry!

Each day small bands of guerrillas, many of them tough Khampa giants,
festooned with pistols, swords, daggers and charm-boxes, would appear
from nowhere to protect their advance. At this stage, the plan was for
Kundun to establish a temporary base at the hill-top fort of Lhuntse
Dzong, sixty miles north of the Indian border, from where he could negoti-
ate with the Chinese about the future of Tibet. So far, they had heard no
news on the battery-operated radio receiver they carried with them: Radio
Lhasa had gone dead. At one stopping-place, they picked up a Voice of
America bulletin which spoke of unrest in Lhasa and indicated that the

Dalai Lama's whereabouts were uncertain; but that was all. They continued to push forward to Lhuntse Dzong, battling with fierce blizzards, crossing high passes every day, some as high as 19,000 feet and encrusted with ice and snow. On 24 March, a broadcast confirmed Kundun's worst fears: two days after they had left Lhasa, the Chinese had shelled the Norbulingka – and opened fire on the crowds milling around it; then had turned their heavy artillery on the city, the Potala, the Jokhang and the main monasteries. Only later would they learn the terrible truth that, after three days of bitter fighting, Lhasa had been reduced to a smoking ruin, with thousands of dead and wounded lying in its wreckage; and thousands more on their way to years of imprisonment in the Chinese Gulag. They heard then that the Chinese still did not know the Dalai Lama had left, and were frantically searching for him among the dead round the Norbulingka. (Whether to kill or capture him was unclear.) Ploughing their way through the piled-up corpses outside the palace, the Chinese soldiers had examined each one, calling out 'Dalai Lama, Dalai Lama' as they did so.

Kundun heard all this in a daze of disbelief and horror. Why, he wondered, had the Chinese responded with such mindless ferocity to the people's heart-felt protest? He could think of only one possible reason:

> Our people – not especially our rich or ruling classes, but our ordinary people – had finally, eight years after the invasion began, convinced the Chinese that they would never willingly accept their alien rule. So the Chinese were trying now to terrify them, by merciless slaughter, to accept this rule against their will.[27]

What he did not know until years later was that when Mao was told that order had been restored in Lhasa, the Chairman had asked: 'And what of the Dalai Lama?' Told that Kundun had escaped, he sighed heavily and said, 'In that case we have lost the battle.'[28]

Tendzin Choegyal was horror-struck by the news from Lhasa. 'I had never for one moment doubted we would win,' he says, 'but when we heard that the Norbulingka had been bombarded and that so many Chinese troops were involved, it came as a terrible shock. It was impossible to absorb.'[29]

On the twenty-eighth, Chou En-lai announced the dissolution of the Tibetan Government and its replacement by the Provisional Committee. The old Tibet was thus officially declared dead.

Further negotiation with the Chinese was clearly out of the question, and nowhere, not even Lhuntse Dzong, would afford them a safe haven. The Chinese, realizing at last that Kundun had escaped, had already crossed the Tsang Po in force, and PLA troops had been ordered to find and block off all escape-routes from southern Tibet to India. It was time for quick thinking. With his options running out, Kundun, in a brief ceremony at Lhuntse Dzong, formally re-established his Government – then sent a small group of the fittest men ahead to India with an urgent request to Prime Minister Nehru for political asylum.

When they set off again next day, two of the highest, most inaccessible passes had still to be faced. It would take them many days more in diabolical weather. On the summit of the Lagoe la Pass, a violent snowstorm hit them; their fingers and hands were numb with cold; their eyebrows and moustaches froze to their faces. They did not have enough warm clothing and the only way to keep their blood from freezing was to dismount and lead their ponies with hands that nearly froze to the reins. As an additional worry, there was very little food left for the exhausted pack animals.

By midday, they had crossed the Pass and after a brief stop for bread, hot water and condensed milk, found their way to the village of Jhora where they rejoined Amala and Tsering Dolma who had travelled by another route. Next day, on the Karpo la, the last high pass before India, they were first buffeted by snow and wind, then, when the sun came out, almost blinded by snow-glare. They protected their faces from the glare with strips of cloth or with their long braided hair. Then, just when they thought the worst was over and sat down with relief to eat their midday meal, a fierce dust-storm whirled over their heads. As they neared the highest point of the Karpo la, out of the blue, a plane appeared directly above them. 'We didn't know whether it was Chinese or from another country,' says Tendzin Choegyal, 'but it flew directly overhead and it couldn't fail to have seen us, hundreds of men and horses on the pure white snow.' Badly shaken, the Tibetans scattered, fearing that the Chinese now exactly knew where they were and would soon be in hot pursuit. 'The mountain was covered with snow and we knew we could all be seen very clearly,' said a monk-official. 'We got down from our ponies. Too late we realized that the horse-blankets were red and would be all too visible from the air. His Holiness told us to reverse the blankets and keep going.'[30]

They journeyed on for two more days, convinced that all was lost. They endured another dust-storm, another exposure to the blinding glare of the snow, before beginning their slow descent, down to the steaming rain-forests that covered the lower approaches to India. On the way, Kundun received the welcome news that the Indian Government was willing to grant him asylum.

In the tiny village of Mangmang, the last outpost of Tibet, the weather chose to wreak its final fury on them. The rain fell in stair-rods, forcing the exhausted Tibetans to erect tents for shelter. Kundun's tent leaked and, as the night wore on, his flimsy bedding got more and more sodden, no matter where he tried to move it. Tendzin Choegyal was with him: 'The water ran in rivulets down the inside of the tent. The fever he'd been fighting off for days developed into a chill and then into dysentery. I watched him become weak and ill.'[31]

By morning he was too ill to go on, so his friends moved him to a small house nearby. This provided scarcely more protection than the tent; it was dirty and black with smoke, and beneath him, all night long, the cattle lowed incessantly. All that day and the next night he tossed in fever. But the following day brought news that Chinese troops were converging on a village nearby, and the need to move on became urgent. This last day in Tibet, knowing that by next morning he would have crossed the border into exile was, says Kundun, one of the unhappiest times of his life. The time for goodbyes had come: 'With a heavy heart, I said goodbye to the group of people who had acted as my escort: my personal bodyguard, soldiers, officials, including some quite important ones. They were staying behind to face the Chinese forces. In other words, they were returning to face almost certain death. They expressed such unselfish devotion. They said they could not serve me in India, where they did not know the language or the way of life, but what they could and must do was stay and fight the Chinese. They said that next day the Dalai Lama would enter India safely and that therefore they had fulfilled their responsibility. Now they must go back. That was an inexpressibly sad moment. I had known some of them for many years, others for just a few years, some for only a few weeks. But they had all become like old friends. Now not only were they leaving, but we all knew in our hearts that many of them would be killed. I was filled with admiration for their courage and their loyalty.'[32]

As he was too ill to ride a horse, his companions placed him on the broad back of a *dzo*[33] and on this lowly beast of burden, 'in a daze of sickness and weariness and unhappiness deeper than I can express', on 31 March 1959 he was carried out of Tibet – and into an uncertain future.

NOTES

1. Jamyang Norbu, 'The Tibetan Resistance Movement', *Resistance and Reform in Tibet*, ed. Barnett & Akiner.
2. Author interview with HH the Dalai Lama, Dharamsala, July 1995.
3. Author interview with HH the Dalai Lama, Dharamsala, July 1995.
4. Rinchen Dolma Taring, *Daughter of Tibet*.
5. Goodman, *The Last Dalai Lama*, p. 286.
6. Author interview with HH the Dalai Lama, Dharamsala, June 1994.
7. Author interview with Tendzin Choegyal, Dharamsala, June 1994.
8. Author interview with Tendzin Choegyal, Dharamsala, June 1994.
9. From the Memoirs of Phuntsok Tashi Taklha (published in Tibetan only).
10. Philippa Russell and Sonam Lhamo Singeri, 'The Tibetan Women's Uprising', in the journal *Cho Yang: The Voice of Tibetan Religion and Culture* 5.
11. Fourteenth Dalai Lama, *Freedom in Exile*, chapter 7.
12. Author interview with Phuntsok Tashi Taklha, London, 1993.
13. Author interview with Tendzin Choegyal, October 1993.
14. Author interview with monk-official, Dharamsala, June 1994.
15. Author interview with Tendzin Choegyal, Dharamsala, June 1994.
16. Heinrich Harrer, 'The Miraculous Escape of the Dalai Lama', *Life*, 4 May 1959.
17. Author interview with Phuntsok Tashi, London 1993.
18. Author interview with Tendzin Choegyal, Dharamsala, June 1994.
19. Author interview with HH the Dalai Lama, Dharamsala, June 1994.
20. Pu Yi. The last (child) Emperor of Imperial China. Deposed in 1912 and was later used by the invading Japanese as puppet leader of the newly-formed state of Manchukuo. He was later imprisoned by the Communist Chinese and died a broken man.
21. Author interview with Tendzin Choegyal, Dharamsala, June 1994.
22. Heinrich Harrer, 'The Miraculous Escape of the Dalai Lama'.
23. Author interviews with Tendzin Choegyal, Dharamsala, 1990, 1993.
24. Mr Ghadrang; the Lord Chamberlain, Mr Phala; and Phuntsok Tashi.
25. Author interview with Gyalo Thondup, New Delhi, July 1995.
26. Author interview with Tendzin Choegyal, Dharamsala, June 1994.
27. Fourteenth Dalai Lama, *My Land and My People*, chapter 11.
28. *Freedom in Exile*, chapter 13.
29. Author interview with Tendzin Choegyal, October 1993.
30. Author interview with monk-official, Dharamsala, October 1993.
31. Author interview with Tendzin Choegyal, May 1991.
32. Author interview with HH the Dalai Lama, Dharamsala, June 1994.
33. Animal rather like an ox.

18

Fugitives

Now, where a society has existed for hundreds and hundreds
of years – it may have outlasted its utility but the fact is – uprooting it is a terribly painful process. It can be uprooted slowly, it can be changed even with rapidity, but with a measure of
co-operation. But any kind of forcible uprooting must neces-
sarily be painful, whether it is a good society or a bad society.
Nehru speaking on Tibet in the Indian Parliament,
27 April 1959

Amala, Tsering Dolma and Tendzin Choegyal went on ahead of Kundun,
with an escort of Gurkhas, down through the dripping jungles of Assam.
The contrast with the dry, light air of the Tibetan plateau underlined
with cruel force that they were exiles without a home. Choegyal has
often reflected that in those first days he was a typical refugee – 'all I
had were the clothes I stood up in, my drinking-bowl, my gun, and Kundun's umbrella'.

For the moment, his main emotion was bitter disappointment: 'I had
had two beautiful torches which I treasured. They even had new batteries
in them. That first night in India, I took them out and put them between
cushions so that they'd be easily accessible. But next morning, we were in
such a hurry to pack up and leave that I forgot them. I was devastated.'[1]

Such minor troubles were forgotten, however, five days later, when they
reached Tawang, in the North-East Frontier Agency territory (NEFA).[2]

Here, at India's largest Buddhist Monastery, they were welcomed by three hundred monks and a vast crowd of tribesmen.

Indian Air Force planes flew in low over a large meadow outside the town and dropped supplies: 'The Indians were extremely efficient and there was nothing half-hearted about their reception of us,' applauds Choegyal.

All sorts of things were provided, food, clothing, medical supplies. We were wearing fur hats and fur-lined chubas in that terrible damp heat, so we needed lighter clothes. I remember our officials asking the Indian Government for more suitable head-gear and they air-lifted crates of trilbies for us. Sometimes the parachute didn't open and you could see the black shape hurtling down to the ground. When it was oil-drums that were dropped they exploded with the force of a bomb, it made a horrible mess – I used to love watching it [3]

The planes flew in every third day. Choegyal discarded his fur-lined Tibetan *chuba* and, even more reluctantly, his pistol. He liked Tawang, 'it was beautiful, on a hill, undulating rather than rugged, surrounded by meadows and evergreen forests'. The weather was pleasant and every day he would stroll around to see how everyone was getting on and catch up on the latest gossip. He had brought five Tibetan silver coins from Lhasa, and exchanging these for twenty-five Indian rupees, 'went into the military canteen and bought a jar of jam, a packet of cream crackers, a packet of butter, and started having a feast'.

From Tawang, they travelled by pony along a bridle path towards the formidable 14,500-feet high Se la Pass, skirting the pass at 9,600 feet above Bomdila, the administrative centre of the area. Here Kundun joined them and was greeted by high officials and by thousands of tribesmen who came in their best finery and danced in his honour. Bomdila, says Choegyal, was 'ugly and full of dust'; but it was there that Kundun received a formal telegram of welcome from Mr Nehru:

MY COLLEAGUES AND I WELCOME YOU AND SEND GREETINGS ON YOUR SAFE ARRIVAL IN INDIA. WE SHALL BE HAPPY TO AFFORD THE NECESSARY FACILITIES TO YOU, YOUR FAMILY AND ENTOURAGE TO RESIDE IN INDIA. THE PEOPLE OF INDIA, WHO HOLD YOU IN GREAT VENERATION, WILL NO DOUBT ACCORD THEIR TRADITIONAL RESPECT TO YOUR PERSONAGE. KIND REGARDS. NEHRU[4]

Choegyal recalls a splendid high tea at the home of the District Commissioner: 'They gave us *rasgulas*, a very sweet and spongy cheese; and they sang Indian songs.' Encouraged by this warm reception, Kundun lingered in Bomdila for a few days, before continuing on his journey. On 18 April the party drove in a cavalcade of jeeps through the forests which shelter Bomdila from the plains. At the road-camp of Foothills, the Indian public caught their first glimpse of the exiled ruler as he alighted from his jeep, followed by his mother, sister, brother, and about seventy Tibetans, among whom were all that remained of his Government. With Indian soldiers providing a guard of honour, he walked across a makeshift carpet of tarpaulins to the camp overseer's cottage where he breakfasted on cornflakes, poached eggs, toast, and fresh bananas.

Much excitement was caused by the arrival of Gyalo Thondup. The latter, says Choegyal, 'wept for joy when he caught sight of us. It was a very moving reunion, and we were all very happy.'⁵ Gyalo Thondup accompanied them to Tezpur, a railway junction thirty miles away. Choegyal loved Tezpur – 'the lush green foliage, Indian bearers in their white uniforms, fans whirring. There was plenty to eat. It had everything, colour, sound, smell, excitement. It really raised our spirits.'

Among the waiting crowds was Heinrich Harrer, apprehensive lest Kundun might not recognize him: it had been eight years since they met. 'I need not have worried,' he reported.⁶

> As the jeep reached me, he waved and smiled in delighted recognition. Then, as he dismounted, my anxiety turned to astonishment. He had grown so tall. And when he greeted me as *trogpo*, friend, his voice, which was just beginning a boyish break when I left Lhasa, was rich and deep. I was surprised, too, at seeing him with spectacles in public, although I had myself suggested that he get them when he was fifteen. In those days he had disliked wearing them, for in Tibet wearing spectacles [was] thought to be a foreign affectation.

Kundun received hundreds of messages, telegrams, letters and cards in Tezpur. Heartened by all the expressions of good will, he felt he must lose no time in telling the world about Tibet. Accordingly he composed a third-person statement to be read out jointly by an Indian and a Tibetan official, summarizing the key events: that the 1951 Seventeen-Point Agreement with the Chinese had been signed under duress; that his Government had been stripped of all power; that broken promises and religious persecution had finally forced him to flee; and that – despite Chinese claims that he had been abducted by rampaging Khampa tribesmen – he had left Lhasa entirely of his own free will. He voiced his unhappiness over the fate of

Tibet, while allowing himself to hope that the situation could be saved without further bloodshed.

A few hours later, Kundun boarded a special Indian Railways steam train for a three-day journey to Dehra Dun, eighteen miles from the former British hill station of Mussoorie, where the Indian Government had provided a house for him.

When Lobsang Samten had chosen not to return to Tibet in 1957, he had convalesced for a while in India, before joining Norbu in New York. 'He felt a bit insecure at first, but he soon settled down,' says Norbu, who had obtained an invitation for Lobsang to enter Georgetown University in Washington. Norbu himself was shortly afterwards invited to the 1958 World Congress of Buddhists in Bangkok, and was able, *en route*, to satisfy an old longing to visit the Buddhist shrines of Thailand, Burma and Ceylon. On his way back home, in early 1959, he visited Gyalo Thondup in Darjeeling – and discovered at last the vocation his restless spirit had been seeking. Ever since his return from Tibet in 1952, Gyalo Thondup and his wife (now called by a Tibetan name, Dekyi Dolkar), had been watching events in Tibet closely, and through the Tibetan Welfare Committee had helped care for the many refugees from Chinese rule. There were so many of them in Darjeeling and Kalimpong that by the end of the Fifties they had become a serious problem: the Welfare Committee could no longer meet even their most basic needs. Worse still, because of its identification with the Tibetan guerrillas after 1956, the Committee was an embarrassment to a nation determined on friendship with Communist China. Gyalo Thondup needed to look elsewhere for funds.

Norbu was just the man he needed, and his brother responded eagerly. Returning to the US via Europe, in both continents he approached powerful institutions and welfare organizations to persuade them to help the refugees. The timing was opportune – 1959 was World Refugee Year – and before long, the first consignments of tents, blankets and tinned foods had been despatched by World Church Services to the destitute Tibetans in Kalimpong.

Norbu found willing helpers at every turn and was grateful to be able at last to help his compatriots. One evening in mid-March 1959 he was in the kitchen of his New York apartment, preparing a Tibetan soup for supper and idly listening to the radio, when suddenly he was transfixed by the announcement of an uprising in Tibet. Leaving the soup to boil over, he heard reports of violent disturbances in Lhasa, of thousands of people surrounding the Norbulingka Palace to prevent the Chinese from kidnapping His Holiness. Norbu was shaken to the core. 'I stood there with my mind in a whirl. What I had most feared for many years had come about at last.' A few days earlier he had been alarmed by an article in *Time* magazine, prophesying an imminent showdown between Tibetans and Chinese. Since then he had been praying that Kundun and the rest of his family would be safe. But now the worst seemed to have happened.

> What was going to happen now? The lives of my relatives were obviously in the greatest danger. Would they be able to escape? The Dalai Lama, I knew, was young, vigorous and in good health, he would be quite capable of the fatigues of any journey. On the other hand, the Chinese would clearly move heaven and earth to prevent his escape? Was he even still at liberty? My mother was already sixty years old, and Tendzin Choegyal…was still a child. All in all, I was worried by the most disagreeable imaginings, and there was no question of sleep for me that night.'

He rang Lobsang Samten in Washington. He too was frantic at the news and arranged to join his brother in New York that very night. To calm his nerves, Norbu tried telephoning various friends, but couldn't handle their well-meant sympathy. Rejecting sundry offers of a meal or a bed for the night, he sat by the radio set in nail-biting silence, waiting for each and every news bulletin. When Lobsang Samten arrived, the brothers tried to calm each other's fears but succeeded only in making them worse – the sense of events lurching out of control induced panic. At about midnight, when the newsboys began to shout special editions of the newspapers in the streets, Norbu 'rushed out and bought every newspaper I could get hold of in the hope of obtaining further news'. But though they devoured every single line, they learned nothing more.

As the days went by, they nearly suffocated with anxiety, the sporadic news bulletins – vague, confused and contradictory – offering no relief at all. Bombarded by conflicting rumours, they swung wildly between hope and despair. Only after days of unendurable suspense did news reach them that Kundun and his entourage had crossed safely into India. The brothers collapsed with relief. 'We were just so happy,' says Norbu simply. They sent a telegram to Kundun, via Gyalo Thondup in Darjeeling; and Norbu determined to go to India as soon as possible.

Kundun was a hero to the Indian people. His journey by train to Dehra Dun was a triumphal progress, with enormous crowds thronging the route, blocking the track, shouting greetings. It was, reported *Life*, 'a procession through adoring throngs, caught between joy at his safety and anger at his enemies. Indians as well as expatriate Tibetans honoured him with smoking incense, fanfares of horns and thousands of traditional homespun scarves thrown in his path.'[8]

What a dramatic contrast to the anguished weeks he had recently spent as a fugitive! Three times, at Siliguri, Benares and Lucknow, Kundun left his carriage to address 'huge, impromptu meetings of flower-throwing well-wishers'. Siliguri was packed with Tibetan exiles from Kalimpong and Darjeeling, among them Gyalo Thondup's wife, Dekyi Dolkar, with Pema, Tenzin Ngawang and Khando, all of them weeping for joy. They had known for some time that the situation in Tibet was grave. 'At Gyalo Thondup's house,' says Pema, then nineteen and in her last year at school, 'we had been aware of an unusual amount of activity. Everyone looked scared. They tried to reassure us, but we became very frightened for Amala, for my sister and her husband, for Tendzin Choegyal and for His Holiness. I trembled at the thought that their lives were in danger.' The Loreto nuns had rounded up all the newspapers they could find for Pema and Khando and morning and evening had the whole school praying 'for Pema's family'. 'The whole school was involved in our anxiety,' Pema remembers,[9] 'Khando and I were so worried, we couldn't sleep, couldn't eat.' 'One day,' adds Khando, 'the nuns told us we were leaving immediately, a car was coming to pick us up and take us home. At home, Uncle Thondup warned us there would be a lot of newspaper people asking questions and we weren't to tell them anything. Well, what could we have told them, we knew nothing ourselves? I remember that Uncle Thondup was very nervous, he had no idea whether our family would succeed in escaping. Then came the wonderful news that they had escaped into India. The relief was overwhelming.'[10] Gyalo Thondup had set off immediately to meet his brother.

As Kundun's train drew into Siliguri station, a shout of joy went up. 'The carriage door opened,' writes Pema, 'the bodyguard got out, and suddenly there was His Holiness, thin and haggard. He looked exhausted and care-worn. The few steps dividing me from him seemed endless. I offered him a *kata*, received his blessing, and then I was literally thrown into the train by the bodyguard. At last I could embrace Amala, my sister and my brothers. For the first time in three years we were together.'[11] The practical

Dekyi Dolkar had brought along a change of clothing for them all, and food, both fresh and canned. 'We had lost everything,' wrote Pema, 'but I was so happy they were all alive that nothing else mattered. Nevertheless, it was at that moment that I realized that for us a new life was beginning, a life of exiles and political refugees.'

Two hours later, despite their protests, Pema, Tenzin Ngawang and Khando, were packed off back to school in Darjeeling. They had, after all, been given only one day's leave.

Mussoorie was about an hour's drive from Dehra Dun. There, at Birla House, the home of a multi-millionaire Indian industrialist, Kundun's epic 1,500-mile journey at last came to an end.

But he was not to be left in peace. The Chinese were incandescent with outrage over his Tezpur statement. A New China News Agency report, referring to it as 'a crude document, lame in reasoning, full of lies and loopholes' insisted that it had been fabricated 'by foreign imperialists', since 'everyone knew' the revolt was the work of an 'upper strata reactionary clique' by whom the Dalai Lama had been abducted. A lengthy editorial in the Peking *People's Daily*[12] claimed that the Chinese military action was justified in order to liberate the Tibetan people from the horrors of their old feudal society, and that the Tibetans had longed for the kind of 'peaceful revolution' that the Chinese had brought. Asserting that the aforementioned 'reactionary clique' had murdered Regent Reting by strangling him in prison, they rather intriguingly went on to claim the Dalai Lama's father as another innocent martyr for their cause. 'The father of the present Fourteenth Dalai Lama, now in Mussoorie,' continued the editorial, darkly, 'because of his patriotic ideas, was poisoned by reactionaries who had connections with foreign countries, in order to facilitate their control over the Dalai Lama.' Both these 'notorious crimes', apparently, had been 'committed by stooges of foreign interventionists within the ruling clique'.[13] (According to a young Tibetan then studying at the Peking Institute of National Minorities, the students were assured that 'the chief trouble-maker' was Gyalo Thondup, who was 'colluding with American Imperialists and foreign reactionaries'.)[14]

Whether or not Kundun had yet seen the Peking *People's Daily*, he was certainly stung by the News Agency report and promptly issued another statement – in the first person this time – in which he stood by his earlier words. 'It astonished me yet again,' he wrote in his memoirs, 'to see how the Chinese blamed everyone they could think of for the revolt – like an injured dog which snaps at everybody...They could not allow themselves to recognize the truth: that it was the people themselves, whom the Chinese claimed to be liberating, who had revolted spontaneously against their liberation, and that the ruling class of Tibet had been far more willing than the people to come to agreement.'[15]

The Chinese reaction put Nehru on the spot. His decision to offer political asylum to the Dalai Lama had been well-received at home: when he told the Indian Parliament of the Dalai Lama's safe arrival, they stood up and cheered. Given the popular mood, Nehru could scarcely have acted otherwise. The snag was that he was still obsessed with the idea of friendship with China, even though the Chinese conquest of Tibet had laid the northern areas of India itself open to Chinese attack. Already embarrassed by the Tibetan Welfare groups in Darjeeling and Kalimpong, he now felt threatened by the fall-out from his decision to stand by a friend in need. In a debate on the Tibetan situation in the Indian Parliament in April, he tried to have it both ways, deploring on the one hand the Chinese predilection for clichés such as 'upper strata reactionary clique' – 'The attempt to explain a situation by the use of rather worn-out words, phrases and slogans is seldom helpful,' he observed.[16] On the other hand, he anxiously reassured the Chinese that his support for the Dalai Lama was a purely humanitarian act, and that the Tibetan leader would not be allowed to make political capital out of the situation.

As soon as Kundun was installed at Birla House – it did not take long, since all his belongings were in four trunks – Nehru came to call. He was affable enough and the two 'old friends' posed smiling for a photograph; but he told his guest bluntly that India would never recognize his Government, nor support the cause of Tibetan independence. Kundun was dismayed, but, not wishing to antagonize Nehru, agreed to be discreet in his public utterances.

For two months he kept the low profile demanded of him. Until, that is, a second wave of refugees started pouring in, thousands of men, women and children, streaming over the Himalaya to Bhutan, Sikkim, Nepal and India, bringing with them tales of horror to curdle the blood. Not only of forced collectivization, class warfare, political re-education, but of mass imprisonments, executions and inhuman atrocities carried out by the new Military Control Commissions which now ruled Tibet. The Chinese had consolidated their position throughout Tibet, replacing the Dalai Lama with their own tame puppet, the Panchen Lama, and warning the rebellious Lhasans to surrender or die. As Kundun would later testify to the International Commission of Jurists:

> Tens of thousands of our people have been killed, not only in military actions, but individually and deliberately. They have been killed, without trial, on suspicion of opposing communism, or of hoarding money, or for no reason at all. But mainly and fundamentally they have been killed because they would not renounce their religion. They have not only been shot, but beaten to death, crucified, burned alive, drowned, vivisected, starved, strangled, hanged, scalded, buried alive, disembowelled and beheaded.[17]

This was the 'peaceful liberation' brought by the Chinese. By the end of June, nearly 20,000 ragged, destitute refugees had arrived, driven from Tibet by starvation and terror. For the most part they were the landless peasants, nomads and yeoman farmers the Chinese claimed to have liberated but whose lives they had instead destroyed. They had braved the terrors of the high uncharted peaks and the ever-vigilant Chinese patrols; and many of those who had set out had died in the attempt. The escape routes were littered with corpses, bullet-ridden, wounded, snow-blinded, starved or frozen to death. The survivors were now on the low-lying plains of India at the start of the hottest season of the year; and the injections given them by the Indian authorities against cholera and typhoid served only to increase their miseries.

This fresh evidence that the Chinese intended to wipe out every trace of the old Tibet was the last straw for Kundun. Anguish for his tortured country overrode his promise to Nehru, made him break his silence and beseech the outside world for help. On 20 June, with obvious emotion he addressed a crowd of international journalists. Once more declaring the Seventeen-Point Agreement to be null and void, he told them of the attempted extermination of his people, their religion and their culture, and he pleaded for an international commission to investigate the atrocities so consistently reported by all the refugees.

That evening, the Indian Government formally refused recognition to the Dalai Lama's Government-in-Exile.

But Kundun's appeal for a commission of inquiry was heard. The International Commission of Jurists – a respected body of lawyers – launched an investigation in July 1959 and a year later concluded that Tibet had indeed been a sovereign and independent nation before the Chinese invasion; and that the atrocity accounts were true. China, the lawyers accused, was guilty of 'the gravest crime of which any person or nation can be accused – the intent to destroy, in whole or in part, a national, ethnic, racial or religious group as such'.[18] Guilty, in other words, of genocide.

Emboldened by the Jurists' report, Kundun tried again with the United Nations. His efforts were partially rewarded: Ireland and Malaya co-sponsored the Tibetan case which was debated at length at the fourteenth session of the UN General Assembly in October 1959. But, predictably, the monolithic Soviet bloc insisted that Tibet was nobody's business but China's and accused Tibet's sponsors of fabricating a 'non-existent Tibetan question' in order to stir the pot of the Cold War. As stirring the pot was something that Britain and the USA would go to any lengths to avoid, the issue of Tibet's sovereignty was cravenly shelved. Tibet's cause foundered on the impotence and moral cowardice of the West. A resolution was adopted, however, expressing grave concern at the forcible denial of basic human rights and freedoms in Tibet and called for these rights – and the distinctive Tibetan way of life – to be respected.

It was better than nothing, perhaps, but it was hardly likely to make China tremble.

In June, Kundun received a visit from Norbu and Gyalo Thondup. Norbu, attending a conference on Tibet in Tokyo, had been drumming up support for the Tibetan cause. A few days later, Gyalo Thondup met him at Delhi airport and drove him to Mussoorie. The brothers arrived early one morning, but were held up for several hours outside the town by a road block set up by the Indian authorities to keep 'undesirable elements' away from Kundun's weekly audiences. When their identity was established, they set off for Birla House, amazed by the crowds:

> The closer we came to Birla House, the bigger the crowds grew until in the
> end they were so dense we had to leave the car and make our way forward on
> foot. We were met in the garden of Birla House by Tendzin Choegyal who ran
> up to us excitedly and embraced us warmly. He then accompanied us indoors
> where the Dalai Lama was waiting for us on the staircase to take us into his
> private apartments. I was about to prostrate myself before him, as I had always been accustomed to do, and to present the usual *kata*, when with a gesture of the hand he indicated that I should not do so here. Wordlessly he

pointed to a *thangka* with a picture of the Buddha Shakyamuni; and deeply moved I laid my good-luck scarf over it. Henceforth our reverential greetings were to honour the Buddhas alone; from now on the Dalai Lama regarded himself only as the first fugitive among his oppressed people.[19]

When it was time for Kundun to show himself to the crowds outside, Norbu went in search of his mother. He knew she would be grieving for Tibet, and for her old mother who had been left in Lhasa with one of his aunts. He found her standing at the window, looking out at the crowds, and as Norbu went to her side she quietly took his hand:

My mother was the first to break the silence: 'Jigme-la,' she said in a low voice, using my childhood name for the first time in many years, 'Jigme-la, from now on we are refugees too.'

I led her back into the room and sat down beside her. The consoling words I wanted to say did not come so easily. Yes, of course, we were all in safety; and we could rely on a certain amount of assistance; but we had lost our country. The enemies of our religion and our way of life had the upper hand there now, and they were intent on destroying everything that we held dear. Our people were forced to bow their backs to the oppressors, and those who refused to do so, lost their lives or were carried off to forced labour. How many of our friends had already suffered so harsh a fate! Many of them had been killed, and others had disappeared, never to be heard of again.[20]

Unable to find words of comfort, mother and son lapsed into silence.

Kundun, however, was a little consoled by Norbu's assurance that people everywhere were anxious to help the Tibetan refugees. In the weeks that followed, he sent his brother to visit the transit camps in Northern India and report back on the condition of the refugees. Together they worked out a plan of campaign, and Norbu was glad to have Kundun's backing for his work. Both of them realized that the stream of refugees would soon become a deluge. And then what would the Indian Government do? Anxiety gave them sleepless nights.

August found Norbu in Vienna, to put Kundun's case at an International Youth Congress. There he sought out Heinrich Harrer, and, in view of the great interest all over the world in the Dalai Lama and the Tibetan refugees, the two old friends decided to collaborate on a book about Norbu's own experiences.[21] But work on it would have to wait, as Norbu must first of all go to Switzerland, to meet a Swiss industrialist, Dr Charles Aeschimann, who was already implementing a plan to bring Tibetan children to the

Pestalozzi Children's Village near St Gallen, founded during World War II to care for war orphans. And as similar children's Homes existed in Germany, Britain and France, Norbu doggedly set off to rustle up support there too. Tibetan children were to be selected in India and sent to these Children's Villages in Europe.

The last visitor to Mussoorie was perhaps the most longed for: Lobsang Samten, the companion of his childhood. Kundun was overcome by emotion: 'When I learned that Lobsang was to come next day, I felt tremendously excited. When he actually came, we just stood and looked at each other for some moments without words. I shed no tears, but my eyes must have betrayed the depth of my emotion. As for Lobsang, the tears were rolling freely down his face.'[11]

As the refugees continued to pour in, Kundun could only mourn his powerlessness to help them. They were being accommodated in primitive conditions in two transit camps, Missamari in the steamy heat of Assam, and Buxa Duar, a former British POW camp further west, in Bengal. Hugh Richardson who visited all the refugee areas between February and April 1960, admired the patience and good humour of the Tibetans in Missamari, twelve thousand of them, living in three hundred bamboo huts. 'It was a horrible place,' he says, 'dusty, no decent water, and they were living in makeshift bamboo shanties.' Richardson had taken a number of statements from the refugees. 'Many of them were people I'd actually known in Tibet and knew to be honest. Their statements were utterly consistent, but the Press refused to believe them.' Most of the cynical Western journalists dismissed the atrocity stories as the whinings of a dispossessed privileged class. To the refugees, this scepticism on the part of the newspapermen (and intellectuals) was a crushing blow, compounding their bewilderment and shock. They had lost their homes, their families and everything they held dear in the most violent of circumstances; they were suffering from humidity, heat-stroke, lack of sanitation and from an unfamiliar diet, as a result of which an outbreak of amoebic dysentery was carrying them off in droves. And journalists, either indifferent or unwilling to believe ill of China's revolutionary social experiment, would not even listen to what they had to say.

The monks and lamas, most of whom were in Buxa Duar camp, were the worst off, housed in thirty concrete barracks, surrounded by high barbed-wire fences. 'It was very unhealthy there, and lots of the monks died of cholera, malaria, dysentery and hepatitis,' says Tendzin Choegyal. 'Apart from the health hazards, they had no electricity, no lamps. Some of them bought kerosene and made wicks, so that they'd have some kind of lamp to read the Scriptures by. But the lamps gave out poisonous smoke and the monks breathed in the fumes. As a result, many of them died from TB – the death-rate was extremely high.' Yet from the survivors of Buxa Duar came many of the scholar-monks who would one day spread a knowledge of Tibetan Buddhism throughout the West.

In Darjeeling, on the site of the house where the Great Thirteenth had passed his exile, Gyalo Thondup's wife Dekyi Dolkar set up a Self-Help Centre, where the refugees could help preserve the traditional arts and crafts of Tibet, while providing employment for themselves either as craftsmen or retail salesmen. With the help of foreign relief organizations, this provided a model for a series of centres which sprang up in the hill-districts of northern India, supporting traditional handicrafts dominated by carpet-weaving.

This kind of self-help programme would eventually be the salvation of the Tibetans. Most of them were illiterate and for the present were glad to be paid a few rupees a day for working on the new military roads being built by the Indian Government in the relatively cooler Himalayan areas to the north. The work was hard but at least the high-altitude climate was more bearable than the torrid heat of the plains; and in earning their own keep they were able to regain some of their lost self-respect.

In Tibet itself, the mainly Khampa guerrillas of the National Volunteer Defence Army did not immediately give up the struggle. But with the Chinese pouring troops and equipment into the area and sealing off the borders, the odds were hopelessly unequal. Three weeks and many deaths later, their field commander, Gompo Tashi Andrugtsang, shut down his HQ in the mountains of Southern Tibet and crossed into India to continue the fight from there. He went to see Gyalo Thondup in Darjeeling, and the two men sought ways of directing Tibetan resistance into more effective channels.

Kundun, realistically accepting that there would be no early return to Tibet, had somehow to assure the survival of his country in exile. He knew that democracy was the only key to survival in the modern world. But introducing it to the Tibetans would not be easy. He had already made some changes, ridding himself of much of the suffocating protocol which he had always hated. His officials were for the most part appalled. They thought of the democratic process as being only a short step away from Communism.

But Kundun persisted, knowing that change was ultimately inevitable and that his Government-in-Exile must have a modern constitution, even if no other nation in the world was prepared as yet to acknowledge its existence.

In December 1959 Kundun went to the Buddhist shrines to give teachings. In the Deer Park at Sarnath where the Buddha had preached his first sermon, he addressed two thousand tearful pilgrims – from all three provinces of old Tibet: Amdo, Kham and Central Tibet. He did not mince matters. 'Tibet's sun and moon have suffered an eclipse,' he told them bleakly, and while one day they would undoubtedly go home it would not be for the foreseeable future. Meanwhile, if they were to survive, they must lay aside their traditional regional antipathies, to unite to preserve what was worthwhile in their culture. Afterwards, pilgrims from all three provinces of old Tibet, gathering together (a unique occurrence) for a traditional prayer service to wish long life to His Holiness, vowed to work together in the future. Then, most of them returned to hard labour in the road gangs of Sikkim.

NOTES

1. Author interview with Tendzin Choegyal, Dharamsala, June 1994.
2. One of the Himalayan hill states which the British had acquired by local agreements, and which the Indian Government had inherited in 1947 after Independence. Today this area is known as Arunachal Pradesh.
3. Author interview with Tendzin Choegyal, Dharamsala, June 1994.
4. Fourteenth Dalai Lama, *Freedom in Exile*, chapter 8.
5. Author interview with Tendzin Choegyal, Dharamsala, October 1993.
6. 'Miraculous Escape of the Dalai Lama', *Life*, 4 May 1959.
7. Norbu, *Tibet Is My Country*, p. 249.
8. 'Miraculous Escape of the Dalai Lama', *Life*, 4 May 1959.
9. Author interview with Jetsun Pema, Dharamsala, June 1994.
10. Author interview, Khando Chazotsang, Utah, USA, February 1996.
11. Jetsun Pema, *Tibet, Mon Histoire*.

12. 6 May 1959.

13. *Concerning the question of Tibet. Collection of documents, speeches, news dispatches, editorials, commentaries and background material concerning the Tibetan question.* Foreign Language Press, Peking, 1959. From Oriental and India Office Collections of the British Library.

14. Tsering Dorje Gashi, *Ten Years in Communist China and Tibet...1956–1966,* Dharamsala, 1977.

15. Fourteenth Dalai Lama, *My Land and My People*, chapter 13.

16. Nehru, Statement in the Lok Sabha on The Situation in Tibet, 27 May 1959.

17. *My Land and My People*, chapter 13.

18. Avedon, *In Exile from the Land of Snows*, p. 80.

19. *Tibet Is My Country*, chapter 21.

20. *Tibet Is My Country*, chapter 21.

21. *Tibet Is My Country*.

22. Author interview with HH the Dalai Lama, Dharamsala, June 1994.

Belonging and Not Belonging

Here we see a strange thing, a society which had been isolated completely for hundreds of years suddenly coming out
into the open, events throwing it into this mad world of ours,
cold wars and all kinds of things happening...Imagine the
contrast in these two. It is a vast gulf. It is inevitable that
painful consequences flow from this type of thing. You cannot simply wish it away.

Nehru speaking on Tibet in the Indian Parliament, 8 May 1959

Kundun had known from the start that his stay in Mussoorie would be
temporary. He was nevertheless surprised when, within a year, Nehru offered him permanent settlement in Dharamsala, in the Himalayan
foothills on the northern edges of the Punjab. Never having heard of the
place, he looked it up on the map. It seemed to be in the middle of
nowhere, 450 miles north-west of – and a day's journey from – New Delhi.
He was dismayed. 'We felt we were being pushed out of sight,' he recalls.'

Indeed they were. Mussoorie was a popular refuge from the heat of the
Indian plains, and while Kundun was there, visitors from India and all
over the world flocked to see him. The Chinese did not conceal their displeasure at this, nor at his continued presence so near to the Indo-Tibetan
border. 'Nehru's Government made the excuse that the Birla family wanted to reclaim their house,' says Gyalo Thondup. 'Then they suggested
Dharamsala, very remote and cut off from everywhere. I think Nehru

hoped that if we were shunted out there we might disappear. If so, he must have been disappointed.'

In the 1860s, British officers had set up a hill-station at McLeod Ganj just above Dharamsala – perched on a ridge of the Dhauladhar spur of the Himalaya. They built over a hundred large bungalows and an Anglican church – St John-in-the-Wilderness – complete with spire and country churchyard. (A former Viceroy, Lord Elgin, was buried in a great Gothic tomb there in 1863.) But, popular though McLeod was, the British abandoned it as a summer resort in 1905 after an earthquake levelled many of the bungalows and destroyed the church steeple.

Their departure spelt disaster to the Nowrojee family, Parsees from Bombay who had set up a canteen in 1860 to serve the British and seen it expand into a flourishing General Store selling 'everything from a pin to an elephant'. By 1960, Nauzer Nowrojee, a descendant of the founder, was wondering how to make ends meet. Having failed to persuade government agencies, businesses, religious organizations, to move to Dharamsala, Mr Nowrojee approached Nehru with the proposal that the Dalai Lama and his refugees should be housed there. Nehru was delighted at this simple solution to his dilemma. Surely the Chinese would be mollified by his shunting the Dalai Lama out of sight to this 'forgotten ghost-town wasting in the woods'?

Kundun was less enthusiastic, but he could nevertheless see that Dharamsala had possibilities. It was a mountainous area with woods and streams, not unlike Tibet. In April he sent one of his Ministers to look the place over. Dharamsala is at its best in spring, and when the Minister reported with enthusiasm that 'the water of Dharamsala is sweeter than the milk of Mussoorie', Kundun's reluctance evaporated. What if it *was* a long way from Delhi, making communication with the outside world difficult – at least there would be room for expansion. In Dharamsala perhaps he and the remnant of his people could make a fresh start.

Accompanied by his mother, Tsering Dolma and about eighty officials, Kundun left Mussoorie on 29 April 1960, travelling by overnight train and motorcade. (Khando had been left behind at the Convent of Jesus and Mary in Mussoorie, as her parents were reluctant to change her school yet again.) Past crowds of cheering, flower-strewing Indians, they drove up steep hills to McLeod Ganj where a floral arch with WELCOME in big golden letters had been erected. The last stage of the journey – by jeep – led them up a hillside covered with pine, larch, rhododendron and Himalayan oak, round a series of frightening hairpin bends to their new home in the clouds, appropriately known as Swarg Ashram, the House of Freedom.[2] Consisting of four colonial-style bungalows perched precipitously on the edge of the mountainside, Swarg Ashram commanded a breathtaking view over the lower slopes of the Dhauladhar mountains and the sweeping valley below.

Kundun's spartan bedroom, his chapel and private office took up the front section, while to the rear lived his mother, Tsering Dolma and Phuntsok Tashi, the Lord Chamberlain and various secretaries and translators. Most of the officials were housed in the remaining three bungalows in the compound, while other Tibetans were scattered through the forests, in small wooden huts, derelict shacks and even cowsheds.

Although the Swarg Ashram compound was surrounded by barbed-wire fencing and patrolled by Tibetan and Indian guards, Kundun none the less knew an unaccustomed freedom there. He could play a little badminton and go trekking in the mountains immediately above the bungalow. But such leisurely activities were mainly crowded out by more pressing concerns for the refugees. 'We were confused and disturbed in those days', he says, 'demoralized by the destruction of Lhasa and the news of so many thousands of dead. When we discovered that the Government of India could do nothing to help us regain our independence, we felt a kind of hopelessness, realizing how powerless we were. So for the next few years, all we could do was concentrate on the present and try to rehabilitate our people in India.'[3]

He was not entirely without resources: various international voluntary agencies offered aid and although the Indian Government refused to give political support, it was generous with grants for educating and resettling the Tibetans. In addition, each refugee paid a voluntary tax of two rupees per month and salaried workers accepted an income tax of two per cent. But those amounts came nowhere near meeting the actual expenses.

It was now that the treasure in gold dust and silver bars which had been sent to Sikkim should have come into its own. But disaster had struck. In 1950, three men had been put in charge of the bullion, none of whom knew anything about business. As the Kashag planned to make the gold and silver work for the possible future benefit of Tibetan exiles, they invited the help of one of the most successful businessmen in Tibet, the Khampa trader, Yarphel Padatsang. The latter came to India to take charge of the treasure, but the three Tibetans, suspecting him of being a Chinese agent, refused to hand it over. Instead, the three asked Gyalo Thondup to advise them. When Kundun and his officials fled to India in 1959, they expected to find that the bullion had been securely invested. Too late, the three trustees realized what they had done. 'Then the trouble started,' says Phuntsog Wangyal, a prominent Tibetan exile in London, 'Everything had already passed under the control of Gyalo Thondup.'[4]

The latter explains that in 1959 he delegated responsibility to others who duly exchanged the bullion for cash.[5] Unwisely, they invested two or three crore rupees (about two or three hundred million) in the stock markets of Calcutta and Bombay. Then, because they were busy with other problems, they gave the share certificates into the care of Indian stockbroker friends – who promptly sold them. The Tibetans invested the rest of the money in some steel-pipe business – which went bankrupt. 'It was terrible,' mourns Gyalo Thondup, 'we lost eighty per cent of His Holiness's money. When we realized what had happened, we tried to chase the money up, but it was too late. It was all lost.' If only, he laments, 'we had bought property in Delhi instead of investing all that money in the stock market! Land at that time was very cheap and it would have been an excellent investment.'

Whatever the true facts of the matter – and they are almost impossible to establish – when Kundun and his officials came to set up a trust to cater for the needs of the refugees, only twenty per cent of the money remained. The Kashag was deeply suspicious of Gyalo Thondup's explanations – it was the beginning of a deadly feud between them.

The Tibetans worked hard to re-establish the Kashag and various departments. Food was basic and eaten 'on the run between jobs'. Everyone was working out of a single room, with two or three portfolios being dealt with by one person. In these conditions, Kundun reformed his Government; set up a Bureau in New Delhi to link the Indian Government with the various foreign relief agencies; established four unofficial embassies, in New York, Tokyo, Geneva and Kathmandu; and created ten civil service ranks. Determined to preserve the best elements of Tibetan culture, he established an Institute of Tibetan Performing Arts, to keep the traditional folk-dances and operas alive; a Tibetan Medical Centre, to preserve and dispense the traditional herbal remedies; and a Library of Tibetan Works and Archives to store what had been salvaged of Tibet's sacred literature and scriptures. Finally, he drafted a new democratic constitution for a future in which there would be free elections to a National Assembly of People's Deputies

– managing to insert a clause whereby he himself could be removed as Head of State if there was a two-thirds majority in the National Assembly in favour. The idea that the Dalai Lama could ever be pushed out, no matter what the circumstances, nearly gave the more conservative ministers heart-failure, but Kundun stood firm and the clause stayed.

There were by now about 30,000 refugees in the road-camps and few of them could be found homes in Dharamsala. Concerned for their poverty, homelessness and vulnerability to disease, Kundun turned to Nehru – who asked the less populous Indian states in the south for suggestions. When Karnataka offered an uninhabited stretch of jungle at Byllakuppe to the west of Mysore, Kundun accepted with gratitude. By December 1960, a contingent of 660 Tibetan refugees was despatched to Byllakuppe, to create the first of what eventually became 57 thriving Tibetan communities in India. But, for these early pioneers, the task seemed utterly hopeless. When they felt the tropical heat and caught sight of the barren wilderness, many of the former nomadic herders and agricultural labourers from the Land of Snows broke down and wept, beseeching Kundun to send them somewhere – anywhere – else. But there was nowhere else to go. In those first terrible years before the survivors learned to adapt, hundreds died of sunstroke, heat exhaustion and despair.

It was the children Kundun worried about most. During frequent visits to the road camps, he had been appalled: 'Children, women and men were all working side by side in gangs…They had to endure a full day's hard physical toil under a mighty sun, followed by nights crammed into tiny tents.'[6] Kundun fretted that the Tibetans were in danger of losing an entire generation. In Tibet itself, children were being deported wholesale to China for brainwashing; while in India orphans and semi-orphans roamed the camps in search of food or family, and died of starvation and disease. Nehru again came to the rescue. 'The children are your most precious resource,' he sympathized. When Hugh Richardson visited Kundun in Mussoorie in early 1960, he reported that two or three houses had been set up, with 'children clean and bright, in white tops and blue shorts or skirts'.[7] These houses would provide the nucleus for the Mussoorie Homes Foundation set up by Rinchen Dolma and Jigme Taring, two of the first Tibetans to have been educated in India. In March 1960, fifty ragged and hungry young men, former monks, Khampa warriors and Government officials aged from eighteen to twenty-five were sent to Mussoorie where, under the guidance of the Tarings, a Tibetan school had been set up in an old house bought cheap from an Indian Army officer. Other residential schools followed, one in Simla, and a school-cum-craft-centre organized by Gyalo Thondup's wife in Darjeeling.

Kundun had been in Dharamsala only two weeks when he heard that a group of refugees being transferred from the Missamari camp to work on the new military roads in Ladakh had been trapped by blizzards and that young children in the group were dying. There was no time to lose. Fifty-one sick and near-starving children, aged between four and fifteen, were rescued and brought to Dharamsala, in so pitiful a condition that Kundun wept when he saw them. They were temporarily housed in the officials' bungalows. But a few days later, on 17 May 1960, Kundun took over two large, derelict British bungalows and, with the Government of India providing the basic rations and international voluntary agencies helping in various other ways, opened a nursery and small infirmary with his sister Tsering Dolma in charge, and nothing but her maternal instinct to guide her.

Conditions were far worse than in Mussoorie. The place, said Hugh Richardson, was 'squalid and muddy and the latrines were terrible'.[8] There was scarcely room even for the original 51, but by the end of the year, their numbers had increased tenfold, and within two years there were over 1500 children. (At one point, 120 were sharing a single bedroom, sleeping five or six to a bed!) They were orphans or children whose parents were unable to support them; they came from different camps all over India, hungry, dirty, ragged and often seriously ill. Overcrowding was aggravated by lack of food, clothing, medicines – and adequate staff. In fact, as Tsering Dolma noted in her first Report from the Nursery in 1962, in those early years there was 'a shortage of everything except children'. When Pema, having left school, came to Dharamsala to help her sister for a while, her first sight of McLeod Ganj filled her with despair: 'Three buildings, just one shop, and nothing but canvas tents everywhere, with Tibetans in rags, children weeping and shivering with cold, women crushed by the weight of their misery. I could not help but wonder how much suffering they had endured in order to reach this wretched village?'

Gyalo Thondup was potentially the Tibetans' trump card, the man best equipped to steer Kundun through his present difficulties. Unlike the Tibetan officials still mired in their medieval past, GT was urbane and articulate; a successful businessman who spoke several languages, knew his way around the international scene and had powerful contacts all over the world. Among the Tibetans, he alone had the capacity to think globally.

He now looked around for allies. The Americans offered help. Before 1959, they had given only perfunctory support to the rebels, but after the exodus their enthusiasm had increased: supporting the freedom struggle in Tibet was, in their view, a good way to destabilize Communist China. But Gyalo Thondup was not sure. As a student of history, he considered that the countries nearest to Tibet – India, Pakistan and the USSR – would be more useful than far-away ones like the United States.[9] A 'man from Moscow' came to see him in Delhi, assuring him that the Russians alone could be trusted to help the Tibetans, the Americans would sell them out to China. GT toyed with the idea of an operation involving India and the USSR, but when he told Indian Intelligence what he had in mind, their reaction, he said was 'furious and frightened'. Disconcerted by this, then remembering that the Chinese now hated the Russians and would never in the future take him seriously if he accepted help from them, he backed off. A tentative approach to British Intelligence (both MI5 and MI6) elicited nothing more helpful than a recommendation to stay close to the Americans. Gyalo Thondup then re-established contact with the CIA – who offered the Tibetans training, arms and money. His Tibetan Welfare Commitee became an office for co-ordinating the activities of the CIA with those of the Resistance – with his cousin Lhamo Tsering in charge. A new fighting force was to be formed from the ranks of the former Chushi Gang-drug warriors working as coolies in the road-gangs of Sikkim. 'We planned,' says Lhamo Tsering,[10] 'to send them back in groups to resume guerrilla operations in areas of Western Tibet where Chinese troop concentrations were not overwhelmingly high.'

A base was chosen – Mustang, a remote area in Northern Nepal which was ethnically and culturally Tibetan and lay close to the edge of the Tibetan plateau. Fifteen thousand feet above sea level, Mustang perched on a spur jutting out over western Tibet. Over a month's trek from Kathmandu, the 750-square-mile territory could only be approached by a deep and narrow gorge to the south, but it had the strategic advantage of being close to the new Chinese road which ran from Kham, along the northern Himalaya, to Ladakh in the west, and from there to the Sino-Soviet border. It would be an ideal launching-pad for raids on Chinese army posts and a fall-back position for the isolated guerrilla units still active in the south and east of Tibet.

Leaders of the Resistance were instructed to recruit the first batch of three hundred volunteers for CIA combat training, bearing in mind that as nobody was quite sure about the operation's legality, the need for secrecy was paramount. Gyalo Thondup went to Kalimpong and addressed the Khampas there. 'We are,' he told them, 'fighters, not farmers, not settlers of the land. We are fighting for the independence of Tibet.' Everyone cheered him. And the exodus began.

'Quietly,' says GT, 'we began sending groups of young men from Sikkim to Nepal.'[11] 'Quietly' was perhaps not the right word. As virtually all the Khampas in the road-camps were itching to take on the Chinese, they exploded with a sort of spontaneous combustion. Suddenly Indian contractors found their workforce was disappearing. On 1 August 1960, the Calcutta *Statesman* reported: 'Mysterious Exit from Sikkim: Khampas Leaving in Hundreds', and alleged that more than seven or eight hundred workers had already left.

'There were too many people arriving, more than we could handle,' says Lhamo Tsering. 'The Americans got very alarmed about this and about the newspaper report, and they temporarily abandoned the whole operation. But that didn't prevent the volunteers from coming.'

Through the second half of 1960, Chushi Gangdrug fighters trekked through the dense jungles of southern Nepal to reach their new operations base on the windswept plateau of Mustang. Though the Americans recovered from their fright and returned, in that first year there were many difficulties, little money and less food. Nobody actually died of starvation, but all came close to it. Some froze to death in the snow. 'Before sufficient supplies could be parachuted in,' wrote John Avedon, 'most of the initial four thousand men were reduced to boiling their boots and saddles for food, with some, according to one account, carrying out raids across the border into Tibet, not to attack the Chinese, but to steal livestock for their own survival.'[12] But, as they slowly built up a network of interconnecting bases, their single-minded enthusiasm was astonishing. 'Even the CIA were amazed by it,' says Gyalo Thondup. 'The Americans who did the parachute training said they'd never seen such spirit. "Your people are really something else," they told me, "they actually laugh as they jump out of the plane."'[13]

Gyalo Thondup came to Dharamsala to recruit. His undoubted charisma was matched by a singular talent for making enemies. (Even Kundun complains of his brother's stubbornness – 'He creates controversy and is difficult to control,' he says. 'Once he's made up his mind about something, no one can change it. Certainly, I can't.'[4] In Dharamsala, GT was disgusted to find that the old officials were still around – and, moreover, suspicious of his handling of the bullion affair. Smarting from this, and from the recollection of 'those years when I was sending all those messages from Mr Nehru to Lhasa, and being ignored', Gyalo Thondup made no secret of his contempt. 'They didn't seem able to understand that times had changed,' he fumes. 'Facing an enemy like the Chinese, we should have been using all the bright intelligent young people we could find for the Government, no matter what their background, even if they were from beggar families. But I couldn't get that through to those corrupt, feudalistic, superstitious old men. We didn't need people like them, we needed people dedicated to change, not lackeys and time-servers from the past. During the Uprising, when His Holiness escaped from Lhasa, I had sent groups of people into Lhasa to find out what the Chinese were up to. None of those officials would have taken the kind of risk those men took. It was because we used people from all strata of society that we were able to get His Holiness out.'[5]

The dislike being entirely mutual, battle was joined. The opening shots were fired by what was generally supposed to be the Kashag's own creation, the Reform Party, formed in an attempt at national unity after Kundun's Bodh Gaya appeal. Its Committee of six front men, representing all three provinces of old Tibet, produced a nine-point manifesto, two of them calculated to put the cat among the pigeons. What exactly, they demanded to know, had happened to the fortune in gold and silver from Sikkim? (The pathetic amount realized had been published in an Indian newspaper.) And what about the yellow parachute full of American, Indian and Tibetan money, which had been dropped in 1958 in Tibet by the CIA? (Before the contents of the parachute could be put to use, the Chinese attack had intensified and the guerrillas had fled.) The loot, alleged the Committee, had been brought out of Tibet by Chushi Gangdrug and had until recently been stashed in a hut in the Missamari camp. It had now disappeared. Where was it? And who was the guilty party? They demanded explanations and pointed an accusing finger at – Gyalo Thondup.

Gyalo Thondup, Machiavellian to his fingertips, would not stoop to a public slanging match. But it was a sticky situation and he knew that if there was to be a showdown with the Reform Party and its Kashag backers, he needed a power base of his own. He had no actual political status, though already the refugees, seeing him under attack from the important Kashag ministers, were putting him on a par with them, giving him the courtesy title of *Tsawang Chenmo*, Mr Senior Minister. He needed a bedrock of reliable support. And he knew just where to find it: Chushi Gangdrug was tailor-made for his purpose. Had not the Khampas always resisted rule from Lhasa? Had they not always fiercely protected their independence? Here, precisely, was their opportunity. In those days, the Khampas were riding high in world opinion, even people who knew almost nothing about Tibet had heard of these warrior tribesmen who had stood alone against the might of the Chinese Army. In exile and no longer paying taxes to a hated Lhasa, they were every man's equal and determined to prove it. They and Gyalo Thondup needed each other.

One by one, the supporters of the Reform Party were winkled out of the road-gangs to join the guerrillas in Mustang, until finally, none but the six leaders remained. 'They had nobody to represent, they were in touch with nobody,' says an observer. 'Their followers were stuck in Mustang with no access to the outside world.'[16] Indian security then stepped in and put the six potential trouble-makers on a train to Calcutta, ordering them to stay there. Well aware that they were finished, there was one last task they wished to fulfil. On the way to Calcutta, one of the six was deputed to return to Dharamsala to explain their failure to the Kashag and to return to Kundun the two thousand rupees which he had initially advanced them. Arriving in Dharamsala with the money in a folder, the man put up in a small hotel. No sooner had he arrived than the rumour-machine got busy, accusing him of being a Chinese spy. A group of thugs went to his hotel and demanded everything he had. Ignoring his plea that at least they should leave him the folder meant for His Holiness, they beat him up, took him outside and lashed him to a large tree. It was two hours before the Indian police arrived and found him. They cut him down, and after taking him to hospital for emergency treatment, put him on the next train for Calcutta. He did not even meet Kundun, and the latter probably heard nothing about his visit either then or later.[17]

It was the end of the Old Guard. They never recovered from the Reform Party's collapse and one by one they resigned from office and emigrated. Soon, there was no one left from the old Kashag. Some still believe that their departure was a sad loss for the Tibetans, for they were for the most part men of experience and wisdom, and in the end would have come to terms with the necessity for change. At the very least, they provided a counter-weight to the ambitious Khampas. But it was not to be. Whether or not the removal of his old enemies had been Gyalo Thondup's intention – and he swears that it had not – now that they were out of the way, he was without a doubt the most powerful man on the Tibetan refugee scene. And there were many who believed that he would stop at nothing to make himself the *de facto* leader of Tibet-in-exile.

Before the Chinese occupied Tibet, the 2,000 mile border with India caused few problems and no defensive measures were considered necessary on either side of it. For over a thousand years, Tibet was a peaceful and friendly buffer state which presented no threat to its neighbours. When the Communists over-ran Tibet, India recognized the dangers, yet Nehru trusted that, in the interests of Asian brotherhood, China would respect his territorial integrity. But China's mounting fury over the Dalai Lama and the Tibetan refugees had led to increased tension. The Chinese huffed that the frontier needed to be redefined, Nehru retorting that the mountains of the Himalaya were clearly India's frontier, according to both treaty, custom and geography.

At 5 a.m. on 20 October 1962, using Tibet as a launching-pad, 20,000 troops of the Chinese People's Liberation Army swept over the border into the North-East Frontier Area of India and into Ladakh 1,500 miles away to the north-west. The strength of the attack winded Nehru; he simply did not have the resources – or the men – to fight a high-altitude war. The Himalaya, his unassailable first line of defence, had turned into his Achilles' heel. Several of the Tibetan work-camps near the border were shut down, Tibetans once again became homeless refugees.

As the Chinese army pushed its way into Indian territory with the ease of a knife through butter, panic set in throughout India. But, having rammed home the point that what they did in Tibet was their business and India could do nothing about it, the Chinese declared a cease-fire and contemptuously withdrew.

Kundun was saddened at this humiliation of his Indian friends. Nehru was devastated – the friendship with China had been the cornerstone of his foreign policy. Admitting that he had been living in a fool's paradise of his own making, he lost all zest for life, became a shadow of his former self – and within two years was dead.

In that time, however, his foreign policy underwent a sea change.

Gyalo Thondup claims that three weeks before the attack, Chushi Gangdrug had warned the Indian Prime Minister that the Chinese intended to attack, 'but at that time he wouldn't listen'. After the invasion, a chastened Nehru abandoned his cherished policy of non-alignment in the Cold War and turned to America for support. He also recalled Gyalo Thondup's persistent request for him to provide some kind of military training for the young, able-bodied (non-Khampa) Tibetans still working in the Sikkim road-camps. As long as Nehru had his dream, he would not risk upsetting China; the road-building programme was all he would offer. 'But as soon as the war started,' claims Gyalo Thondup, 'Mr Nehru came looking for me. His attitude towards us had changed overnight. Suddenly he was a man in a hurry, in search of men who would be able to withstand the cold and fight at high altitudes without getting sick. "Now," he said briskly, "about training those Tibetans of yours. We'll do it, if you can provide the men." "Of course," I said. "How many do you have?" he asked. "Five thousand," I said. "Right," he replied, "will you work with the Defence Ministry or with Indian Intelligence?" I chose Intelligence. I knew the CIA would prefer them, and anyway I'd been in contact with Indian Intelligence ever since 1952.'[18]

Thus was born the Special Frontier Force (known as SFF or, more usually, Establishment 22[19]), a high-altitude army of paratroop commandos which would be trained by the CIA to defend India's Himalayan border against further Chinese attack; and to be ready to parachute into Tibet, to make contact with the underground and disrupt the PLA, should fighting break out again. It was formed in November 1962 under the auspices of Indian Intelligence, and it consisted entirely of Tibetans. Informed that a new unit was being formed, independent of the Khampa guerrillas, Tibetan refugees left the road-gangs in droves to join it. After six months basic commando training not far from Dehra Dun, an embryo Tibetan Army of 10,500 men and its own officer corps was operational. Thanks to them, India was able to build up a network of bases from Assam to Ladakh. But China did not invade again.

In Mustang, the Khampas' morale had soared when the Americans made their first arms drop – just inside Tibet, on the mountainous border between Tibet and Mustang. There were arms and ammunition enough to equip four companies of soldiers; and plans were instantly made for raids on seven different sites inside Tibet. The raids were carried out successfully, and caused much disruption to the Chinese military and civil administration in all seven places. On another occasion, the guerrillas isolated a Chinese truck from its convoy, killed everyone in it and seized the contents of the vehicle. 'The truck happened to have been carrying a regimental commander bearing many confidential documents – complete sets of Party directives to area commanders, political manuals and so on. The documents were of great importance. Among them was one which gave the disposition of army groups in Tibet – and revealed the entire system of information-gathering by various spy networks on the Tibetan borders.'[20]

Every year after that, in winter when the rivers were frozen and could be crossed, Chushi Gangdrug sent raiding teams inside Tibet. By 1963–4 the Xinjiang–Shigatse section of the road to Lhasa became virtually unusable by the Chinese. But inside Tibet itself resistance had been crushed. Though the last remaining guerrilla units had held out until 1962, the CIA had already written them off a year before that and were concentrating on the secret underground activities which might have more chance of success. At Camp Hale in Colorado Springs they were secretly training about 500 Tibetans, to be parachuted into their native areas to organize a network of resistance groups throughout the country.

Gyalo Thondup's office in Darjeeling worked round the clock to co-ordinate the various activities, setting up spy networks from Ngari in the west to Kongpo in the south-east, eight networks along the borders and others operating further inside the country, even in Lhasa. Small teams were sent in to carry out reconnaissance, establish safe houses, find food supplies and so on. They had to travel over the mountains and over land, and their assignments were difficult and dangerous. One by one, the teams were blown by Chinese Intelligence. The Chinese would later claim that they had captured fifty-two foreign agents in Tibet to most of whom they had awarded life-sentences. The price of resistance was very high.

But in Dharamsala, Tibet-in-Exile was painfully coming to birth. Kundun had democracy firmly in his sights when in March 1963 he managed to push through a new draft constitution. In the National People's Assembly elections which followed, Tibetans were introduced for the first time to the mysteries of the ballot box. The changes did not as yet go far – how could they? – and democracy was still a long way off. But the first tentative steps towards it had been taken.

NOTES

1. Author interview with HH the Dalai Lama, Dharamsala, June 1994.

2. To the British it was Highcroft House, the seat of the District Commissioner; and today it has become a Mountaineering Centre.

3. Author interview with HH the Dalai Lama, Dharamsala, October 1994.

4. Author interview with Phuntsog Wangyal, London, February 1996.

5. Author interview with Gyalo Thondup, New Delhi, July 1995.

6. Fourteenth Dalai Lama, *Freedom in Exile*.

7. Letter to the author, 12 December 1993.

8. Letter to the author, 12 December 1993.

9. Video interview with Gyalo Thondup by a monk of the Namgyal Monastery, Dharamsala.

10. Author interview with Lhamo Tsering, Dharamsala, October 1993.

11. Author interview with Gyalo Thondup, New Delhi, July 1995.

12. Avedon, *In Exile from the Land of Snows*.

13. Author interview with Gyalo Thondup, New Delhi, July 1995.

14. Author interview with HH the Dalai Lama, Dharamsala, June 1994.

15. Author interview with Gyalo Thondup, New Delhi, July 1995.

16. Author interview with Phuntsog Wangyal, London, February 1996.

17. This account was given to the author by Phuntsog Wangyal (see note 4 above).

18. Author interview with Gyalo Thondup, New Delhi, July 1995.

19. Gyalo Thondup provided the first five thousand men within six weeks and soon exceeded the target.

20. From an unpublished manuscript shown to the author by Jamyang Norbu.

Family Matters 1960–5

Cast from Tibet while most countries stayed mute
all those who fled tasted the bitter fruit –
of exile, and the deep, heart-searing pain,
that they might never see their homes again.

Dr Louella Lobo Prabhu, an Indian journalist
and social worker in Karnataka[1]

From now on, the family had lost its central focus – Lhasa. They were scattered, and would become even more so, throughout the Tibetan diaspora, united only by their loyalty to Kundun and their devotion to Amala.

Amala herself, nearing sixty at the time of the hazardous escape, was having problems with her health. Since her arrival in Dharamsala, she had suffered from a blockage in the throat. A doctor in Delhi discovered a polyp but, assuring her it was benign, arranged for its removal at St Mary's Hospital in London. On the journey back from Delhi, the car was hit by a speeding vehicle just outside Pathankot. Anyone who has travelled the road between Delhi and Dharamsala knows only too well what a death-trap it is, the proof lying everywhere along the roadside – vehicles burned out, crushed, overturned, mangled. Amala's injuries, fortunately, amounted to no more than a whiplash neck and a dislocated arm.

Rinchen Dolma Taring, who was to accompany Amala to England as companion and interpreter, began teaching her some basic conversational

English and how to write her name in English script. The two friends stayed first in a small boarding-house in Welwyn Garden City, then, after the operation, crossed to the Isle of Wight, where Sir Basil Gould's widow, Cecily, lived. 'I had a phone call from the Tibet Society one day,' says Lady Gould, 'asking me to arrange for two weeks' convalescence, nothing too expensive. I booked them into a small guest-house in Freshwater, insisting that the ladies should be incognito. I was told that the Great Mother's son, Jigme Norbu, would come down and see if the place was auspicious, but in the end he gave his consent without actually visiting it. He said he would trust me.'

The two ladies stayed on the island for six weeks: they had the homely guest-house to themselves, and the weather was glorious. Cecily Gould found them both delightful: Mrs Taring, the highly-educated aristocrat who spoke perfect English, and the Great Mother, 'a peasant woman with the grace of a queen, so very composed, with a gracious, lovely demeanour. She just radiated warmth and peace.' Lady Gould drove them around the island, took them for pub lunches and arranged sightseeing trips, though what they liked best was to stay indoors playing draughts. Occasionally, they would prepare trays of the Tibetan dumplings known as momos and invite Lady Gould and the doctor – a daily visitor who made no charge for his services – to supper. Amala, her bad arm supported in a sling, supervised Mrs Taring in the cooking. Amala loved momos. 'Once or twice,' says Mrs Taring, 'I used to suggest that she should eat a bit less as she was putting on weight and complained of pains in her legs. She joked that everyone else told her to be sure and eat well to stay healthy, and here was I telling her the reverse.'[2]

One day they spotted a couple of local police constables at the door. With police-state memories still uppermost in their minds, Mrs Taring bravely insisted that Amala should lock herself in her bedroom, while she confronted the unwelcome callers. Luckily, the constables were just searching for a missing cat!

Amala fretted constantly about her old mother who, for reasons of security, had had to be left behind in Lhasa. 'My mother must really have suffered over leaving my grandmother behind,' says Kundun. 'They were very close – they even looked alike. When we left Lhasa, one of my uncles and my mother's youngest sister went to live in the family house and look after the old lady.'[3] Amala was almost sick with anxiety, saying over and over to Mrs Taring, 'If only we could go back to Lhasa to see my mother and your children.'⁴ (Mrs Taring herself had been stranded on the far side of Lhasa during the Uprising, unable to make her way home, and had had no news of her husband, his mother, four small grandchildren and two other daughters and their babies.) But in spite of all the terrible things that had happened, says Mrs Taring, 'the Great Mother believed that everything was taken care of, and there was no real point in worrying. She would say that politics was not our concern, our task was to pray and watch our own minds so that we committed no sin.'

Nevertheless, Amala went on worrying, not least about Tendzin Choegyal who was at boarding school in India. Within six weeks of his arrival in exile, he was on his way to St Joseph's College, North Point, Darjeeling. 'Gyalo Thondup drove us to Delhi, which was terribly hot and I couldn't sleep,' he remembers. 'My sister, Pema, was with us. She was going back to the Loreto Convent in Darjeeling, after being allowed to come and visit us in Mussoorie.'⁵

In Darjeeling, he was taken to meet the Rector of North Point, Fr Maurice Standford. His uniform was assembled in two days and on 6 June he began school. 'I had to wear short grey trousers, long socks, shirt, tie, pullover, all very British public school, not at all what I was used to. I couldn't communicate with anybody, I only knew a few words of English. It was very frustrating. I used to lock myself in the urinals and cry my heart out.'

There was nothing for it, however, but to buckle down. Though at first his English and Maths were way down at kindergarten level, he learned fast. Within six months, he had made good progress in English, and was soon being pointed out to beginners as an example of what was possible. Initially placed with much younger children in the Primary Division, before long he was holding his own with boys nearer his own age, not only in Tibetan and English but in French, Scripture, Arithmetic, General Science, Elocution, Spelling and Art. (Art was his favourite.) It was a far cry from the life of an incarnate lama at Drepung, but Tendzin Choegyal adapted to his new life with the natural ease of a chameleon. And he was comforted by the presence of Tsering Dolma's son, Tenzin Ngawang, the nephew six years older than himself who was already studying for his Senior Cambridge Certificate. 'Tenzin Ngawang used to give me reading lists and urge me to read as much as I could, and study hard. He loved literature and music, especially Bach, and he conveyed something of that love to me as a child.'⁶

Earlier that year, in January 1960, Norbu had moved from New York to Seattle University, to take up a one-year assignment in the Tibetan Studies Department, where another eminent Tibetan was also in residence: the Head of the Buddhist Sakyapa sect, the direct descendant of the lama whom the great Kubilai Khan had adopted as spiritual adviser and to whom he had handed the overlordship of Tibet. Throughout the thirteenth and fourteenth centuries, the Sakyapa ruled as priest-kings in Tibet. But eventually the sect lost out, in a civil war, to the reforming Gelugpa sect, to which the Dalai Lamas have all belonged. Nevertheless, the Sakyapa still command a large following. They preserve their hereditary priesthood, not by the celibate *tulku* system of the Gelugpa but by insisting that the eldest son of the sect's head – the 'Holder of the Throne' – must marry and produce an heir, the rest of the family embracing celibacy as monks or nuns of the Sakya order.

The current 'Holder of the Throne' was married, his younger brother was already a monk, and his young sister, Kunyang, was about to enter a nunnery. Then Norbu arrived in Seattle. When he had first met seventeen-year-old Kunyang a year earlier in Darjeeling, he had dismissed her as 'a little wisp of a girl', merely the sister of an important lama. Now he fell in love with her. Kunyang, for her part, abandoned all thoughts of a nunnery, and within three months they were married. A year later they returned to New York, where a friend of Norbu's had found him a job as assistant curator of the Tibetan collection at the Museum of Natural History. Cataloguing Tibetan artefacts and works of art, Norbu slowly began to appreciate the value of the ordinary, everyday objects which at home in Tibet he had taken for granted.

Norbu's marriage, which made newspaper headlines in the USA, where the activities of the Dalai Lama's brother were hot news – was unsettling for Amala. Upset that her Rinpoche son should have forsaken his vows and decided to marry, her anxiety was all the more acute since Lobsang Samten too had renounced his monastic vows and was with Norbu in New York. He was known to have a Japanese girlfriend – what if he were to marry her, or, even worse, an American girl? At the time in question, most Tibetans had still not emerged from their cocoon of isolation, and the idea was horrific. Amala and Tsering Dolma decided that Lobsang must marry a Tibetan girl without delay. And who better than Pema's friend, Namlha Tsarong?'

Namlha and her sister Norzin had attended a Protestant school in Darjeeling, while Pema and Khando were at the Loreto Convent. Their paths did not cross until some mutual friends brought them together in Calcutta after the Buddha Jayanti of 1956. (Gyalo Thondup had persuaded his mother to return to Calcutta for a holiday with the rest of the family, after Kundun returned to Lhasa.) After that the four girls began exchanging letters during term-time and occasionally met at weekends at Gyalo Thondup's house.

It was during winter holidays in Calcutta that the friendship really took off. 'Darjeeling was so terribly cold in winter,' remembers Namlha, 'we used to go to Calcutta for two weeks to escape being frozen.' Amala would be there with Tsering Dolma and Tendzin Choegyal. 'She was always very warm and welcoming, very motherly. Whenever my sister and I went to see Pema and Khando, she would take sweets or chocolates out of a cupboard for us. Sometimes she would come with the four of us when we went shopping or to the movies – and then she'd buy us tea and cakes in a café afterwards. We loved films, especially English-language ones; and we loved rock 'n' roll dancing. Actually, Pema didn't do rock'n roll, she would just stand and watch us – though I remember she danced the Charleston really well. She and I were rather shy and reserved, unlike Khando and Norzin who were far more extrovert. They liked to wear print dresses with big flowers and laughed at us for being old-fashioned and boring. They nicknamed us Grandmother One (Pema) and Grandmother Two (me).'

One day in 1961, Namlha received a letter from Pema, asking what she would think about marrying Lobsang Samten. She was taken aback. 'I'd known Lobsang from a distance, I'd met him once at an official dinner in Lhasa, but then he was a very important monk, and, besides, he was ten years older than me. I had seen him only once since those days, in Calcutta when he and Norbu had briefly joined the rest of the family. They didn't waste any attention on us girls, they were so much older; and in any case they had had to look after Tendzin Choegyal, such a bright, intelligent little boy, but unbelievably naughty.'

Pema enclosed a photograph of Lobsang taken outside the UN building in New York. Namlha thought him attractive, but laughed off Pema's idea as 'girl-talk', such as they'd often indulged in. She had her own plans for the future: she had just taken the Senior Cambridge Examination and was doing a secretarial course with French, after which she intended to go to the States. 'A friend of my grandfather's, Ilia Tolstoy, had come to India to see how the refugees were coping. He asked me what I wanted to do, but I didn't know: Tibetan girls at that time didn't really think about a career, we simply got married and looked after the house. But when he found that I was quite good at Art, he invited me to New York to study at an Institute owned by a friend of his. I jumped at the chance, it seemed almost too good to be true.'

But Pema did not let the matter drop. One day Gyalo Thondup came to see the Tsarongs, with a formal request that their daughter might marry Lobsang Samten. 'My parents asked me what I thought,' says Namlha. 'My father said it was entirely up to me, but marrying into a Dalai Lama's family would not be easy. There would be a lot of pressures, over-exposure to limelight and so on. At that point, my mother broke in and said they mustn't interfere, it was my life and I had to make my own decision. I said that at least I ought to meet Lobsang before deciding.'

Lobsang was persuaded to return to India. Arriving in Madras, he rang Namlha to arrange a meeting. She recalls that he was as nervous as she was, they 'just talked a bit awkwardly about Pema' and arranged to meet some time later in Calcutta. The second meeting went much better: they liked each other instantly, the ten-year age gap seeming not to matter at all. 'What I liked about Lobsang was his wonderful sense of fun,' says Namlha. 'He was utterly straightforward and very kind. We spent just over a week getting to know each other, and then he went to Dharamsala to see His Holiness. We were already writing to each other by then, and I had de-cided to stay in India and marry him.'

Though he did not tell Namlha, Lobsang's encounter with Kundun was not easy. The latter was angry that first Norbu and now Lobsang had aban-doned the celibate state for marriage. Perhaps because he had always been so close to Lobsang, his anger against him was the greater. 'I didn't really speak to either of my brothers for some time,' he says wryly, uncomfortable now at the recollection,[8] 'but I was particularly mad with Lobsang Samten. I remember shouting at him, "Even a dog doesn't copulate while it's actual-ly being beaten." It really did seem to me at that time that Tibet was like a dog being viciously whipped and that all our efforts ought to be directed to saving it. But later, when I thought about what I'd said to Lobsang, I realized that if my comments were to be taken literally, there would be no more Ti-betans born inside or outside Tibet. I understood that I'd been illogical as well as unfair, I'd allowed my emotions to run out of control. I was sorry for that. But,' he adds feelingly, 'at the time I was very angry indeed.'

Lobsang and Namlha met again in August 1962 and decided to marry as soon as possible. Amala and Tsering Dolma disapproved of their impatience.

'That year was said to be inauspicious for us,' says Namlha, 'it was a bad-luck year! Neither Lobsang nor I was superstitious, we were very much in love and we didn't care, but Lobsang had a hard job persuading his mother. But in the end she withdrew her objection and we were married that same month.'

After a traditional wedding ceremony in Gyalo Thondup's house in Darjeeling, the young couple went on a honeymoon trip to Srinagar in Kashmir, a wedding present from Gyalo Thondup.

> There was some political trouble there, and we were subjected to curfews. We didn't really mind that. But Srinagar was so very like Tibet, so like Lhasa itself, that it made me terribly homesick for my family and sad about those we'd left behind. During the Lhasa Rebellion, my 74-year-old grandfather, the one known as the Great Tsarong, had been chosen as a People's Representative, to negotiate with the Chinese. We heard later that when the Chinese had stopped shelling Lhasa they came to our house – Tsarong House – and took my grandfather and youngest uncle away. They were both imprisoned in the Potala and made to do hard labour. A fellow-prisoner who escaped to India afterwards told us what happened to my grandfather. One day the Chinese ordered his former servants to humiliate and beat him up at a *thamzing* session next morning. When morning came, my grandfather was found dead. He'd apparently just had a heart-attack! Then there was my youngest brother, an Incarnate Lama who'd been left behind in Tibet, I kept wondering if he was still alive. So, even though it was my honeymoon, it was a sad time.

On their return to Dharamsala, Lobsang took Namlha to Swarg Ashram to present her to Kundun. She was terribly nervous. 'I'd only seen him twice before in my life, once when I was a small child and once when I was at the Chinese school in Lhasa. When he left for the Buddha Jayanti, we schoolchildren all lined up to wish him goodbye. And now here he was, my husband's brother. I don't even remember what he said to us, I was shaking so much. But he was very kind and gave us several wedding presents. There was a lovely charm-box with a Buddhist picture in it, a set of seven silver bowls and a length of beautiful dress material.'

Lobsang who was working in the Refugee Rehabilitation Department in Dharamsala, was awaiting transfer to the Tibet Office in Delhi, where Namlha also had found work. Kundun had appealed to young, educated Tibetans to forget self-interest and put their talents to work for the refugees – 'We are not just one big family,' he had reminded them, 'we are trying to rebuild a nation.' Namlha had responded to the call. 'There were so few of us who spoke good English, and English-speakers were desperately needed. So I had agreed to go to Delhi as a secretary/interpreter.'

While waiting for his transfer, Lobsang stayed at home and did the cooking, while Namlha went to work. He was an excellent cook – 'The only fights we ever had were over cooking,' says Namlha, admitting that preparing food was not really her forte. At first she went home each day for lunch, but as the journey by auto-rickshaw cost her more than a month's wages, she soon stopped. When Lobsang was appointed Assistant to Kundun's Representative in Delhi, they acquired a bed-sitting room, bathroom and shared communal kitchen above the Tibet Office. 'It wasn't much, but we were happy. Whenever Lobsang wanted to cook something special, we went into the bathroom where we had a tiny stove. Lobsang was always a realist. He never put on airs. When the others left the kitchen dirty, as they often did, he would come down on Sundays in his shorts and clean it up.'

Even after their daughter, Choekyi, was born (1963), they continued living in their one room above the office. 'There was just one cupboard for our clothes, another for the baby's things. We were terribly cramped. I was so stressed that I didn't have enough milk for the baby and had to supplement it with a bottle. But Lobsang was a fantastic father. He would often get up to give the baby her bottle during the night when I was sleeping so heavily I didn't know anything about it till morning.'

Their son, Tenzin Namdhak, was born two years later. Between the refugees and their own children, life became a constant struggle against exhaustion, their social life limited to an occasional visit to the cinema – where Lobsang invariably fell asleep.

On returning to Dharamsala, Amala found it swarming with orphaned and sick children. She would go down to the Nursery every day, helping with the laundry, showing the ayahs how to handle the children and so on. But, with fifty or sixty new children crossing the border into India every day, conditions in the Nursery were inevitably, as Tsering Dolma admitted, 'shocking to some visitors whose imagination was not vivid enough to realize that it was an emergency, in fact a war situation'.

One of these visitors was an Irish writer, Dervla Murphy, who arrived in 1963 to do voluntary service at the Nursery and was indeed shocked by what she found:

...bronchitis, pneumonia, TB, whooping-cough, chicken-pox, measles, mumps, amoebic and bacillary dysentery, round-hook, tape- and wire-worms, scabies, septic headsores from lice, septic bed-bug bites, boils, abscesses of incredible size, rickets, bleeding gums, weak hearts, asthma, conjunctivitis, trachoma and otitis media. The majority suffer from calcium and Vitamin C deficiency and a heart-breaking number, no matter what is done for them now, will probably be partially blind or deaf or both in maturity...Many of the children are so covered with festering, open sores that you couldn't find room for a six-pence on a clear bit of skin. And when put to bed – six children lie across each bed – the heat so aggravates the itch and pain that they often lie awake whimpering quietly for hours.[9]

At their first meeting in early August 1963, Ms Murphy took an instant dislike to Tsering Dolma. The Principal welcomed her warmly, was 'very sweet and charming and apparently deeply concerned about my comfort while in the camp; she was effusive in her expression of sympathy for the children and of gratitude to all Western helpers'. But even on such scant acquaintance, the new volunteer decided that Tsering Dolma was too 'enjoyably aware of being the Dalai Lama's sister'. The more the Irishwoman grew to love the Tibetan children (Tiblets, she affectionately called them), the more hostile she became to Tsering Dolma, dismissing her as 'a completely uneducated peasant woman who just happens to be His Holiness's sister', a high-handed authoritarian 'with a genius for alienating even those who are best disposed towards Tibetan officialdom'.

The temperaments of the two women made battle inevitable. By November Dervla Murphy's tolerance was wearing thin. In her book *Tibetan Foothold* she writes that 'Tsering Dolma is becoming more and more difficult to deal with', and speaks of 'flaming rows' which have resulted from 'her incomprehensible attitudes'.[10] When the Principal refuses to allow a sick orphan child to leave the Nursery for a camp with a better standard of living in Simla, Ms Murphy accuses her of using the Nursery as a power-base. 'Undoubtedly,' she writes, 'she has compensated herself for the loss of the nationwide power she enjoyed in Tibet by asserting her authority here beyond all reasonable limits.'

The gloves were off and all pretence at politeness was dropped. Suspecting that the interpreters were toning down her own pungent comments when reporting back to Tsering Dolma, Dervla Murphy shrugged, 'I don't blame them. If *I* were constantly in Mrs Tsering Dolma's company I'd be very careful indeed not to translate anything that might worsen her temper during the next twenty-four hours.'

Kundun was not aware of the unpleasantness at the time, but acknowledges that his elder sister may have been difficult to work with. 'My sister, like the rest of us, had a very short temper,' he says. 'I think it was probably true that she was over-conscious of being the Dalai Lama's sister and it may have gone to her head. Don't forget she was an uneducated peasant girl and she was already grown-up and married when her life was turned upside down. She was expected to handle situations and jobs which would ordinarily never have come her way.'[11]

Khando defends her mother more robustly. 'She had the will and the heart for the job, but she knew nothing about management. She cared deeply about those children, some of whom were only babies. She wept because so many died and because she didn't have the means to save them. When my brother and I came to Swarg Ashram for the summer and winter holidays,[12] she had no time to look after us – we had a roof over our heads, we had food to eat, we could look after ourselves, we didn't need her as those poor children in the Nursery needed her. She used to bring some of them to Swarg Ashram, and we'd all try to look after them. To her, those children were not just a job, she was totally involved in them.' Khando feels that Dervla Murphy was unfair. 'She made a lot of petty accusations, such as that my mother wore dark glasses so that nobody could see where she was looking. That was quite unjustified. My mother wore dark glasses on orders from her doctor – to protect her one good eye, as she was blind in the other one. All these personal attacks on my mother, in my view were more demeaning to Ms Murphy than to her. Actually, had my mother spoken English or had a better translator, they might have communicated more successfully.'[13]

Volunteers from other foreign organizations – among them the Swiss Red Cross, the French Service Civil International and the British Save the Children Fund – worked well enough with Tsering Dolma. In fact it was a woman doctor with the Swiss group who first alerted Tsering Dolma to the fact that she was ill. 'Dr Anderhof said she could tell from the texture of my mother's hands, and she begged her to go to the hospital for treatment. But at that stage she was not feeling any physical pain, so she ignored the advice – and we were all too busy to notice.'

By the time Tsering Dolma went to the hospital in Calcutta for a medical check-up, it was too late. Told that she had cancer of the lung and womb, she battled on valiantly. 'No matter how ill she was,' says Kundun, 'she still put her entire self into what she did. She had an enormous capacity for hard work and a deep sense of responsibility.' Though in considerable pain, she got up early every morning for the long walk to the Nursery. As late as 1964, only six months before her death on 21 November, she joined in ball games with the helpers and the bigger girls during the Nursery's fourth anniversary celebrations.

When Pema took her back to Calcutta in June, her doctor, an expatriate Englishman, recommended major surgery at the Westminster Hospital in London. Tendzin Choegyal telephoned her in Calcutta before she left for England. 'I can still hear her voice,' he says sadly. 'She said, "Don't worry about me. I'm not in much pain." The way she said it, I felt she was at peace, but I think she knew she wasn't going to make it. That phone call was our goodbye. When she got to England, she was told they could do nothing.'[14]

Khando had finished school in 1962 and after an eighteen-month period with a Swiss family in Neuchâtel to learn French was studying in England at the House of Citizenship, an international school for young women in Aylesbury. ('We were taught to read newspapers properly, research certain issues, debate them in class, make intelligent conversation on every subject under the sun. We learned how to entertain and how to deal with conflict situations. It was wonderful and the teaching was first-class. But for the life of me, I couldn't think how any of it was relevant to my own life. Later, of course, it turned out to be incredibly useful.') When news came of her mother's illness, she dropped everything and went to London. 'We talked and talked,' she says. 'After she'd had the surgery, my mother was full of plans for the future. She didn't really believe she was going to die.'

One day Khando received a letter from an old school friend of her brother's, Rapten Chazotsang, who, after a period of working in the Dalai Lama's Private Office in Dharamsala, had won a scholarship to the United States to study Political Science. They had known each other on and off for years, had lent each other books and records. 'But he thought I was a fat, ugly school-girl,' says Khando, 'I just wasn't his type.' Since going to the States, however, he had kept in touch occasionally, and, hearing of Tsering Dolma's illness, wrote again to offer sympathy.

'When I saw my mother in hospital and told her about Rapten's message,' says Khando, 'she got very excited and said she had always felt sure we liked each other...My mother said I must write back to him, that he was a wonderful young man, very steady and likeable. Sadly, it was then when she was dying that my mother began to weave plans for the future. "When I get better," she told me, "I shall take life more easily. I'd like a little home of my own where you, Tenzin Ngawang, your spouses and children, can come and I can be a real grandmother." It made me weep, it was so sad. When I thought about it later, I realized she'd never had a family life. She had lived her life in the shadow of my grandmother, always, as the eldest daughter, at her beck and call. She didn't resent that and she knew she would go on doing it. But she still had her dreams. She longed to have her own home, just like other women. She even knew the house she wanted, she'd picked it out, a tiny little cottage in Dharamsala. She thought it was the most beautiful place she'd ever seen, and she dreamed about it. But the dream didn't come true.'

Tsering Dolma died on 21 November 1964, aged forty-five, in the Westminster Hospital, with Phuntsok Tashi, Khando and Tenzin Ngawang at her bedside. 'My father,' says Khando, 'went to pieces and wept. It was heart-rending.' Norbu who flew in from the States, arrived just too late.

The body was cremated in England and the ashes taken to Dharamsala for disposal in accordance with Buddhist ritual. Kundun himself moulded them with clay and imprinted them with images of the gods, the clay images being then enclosed in the casket. Describing himself as 'I, Tenzin Gyatso, Buddhist *bikkhu*' (which is to say, 'a simple monk'), he prayed that her rebirth would be a good one. 'Beloved sister,' he said, 'who was here a moment ago, smiling, talking and telling of her joys and sorrows, is just a memory. She is afar from the field of our vision and hearing. My heart is heavy with grief.'[15]

Whatever the criticisms of her, Kundun has never doubted that Tsering Dolma was the right person in the right place: 'My sister...never gave in to despair,' he wrote in his memoirs.[16] 'She was a powerful woman and quite strict, having inherited the family temper in full measure. At heart, though, she was a very kind person with a good sense of humour. Her contribution in those difficult times was invaluable.' Khando agrees, insisting that her mother was never 'Dervla's devious and scheming harpy', but a simple, warm-hearted woman with no airs and graces, a woman who was inadequately prepared for some of what life threw at her. 'I'm proud to have been her daughter. She had no education, yet she acquitted herself as well as could be expected in the positions she was thrust into. She looked after her mother, had an unquestioning love and devotion for His Holiness, and was a good sister to all her brothers – one of her greatest regrets at the end was that Gyalo Thondup had caused His Holiness such difficulties in Dharamsala – and the other was that she had let down a few very close friends in Tibet by being unable to let them know of the secret plans to flee Tibet. I'm just sorry she died so young, before my brother and I had families of our own and might have been able to make her life a lot happier.'[17]

Tsering Dolma was succeeded at the Nursery by her 23-year-old sister, Pema. Pema's schooldays in Darjeeling, amid nuns who 'instilled high principles into us', had on the whole been happy. 'We were taught to be kind and compassionate above all, and that, of course, was also the basic teaching of Buddhism.'[18] Leaving school, she had gone to La Pelouse, a finishing school in Switzerland, and then to Mrs Hoster's College for Young Ladies in London for a combined Secretarial and Office Administration course. She intended then to return to India and work in the Private Office, recently set up to handle Kundun's income and expenditure (including his daily twenty-rupee allowance from the Indian Government[19]). But on reaching Dharamsala in March 1964, she realized that her sister, Tsering Dolma, was ill and needed her help.

Pema admired her sister's courage and what she had achieved in the face of enormous difficulty. 'She did a great deal for the children in the Nursery,'[20] she said, 'at a time when we had almost no facilities. She was the original moving spirit behind what eventually became the Tibetan Children's Village, with almost a thousand children to take care of and precious little to do it with.' Pema, in common with many others, believes there was a deeper reason for the feud with Dervla Murphy. 'I felt hurt by Dervla's criticisms of my sister, but then Dervla had been hurt too. She actually wanted to adopt a Tibetan child and my sister would not allow it. That was why Dervla felt resentment; and where there is resentment, people overreact. It was all rather sad.'

Younger, educated, energetic and flexible, Pema was more in tune with the foreign volunteer workers than her sister – though she too had inherited the family temper. While waiting to go to Switzerland, she had been roped in to teach English to Kundun's two personal monk-attendants. The two monks were slow learners, and Pema was as impatient as the rest of her siblings. 'She used to pinch their hands and dig her nails into their knuckles as a punishment for being so slow,' recounts her brother,

Tendzin Choegyal. 'In the end, they went on strike and said they didn't want to learn English any more.'[21]

When Pema talks about the early days, she can barely resist a shudder. 'Shortage of staff, shortage of funds, shortage of facilities, shortage of food, clothing, space, shortage of just about everything. The children just came flooding in, and we had to devote our energies to keeping them alive, finding enough for them to eat. Everyone was very dedicated, the house mothers, the cooks, the office workers, but we were desperately short of trained teachers. With so many of our teachers unqualified, the children's basic general education left a lot to be desired.' But, against all the odds, they survived, and under Pema's careful guidance the Nursery grew and flourished. In September 1964, Dervla Murphy received an enthusiastic letter from Judy Pullen, a Canadian volunteer teacher at the Nursery:

> Lois and I have seen a lot of Pema (younger sister of His Holiness, who has replaced Mrs Tsering Dolma) and the more we see her the more we like her. She's a wonderful gal and is working like a dog at the Nursery. She's there from 9 a.m. to 8 p.m. seven days a week. She was sick with tonsillitis one week and Thomas [the doctor] ordered her to bed but she refused to go and came to work every day. Everyone is just thrilled with her, and things at the Nursery have improved 100 per cent...You can rest assured the Nursery is in good hands.[22]

When, in April 1965, Dervla Murphy returned briefly to Dharamsala, she could scarcely believe her eyes. Her diary for 23 April records:

> Hard to believe that the miserable children among whom I worked less than a year and a half ago have been transformed into these bouncing, bright-eyed, rosy-cheeked Tiblets. Had I been dropped into the compound by helicopter I would never have recognized the place; there are now twice the number of buildings – and half the number of children...the present policy is to keep numbers down to a maximum of 500, and Pema-la very wisely refuses to admit any but orphans from the road-camps.

It was to Pema, her 'intelligence, common-sense and flair for leadership' that she attributed the transformation. 'Young people like Pema,' she wrote, 'gave one hope for the future of their country.'

NOTES

1. Published in the *Tibetan Bulletin*, March–April 1995.
2. Letter to the author from Rinchen Dolma Taring, 1993.
3. Author interview with HH the Dalai Lama, 1993.
4. Letter to author from Rinchen Dolma Taring, 1993.
5. Tenzin Ngawang and Khando were to pursue their studies in Mussoorie.
6. Author interview with Tendzin Choegyal, UK, 1996.
7. All the information that follows is the result of various conversations with Namlha Taklha in Dharamsala, 1993, 1994 and 1995.
8. Author interview with HH the Dalai Lama, Dharamsala, June 1994.
9. Dervla Murphy, *Tibetan Foothold*, John Murray, 1966; Pan 1969.
10. Murphy, *Tibetan Foothold*.
11. Author interview with HH the Dalai Lama, Dharamsala, July 1995.
12. K ndo was still at school, but Tenzin Ngawang was studying at St John's Col-

13. g, Utah, February 1996.
14. Dharamsala, June 1994.
15. h either as human or animal. A good na carns rebirth onto a higher plane ient or Buddha-hood.
16. .
17. ng, Utah, February 1996.
18. ramsala, June 1994.
19. ian a pound sterling.
20 aramsala, June 1994.
21 al, Dharamsala, 1993.
22

...And 1965–70

A nation is a soul or spiritual principle. These are but two aspects of the same thing. One is in the past, the other in the present. One is the common possession of a rich legacy of memories; the other is the present consent, the desire to live together, the wish to continue to assert the undivided heritage that has been handed down. A nation is therefore a huge solidarity, constituted by the feeling of sacrifices that have been made, and which will continue to be made. It supposes a past, but it nevertheless comes down to the present in a tangible fact: the consent, the clearly expressed desire to continue living together.

Ernest Renan, Discours et Conférences

'Springtime has come to Tibet...serfdom is finished...the moment the people have waited for has come,' a Chinese propaganda film burbled joyously. But the Lhasa Uprising had brought home to the Chinese that they could never govern the Tibetan people by consent. With the entire country now at their mercy, they divided Tibet into eight military zones and imposed a reign of terror. By the end of July 1960, sixty thousand refugees had fled Tibet for India. Over the next few years, as forced collectivization brought about a constantly repeated cycle of starvation, resistance and repression, the number would increase to more than one hundred thousand. It was partly anger at this continuing haemorrhage that drove the Chinese to invade India in 1962; since when they had used different tactics to try and staunch the flow. In 1964 hoardings in major towns offered tempting incentives to any Tibetans who might return to the new 'socialist paradise' – accompanied by unmistakable threats to the families of those rash enough to refuse. Few responded.

In 1965, when Tibet officially became the Tibet Autonomous Region, the same old puppet 'leaders' were still in place. With, however, one surprising exception: the Panchen Lama. Ordered in 1962 to move to the Potala, denounce the Dalai Lama and take his place as Chairman of the PCART, 'Mao's Panchen' had refused, advising the Tibetans instead to preserve their cultural heritage at all costs. For two years, he was banned from appearing in public. Then, one day in 1964, he was given a last chance to redeem himself by denouncing his predecessor. On that day he earned his place in Tibetan history and in Tibetan hearts when, in front of ten thousand people, he affirmed that the Dalai Lama's survival was a sign of hope for Tibet; and proclaimed his belief 'that Tibet will soon regain her independence and that His Holiness the Dalai Lama will return to the Golden Throne'.' The Tibetans wept at his brave words, and knew he would have to pay for them. Arrested and subjected to horrific *thamzings*, he was taken to Peking and was now in solitary confinement in China's top security prison. With their two religious leaders gone, most Tibetans were in a state of shock and grief, far removed from the determined Chinese portrayal of a happy people whose dream had just come true.

Just under a year later in 1966, Chairman Mao, in a crazed attempt to restore his flagging personal power, let loose his young Red Guards in the barbaric Cultural Revolution. Its aim was to erase the past by destroying 'the Four Olds' – old culture, old customs, old habits, old ways of thinking; the definition of 'old' being left to the Red Guards who were allowed to rampage at whim. For Tibet, last bastion of 'the old', that period of collective insanity meant an orgy of undiluted horror. Buddhism was the main target. Most of the remaining monasteries – they had once numbered over six thousand – were destroyed; sacred scriptures were burned or used as paper for the latrines; statues – stripped of their gold and silver – were mutilated and beheaded. Tibetans were forced to throw their prayer-wheels into the river and replace their mantras with the Thoughts of Chairman Mao. Even to be seen moving one's lips in prayer was a crime punishable by death. Celibate monks were made to copulate in public, abbots of great monasteries were crowned with dunce caps and ritually humiliated before being murdered or sent to the gulags in the far north to be worked and starved to death. Anyone remotely connected with the Dalai Lama or the old system was thrown into prison and subjected to *thamzings*. 'The word Hell,' wrote one observer, 'is too soft to describe what happened in those years.'[2] The British writer Bernard Levin has described it as nothing less than genocide.[3]

The Cultural Revolution was even more brutal and lasted longer in Tibet than anywhere else in the People's Republic of China. For well over a decade, Tibet disappeared into the darkness of total night. 'We heard very little,' says Kundun, 'just occasionally, from Nepalese traders who had crossed the borders, and their news was always long out-of-date. We knew the Cultural Revolution had begun and that there was immense destruction. But we had so often been overwhelmed by negative events that this seemed like just one more terrible chapter to be added to all the others. We didn't yet realize that it eclipsed in horror everything that had happened before.'[4] What he did know was that the Chinese leaders in Peking had launched a character-assassination campaign against him, denouncing him as 'that wolf in monk's clothing', hypocrite, thief and even rapist, the Number One Enemy of the Tibetan People!

Mercifully unaware of the events which were crucifying their homeland, by the mid-Sixties the Tibetan exiles in India and Nepal were experiencing a kind of rebirth. In southern India they were fast becoming skilled agricultural workers in a tropical climate; in the north and in Nepal they had established handicraft centres, set up market-stalls, ramshackle shops, tea-houses and even small hotels. Dharamsala continued to be the home of the Tibetan Government-in-Exile, and here Kundun was preserving elements of the old Tibet while coaxing his people politically into the twentieth century.

Nehru's successor, Lal Bahadur Shastri, not only sympathized with the Tibetans but, unlike Nehru, was prepared to uphold their cause in public. In autumn 1965 when the UN once again discussed Tibet, Shastri's India actually voted in Tibet's favour. Though the UN again contented itself with pious exhortation, calling for 'respect for the fundamental rights of the Tibetan people', Kundun felt hopeful that India at least might be near to recognizing his Government-in-Exile. Alas, on 1 September 1965, war broke out between India and Pakistan and, although the fighting was over in six months, within a few hours of signing the peace treaty Mr Shastri was dead. It was a cruel blow. Not only, grieved Kundun, had India lost one of her finest statesmen and the world an enlightened leader – but Tibet had lost one of its few friends in high places.

Since Dharamsala was less than one hundred miles from the Pakistan border, when Kundun left to visit the Tibetan settlements in the south later that year, a total blackout was in force. His driver had to make the dangerous descent to the station at Pathankot without headlights. From the station, they could hear shells exploding over the airport nearby.

At Byllakuppe, the progress made by the settlers was heart-warming. The land had been cleared and, thanks to the International Red Cross and others, most of the refugees at least had access to medical care. 'No longer,' he wrote, 'did I have to confront people who were on the edge of despair.'⁵ Because of the war, his visit to the south was extended: two bombs had already fallen on Dharamsala and the Kashag insisted on his staying in South India until the trouble was over. So from Karnataka, he travelled to Mysore, Madras and Kerala, to give teachings.

In Kerala he decided to become a vegetarian. As noted earlier, the assumption in the West that Tibetan Buddhists are all vegetarians is a fallacy. Nevertheless Kundun, though an enthusiastic meat-eater all his life, believed in vegetarianism as an ideal for monks and nuns. When, in Kerala, he saw a chicken being strangled for his lunch, he decided the time had come to put the ideal into practice!

Two months later, when the war ended, he returned to Dharamsala with all the fervour of a new convert. For the next eighteen months he ate 'no eggs, no fish – and, of course, no chicken'. Following the advice of Indian friends, he supplemented his diet with plenty of milk and different kinds of nuts. His mother was appalled, protesting to her friends that 'he'd been fed on meat all his life and if he didn't have it he'd die.'⁶ But he persisted – until, one day in the autumn of 1967, he collapsed with a severe dose of Hepatitis B. Nauseous and without appetite, he lay for several weeks in a state of total exhaustion. When, after a long course of Tibetan medicine, the doctors pronounced him cured, they scolded him for being foolhardy. 'They insisted that not only must I eat less greasy food, cut out nuts and reduce my milk consumption, but I must start having meat again instantly. They feared that the illness had caused permanent damage to my liver and had probably shortened my life.'⁷ As several Indian doctors agreed, Kundun reluctantly resumed his meat-eating. Amala breathed again.

Lobsang had been posted to Geneva as Assistant to Kundun's Representative. The Swiss Red Cross had already found homes for hundreds of Tibetan orphans, having them adopted into Swiss families while encouraging them to preserve their Tibetan culture and identity. More recently they had undertaken to resettle a thousand Tibetan adult refugees, providing food, clothing and medical assistance as well as accommodation. 'They were bringing the Tibetan adults over from India, and some of them arrived looking very tidy and neatly dressed,' recalls Namlha. 'When they stepped off the plane, the press were waiting and of course their pictures were in the papers. There was an outcry, people protested that they were supposed to be helping poor Tibetans, not well-dressed ones. The Swiss were very upset about it, they felt they were getting the wrong kind of people. They turned to Lobsang and asked if he would go to India and personally select the refugees for resettlement. So he went back and made his way to the road-gangs in Kulu, gathered the workers together and told them to pick out the very poorest among them. The Red Cross then brought these people to Switzerland and everyone was happy.'[8]

Lobsang travelled all over Europe, wherever there were Tibetan refugees. Namlha worked as interpreter and secretary, but both of them spent most of their time just listening to the problems of the refugees and co-ordinating the efforts of the various international agencies. They were expected to attend the usual round of diplomatic functions, but being 'simple people who like fresh air, walking and simple pleasures', they cared little for these formal occasions. Their budget did not allow of elaborate entertaining: when it was their turn to invite guests to their sixth-floor apartment, they cooked the meal themselves. 'The diplomats seemed to love our informality,' says Namlha.

When Amala came to Geneva to spend a year with them, 'we insisted she was to have a rest and not do any work,' says Namlha. 'We thought we were being kind, but she absolutely hated it; she wanted to help and we wouldn't let her. One day I went to her room and found her sewing up the hem of her dress, looking very depressed. When I asked her what on earth she was doing, she said, "Sitting around waiting for death. You two won't let me do anything, and I can't stand being idle. So I've unpicked this hem and am sewing it up again." Well, naturally, we were very upset, and after that we let her help as much as she wanted. She joined me in the kitchen and taught me how to bake that wonderful yeasty Amdo bread sprinkled with turmeric and fenugreek. "You young girls don't know how lucky you are," she would scold me if I ever dared grumble. "When I was young, as soon as the cock had crowed, I had to get up and make bread, clean the house, prepare the altars. And in the evenings I'd still be embroidering and mending clothes till after midnight. I never got more than four hours' sleep. Girls today don't know they're born."'

Khando also came to Geneva to recover from a serious illness. After four and a half years of study in England she had returned to India. 'His Holiness and my father had decided I needed to be brought down to earth and experience a bit of real life.' Phuntsok Tashi took her to Mustang, where he had some business with the guerrillas. 'There I was, in my best clothes, fresh from England, suddenly looking round for walking shoes and borrowing my father's jacket to go into the wilderness. The experience did me a lot of good, but unfortunately I caught some rare stomach bug in Kathmandu and became very ill.' She was packed off to Zurich for treatment in a clinic run by a Swiss doctor friend.

Convalescing in Geneva was a rare opportunity for her to get to know her grandmother better. 'I remember she used to say extremely long prayers, and as she was very self-disciplined, she'd get up at the crack of dawn and get them all over with at once. When breakfast time came, she would say cheerfully, "Well, the prayers are said, so I'm free for the rest of the day." Then we used to go out for walks or go shopping together.' Khando's brother, Tenzin Ngawang, had come fifteenth in all Bengal in the Higher Cambridge examinations, and had gone on to study Sociology at King's College, Cambridge. On his way back to India, he fell in love with Dr Charles Aeschimann's daughter, Danielle, and decided to marry her. When his father protested that they were temperamentally unsuited to each other, Tenzin enlisted Kundun's help, and Phuntsok Tashi was persuaded to withdraw his objections. Tenzin then went to work in the Education department in New Delhi, before moving to Darjeeling to be editor of the Government's *Tibetan Review*. He and Danielle were married in 1964.

His schoolfriend, Rapten Chazotsang, who had acquired a Sociology degree in the USA, wrote to Khando to say that he was passing through Geneva on his way home to India! On his first evening, the pair went out to the cinema and did not return until the small hours. Amala was shocked. 'My grandmother was cross with me next day. She said I'd spent far too long with him and if we went out together again I was to come home earlier. But I know she liked Rapten really.'

When Khando returned to New Delhi and moved in with her father, she and Rapten had already decided to marry. To her relief, her father approved the match. Maybe Phuntsok Tashi was relieved too, since, though he had not yet told his daughter, he was planning to get married again, to Kesang, a young Tibetan woman many years his junior, who was working at the Nursery in Dharamsala. When Khando first found out, she was furious. But as time went by she relented and grew quite close to Kesang. Amala, however, found it difficult to forgive her son-in-law for remarrying.

Norbu, as Assistant to Kundun's Representative in New York, divided his day between the Tibet Office and the Museum. He and Kunyang had moved out of their tiny apartment to a larger flat near Central Park in 1962 when their first son, Lhundrup Namgyal, was born. A second son, Kunga, arrived in 1963, followed by a third, Jigme, in 1965. By this time Norbu was engaged on a six-month lecture tour about Tibet, visiting colleges and universities in almost every state of the US and Canada. Towards the end of the tour, he was invited to join the staff of Indiana University in Bloomington. Having spoken on the campuses of a number of colleges, many of them quite small, he formed a mental image of the university in question as a small insignificant rural outfit 'surrounded by a vast number of cornfields' – though, with three young sons, and a dog, there was something to be said for moving from New York to a place where 'grass and trees grew around houses' and where they would have space to run around. He decided to take a look at Bloomington.

He was in for a surprise. 'Instead of a small college in a sleepy town with perhaps a thousand students, I was astonished to discover a beautiful sprawling campus bustling with activity and with a student population of almost thirty thousand.' After talking the matter over with Kunyang, he accepted the offer and the family moved to Bloomington in time for the beginning of the 1965 academic year. The university provided him with a two-bedroomed house which, though small, was palatial compared to their New York apartment. The boys were delighted to be in the country – seeing, for the first time in their urban lives, real fruit growing on real trees. They settled into Bloomington life with ease.

In his first semester, Norbu, with only one language course – in elementary Tibetan – and only three students, had time on his hands. He spent it getting to know the place and making new friends. In the years that followed he was given more demanding language work, as well as courses on Tibetan oral literature, religion, the monastic orders and the political system in Old Tibet.

In 1967, to Norbu's great delight, Amala came to visit. He had been eight years old when he left home for Kumbum. After that, though he had sometimes visited his family in Taktser, and had had a room in his parents' home in Lhasa, the monastery had been his real home. Following his flight from Tibet in 1951, he did not see his mother again until the Buddha Jayanti in 1956, and after that not until she reached India as a refugee in 1959.

He was overjoyed at the prospect of seeing her. 'I felt that my mother's presence under my roof would bring us some degree of the home life and family atmosphere of Amdo that I had sorely missed since my childhood, and especially throughout my life of exile.' The boys were thrilled to realize that, like all their American friends, they would have a real 'Grandma' with them for Thanksgiving and Christmas. As Amala spoke no English, they would have to polish up their own Tibetan.

Norbu went to meet Amala in New York, and showed her the big city before bringing her home in triumph to Bloomington. She immediately took the whole family under her wing. 'She helped organize our household, taught my wife special Amdo dishes, constantly fussed over the children, and behaved in every way like an adoring grandmother.' Fortunately Amala and Kunyang took an instant liking to each other. Kunyang, an orphan from early childhood, was soon telling her friends that Amala was a real mother to her. Norbu – perhaps realizing more than ever how much he himself had been deprived – loved to see her playing with the boys. 'She had a wonderful way with children,' he wrote. 'My boys all adored their Mo-la and even the neighbours' children would gather round her calling her Mo-la.'

Throughout that year, Norbu marvelled that his mother had retained her unassuming simplicity, despite the high station to which she had been elevated. 'She had a natural dignity that sprang from her inner strength of character and self-reliance; she never assumed the airs of a grand lady.'

Planting and replanting – 'every morning she was in the garden watering the flowers' – mending the family's clothes, rearranging furniture, playing with the children, Amala's year passed all too quickly. When it was time for her to leave, the parting was difficult for them all. 'She had,' said her son, 'immeasurably enriched our household with love and care and with the peace and serenity that she inspired in all of us.'

Tendzin Choegyal was still at school in Darjeeling. Though two of his elder brothers had abandoned the monastic state, it was taken for granted that he at least would continue to be a monk. He was Ngari Rinpoche, an important Incarnation, destined to take charge of a number of monasteries in Ladakh and Zanskar. At the same time, he was an adolescent who had been torn, at the formative age of thirteen, from a Tibetan Buddhist monastery and transplanted into a Roman Catholic, English-speaking boarding school. Somehow, he had survived. In the higher forms now, he was studying Scripture, Moral Science (i.e. Religion), History, Geography, Chemistry, Physics, Biology, Maths, PE, Arts and Crafts, English Language and Literature – and Tibetan. It was a general education such as Kundun might have envied.

In the lower school, Religion had been just another lesson, involving little more than the mechanical repetition of scriptural texts, a routine which reminded him of home. As he grew older, the lessons became more challenging and controversial. 'Some of the non-Christian boys became quite hostile towards Christianity,' he remembers, 'they asked snide, aggressive questions in class. But I never wanted to mock. I think that in spite of appearances I had always been drawn to the spiritual life, and these Christian teachings began to rekindle the flame. Having been brought up in a monastery, and in a national culture dominated by religious beliefs and spirituality, I was quite open to learning what I could from Christianity.'

Studying the Gospels, he was happy to find them close in spirit to Mahayana Buddhism, the Beatitudes and the Sermon on the Mount in particular sounding a familiar note. 'The Christian message of altruism and love just reinforced my Buddhist beliefs. The Mahayana ideal is also love: we search for enlightenment in order to help other sentient beings along the path. Christianity and Buddhism both worked in me, the one feeding the other, and for me the synthesis of the two was something positive.'⁹ Sometimes, when all was quiet, he used to go to the chapel – to meditate in silence or recite his Buddhist prayers. There he was at peace.

That the Christians he met seemed to live their beliefs impressed him. 'With our monks, it was so often just a matter of lip-service...But here it was different...Priests were doing all kinds of social service, becoming teachers and so on. I liked that and made a lot of friends among them.'

At the end of that year – his last but one at the College – Tendzin Choegyal, to everyone's surprise, failed his exams. Unable to face repeating the year, he decided on impulse to pick up his monastic studies in Dharamsala. Joining the rest of the family at Swarg Ashram, he enrolled in Buddhist philosophy classes given by the Abbot of Namgyal Monastery.

One of his fellow-students was a young monk working in the Private Office, Tenzin Geyche Tethong. Tenzin Geyche, from an old aristocratic family, had been sent to a Methodist school in Darjeeling from an early age. He and Tendzin Choegyal had met only after the latter came to India as a refugee. 'I'd already been out of the country for about ten years and his Tibetan was so much better and more fluent than mine,' says Tenzin Geyche. 'I was very impressed.'

When they met again in Dharamsala, Tenzin Geyche was impressed in a different way. 'As Ngari Rinpoche, he was responsible for all those monasteries in Ladakh. I used to tease him about it, calling him King of Ladakh. It really was a small kingdom that he had inherited.' When studies were over for the day, the two boys would escape to the hills. 'Up there in the mountains we used to let off steam, yelling and shouting our heads off for the sheer joy of it,' says Tenzin Geyche. 'Sometimes we would recite Shakespeare at the tops of our voices. Or make paper gliders which used to fly very well if you made them properly.'

Tendzin Choegyal did not find the transition altogether easy. 'Rinpoche had a brilliant mind and an excellent memory, but he was terribly impatient,' remembers his friend. 'The philosophy lessons given by the Abbot were really quite short, only about an hour. But Rinpoche had a wrist watch with an alarm on it, and as the lesson began he used to set the alarm to go off in exactly one hour's time. He had no intention of staying any longer than he had to.'[10] Fortunately, the Abbot was a tolerant man.

While in Dharamsala, Tendzin Choegyal was ordained as a monk.

In the summer of 1966, the monks of Rangzom in Ladakh, the chief monastery associated with the Ngari Rinpoches, requested a formal visitation: as Tenzin Geyche had teased, he *was* virtually king of Ladakh. 'Well,' he explains – with some embarrassment – 'Ladakh and Zanskar are my territory, rather like a bishop and his diocese.' As Kundun was making an official visit to that extreme north-west area of India, they travelled together. Choegyal visited all seven of his monasteries and stayed on for a month after Kundun had left. He was miserable: 'It was difficult to sleep at such a high altitude, the food was terrible, everything was dirty and the people were appallingly superstitious. I felt I had travelled backwards in time into a medieval world.' The solemn ceremonial with which he was received unnerved him and on at least one occasion embarrassment pushed him into behaving outrageously. 'They were very solemn, but I wasn't,' he explains. 'At Karsha monastery, one of the biggest in Zanskar, they had set up a formal welcome, banners everywhere, the Abbot in attendance, horns, trumpets and all that. We rode in solemn procession, and our progress was dismally slow. I ran out of patience and said to the Ladakhi official who was riding next to me, "Oh, come on, let's gallop!" He took his whip out from under the saddle and slapped the rumps of the monks' horses in front of us. So the whole procession galloped the last five kilometres, straight through the crowd and up to the monastery. I really enjoyed myself and the villagers laughed their heads off, it was the first time they'd ever seen an Abbot gallop. Nobody minded; we are, don't forget, a fun-loving people. But I must admit it was unusual.' What the Abbot felt – or said – he does not reveal.

Choegyal's inability to take his prestigious role seriously may have been symptomatic of a larger confusion already making itself felt. With hindsight, he thinks that, despite his so recent ordination, he was already doubting his vocation as a monk. 'You either have it or you don't, and I don't think I ever had it.' He didn't mind the studying, nor even the rigours of the life. But somehow he could not identify with what Buddhist monks were meant to be about. 'We spent our time assimilating knowledge. But what good was all that learning without practice? Philosophy should hold the key to the meaning of life, but here it did not.' Knowledge on its own was of little use in confronting one's personal demons. 'Our one real aim in life should be the practice of *dharma*, any act, word or thought aimed at eradicating the three afflictive emotions of hatred, greed and ignorance.'[11] But it seemed to me that most of the monks concentrated on learning for its own sake, not on putting that learning to good use, nor on trying to grow in happiness and holiness. I really felt they were missing the whole point.'[12]

Helping Tibet in some way was the point for him. Answering Kundun's appeal to young Tibetans – to rebuild their nation in exile. That, in Tendzin Choegyal's book, was the true practice of *dharma*.

Towards the end of the Sixties, things began to go wrong for Gyalo Thondup. Acting on complaints from some of the younger, CIA-trained officers in Mustang, he had sacked the Commander of the National Volunteer

Defence Army, the Khampa General Baba Yeshi, replacing him by General Gyatso Wangdu, sole survivor of the first group of Tibetans trained by the CIA.[13] Baba Yeshi retired to Dharamsala to lick his wounds, before returning to Mustang, publicly breaking with the NVDA, and accusing Gyalo Thondup of misappropriating the contents of the famous yellow parachute. Then, with about two hundred disgruntled Khampas, he set up a private army. A dangerous stand-off resulted, not only in Mustang where the two groups actually came to blows, but also throughout the Tibetan settlements, where the refugees lined up on either side of the old tribal fault-lines: Khampas versus the rest. Refusing to join any of the regular Tibetan settlements such as Byllakuppe, Khampa leaders set up thirteen breakaway settlements of their own. Like Baba Yeshi they believed that Gyalo Thondup had betrayed them and that he was part of a sinister Dharamsala (i.e. old Lhasa) plot to keep them down.

Gyalo Thondup had belatedly realized the danger of depending solely on the powerful Khampas for his support, and had been slowly distancing himself from them. When he actually formed a new political group, the United Party, culled from all three of the former provinces of Tibet, the Khampas turned against him, regarding him from that time forward as the arch-betrayer. The situation got so out of hand, Tibetan loyalties became so polarized, that the fragile unity of the refugees in Dharamsala seemed about to collapse.

The CIA chose this of all times to announce that they were closing down the Tibetan operation. They sugared the pill somewhat by offering a three-year programme which would supposedly enable the Tibetan SFF to become self-sufficient, but it was no more than a face-saver. Gyalo Thondup's right-hand man, Lhamo Tsering, is still bitter. 'It was just a ploy to keep us from making too much of a fuss,' he accuses. 'They had us completely fooled.' By the time American aid was cut in 1970, Gyalo Thondup had had enough of Dharamsala and had retired in disgust to Hong Kong. (Without, however, breaking his ties with the Indian Secret Service.) The Tibetans would not see him again for almost a decade.

Many of the younger Tibetan refugees had idolized Gyalo Thondup and, like him, wanted radical change. Chafing at their elders' reluctance to move with the times, they talked incessantly about how to harness the energy of Tibetan youth in the cause of their country's independence. Four young men[14] came up with the idea of a Youth Congress, with leaders who would be forward-looking and accountable to the members. 'We needed some kind of youth forum where people could come together and pool their ideas. We all felt the voice of Tibetan youth had to make itself heard; their energies had somehow to be channelled to help Tibet,' says Tendzin Choegyal.

Kundun gave the youngsters his blessing, and offered to meet the costs of an inaugural meeting, with the one proviso that it must represent refugees from *all* three regions. On 7 October 1970, three hundred eager young Tibetans gathered in Dharamsala to ask some pointed questions of their elders. Why, they wanted to know, had the Chinese been able to walk into Tibet so effortlessly in 1950; what had the Kashag been doing to let it happen; and why hadn't the army in the east put up a credible fight? It was obvious that a vibrant new political opposition party was in the making, one that might eventually replace GT's United Party. The more conservative Tibetans were unhappy about it, but, like it or not, half-way through that week of tough talking and debate, the Tibetan Youth Congress was officially inaugurated by Kundun.

Tenzin Geyche was elected first President of what was, in those early days, a pretty chaotic organization. 'We didn't have an office,' says Tendzin Choegyal, 'just a tin trunk in which we kept all the documents and papers. Sometimes we held our meetings in empty rooms with no furniture, so the tin trunk had to act as table as well.'[15] But what they lacked in comforts, they more than made up for in enthusiasm. Their aims were unambiguous: to preserve their Tibetan identity and culture; to stay united under the leadership of the Dalai Lama; and, last and most aggressively, to regain Tibet. 'For the first time since the exile,' claimed Jamyang Norbu, a member of the first Central Executive Committee, 'we had an organization which knew what it wanted to do; which was not a court organization, not regional, not sectarian. It was something new: it was national.'[16] The Kashag viewed them sourly as the thin end of a highly undesirable wedge. The Youth Congress saw itself as a loyal opposition, but, as Jamyang Norbu put it, 'the Kashag did not want *any* opposition, loyal or otherwise'. As over half of the Youth Congress members were actually employed within the Government service, squalls could safely be predicted.

The founders of the new movement all belonged to that new breed of young Tibetans who had received a modern Western-style education outside of Tibet. They spoke English and Hindi along with Tibetan. They were not emotionally bound to their old outdated system; and they could clearly see the problems which their society faced as it struggled to join the modern world. They recognized that there were now two kinds of young Tibetans: those born inside Tibet, under a Chinese military dictatorship, with no experience of freedom, no knowledge of their own traditions or of the Dalai Lama; and those others who had been born as refugees in exile, affected by Western values, knowing nothing of the Chinese, nor of Communism.

The central executive (CENTREX) of the Youth Congress was to be in Dharamsala, with branches set up wherever there were young Tibetans. Darjeeling, for example. For no particular reason that he can think of, Tendzin Choegyal had gone there for a holiday in the summer of 1969, after revisiting his monasteries in Ladakh. (This time, with his social conscience working overtime, he had applied himself to introducing democratic principles, making radical changes in the distribution of his monastic wealth. 'There were certain monasteries which had accumulated wealth but were not putting it to good use. Their excuse was that this wealth was mine, intended for me personally. So I sent out letters to all the monasteries, insisting that whatever money there was belonged to them and was to be used for the benefit of all, not just for certain monasteries and certainly not for me. In the end I just renounced my personal claim to any of it.'[17]) Meeting his old Headmaster, Fr Maurice Standford, he was persuaded to return to St Joseph's College and finish his interrupted studies. He enrolled as a day boy, living in Gyalo Thondup's house until the last month of the school year when he once again became a boarder. By dint of working hard, at the end of the year he 'managed to scrape through' his leaving examinations. 'My results were just about good enough,' he shrugs. In the circumstances, he had expected no better.

Accepting belatedly that he had no vocation to the monastic state, he announced that he was abandoning it. It is said that his mother was deeply distressed by his decision, but if so she hid the fact from him. 'You're not the first high lama to disrobe,' she consoled him, 'it's happening more and more now, in exile.' Kundun admits that for a while he felt disappointed that yet another brother had reneged on his calling. But he too was a realist and soon accepted the situation. Rinchen Khando, whom Choegyal would later marry, believes that his decision to abandon the monastic state took a great deal of courage. 'He was desperately anxious to lead a good life without hypocrisy and I think that his being an Incarnation and a monk set up a terrible conflict within him. The very fact that he was able to stand up and say he could no longer be a monk, well, it took a lot of guts. Many men in that position couldn't have done it.'[18]

For a few months Choegyal continued to study at St Joseph's, underlining his new lay status by outlandish behaviour and a style of dressing which can only be called bizarre. 'There was a Humphrey Bogart-style trench-coat which I loved...teamed with a broad, pale blue tie with polka dots. I'd stick a pipe in my mouth and wear sideburns plastered in place with egg-white.' He swears that as a technique for attracting the attention of girls, it worked, 'if only because no one else looked quite so odd'.

At their first meeting since Tendzin Choegyal had disrobed, Kundun treated him gently. 'You've been passing through a wild phase,' he said, 'but, even if you're no longer a monk, you're still a follower of the *dharma*. Hold on to that. Get married,' he went on to advise, then, mindful of his younger brother's impulsiveness, 'but don't rush. Take your time. Find a really suitable girl.'

In September, at a Youth Congress meeting, Choegyal met Rinchen Khando Tasotsang, a student at the Loreto College in Darjeeling. He remembers thinking quite dispassionately, when he first set eyes on her, 'If I ever marry, that will be the girl.' Their meeting impressed Rinchen Khando too, for a quite different reason. Since childhood, she had been devoted to the Great Mother. 'In my mind I always felt very close to her. I was sure she was the reincarnation of the Goddess Tara, not because I knew much about her but because she had given birth to someone as outstanding as His Holiness. In college I had a picture of her on my desk. But it was past its best, so one day after a Youth Congress meeting, I plucked up courage to ask her son for a new one. That was my first meeting with Rinpoche. [Like most people, even his closest friends, Rinchen Khando still refers to her husband as Rinpoche.] He asked me why I wanted it and seemed a bit surprised when I told him. But he found a photograph for me, so I was quite content.'

The Tasotsangs were a family of prosperous Khampa traders who had lived very simply in Kham. 'We all used to eat together in a big room, the village children, the servants, ourselves, sometimes about thirty-five of us. There were no differences between us. People were happy then.' She was about four when the Chinese came and tore everything apart. 'They started dividing people into ranks and setting them against each other, interfering in the way the village was run. They used to watch our every movement, everything we did, how we behaved towards each other.' In 1956, when Rinchen was seven, the family moved to the apparent safety of Lhasa. There for a while she attended a Tibetan school until her parents decided to follow the example of several other families and send their children to schools in India. Enrolled as a boarder at St Joseph's Convent in Kalimpong, Rinchen dreaded being parted from her parents, and when she found herself actually in Kalimpong, with her school uniform already packed, and her parents preparing to return to Tibet, she was inconsolable. Fate then took a hand, in a way that at the time she was too young to understand. 'Suddenly my parents had a letter from my uncle telling them not to go back to Tibet. I was so happy that they were not going to abandon me that I didn't really bother about the reasons.' It was March 1959!

Unable to return home, Rinchen's parents stayed in Kalimpong for a year and then moved to Darjeeling. But when China invaded the border territories of India in 1962, the Tasotsangs like many other Tibetans abandoned the town which was so uncomfortably near to the war zone, and settled instead in Mussoorie.

The Tibetan school in Mussoorie had an excellent reputation. It had been opened in 1960 for fifty young men from the Missamari transit camp, and, at Kundun's request, Rinchen Dolma Taring and her husband Jigme had taken charge. The young men were in rags and permanently hungry, there were no toilet facilities – but no one complained. Gradually, as individuals and charitable organizations came to the rescue, (and eventually the Government of India took over the school) things improved. By the time the young men had finished their education and dispersed to train as teachers themselves, the school was already a recognized High School, with Jigme Taring as Principal. Those first students were replaced by about six hundred boys and girls, of whom Rinchen Khando was one. Later she was admitted to a Protestant school in Mussoorie, where she obtained her Senior Cambridge Certificate.

From Mussoorie, Rinchen moved to Darjeeling to train as a teacher at the Loreto College for Girls – just at the time when delegates were being chosen for the inaugural meeting of the Tibetan Youth Congress in Dharamsala. She and Tendzin Choegyal were both selected. Afterwards, they both worked enthusiastically to set up a Darjeeling branch, devoting all their Sundays to the task. 'We worked together and got to know each other very well,' says Choegyal.

Choegyal, however, went off to the USA to pursue his studies. He applied to do student counselling at Seattle University, but unfortunately his qualifications were not good enough and he was despatched to a Junior College to acquire the necessary credits. It was demoralizing for a young man of twenty-three, beset by confusion and low self-esteem. As his sense of inadequacy deepened, so did his depression. Then, filled with a sharp longing 'to go back to India and help the refugee community', he left Seattle and returned to Dharamsala.

It was the onset of a long period of clinical depression. Tenzin Geyche was alarmed at the change in his friend: 'Rinpoche found life almost unendurable at this period,' he recalls. 'He was staying with Jetsun Pema at the TCV. At one point he would stay in his room all day long, refusing to get dressed or to eat, unwilling to talk to anybody. As I was one of the few he would see, I used to go and visit him, doing anything I could think of to drag him out of his misery. Once I even resorted to standing on my head – in my monk's robes – just to make him laugh. Sometimes I'd stay with him all night. He couldn't sleep, and he wouldn't let me sleep either.'[19]

Gyalo Thondup stepped in with a practical suggestion: if his brother really wanted to help his fellow exiles, he should go to Nepal and work in one of the Handicraft Centres. Still in a state of shock, Choegyal bowed to GT's wishes. 'I wasn't keen on the idea of exporting carpets and things like that. But, as GT wanted it, that was what I did. It was no good, though. I could work up no enthusiasm for what I was doing and after six weeks I gave up.' But he had resolved to pull himself together and make something of his life. His sister Pema found him a job at the Nursery which, thanks to continuing aid from international voluntary organizations had become the Tibetan Children's Village, modelled on the Pestalozzi Villages in Switzerland. (They had moved to a house (originally called Egerton Hall) further up the mountainside and were busily expanding all over it. The TCV was beginning to resemble a small city, with over one thousand destitute children ranging from six months to eighteen years.)

Pema charged him with finding sponsors for the children of Tibetans working in the road-gangs. 'We were supposed to go and take photographs of the children to be sponsored and write up their case histories,' he says. 'It was my first real job of work. I went off with two companions to find the children. As we had to pass through the Kulu Valley on the way to the road camps, we saw a lot of marijuana growing wild. I'd never had anything to do with drugs before, but it seemed a good time to try. Every time we reached our destination for the day, we used to cut some grass, rub it, roll the resin into small balls, dry it off and try and smoke it. We would get stoned out of our minds and go to sleep. It was certainly effective, it changes your consciousness, lifts you onto a different level. But I didn't like it, it made me sick – possibly because we were so eager to smoke the grass we had cut that we didn't dry it properly, we just heated it in a fry-ing-pan like tsampa. This first experience with drugs wasn't exactly a plea-sure and I never touched the things again.'[20]

He 'found over one hundred children, took their photographs, gave them all numbers and wrote brief case histories of them all'. When the job was done, Pema offered him a teaching job at the TCV. 'They were very short of teachers, and anyone who knew English and had a little Maths was good enough,' he says. He taught most subjects in the lower forms, and PE as far as Class 5, and feels immense pride that 'his' Class 2C all went on to gain university degrees.

Amala was as anxious as Kundun for Tendzin Choegyal to settle down. She was relieved to learn that he already had a Tibetan girl in mind – Rinchen Khando Tasotsang. Arrangements went ahead and in 1972 Norbu accompanied him to Mussoorie where he and Rinchen were married with a simple ceremony in her parents' house. 'Everyone expected us to have a very traditional ceremony with a big party to follow,' says Rinchen. 'But neither of us liked a lot of fuss. All we wanted was a blessing from His Ho-liness and from His mother.'[21] 'Besides,' adds Choegyal, 'we didn't have money to throw around. After all, we were refugees.' They went straight back to Dharamsala.

Since 1968, Kundun had been living in his new quarters, aptly renamed Thekchen Choeling, the Island of Mahayana Buddhism. In these surround-ings, he was more relaxed, free at last to indulge his talent for gardening. He had planted many new fruit trees and flowers, and, delighting in the numerous small animals and birds which came to visit, had constructed a bird-table just outside his study window, surrounding it with netting to keep out the huge circling birds of prey. Occasionally the netting was not sufficient deterrent and then he had recourse to his air-pistol. 'Having spent a great deal of time as a child at the Norbulingka practising with the Thirteenth's air-rifle, I am quite a good shot,' he chuckles, hastening to ex-plain that the air-pistol is for scaring the birds, not killing them.[22]

He was pursuing other old hobbies too, like photography and mending watches, and as his new residence had rooms to spare, he had acquired a set of tools and converted one of the rooms into a workshop. He had lost none of his taste for taking things apart and putting them together again. At the same time, he was trying to learn something of Western thought, particularly in the fields of science, astronomy and philosophy. Even more seriously, he was 'putting more effort into meditation and study. At long last I found the enthusiasm and determination to meditate properly on Compassion and Emptiness. These two practices really did change my life. I began to understand something about the possibility of salvation, the permanent cessation of all negative emotions. Once you're convinced that salvation is possible, you work towards it steadily and your faith becomes much stronger. The more I concentrated on Compassion in the late Sixties and early Seventies, the more patient I became, the less prone to anger. Anger still comes but it's more like a lightning flash now, it doesn't last.'[23]

NOTES

1. Avedon, *In Exile from the Land of Snows*, p. 274.
2. Harrison E. Salisbury, 'Hell – and Hope – in Shangri-La', article in *From Liberation to Liberalisation: Views on Liberalised Tibet*, Dharamsala, 1982.
3. *The Times*, 7 September 1990.
4. Author interview with HH the Dalai Lama, Dharamsala, June 1994.
5. Fourteenth Dalai Lama, *Freedom in Exile*, p. 195.
6. Letter from Rinchen Dolma Taring to the author, 1991.
7. Author interview with HH the Dalai Lama, Dharamsala, 1993.
8. Author interview with Namlha Taklha, Dharamsala, 1993.
9. Author interview with Tendzin Choegyal, Dharamsala, October 1993.
10. Author interview with Tenzin Geyche Tethong, Thekchen Choeling, October 1993.
11. Known in Buddhism as 'the three afflictive emotions'.
12. Author interview with Tendzin Choegyal, October 1993.
13. *In Exile from the Land of Snows*, chapter 5.
14. Tenzin Geyche and his brother, Tenzin Namgyal Tethong, Lodi Gyari and Sonam Topgyal.
15. Author interview with Tendzin Choegyal, October 1993.
16. Author interview with Jamyang Norbu, Dharamsala, September 1991.
17. Author interview with Tendzin Choegyal, October 1993.
18. Author interview with Rinchen Khando Choegyal, June 1994.

19. Author interview with Tenzin Geyche Tethong, Thekchen Choeling, October 1993.

20. Author interview with Tendzin Choegyal, October 1993.

21. Author interview with Rinchen Khando Choegyal, October 1993.

22. *Freedom in Exile*, p. 203.

23. Author interview with HH the Dalai Lama, Dharamsala, July 1995.

Stones and Stars 1970s

...your own life, timid and standing high and growing,
so that, sometimes blocked in, sometimes reaching out,
one moment your life is a stone in you, and the next, a star.
Rainer Maria Rilke, 'Sunset'

After six years in Geneva, Lobsang Samten was restive. Though life there was enjoyable and the children were well settled in school, Switzerland was an expensive country, especially on the sort of pittance he earned from the Government-in-Exile. Besides, Lobsang felt he was existing in a goldfish bowl. As the brother of the Dalai Lama, he was too exposed, his every action was watched. Part of him – the private self who longed for freedom and anonymity – wanted to go back to the United States and become an American citizen. He loved America, with its rich racial mix, its hotch-potch of cultures. In America he could wear what he chose, go where he wanted, lead his own life, instead of being placed on a pedestal as the Dalai Lama's brother. He and Namlha both had the Green Card that would allow them to work in the US. In 1971, they packed up and went. 'We started life all over again,' Namlha says cheerfully.

Staying first with Tibetan friends in New York, they helped set up a Tibetan Arts and Crafts Centre on Madison Avenue. Five Tibetan families put up the money and Gyalo Thondup and his wife (who were shareholders) sent handicrafts made by the refugees in Darjeeling. A Tibetan accountant worked the till, Namlha did the window display, and she and

Lobsang 'worked as cleaners, sellers, packers and as an information centre about Tibet for the many people who came to ask.'

When the venture collapsed, Namlha found work in the New York offices of 'The Board Room', an executive lunch-and-dining club in Park Avenue, 'replacing all five girls in the office in turn, when they went on holiday, and doing the payroll for the telephone switch-board operators.' Lobsang, on the other hand, was jobless. He and a few friends wanted to open a small Tibetan café, but as they could afford neither the initial overheads nor the insurance premiums, the idea was a non-starter. Lobsang then vainly searched for casual work as a cook. 'You have to remember,' says Namlha, 'he had no qualifications, no degrees or certificates, he hadn't even been to a modern school. It was difficult to think what he could do.''

Their first priority, however, was to find a suitable school for their children, Chuki (13) and Tenzin Namdhak (11). They could not afford private school fees and wanted to avoid inner-city schools with their reputation for violence and drugs. When a real estate man from New Jersey told Lobsang of a good school in Scotch Plains, they moved there, even though it meant Namlha commuting daily by bus to New York. With the help of friends and a 25-year mortgage from the bank, they bought a small shingled four-roomed house in Scotch Plains. And as Namlha did not arrive home before seven and the children could not be left alone in the evenings, Lobsang looked around for a day job. One day, a neighbour told them that the local school needed a night caretaker, and he decided to apply for the job. It was better than nothing.

So Lobsang Samten, who once had been Lord Chamberlain of Tibet and head of the Dalai Lama's Household and Treasury, became a night-shift school janitor in Scotch Plains, New Jersey. 'It worked all right,' says Namlha, 'though we scarcely saw each other except at weekends. By the time I got home, Lobsang was ready to leave for work, and in the mornings I had to go off straight after breakfast. But at least we ensured that one of us was always there for the children.'

Some of the Tibetan exiles were scandalized to hear that His Holiness's brother was doing such menial work. But Kundun took a more realistic view. 'Lobsang didn't mind being a caretaker,' he says. 'In fact I think he enjoyed it. He was a very happy person with a natural humility. He had no false pride. It was very endearing.'

For the next two years, Lobsang and Namlha lived in Scotch Plains, with little money but many friends. When they wanted to get away or simply to be reminded of their Tibetan mountains, they climbed in the nearby Watchungs, which boasted a somewhat less exalted elevation of 400–500 feet. Chuki and Tenzin enjoyed school and found nothing strange in their father's being janitor. Their parents were anxious for them to have as normal a childhood as possible and hardly ever mentioned Lobsang's past. 'Our children had no sense of coming from a privileged or famous background,' says Namlha, 'we brought them up to respect people whoever they were or wherever they came from, so it would not have occurred to them to boast about the Dalai Lama being their uncle.'

Lobsang declared the work 'wonderful'; and as the teaching staff swore they had never before had such a conscientious janitor, everyone was happy. 'They called him Sam,' smiles Namlha. 'He was very popular. Whenever we went shopping in the market on Saturdays, there were people shouting "Hi, Sam!" He kept the school so clean that some of the parents tried to talk him into cleaning their apartments too. But he wouldn't do that. He said the school was quite enough.'

After two years of janitoring, however, he began to feel the lack of mental stimulus. He was 44 and life seemed to be passing him by. But however ready he was for a change, he was unprepared for what happened next.

His story came to the attention of Morris Kaplan, a *New York Times* reporter who asked for an interview. Lobsang ignored the request. 'He was a very private person, didn't want any publicity. He told the man he was an ordinary middle-class American and wanted to be left alone.' But Kaplan knew a good story when he saw one. Having failed to persuade Lobsang, he went to the school. And then, of course, the cat was out of the bag. 'People just didn't know what to think,' says Namlha. 'They were stunned when they first found out that the school janitor wasn't what he seemed to be. Then they started urging him to tell his story to the newspaper.'

Thus did Kaplan gain access to the little house in Scotch Plains, and thus was Lobsang's precious anonymity shattered. On Monday 19 July 1976, the *New York Times* carried the article on its front page: DALAI LAMA'S BROTHER, NOW A JERSEYAN, ENJOYS HIS JOB AS A SCHOOL JANITOR. The headline was scarcely pithy, but the story could not fail to attract attention. Lobsang was pictured shaven-headed like a Tibetan monk; and then with an all-American crew-cut and summer shirt, polishing chairs in the school cafeteria, grinning self-consciously at the camera. 'In Peking, he dined with Mao Tse-tung and Chou En-lai,' readers were breathlessly told:

In his native Tibet he dealt familiarly with Sir Edmund Hillary and Tenzin Norkay, conquerors of Mount Everest...Lobsang Samten is now a $8,100-a-year custodian at the Scotch Plains-Fanwood High School in central New Jersey. To fellow-workers, neighbours and students, the 44-year-old copper-skinned Tibetan is known as 'Sam'.

'Until he got a haircut a few days ago, we also called him 'Kung-Fu,' said Louis Santacross, the head custodian...

'He's well-mannered, well-respected, a damn good worker and he's learning a lot,' Mr Santacross volunteered. 'He's my right-hand man, a wonderful guy.'

The 'wonderful guy' modestly explained to the reporter why he was doing such work. 'I never went to school, except in the monastery where I studied Buddhism. I did some social work with Tibetan exiles in India, but I have no truly modern skills.'

His brother, Norbu, 'professor of Tibetan language, culture and history at Indiana University' rated a mention, Namlha too, though the fact that her family was one of the most historic in old Tibet did not emerge. A single sentence in Kaplan's article referred to 'Mrs Samten, an alert, well-spoken office employee' who 'learned English at a Methodist mission school in Darjeeling, where she was married in 1962'.

Such nation-wide exposure put paid to their anonymity. 'After the article appeared,' says Namlha, 'we were no longer just Sam and Namlha. Suddenly Lobsang was the most famous man in Scotch Plains. People used to drive over in their cars just to look at the house and gawp at us. It was terrible. We absolutely hated it.'

Ruefully they decided to return to India, not only for their own but for the children's sake. It was time for Chuki and Tenzin Namdhak to rediscover their Tibetan roots. 'We worried about them becoming so Americanized,' Namlha says. 'Their lifestyle was a little too free and unrestrained. Scotch Plains was a small town and the school was good, but some of the children there were quite violent, and drugs were beginning to be a problem. It was what we had always dreaded.'

Thirteen-year-old Chuki was actually relieved. 'She told us she didn't want to go to High School. She was a very attractive girl and was beginning to be hassled by boys who wanted to date her. She wouldn't go with them. Her friends thought she was mad, but she just didn't want that kind of life.'

In the winter of 1976, the news that Amala had had a stroke clinched the matter. They sold up and prepared to uproot themselves yet again. 'I knew Lobsang would always regret it if he didn't see his mother before she died,' says Namlha.

When Kundun had set up a Library of Tibetan Works and Archives in Dharamsala, to preserve Tibet's written treasures for the exile community, he invited his brother, Norbu, to be its first Director. It was 1972, and Norbu was due for a sabbatical. And though it meant his sons missing a year's schooling in America, he reckoned 'they would more than make up for it by learning Tibetan and living in a Tibetan community'. So, renting out his house in Bloomington for the academic year of 1972–3, he moved his family to Dharamsala.

In his own book,[2] Norbu writes that he found a small cottage in Dharamsala which he renovated and furnished. Kashmir Cottage, later to be known and loved by many overseas visitors to Dharamsala, was, in fact, a large-ish bungalow built by the British at the turn of the century. Since then, it had come down in the world. When Kundun first opened the Nursery, the Indian Government loaned the place to him as a sort of halfway house for sick and undernourished children. A few years later, in 1966, Kundun's Private Office managed to buy it to use as a Guest House for foreign visitors. Unfortunately, the venture misfired. 'The person in charge was misusing the income,' explains Tendzin Choegyal, 'and Kashmir Cottage was getting a bad name. There was a lot of argument about what was to be done with it.'[3] Norbu's arrival was timely. He bought Kashmir Cottage from the Private Office and installed his mother there with his own family.

After his long exile from Tibet, 'it was a wonderful change to be surrounded by the sights, sounds and smells of Tibet,' to be free to spend his days collecting folklore and oral literature from exiles of all classes and occupations and from every region of Tibet. And for the leisure hours, it was a joy to have Pema, Tendzin Choegyal, and various other relatives living nearby. 'My boys soon found themselves swimming in a sea of assorted cousins, uncles, aunts, nieces, nephews, and so on.'

When Norbu was ready to return to Bloomington, in the autumn of 1973, Amala decided to sell her Lhasa jewellery and buy Kashmir Cottage from him. In those days, property was still relatively cheap.

To everybody's satisfaction, Tendzin Choegyal and Rinchen Khando were to move in with her. After their marriage in 1972, Choegyal had returned to his teaching job at the TCV and Rinchen, seeing that they 'were short of staff, had few resources and the health of the children was deplorable', volunteered for secretarial work in the Sponsorship office. The young couple were found 'very restricted accommodation' within the TCV precincts. A few months later, Choegyal was transferred to work for his friend Tenzin Geyche in Kundun's Private Office as 'one of the minions who dealt with things in English' and Rinchen – by now pregnant – continued working until just before their daughter, Choezom, was born in October 1973.

She intended to find someone to look after the baby while she returned to work. But Amala intervened and asked her if that was what she really wanted. 'She made it clear that if she were me she would want to look after the baby herself, but she would fully understand if I decided otherwise. When I thought about it, I realized she was right. Then, when she suggested that we should move in with her at Kashmir Cottage, we were delighted. Not only would it be easier for Rinpoche to get to his job at the Private Office from there, but Amala herself would have company. Staying with her and my baby would have much more meaning than continuing with a job that required no special skill.'[4]

Rinchen's relationship with her mother-in-law was unique, both women feeling sure they had known each other in a previous life. 'I called her Amala,' says Rinchen. 'It came naturally to me to call her mother, but some found it lacking in respect. All the other daughters-in-law called her Gyayum, Great Mother, but I couldn't bring myself to call her anything so formal. She was a real mother to me. We shared so much, she was so kind to me, and I loved her – not just because she was the mother of His Holiness, but for the sort of person she was.'

'Amala loved gardening and looked after all the flowers herself,' remembers Rinchen. 'We'd be walking in the garden and she'd say, "Gather the seed of this or that plant and we'll take it back to Tibet with us when we go." There was one particular tree that she was quite sure she would one day replant in Tibet. I felt quite sad, because I knew that she'd never see Tibet again. But she was always an optimist. She planted these orange trees in the garden. People kept saying they would never bear fruit, but she said it didn't matter. "Look," she'd say, when the blossoms came, "there may not be any fruit, but aren't the blossoms beautiful?" Then one day, the fruit did come, and the oranges gradually grew bigger. So then she said, "You see, if you do things with hope, something is sure to happen. But if you do nothing at all, then nothing will happen." She was a person who lived in the present moment.'

Amala didn't waste time grieving for past grandeurs. She had always taken responsibility for her life – as she once told Rinchen, with a husband like hers she had had to take a double share. Exile was no different. She had her health and strength, and that was as much as anyone could ask. 'So many things had happened to her,' reflects Tendzin Choegyal, 'that she had come to have a very clear idea of the meaning of life. She knew that suffering was important because it increased a person's compassion for others. To her dying day, my mother was unfailingly kind to any who sought her help.'

In 1974, Rinchen gave birth to a son, Tenzin Lodoe. And in August of that year, Tendzin Choegyal enlisted in the Special Frontier Force of the Indian Army.

The SFF was now the only fighting force that the Tibetans had, for the guerilla army no longer existed. It had finally fallen victim to American President Nixon's determination to seek better relations with China. The guerrillas received their last instalment of American aid in 1973. Lhamo Tsering (whom GT had left in overall charge) was bitter. 'There was no getting away from it,' he said, 'It was no longer in America's interest to support Tibet.'

Pursuing its advantage, in 1974, China asked the Nepalese Government – threatening attack if the request was ignored – to ensure that all arms held by Tibetans were handed over. The new King of Nepal, anxious not to antagonize China, offered to re-settle the Tibetans in Nepal if they surrendered their arms. The Khampas refused outright. Nepal issued an ultimatum, calling on the Tibetans to leave Mustang by 30 July – or be driven out. The guerrillas were unconcerned – the Nepalese Army did not exactly scare them.

Kundun now faced an agonizing dilemma. He could never accept the guerrillas' use of violence, but he had always admired their courage and determination, and knew how much the Tibetan people – and he himself – owed them. But the present situation in Nepal – with its implicit threat of huge loss of life – could not be allowed to continue, and he alone had the power to stop it. So he sent Phuntsok Tashi, his Head of Security, with a taped message in which he 'said that it would be senseless to fight the Nepalese, not least because there were several thousand Tibetan refugees settled in Nepal who would also suffer if they did. Instead they ought to be grateful to the Nepalese Government. They should therefore lay down their arms.'[5]

The guerrillas listened to the tape in incredulous dismay. 'How can I surrender to the Nepalese when I have never even surrendered to the Chinese?' cried one of the leaders, in horror. 'We should all return to Tibet this minute and die there fighting rather than live in shame.'[6] When the other leaders decided – reluctantly – that the Dalai Lama must be obeyed, this man went outside and cut his throat. Another jumped into a river and was drowned. Phuntsok Tashi returned home with his thoughts in a turmoil, his heart going out to the guerrillas, knowing that 'they were right, they could have handled the Nepalese, they commanded the heights'. It was one of the most difficult things he ever had to do, he says, 'and it still chokes me to remember it'.[7]

No sooner had the Khampas started to disarm than the Nepalese reneged on their promises. Entering Mustang, they seized Tibetan property and arrested those guerrillas who had already surrendered their weapons. With about forty of his men, General Wangdu fled, to continue the fight elsewhere. But just before the Indian border, they fell into a Nepalese ambush, and most of them, Wangdu included, were killed. The sacked Commander, Baba Yeshi, in exchange for protection and political asylum, had handed over to Nepal details of the guerrillas' troop strength, supplies, weaponry and positions, together with information about resistance networks in Tibet. The Nepalese gave them to the Chinese and the whole Resistance operation was finally blown. Such was the tragic end of a struggle which the Khampas had waged with outstanding courage for almost two decades.

So only the SFF remained. The Tibetan Youth Congress (which, with forty branches, had become the community's largest opposition party) believed that responsibility for the Tibetan struggle had now passed to them, and decided to develop a freedom-fighting wing. All graduates of Tibetan schools were urged to support the SFF for a period of six or twelve months. Tendzin Choegyal, who had recently succeeded Tenzin Geyche as President of the Youth Congress, resigned his position and volunteered. 'Most people said I was only a rubber-stamp for the Committee anyway,' he shrugs.[8]

The HQ of the Special Frontier Force, codenamed Establishment 22, was in New Delhi, but active units were scattered around the Himalayan border areas, wherever there was danger of Chinese attack. One was at Chakrata, just north of Dehra Dun. Rinchen and the children moved in with her parents in Mussoorie, though later she joined her husband at Chakrata where she taught English (unpaid) and acted as general counsellor to about a hundred Tibetan girl soldiers in the Girls' Company. Choegyal was plunged in at the deep end of a new way of life – and revelled in it. 'We were a crack body of Paratroop Commandos, trained in infantry tactics and guerrilla warfare,' he says. 'We did map-reading, field-craft, demolition, weaponry, parachuting, survival techniques, and the arts of ambush and sabotage.' It seemed possible, even likely, that his restless spirit had at last come home.

After six months basic training – during which he proved himself a crack shot – he was urged to stay on. Though Indian officers filled the highest ranks, nevertheless there was a Tibetan officer corps. He was made a Deputy Leader – equivalent to the rank of Captain in the British Army – and put in charge of a platoon. Within a further six months he was promoted to Company Leader and volunteered to run one of the special centres for the training of new recruits – a posting he enjoyed greatly. The prospects looked good, and when he was again promoted, to Political Leader (equivalent to a British Colonel), it seemed that he had truly found his niche.

But it didn't work out – largely because of Tendzin Choegyal's impossible idealism. For a start, he was disillusioned by the lack-lustre attitude of the Tibetans: 'It was a Force made up of Tibetan refugees for the sake of Tibet,' he argues passionately, 'yet many of the Tibetan officers seemed to have lost sight of that. They were behaving as though they weren't Tibetans at all. Our situation needed real dedication and commitment, yet the majority were merely concerned with pleasing the Indians and not rocking the boat. There were many Judases.' When he told his compatriots that they ought to be speaking Tibetan not Hindi, his Indian superiors took it as a declaration of war. Many of the latter, he believes, hated him because of his education and because of who he was. His own *bête noire* was the most senior officer in the Force who, he says, showed public contempt for the Dalai Lama, when the latter visited the station one day. 'How could they have put such a boor in charge of men who, whatever their shortcomings, were undeniably devoted to His Holiness? I really hated that man.'

The SFF was meant to be a crack force of Tibetans trained to defend the Himalayan borders and if necessary fight inside Tibet itself. 'The potential was there,' Choegyal insists bitterly. 'Even if we were never called on to fight the Chinese, we could have formed the nucleus of a fighting-force for a future Tibet. We could have created a body of first-rate troops if all the officers had been prepared to pull their weight. But many of the Indian officers were only concerned with lining their own pockets; they had only volunteered for the SFF because their own Indian Army regiments threw them out. Far from being willing to give a proper training to the Tibetan troops, they were just bullies who thought they could trample all over them.'

The fur flew in all directions, but in the nature of things Choegyal was bound to lose. 'The Security Office in Dharamsala had hoped I would be put in overall charge of training in the Force. Instead I was side-lined into a school for soldiers' children. It was all very sordid,' he complains. The experience was traumatic. Not only did it pitchfork him into a second bout of clinical depression, even worse than the first; it also developed in him a cynicism about authority which has never left him. 'I saw that power always went hand in hand with corruption; people who had power would always abuse it.' Overwhelmed once again by a despairing sense of failure, in May 1977 he resigned from the Special Frontier Force. 'A few people understood what had happened, though they didn't know how to help. But most of them thought I was a spoiled brat. They said I was depressed because I couldn't get my own way. That still rankles.'⁹

'Rinpoche went through a terribly difficult period,' says Rinchen loyally.¹⁰ 'The trouble is that he can see much more clearly than most when things are not as they should be. He is sensitive and intelligent, and feels things very deeply. I believe he had to go through what he did because of these characteristics. He's a perfectionist in everything he does...He expects too much of people, and when reality falls short of expectations, he gets very upset and depressed.'

Rinchen needed all her powers of understanding and sympathy. 'What gave me strength was being able to see what was happening. Here was a man who was honest, crystal-pure in his motives, longing to do something for other people, for the cause of Tibet, for His Holiness himself. And when it proved to be impossible, he became miserable and angry. It wasn't *him* getting angry, it was all these factors driving him. When I understood that, it was easier for me to walk the path with him wherever it might lead.'

During the absence of her son and daughter-in-law, Amala had lived on at Kashmir Cottage, with three servants to help in the house and garden. One of these, 17-year-old Lodoe, spent seven of the happiest years of his life in her service.[11] She had saved his life when as a child he had epileptic fits and his parents believed he was possessed by evil spirits. Amala had no time for such superstitious nonsense and whisked him off to a Western doctor for treatment. Lodoe adored her. 'She was like a mother to me, she cared about me. We used to work together in the garden and she'd tell me about her life in Amdo, the cooking, the farm-work, the sewing and so on. She was always patient if I made mistakes, never got cross, always explained things. She taught me to cook. His Holiness used to come and see her and we all helped to get the lunch and tea ready. We didn't do anything special, but we always cleaned the house thoroughly. When he came, there was no ceremonial, his mother just used to go out and greet him at the car, then they'd go in and have lunch together in the dining-room.'

The Tibetans, says Lodoe, regarded Amala as an Incarnation of the goddess, Green Tara, because she'd given birth to three high *tulkus*. They revered Kashmir Cottage as highly as His Holiness's residence. 'Some people came to ask for her cast-off clothes, believing they could cure sickness. She didn't believe that, but she would never turn anyone away. If anyone came to her door, she would give them some tea first, then food or shelter or clothes, just as she had done all her life. She had real compassion.'

Khando was back in Dharamsala. She and Rapten, with their three young daughters – Youdon (7), Diki (5) and baby Dolkar – had spent three years in Bhopal (Central India), where Rapten had managed a paper mill that the Tibetan Government had bought. But the mill had to be sold, and they returned to Dharamsala. The Kashag sent for Khando and asked her to take over from Mrs Taring who was retiring from the Mussoorie Homes Foundation.[12] She protested that she wasn't up to such a demanding job and would need time to think it over. (The Foundation, which was run on similar lines to the Tibetan Children's Village in Dharamsala, had six hundred Tibetan orphans in twenty-five family groups staffed by live-in house-parents). Then Kundun summoned her. 'Normally, I would go in and prostrate myself before him, and then he would greet me affectionately. On that particular day, he didn't even allow me to finish my prostration. "What is there to think about?" he asked furiously. "You've been lucky enough to receive a first-class education, which not many of our people have received. And now you must give something back, no matter how difficult it may be." He really made me see things quite clearly, and I knew he was right. I was silly to have been so cautious and afraid.' She and Rapten, who was to replace Jigme Taring as Rector of the Tibetan School, duly went off to Mussoorie, where Rapten remained for six years (before being appointed as General Secretary to the Council for Education in Dharamsala) and Khando stayed for almost thirteen.

As Phuntsok Tashi had predicted, Tenzin Ngawang's marriage had ended in divorce.[13] Though the Tibetan Government asked him to return to Dharamsala to work for them, he refused. Disenchanted with the slowness of change within the Tibetan community, he was turning his back on his past. Somewhere along the way, he had lost his Buddhist beliefs, though Tendzin Choegyal, the younger-than-himself uncle to whom he had always been part elder brother, part spiritual mentor, insists that he was a deeply spiritual man who could not tolerate the way spirituality was expressed in his own society. 'He was much misunderstood,' claims Choegyal. 'He rejected rituals and superstition, and he wanted to go and live in China. He even talked to His Holiness about it, and the latter asked him to wait a bit before making up his mind. But from then on the Tibetans labelled him as a Marxist. Well, perhaps he was. But I would rather call him a humanist of the best sort.' Tenzin Ngawang bowed out. He had diabetes, but, in spite of all urging, refused to take proper care of himself. He retired to lead an almost spartan life in America, earning his living as a freelance teacher of computer science.

In the winter of 1976, Amala suffered a stroke, and it was a matter of general concern that none of her children was with her when it happened. Kundun's personal attendants came regularly to Kashmir Cottage to see how she was, as did Pema when the demands of the TCV allowed. But the old lady was fretting for her youngest son. Again and again she would ask when Tendzin Choegyal was coming home, when his next leave might be. She did not know of his breakdown, so when he came home in May 1977 her joy knew no bounds.

But the truth could not be hidden. For eight months Tendzin Choegyal remained in a state of chronic depression and anxiety, rarely sleeping more than one hour a night. His mother buried her own pain in his, trying to reassure him that the darkness would pass, while Rinchen and his friends did everything they could to help. Once, to goad him into some sort of response, Tenzin Geyche picked him up bodily and dropped him into a tub of cold water. But he remained alienated and hopeless. Only when he at last agreed to accept some kind of treatment did the nightmare begin to recede. To aid his recovery, Tenzin Geyche, with Rinchen and Pema, took him to the Kangra River some miles away for a swim. 'He wasn't keen, but we insisted. Unfortunately, when he came out of the river, he discovered he'd lost his wedding ring. I was terrified that all our good work would be undone, but fortunately Rinchen dived into the water and found it.'14

The worst was over, but with his army career blighted and its memories still raw, there was little now to motivate him. He was found employment in the Security Department of the Tibetan Administration, and worked there diligently but without enthusiasm until December 1979, when Tenzin Geyche asked him to help in his office for a week or two. 'He didn't explain and I had no idea that I was actually being tried out for his job,' says Choegyal. 'Then after about ten days, he told me he was being transferred to Education and I was to take over.' So Choegyal became one of Kundun's Private Secretaries, dealing with English correspondence and acting as interpreter during the audiences with English-speaking visitors. 'It was a job I loved. I had daily contact with His Holiness, and though he was quite strict and not above giving me a rocket when I forgot things or made mistakes, mostly we had a very warm secretary/boss relationship.' It could also have been that Kundun was keeping a watchful eye on his mercurial younger brother.

Before 1977 was out, Lobsang Samten and Namlha had returned to Dharamsala. Lobsang was relieved to see his mother again, and Namlha too had cause for rejoicing: her younger brother, Drikung Chetsang Rinpoche, whom the whole family had believed to be dead, was alive and in Dharamsala. He was a 10-year-old *tulku* when the Chinese came to his monastery in 1959, arrested all the older monks, but sent home those under the age of twelve. 'They just told them to go, though they'd nowhere to go to,' says Namlha. 'My brother walked all the way to Lhasa and came to Tsarong House, but of course there was nobody there. He had to beg for food, and live as best he could.' Seventeen years later, he managed to escape, the first Tibetan from a prominent family to do so since the start of the Cultural Revolution. To Namlha his escape was little short of a miracle, 'We were convinced he was dead. At least, all of us except my mother. I remember her coming to see us in America and saying she knew she would see him again. I told her, "No, no, you mustn't even think it, it's all over, we'll never see him again, we just have to pray for him, that's all." Then one day my father got a telegram saying, "Rinpoche has arrived in Kathmandu". We couldn't believe it. My father took some photographs out of the album so as to be able to be sure it was him, and he came up to Dharamsala and recognized his son.' Not surprisingly, when the young man turned up in Dharamsala, the Tibetan Government suspected him of being a Chinese spy, for how otherwise could he have escaped? The Chinese must surely have had him under surveillance! 'They refused to receive him officially,' Namlha says. 'It was awful for him. He walked up the hill towards the TCV, and to get to our brother Jigme's house, he had to pass Pema's. He looked up to see my mother-in-law standing on the verandah, looking at him and smiling. She shouted down, "I don't care what they're all saying about you, you just come right in here and have something to eat." He almost wept, it was the first time since he had arrived in India that anyone had made him feel welcome.'

To leave behind the everyday luxuries of America and settle for a couple of rooms and a kerosene stove at the Tibetan Children's Village could not have been easy. 'It was an interesting time, though,' Namlha insists, 'especially for the children, because there were so many new things for them to discover.' Namlha soon discovered that the American love of making a fast buck had rubbed off on her son. 'One day, he came home from school and said he'd made a lot of money. When I asked him how, he said he'd taken some packets of Wrigley's Chewing Gum that friends of ours had sent from the States, and had sold them to the other children. Just what an American schoolkid would do! I had to explain to him that most of the children at the TCV were very poor, and he must give the money back to them. He wasn't keen, but he did it.'

While Namlha studied Buddhist philosophy with a lama, Lobsang went walking in the mountains above Dharamsala. Often he would call on Kundun and the two brothers would enjoy a simple meal together. 'Lobsang was good company. He was a very happy person, always telling jokes, most of them, I'm afraid, rather bawdy,' laughs Kundun. Tenzin Geyche was impressed by Lobsang's incredible humility. 'He'd held top positions and, as His Holiness's brother, was held in great esteem among Tibetans. Yet, whenever His Holiness was leaving Dharamsala on a journey, Lobsang would line up with the rest of the public to see him off. It was very touching the way he simply mingled with the crowds waiting to say goodbye – and later to welcome him back. I don't think Rinpoche [Tendzin

303

Choegyal] would have done that. Nor would I. But Lobsang Samten was completely without self-importance.'¹⁵

Every Sunday, Lobsang, Namlha and their children came to spend the day at Kashmir Cottage. 'We'd arrive very early and would all be milling around in the kitchen, helping my mother-in-law to prepare lunch, ourselves, Pema and her two children, Rinpoche and his family. There was a lot of teasing and laughter.' These gatherings are among Choegyal's son Tenzin Lodoe's earliest memories. He was a small, round-faced boy, and his uncles and aunts teased him about his Mongolian features. 'Uncle Lobsang used to greet me in the Mongolian language, and ask me where my camel was. I would say that I'd left it down the hill at the Tibetan hospital. I didn't mind being teased, I loved Uncle Lobsang. He was kind and played lots of games with me.'

When evening came, they would set off on the long uphill walk back home to the TCV. 'We didn't even notice,' says Namlha, smiling, 'those were wonderful days.'

They were among the last they would ever know.

NOTES

1. Author interview with Namlha Taklha, Dharamsala, October 1993.
2. Norbu, *Tibet Is My Country*.
3. Author interview with Tendzin Choegyal, Dharamsala, October 1993.
4. Author interview with Rinchen Khando, Dharamsala, June 1994.
5. Fourteenth Dalai Lama, *Freedom in Exile*, chapter 10.
6. Avedon, *In Exile from the Land of Snows*, chapter 5, p. 127.
7. Author interview with Phuntsok Tashi, London, 1993.
8. Author interview with Tendzin Choegyal, Dharamsala, October 1993.
9. From author interviews with Tendzin Choegyal in 1993, 1994 and 1995.
10. Author interview with Rinchen Khando, June 1994.
11. Author interview with Lodoe, October 1994.
12. At that time, such appointments were made by the Dalai Lama in consultation with the Kashag and his Private Secretaries.
13. There were two daughters from the marriage.
14. Conversation with Tenzin Geyche, Dharamsala, 1993.
15. Conversation with Tenzin Geyche, Dharamsala, 1993.

23

New Dawn – or False Hope? 1979–80

I feel that the struggle of the Tibetan people is not only for freedom but also for survival as a race. Our country is being ransacked, our temples and monasteries have been destroyed and our people face the danger of extermination.

Jetsun Pema, 1980

Mao died in September 1976, his death being followed by the arrest of his wife, Chiang Ching, and the other members of the 'Gang of Four', evil geniuses of the Cultural Revolution – and handy scapegoats for every crime committed in China before, during or since. Very senior voices were heard admitting that the Cultural Revolution had been a disaster. Was this just another swing of the pendulum which in nearly thirty years of Communism had so often sent China lurching from left to right and back again? Or might there be hope of a lasting improvement? The Tibetans held their breath.

After Mao's death, Peking's attitude to Tibet appeared to soften. As one cynical Tibetan intellectual remarked, there was 'a moulting of the Peking Duck'.[1] A few of the more draconian rules concerning religious practice were relaxed, the Panchen Lama was released after fourteen years in prison, and Peking declared that the Dalai Lama and his followers would be welcome to return to Tibet whenever they wished! Towards the end of 1978, Deng Xiao-ping emerged as the new leader of China. One of the earliest and most committed of the Communist hierarchs, Deng bore a fair share of responsibility for the repressions, murders and massacres which had long predated the Gang of Four, but – thanks to his hounding by the latter – he was currently being hailed as a moderate. At any rate, Deng, while leaving the political situation intact – and whatever criticisms were permitted about the Cultural Revolution no one had dared speak against the system itself – introduced a flurry of economic reforms which would propel China into the international market and earn him plaudits in the West as the Great Liberalizer. His popularity – and the continuation of his draconian regime – were alike assured. Deng was an astute politician.

Events began to move fast. In November 1978, thirty-four Tibetan prisoners (mostly elderly members of Kundun's administration in Lhasa, in prison since the 1959 Uprising) were released – and allowed to emigrate, if they so wished. Then the Panchen Lama made his first public appearance for fourteen years, calling for the Dalai Lama to visit his homeland – 'I can guarantee,' he urged, 'that the present standard of living of the Tibetan people in Tibet is many times better than that of the "old society".' (If the Panchen Lama had once again become the mouthpiece of Peking, after so many years of imprisonment and torture, who could blame him?)

In Dharamsala, hopes soared. Did this mean the exiles could now return home? Few seemed to notice that in effect little had changed, that in April Deng had banned all criticism of the regime, and warned that a Western-style human rights movement would not be tolerated.[2] 'The totalitarian regime still stands,' commented a Tibetan critic, 'and is, maybe, further strengthened by its decision to provide its cowed populace with the latter-day equivalent of bread and circuses – Coca Cola and foreign movies.'[3]

Out of the blue, Gyalo Thondup turned up from Hong Kong – with the news that Deng Xiao-ping had invited him to Peking for talks. 'I was expecting it,' he says airily. 'I knew that if the Chinese wanted to take things forward, they would contact me. The director of the Xinhua News Agency, which represents the Central Government of China in Hong Kong, came and asked me to go to Peking. He said, "It won't take long, you can go there and back in a day." I reminded him I was just a hard-working businessman with no authority to talk to anyone in Peking. But he wouldn't take no for an answer.'[4]

Insisting that he must first consult the Dalai Lama, Gyalo Thondup set off in search of his brother, whom he found giving religious teachings somewhere in Central India. Kundun was initially doubtful – 'as the ancient Indian saying goes, "When you've once been bitten by a snake, you are cautious even of rope".'⁵ All his experience suggested that the Chinese leadership did not know what it was to tell the truth or keep a promise. But in the end he felt he owed it to his people to investigate this latest opening. With Kundun's cautious blessing, therefore, Gyalo Thondup flew to Peking, only to find that in the meantime war had broken out between China and Vietnam and Deng was somewhere on the border 'directing the war personally and talking about giving the Vietnamese a lesson they would not forget'. (Of course, gloats GT, 'what happened was that it was the Vietnamese who taught *him* a lesson, not the other way round.'⁶)

GT was no admirer of Deng Xiao-ping, whom he referred to as 'the dwarf' and regarded as an unreconstructed Maoist at heart. 'After all, in 1949, it was Deng who directed the South-West Military Bureau, charged with destroying Tibet's monasteries. He blames all that on the Gang of Four now [1995] but most of the monasteries were destroyed while he was in control, long before the Cultural Revolution. I actually saw some 1962 documents in which the military authorities asked Deng's permission to dismantle the monasteries in Tibet. He replied, be careful with the monasteries on the border because the border is sensitive internationally, but do whatever you want in the interior of the country. All the looting and killing, all the massacres in Central Tibet and in Kham were all directed by Deng. But in 1978 he was doing his utmost to conceal his own part in the tragedy of Tibet and was claiming to be very concerned about its future.'

It was three weeks before Deng returned from the war zone. The two men greeted each other warily. 'Deng asked me why I hadn't been back to China in all those years – 29 years in fact – and asked me if I was surprised at all the changes. I said no, I was a China-watcher in Hong Kong and everything was more or less as I'd expected. Deng then said he wanted to meet the Dalai Lama for discussions, and that everything would be negotiable – except Tibetan Independence. No Chinese leadership could ever agree to that, he said. On behalf of His Holiness I asked if he proposed doing anything about the way Tibetans in India and those in Tibet had been cut off from each other for twenty years. And as we'd heard that in a number of Tibetan areas there were neither schools nor teachers, I also asked if we could send some of our young people from India who had been newly-trained as teachers. Thirdly, I asked if we could send teams of representatives to see for themselves what "New Tibet" was like. To my surprise, he agreed on all three counts – and was especially enthusiastic about

the teachers, saying they weren't just needed in Tibet, but even in the Minority Colleges in Peking. When I suggested fifty for a start, he said "no
good, we need at least one thousand"!'

Kundun was heartened by his brother's report and asked him to continue as 'bridge-builder'. Deng agreed to an official fact-finding delegation
from Dharamsala visiting Tibet to examine conditions there. It seemed a
reasonable arrangement, though Kundun knew that a number of the exiles
– particularly the younger ones – would consider any *rapprochement* with
China which ruled out the possibility of independence to be a sell-out.
The thirteen (Khampa) settlements were loud in their accusations that
Gyalo Thondup was up to his old tricks again.

Plans for the first fact-finding visit to Tibet went ahead in such secrecy
that news only leaked out the day before the group's departure. Kundun
had chosen as delegates men who were familiar not only with old Tibet but
with the modern world as well. He had included Lobsang Samten in this
five-man group, despite initial misgivings: '[Lobsang] was going through a
very modern phase in terms of dress and appearance. He wore his hair long
and had a thick, droopy moustache. His clothes were very casual too. I was
a little worried that he might not be recognized by those in Tibet who
should remember him.'⁷ Lobsang had no such qualms. Since returning from
America, he had again been suffering from the 'goldfish bowl' syndrome:
that careful deference, mixed with envy and mistrust, accorded to a brother
of the Dalai Lama. He missed America, the free and easy life, the fast food
and standards of hygiene, but beyond everything he missed Tibet. When
Kundun asked him to join the first delegation, 'he felt he was going home,'
says Namlha. 'He had always talked about Tibet, wherever we went, whoever he was with. Going back there was his dream.'

On 2 August 1979, the group flew to Hong Kong.⁸ At an official lunch in
the Xinhua News Agency offices, their Chinese host proposed a 'Welcome'
toast and bluntly told them exactly where they stood. 'We are the great
land of China and you are a minority people. For too long you have been
separated from your motherland. We two peoples, the Han and the Tibetans
– one of the most important minority groups – should never be apart. Now
we are very happy that you have come back to visit...You must understand that you have such a good opportunity only because of the enlightened policy and excellent qualities of the Communist Party leadership.'
The Tibetans nearly choked on their drinks, but apart from pointedly ignoring the toast, there was little they could do.

In Hong Kong they met Gyalo Thondup. 'Don't talk politics,' he advised, 'simply tell the people His Holiness has sent you with his best wishes for the people of Tibet. That's enough. All we want is to restore the thread that has been broken for twenty years. Talk to people, find out about their lives. But no politics.'[9]

At the Canton airport terminal, Lobsang Samten had a moment of panic when he and his friends stood, surrounded by Red Army guards, under a life-size portrait of Mao Tse-tung. Had they walked straight into a trap? The feeling resurfaced in Peking, when they were lodged in an army guesthouse with hundreds of high-ranking PLA soldiers. Lobsang was in no doubt that the place had been deliberately chosen to show the Tibetans where the real power lay.

After two weeks in Peking, working out a 2,500 miles itinerary, they set off on the morning of 28 August, in two white Toyota minibuses and accompanied by a Chinese escort. Driving due west, they headed towards Amdo, where Lobsang Samten had been born. At an altitude of ten thousand feet,[10] Lobsang spotted a yak, and, overcome with emotion, insisted on leaving the minibus for a photograph. 'We didn't care what the Chinese thought,' he said afterwards, 'You can't imagine how it felt just to see a yak after all those years.'

A single moment of pure pleasure, to be followed by a thousand unpleasant surprises. As they approached the town of Tashikiel, once renowned for the glories of its monastery, news of their arrival had spread and a crowd of 6,000 had gathered. Since freedom of assembly had been denied to the Tibetans for twenty years, the Chinese were terrified. Having swallowed their own propaganda that the Tibetans hated the Dalai Lama and all he stood for, they warned the visitors to keep the doors and windows of the minibus shut, for fear of being lynched by the mob! This, however, was no angry mob, but a crowd of famished Tibetans, weeping for joy that their exiled countrymen, among them a brother of their beloved leader, had come at last. 'We opened our windows,' reported Lobsang Samten. 'It was unbelievable. Everywhere people were shouting, throwing scarves, apples and flowers...They broke the windows of all the cars. They climbed on the roofs and pushed inside, stretching out their hands to touch us. The Chinese were screaming, "Don't go out! They'll kill you! They'll kill you!" All of the Tibetans were weeping, calling, "How is the Dalai Lama? How is His Holiness?" We yelled back, "He's fine. How are you?" Then, when we saw how poor they were it was so sad, we all started crying too.'

The people would not go away. Hundreds camped all night outside the locked gates of the military guest-house where the delegates stayed. By next morning, the crowd had swelled to ten thousand, and they surged around the visitors as they left, no matter how hard the police strove to keep them apart. 'Everyone rushed at us, weeping and calling for His Holiness,' said Lobsang Samten. 'People were crying hysterically. There were some who just collapsed in tears on the ground. The others pulled our hair and tore our clothes for mementos – blessings, in fact. From that time on, I lost so much hair, my hands were always cut and my voice was constantly hoarse from shouting. Altogether one overcoat, a raincoat, two shirts and a cap were torn off [me] during the trip.'

The few hundred small pictures of the Dalai Lama they'd brought with them had disappeared long before they reached the entrance to the Tashikiel monastery, which Lobsang had last visited in 1955 on returning with Kundun from China. Outside the monastery, which had been razed almost to the ground by the Chinese, a few hundred elderly Tibetans stood in a long row, weeping as the visitors passed by. 'God! They were crying so much,' recounted Lobsang. 'We have nothing left,' they kept saying. 'Everything has been destroyed.'" Though the Chinese enthusiastically blamed the Gang of Four, Lobsang learned from an old monk that the monastery had actually been destroyed before 1959.

A new Chinese town had grown up round the old Tashikiel, and the old Tibetan section was 'little better than an open grave,' commented Lobsang. 'Its buildings were in total disrepair, its streets muddy and impassable. The people lived in dark, decaying rooms with barely any furniture or utensils and no running water and only intermittent electricity. On the other hand, the Chinese quarter, though itself showing signs of neglect, was newly built, its inhabitants far better fed and clothed than the Tibetans.' Yet their Chinese minders kept up an incessant chorus of praise for the benefits showered on the Tibetans by China. Were they blind, brain-washed, or just stupid, the visitors wondered?

For four days, they were besieged by visitors begging to be allowed to see them, to touch them. 'Whenever we asked people what had happened since the revolt,' related Lobsang Samten, 'they would just start crying. Then, after composing themselves, they'd reply, "Our country has nothing now. Everything is finished. But...our spirit is strong. As long as His Holiness is not in the hands of the Chinese we have hope."' Lobsang felt crushed by so much misery, his shock and outrage compounded by the sight of an old Amdo friend, a former village headman released only a few days earlier after twenty years in prison. Lobsang was stunned. 'He had been such a strong, heavily-built man. Now I could barely recognize him. The fellow was just broken. He said everything he owned, his land, his home and possessions, were taken. His family had been separated. He had never seen them again. He had just heard that his son had died in prison. "Look at me, Lobsang," he said. "I have nothing left except this one suit of clothes they gave me."'

Over the next three weeks, criss-crossing the desolate landscapes of Amdo, visiting towns and villages, communes and nomad encampments, their despair increased as the tales of suffering and death unfolded. They heard of 'years of famine, mass starvation, public execution and gross and disgusting violations of human rights'.[12]

In Lhasa, the authorities, forewarned, were taking no chances. At the obligatory political assembly each evening the citizens were given their orders: Lhasa's streets and buildings were to be scrubbed and tidied, the people were to wear their best clothes and look cheerful at all times; if spoken to by the visitors – by definition, 'counter-revolutionaries' – in a firm, convincing tone they should relate how good life was under the new order. Families likely to be visited by the delegation were given coupons for new work suits and gaudy pink and blue ribbons for the women's hair. Thermoses, blankets and quilts were handed out and rooms inspected to make sure that portraits of Mao and Party Chairman Hua Guo-feng were prominently displayed on the walls.[13]

A few days before the delegates were due to arrive, the people were given a politically correct version of the facts. The delegates, they were told, were coming from Amdo where the people had been so incapable of restraining their hatred of counter-revolutionaries that they had attacked them on every possible occasion. Hundreds apparently had turned out to throw dirt and stones and denounce and spit on the visitors. Such inhospitable behaviour would not be allowed in Lhasa, the officials threatened piously.

On 26 September, the group reached Lhasa and as Lobsang caught his first glimpse of the Potala's golden roof-tops, he was overcome by nostalgia. 'My whole childhood, living with His Holiness in that beautiful building, came into my mind. Then it was full of life; people worked in the offices, prayed in the chapels, walked on the outside stairways and on the rooftops, and at night its windows were always lit by hundreds of butter-lamps. But now it looked completely dead – empty and cold. All of its dignity was gone.'[14]

Despite their protests, they were driven to a guest-house outside the city. When Lobsang suggested his family's house as an alternative, the Chinese informed him that the house now 'belonged to the public'. 'What public?' Lobsang could not help asking. 'Tibetans or Chinese?' 'Oh, just the public,' they said, and changed the subject. A few days later, the delegates were quietly removed to a guest-house inside the city.

Order had already broken down. On the first morning, the delegates had gone to the Jokhang Temple, parts of which had been turned by the Red Guards into a pig-sty and slaughter-house during the Cultural Revolution. It had recently been reopened in a modest revival of at least the external forms of religion. (Of Buddhist teaching there was none. Religion was still officially viewed as counter-revolutionary poison, and in any case nearly all the teachers were in prison, in exile or dead.) That morning, seventeen thousand Tibetans trampled the security police underfoot in the rush to greet their compatriots. It was Amdo all over again. Stern warnings were given at that night's political meeting. But, though hundreds bowed to official pressure to remain indoors next day, thousands took to the streets, on the off-chance of speaking to – or just touching – the visitors.

There was a moment of pure farce when the delegates were conducted round the Norbulingka and its (sadly untended) gardens where Lobsang Samten and Kundun had played as children. When they came to the two-storied palace built in 1956 for Kundun under Lobsang's supervision, the guides burbled on: This is where the Dalai slept, where he ate, where he met his mother, and so forth. Lobsang reminded them that he'd built the place himself and worked in it every day, and that *he* would be happy to give *them* a guided tour if they wished, but irony was wasted on them. Lobsang's irritation turned to distress when, through the broken glass panes of the larger Kelsang Palace where he and Kundun had stayed when first they came to Lhasa, he saw the heaped-up shards of broken statuary. It was too much, and though he had promised the Chinese not to speak in public, he stormed out to the front steps of the palace and began to address the large crowd assembled on the flagstones. 'Long live the Dalai Lama,' chanted the crowd as soon as he appeared, and a man offered him a white scarf draped over the end of a long stick. 'His Holiness misses you,' shouted Lobsang, accepting the proffered scarf, 'and he knows how you have suffered. We hope that one day he will come to see you...When we return we will report the truth.'

As he turned to walk back inside towards the glowering Chinese, hundreds broke through the police cordon and followed him. Ignoring the protests of the officials, he whipped around again and plunged into their midst. As John Avedon recounts: 'Ten young men linked arms to protect him from the commotion. In their midst he spent the next five hours walking back and forth across the Jewel Park. Several times, the whole group was inadvertently pushed over, once waist-deep into a pond. 'It was so chaotic that I only managed to sit down and picnic with people in a few spots...When I did, after only a few minutes of polite conversation, the people's real feelings would pour out and they would start to cry uncontrollably. I'd try to get up to move on, and they would beg me to stay. Then they'd insist that we all have just one dance. So, for a little while, everyone, old men, women and children would join arms and try to do a few of our own Tibetan steps, laughing, singing, crying and dancing all at once.'[15] One of the delegates overheard a high-ranking Chinese cadre remark bitterly to a colleague, 'The efforts of the last twenty years have been undone in a single day!'[16]

There was a tragic footnote to these extraordinary events. Tsering Lhamo, the 56-year-old wife of one of the Norbulingka gardeners, was so carried away by the excitement of the moment that she cried out, 'Tibet is independent!' She was taken away for interrogation and three days later was brought before her 600-strong neighbourhood committee and given thamzing to the accompaniment of severe beatings. Protesting her innocence, she was returned to prison and tortured with electric shocks. When news of this reached the delegates, and they realized the danger to which their presence was exposing their compatriots, they told their Chinese hosts that they would cancel all further engagements and return home. Hastily, the Chinese released the woman. How could the Tibetans have guessed that as soon as they had gone, she would be rearrested and subjected to electric shocks so violent that she was reduced to a permanent vegetable state?[17]

By late December, the group was back in Dharamsala, with audio recordings, hundreds of rolls of film, more than seven thousand letters from Tibetans to their relatives; and countless requests for prayers.

Why did the Chinese get it so wrong? They had planned to show the visitors that the new Tibet was now an earthly paradise. So convinced were they by their own official propaganda they had even invited forty-four Peking-based journalists to Lhasa. It did not seem to have occurred to anyone that the visit would instead reveal the Tibetans to be in mourning for the destruction of their ancient culture and for the exile of their leader, the Dalai Lama. Peking had been woefully misled by the local Government of Tibet. (Heads inevitably rolled, the local Party leaders being sacked and replaced by more moderate men.) The question now was, would the Tibetan Government-in-Exile present this evidence of Chinese failure to the outside world, thus wrecking all chance of dialogue and risking further misery to their compatriots inside Tibet? The Chinese had impressed on Lobsang Samten that negative criticism would not be tolerated. The unspoken threat hung in the air. So, although Lobsang and his colleagues drew up a detailed report of their findings, the Dalai Lama reluctantly decided not to release them to the outside world. A small item appeared in Dharamsala's official *Tibetan Bulletin*, thanking the Chinese for making the visit possible! The dialogue with China was set to continue.

Critics angrily pointed to this evidence of a sell-out. Where now was the talk of Tibetan independence, they asked bitterly? It had become a bargaining chip, pushed out of sight by the human rights issue.[18] Tibetan officials denied the charge, claiming that the way of dialogue was the only way forward. The Chinese had already agreed to accept a second delegation, and after that a third and a fourth. There was much to be hoped for from such continuing contact.

The story of the second delegation cannot be reported in detail here, since no member of the family was a member of it. Yet neither can it be completely ignored, for it set the pattern for what was to follow. To demonstrate that the younger generation of Tibetan exiles was educated and articulate, it was made up of young men in their early thirties. They travelled through southern Amdo and Kham to reach Lhasa, where the Chinese had already taken steps to prevent a repetition of previous events, warning that nobody was to have any contact, whether by word or by gesture, with the visitors. They made it ominously clear that the names of those who had greeted the first delegation were on file, and that if any of them dared put in an appearance this time, they could expect to share the fate of the unfortunate Tsering Lhamo. But their warnings fell on deaf ears. Everywhere, the delegates were mobbed by desperate crowds, and cries of Tibet is Independent rent the air. In Lhasa, the young delegates' patience snapped and they launched into passionate – and very public – denunciation. They were accused of deliberately inciting the Tibetans to break with the motherland and were expelled from the country in disgrace.

In the light of this débâcle, if the third delegation, led by Kundun's sister, Pema, and composed of six educationists – one of them Khando's husband, Rapten Chazotsang, now General Secretary to the Council for Education – had not already been in Tibet, it might never have got off the ground.

Pema had reluctantly agreed to lead the third delegation, calming her fears with the knowledge that the first had returned unharmed. (Had she known what was to befall the second, she might have been even more apprehensive.) She had a fright when they arrived in Hong Kong and the Chinese took the group's passports away. 'That was a bad moment,' she says. There would be many bad moments, for the hosts' bonhomie had quite evaporated.

The itinerary itself was a problem. Pema's brief was to visit as many schools as possible and to see what kind of education Tibetan children were receiving; she planned to visit those areas of Tibet not covered by the first and second groups. But the Chinese would not hear of it. In Peking, she was told that the plan was impracticable: too many places on the list, not enough time, no motorable roads, not enough money. They were ordered to provide an alternative plan – with Chinese assistance. When they reached Tibet, this revised journey-plan would be followed to the letter; there would be no unscheduled stops, even where – or perhaps especially where – thousands of people lined the roadsides in the hope of speaking to them.

Pema at first seethed in silence. 'We visited fifty different towns and villages and everywhere we went it was the same old story. They wouldn't allow the people to come and see us. Even when we went into our guest-house for the night, they would lock the gates so that the people couldn't get near us.' But the legendary family temper was rising: 'I let it pass for four or five days. But on the fifth or sixth day, I really blew my top. I flatly refused to go any further if they didn't allow us to meet the people. We might as well go home, I said. After that, they allowed the people to come and talk to us. People would crowd round us, wanting to touch us – especially me, because I was His Holiness's sister. Everyone was wanting to talk about His Holiness, to have a picture of him. When they found that we had lamas in the group, everyone wanted a blessing. Of course, it was one horror story after another. They all spoke of terrible suffering, of torture, of death, of starvation. The commune system was still in existence and most of them didn't have enough to eat, the rations given them for a month being scarcely enough for two weeks. We wept to see how poor they all were, they were dressed in rags and so very unhappy.'[19]

315

Everything was so much worse than they had anticipated, says Rapten. 'Wherever we went, the Chinese organized meetings of public dignitaries – who, despite their titles were no more than mouth-pieces. They would spout statistics and make propaganda points, but they were quite incapable of answering our questions, and they would look at the Chinese for permission to speak before they dared open their mouths. The Chinese who had accompanied us from Peking were obviously trying to set us against each other, enjoying seeing us at each other's throats. After a time, we realized what their game was and stopped provoking arguments. Why should we argue with our own countrymen when they were not free agents anyway?'[20]

Almost every experience in the 105 days they spent in Tibet was disturbing. It was partly the constant wrestling with Chinese bureaucracy and the systematic lack of co-operation from the local authorities; partly the surreal experience of reconciling Chinese lies and fantasies with the reality they found – 'The Chinese have absolutely no shame,' wrote Pema afterwards in a personal account that pulled no punches. 'They can tell you one thing at one time and the very next moment either deny having said it or tell you something quite different...Time and again they would give us elaborate figures when they knew that only hours later we would find out the truth.'[21] There was also the crushing sadness of reality itself. The once flourishing monasteries, for example, now no more than hastily rebuilt show-pieces from which the gods had fled. Throughout Tibet, 6,254 monasteries had been destroyed (their contents mutilated or sent to Peking to be sold); only 37 remained more or less intact. 'Our monasteries,' mourned Pema, 'were places of worship where anyone could come anytime to pray and to seek spiritual guidance. They were also places of learning and religious practice – where prayer, meditation, the practice of good and the avoidance of evil had become a way of life. The Chinese have turned them into sterile museums with false exhibits [intended] to show what a luxurious life the monks led in the old society and how cruel and ruthless they were.'

After her return, Pema agonized over the impossibility of finding words to convey Tibet's tragedy to the outside world. She was stricken by the horror of all she had seen and heard: 'Parents had to witness their sons being murdered and if they failed to smile and clap and thank the Chinese for killing their own children they too would be condemned.' She spoke to a mother who had made soup from her own blood to keep her children from starvation, and such cases were not unique. It was far worse even than they had expected. 'When I saw their emaciated bodies and heard their tales of suffering, there was no way to hold back my tears. Throughout our stay in Tibet most of us were crying at one time or another.'

As for the education they had come to investigate, they were constantly told of the unprecedented progress being made. Impressive statistics about students and teachers and government expenditure were always to hand. But the statistics could never be verified. 'What we did find out,' complained Pema, 'was that it was extremely difficult to arrange a visit to a school. We were not demanding to see hundreds and thousands of schools. All that we requested was to see one or two.' But somehow, wherever they went, the schools were 'closed for the summer holidays,' the excuse offered on every one of the 105 days, from 10 June until 23 September. Strange, in a country which practically came to a standstill during the paralysingly cold winters and could be expected to spend the summer months making up for lost time. 'At first we insisted that we should visit the school just to see the empty building. Later I realized that "the school is closed for summer vacations" was their way of saying "there is no school" or "we don't want you to see this school".' 'The Chinese,' commented Rapten Chazotsang, 'must have been incredibly naïve to think we'd swallow all the propaganda they threw at us.'

In one place where a school was 'closed for lunch' – at ten in the morning – closer investigation revealed the classrooms to be stacked ceiling-high with timber. Elsewhere, they were shown a nomad 'tent school' in which everything was brand new 'from the tent to the children's clothes, the tables, the mats and the blackboard, even the grass was fresh and green inside the tent and a classroom where intricate Tibetan grammar was being taught to children who did not even know the alphabets'. Pema was speechless with indignation, and even their Chinese escort had the grace to look embarrassed.

In spite of these *opéra bouffe* attempts to fob them off, the delegates visited seventy primary, middle and high schools and found the overall standard abysmally low, with a seventy per cent illiteracy rate among Tibetans. 'Where we found Tibetan teachers,' says Rapten, 'we were astounded to find that their basic qualification was their social background: if they were poor farmers or had collaborated with the Chinese, they would have been given a reasonable education. After reaching about the third grade, they were then sent for teacher-training.' But almost all the teachers were Chinese, the Tibetan language was almost a thing of the past and few children spoke it correctly. Tibetan children were being taught to despise their own culture, while absorbing the alien ideology of Marxism-Leninism. When the group returned to Dharamsala, they reported that while there had undeniably been an improvement in the standard of education over the past twenty years, 'to the Chinese, the real value of reading was to enable children to study the Thoughts of Chairman Mao, and of writing to enable them to produce "confessions"'.[22]

How could one come to terms with such a harrowing of the soul? 'When I came back from Tibet, I was terribly emotional,' Pema shudders. 'I could feel only hatred, bitterness and disgust, and I could not stop crying. I kept seeing the faces of the people we had met, and I could not for one moment shake off the memory of their terrible sufferings.'[23] Rapten, too, had been mentally scarred by the encounters with his compatriots. 'They'd all been shunted around the country. Those from Lhasa had been sent to outlying parts, while the Tibetans in Lhasa itself all seemed to come from other parts of Tibet. Once, when we were coming down from the ruins of Ganden Monastery, a lot of Tibetans had gathered on the roadside waiting for us. I heard someone calling my name, saying, Rapten, Rapten, don't you know me? It was an old friend, from my own district of Kham. He was about the same age as myself, but his face was that of an old, old man. He couldn't really speak, the tears were just coursing down his cheeks. When I came back, I kept on having nightmares about that face. Memories like that stay with you, they affect you for the rest of your life.'

Between them, the three delegations drew up a devastating indictment of the Chinese record in their country: One-fifth of the population had been murdered or had died of starvation; 6,254 monasteries and nunneries had been destroyed, their contents looted, melted down or sold on foreign markets; sixty per cent of Tibet's sacred literature had been incinerated; Amdo had become the world's biggest gulag, with the capacity for holding ten million prisoners; one in every ten Tibetans was in prison; one hundred thousand had disappeared into labour camps; mountains had been shorn of their forests and the abundant wildlife of Tibet had almost become extinct.

And in all those who had revisited their homeland, something had died.

NOTES

1. Jamyang Norbu, article with that title in *Illusion and Reality: Essays on the Tibetan and Chinese Political Scene from 1978 to 1989*, Tibetan Youth Congress Books, 1989.

2. Noted by Jamyang Norbu, writing in the *Tibetan Review*, April 1989.

3. Jamyang Norbu, 'A Moulting of the Peking Duck', article in *Illusion and Reality*.

4. Author interview with Gyalo Thondup, New Delhi, July 1995.

5. Fourteenth Dalai Lama, *Freedom in Exile*, chapter 13.

6. Author interview with Gyalo Thondup, New Delhi, July 1995.

7. *Freedom in Exile*, p. 253.

8. For the following account of the first delegation's visit to Tibet, I am indebted to Avedon's *In Exile from the Land of Snows*, chapter 11.

9. Author interview with Gyalo Thondup, New Delhi, July 1995.

10. Yaks cannot survive at a lower altitude than this.

11. This quotation, like most of those concerning the delegation's visit, are from *In Exile from the Land of Snows*.

12. *Freedom in Exile*, p. 256.

13. *In Exile from the Land of Snows*.

14. *In Exile from the Land of Snows*.

15. *In Exile from the Land of Snows*.

16. *Freedom in Exile*, p. 254.

17. Amnesty International Report 1983.

18. Jamyang Norbu, 'There and Back Again', article in *Illusion and Reality*.

19. Author interview with Jetsun Pema, October 1994.

20. Author interview with Rapten Chazotsang, Utah, February 1996.

21. *Three Months in Tibet: a personal viewpoint*, pamphlet by Jetsun Pema published by the Tibetan Children's Village, Dharamsala.

22. *Freedom in Exile*, p. 263.

23. Author interview with Jetsun Pema, October 1994.

24

A Time for Grieving

Neither in the sky, nor deep in the ocean, nor in a mountain-cave, nor anywhere, can a man be free from the power of death.

The Dhammapada

'After Amala had the stroke, I felt the need to be with her more than ever before,' declared Rinchen. 'There were so many things that I could do for her that no one else could. Like sitting with her for hours on end and changing her clothes. There was a big change in her after the stroke. She hated not being able to do many of the things she liked doing. Most of all that she couldn't do things for other people, they had to do things for her instead. She thought she was being a burden – yet everyone felt it was a privilege to be able to help her.'

Kundun was relieved that his mother was in such caring hands, but feared that the strain would be too much for Rinchen. 'One day, His Holiness came to Kashmir Cottage and he suggested that if I wanted to go back to work, he might be able to find someone to look after Amala. I was astounded. After all, I'd not complained. I knew I was in the right place and there was no better thing I could be doing. So I answered, "For me, serving His Holiness's Mother and serving His people are one and the same thing. I'm happy and proud to look after Your mother."'[1]

Khando made a fourteen-hour journey from Mussoorie to see her grandmother, and was shocked at the change in her. 'She had been so full of a zest for life and suddenly she was helpless and frail. I felt quite frightened.

All I could do was sit with her and hold her hands'. But, with her in-
domitable will and with treatment both Tibetan and Western, Amala ral-
lied. One evening, while helping her into her nightdress, Rinchen was
moved to exclaim, 'Amala, what a lot of muscle you still have!' 'What's
surprising about that?' came the reply. 'After all, I *am* a farmer's wife!' But
Rinchen noted that 'she no longer talked about taking seeds back to Tibet'.

Her capacity for laughter remained strong. 'After she had the stroke,'
says Rinchen, 'we begged her not to laugh so much. She would try, but not
always successfully. One afternoon, when the children were small, I was
rubbing ointment into her leg as we watched TV together. (She had
rheumatism in her legs every autumn when the house got damp.) Suddenly there was an earthquake tremor. I panicked: she couldn't walk, what on
earth was I to do?...I got the children outside and tried to lift her, but she
was so heavy, I couldn't move her. I was so frightened. But she wasn't, she
thought it was hilarious, she just laughed and laughed.'

But the laughter died when first Lobsang then Pema returned from Tibet
to report the destruction they had seen. Norbu too. In 1979, he had spent
his second sabbatical as a visiting scholar at the Institute for Studies of
Languages and Cultures of Asia and Africa in Tokyo. From there he was
invited to the USSR, and after visiting the Oriental Institute in Leningrad
with its large collection of Tibetiana, he had flown to Moscow and on to
Ulan Ude. There, in the heart of Soviet Siberia, he attended a service at a
Tibetan-style monastery:

> Soon there came the familiar sounds of chanting, the deep tones of the Tibetan
> long trumpet, the piercing cries of the Tibetan shawm, the booming sounds of
> the drum, the clashing of cymbals, the tinkling of bells, the smell of incense,
> the flickering of butter-lamps, and the rows of sacred images and *thangkas*.
> These were sights, sounds and smells so familiar to me from my early child-
> hood, youth and young manhood, worlds away from my daily life in Blooming-
> ton, and yet always and ever a part of me. I was swept away in nostalgia, and
> tears brimmed in my eyes. I wanted to remain there as long as I could.[2]

To his surprise, he was granted a visa for Mongolia and took off almost immediately for Ulan Bator. As the plane flew over Lake Baikal, the Kokonor
of his childhood, nostalgia increased a hundredfold. The closer they approached the hills and grasslands of the Mongolian steppes, the more he
was reminded of Amdo, and visiting Mongolia's most famous monastery,
he could almost believe himself back in Tibet.

In fact, he was to go there. In Tokyo, he had been invited by Peking to visit Tibet, and now embarked on a nostalgic journey to Kumbum, the monastery which had been his home for so many years and whose Abbot he had once been. He was depressed to find that, though a few temples were in use as tourist attractions, of the once-thriving monastic town of over three thousand monks there was no sign.

In his home village of Taktser he was overcome with grief. Not only were the Tibetans now a tiny minority in the village but more than twenty of his relatives were dead:

> Only one cousin was still living, and I visited her home and met her child. When I asked her what happened to her father, she replied, 'He is dead.' When I asked her how and where, she did not know. Their farm had been taken, and their house torn down. Many of the people I talked with had such sad stories. When I asked them about their life now, they would just cry, they had no words. Others told me how their families and friends were killed, imprisoned, sent to labour camps, maimed and crippled. Some were beaten so severely over and over again with clubs and boards, that they lost their hearing or sight. Others had bodies that were bent and twisted from being forced to pull heavy carts, like animals...They told me that in 1959 or 60 all men were rounded up, put in trucks and sent away to labour camps; that the only people you saw then were women, children and the aged.[3]

Whatever grief these revelations caused Amala was compounded later in 1980 when her youngest sister arrived from Tibet.[4] It was the first time the two had seen each other for twenty years. 'This aunt was the one who had looked after my grandmother when we left,' explains Kundun. 'My grandmother, fortunately, had died before the Cultural Revolution started, but my poor aunt suffered greatly, was forced to undergo *thamzing* and was imprisoned. She had dreadful digestive problems afterwards and her husband was semi-paralysed. After she was released from prison, she earned some money by dress-making.'[5]

The sisters laughed and wept in turn over their reunion, but its net effect on Amala was catastrophic. 'Her sister was a sweet woman,' says Rinchen, 'but not very subtle. She told everything exactly as it had happened, all the awful things the Chinese had done to their family and friends, down to the last terrible detail. So-and-so died, so-and-so starved to death, so-and-so's house was burned down, so-and-so was in prison. On and on, each story more depressing than the last.' 'My aunt,' agrees

Tendzin Choegyal, 'spent the whole time relating horror-stories. Most of our relatives had either died of starvation or been liquidated – just like almost everyone else's relatives, really. The constant repetition took its toll of my mother and she became terribly depressed.'[6]

Rinchen noted that from then on 'Amala finally understood that the Tibet she had known and loved had gone for ever, and the realization killed her.' When her sister returned home (where she died a few months later), Amala had lost the will to live.

In the winter of 1980, Tendzin Choegyal accompanied Kundun to Bodh Gaya where the latter was to give teachings. Amala had always gone to Thekchen Choeling to say goodbye to him. But this time she could not. The cold, damp Dharamsala winters were increasingly hard for her, in spite of Rinchen's struggles to keep the house warm. Amala had a chill. Kundun therefore came to Kashmir Cottage to say goodbye.

For Rinchen, this last meeting between the two is an unforgettable memory. 'His Holiness sat by her bed and talked to her, just like a little boy coming home to see his mother. It was very beautiful. "So," he asked in a matter-of-fact way, "is there anything you want to tell me?" I can hear her so clearly saying, "No, nothing at all." He told her gently not to be afraid of dying, but to concentrate on the *thangkas* (sacred scrolls) and say the *mani* prayers. He asked her, "Are you afraid?" and she answered confidently, "No, I'm not afraid." It was a lesson in how to die. He said goodbye to her then, adding "Who knows, we may perhaps see each other again." But I think both of them knew it was goodbye.'

Khando came again to Dharamsala, *en route* for a family backpacking holiday in Goa. Rapten was still suffering nightmares and was profoundly depressed (his father had died while he was in Tibet) and she had been advised by friends to get the family away for a break. 'I came to Dharamsala and Mo-la (Grandma) asked me to stay with her for a few days before going to see my father. She kept giving me dresses, old photographs, and other things. As I left her, she hugged me so tight and for so long that I wept for a long time afterwards. I knew in my heart that we both knew this would be the last time we'd ever meet. We were right: on the day I reached Bombay, I heard that Mo-la had passed away. It was one of the saddest times of my life.'[7]

Lobsang Samten scarcely left his mother's side. Perhaps because he was the gentlest and most vulnerable of her seven children, he had always been her special favourite, a fact she admitted towards the end of her life.

Kundun recounts with distinct glee that Tendzin Choegyal had asked her point blank which of them was her favourite, expecting it to be himself. He was devastated when, after a brief pause, she said 'Lobsang Samten'. Kundun admits that he too felt a stab of disappointment, but is consoled by the knowledge that it was Lobsang Samten who was with his mother at the end.

Amala had come to terms with death. Often now she was quiet for long periods, but sometimes she would talk. 'Once,' says Rinchen, 'when we were discussing the death of one of the lamas from Amdo, she said, "We have all these wonderful teachers around us and we feel sad when they leave us. But the important thing to remember is that they *never* leave us; their teachings are always with us. If we have really loved them, we should follow their teachings so that they become part of us." I have never forgotten her words. I have always tried to live as she would have wanted me to live.'

She died of pneumonia within two months of her eighty-first birthday, on 12 January, 1981. 'The day before,' says Rinchen, 'she called all of us in – Lobsang Samten, Namlha, myself, the children, the doctor, the servants. She said, 'You've all been so good to me, thank you for your kindness, and I'm sorry to have been such a nuisance.' She was quite matter-of-fact about it; there were no tears, it was as though she was about to set off for England on a holiday or something. She was completely unafraid, she had detached herself from earthly things, and now she was saying goodbye. Late that night, she told me to unroll the *thangka* in her room. She didn't want to lie down, she wanted to sit up and meditate on the *thangka*, just as His Holiness had told her.'

'It was a cold winter's morning,' remembers Tenzin Lodoe, who was then about eight. 'Normally I slept late. But that day I got up just before the sun had risen and went to my grandmother's room. I sat with her for a bit, she patted my head and said, "Tenzin Lodoe, when you grow up, you must remember to be a good man." Then I massaged her feet and rubbed her hands a little because they were so cold. I stayed about two hours, then went away and got myself some breakfast.'

'Amala was still looking at the *thangka*,' said Rinchen, 'when the end came. She died in my arms. She was the very first person I had ever seen die, and it was a wonderful example of what death can be like.'[8]

Tenzin Lodoe returned to his grandmother's room at about ten, in search of the sticky sweets she kept in a wall cupboard – 'My grandmother would always give me some when my mother wasn't looking.' That morning, hoping his mother was busy elsewhere, he slipped into the room. 'Then I saw my grandmother on the bed, covered up to her neck with a white sheet. Her eyes were closed. In the right-hand corner of the room an old monk, a hermit from the mountain, was murmuring prayers. In front of him were two big bowls filled with saffron water. As I moved towards the bed, he saw me, and got very agitated. "Get out, get out," he shouted. I ran out, very confused, not knowing what to think. I ran into my mother and Auntie Namlha, and asked them what was happening. Auntie Namlha turned to my mother. "Didn't you tell the kids?" When my mother said no, Auntie Namlha said, 'Well, you'll have to tell them now.' Then my mother told me very gently that my grandmother had passed away. It came as a great shock, because nobody close to me had ever died before. I started crying. My mother said, "Don't cry. Just keep in mind your grandmother's last words to you." But I couldn't stop crying, and rushed out of the room to find my sister, Chozoem, and tell her. She just wouldn't believe it.'

'Both children were terribly upset,' says Rinchen. 'I could only tell them "If you really loved your granny, let's all remember what she wanted us to be, and do the things that would make her happy. She will always be with us."'

The death of Dekyi Tsering, Amala, the Gyayum or Great Mother who had given birth to three *tulkus*, was, of course, an occasion for deep mourning. Immediately the Tibetan Administration Offices in Dharamsala were closed, one thousand lamps were lit and prayers were started at the Tsuglakhang Temple. The Minister for Religious Affairs and his staff all came round to Kashmir Cottage to pay their respects, and, accompanied by a crowd of several hundred, to recite the Great Mantra, *Om mani padme hum* (All Hail to the Jewel in the Lotus).

The Kashag worried about how to break the news to Kundun in Bodh Gaya, feeling that to telephone or send a telegram would be insensitive. Instead, says Kundun (and one can imagine that Dekyi Tsering would have enjoyed the joke), 'they sent a letter to my Senior Tutor, Ling Rinpoche, asking him to convey their condolences to me. But as Ling Rinpoche was teaching at the time, the letter was handed directly to me. I opened it, read its contents, and handed it to Ling Rinpoche who had then formally to tell me of my mother's death.'[9] At the end of his teachings that day, Kundun asked the pilgrims to pray for his mother beneath the Bodhi tree where the Buddha had received Enlightenment.

At daybreak on 14 January, the wooden casket containing Amala's body was carried by a group of monks to the old palace of Swarg Ashram. Prayers were offered by the abbot of the Dalai Lama's own Namgyal monastery – and the body was placed on its funeral pyre. Lighting one end of a stick wrapped in a paraffin-soaked white scarf, Lobsang Samten performed the last rites for his mother. The mourners circled round the pyre, placing scarves and incense sticks on it as they chanted prayers. Pema, returning from TCV business in Amsterdam next day, too late for the funeral rites, found an immense crowd still massed on the hillside. She joined her tears to theirs, acknowledging that Amala had been 'more than a mother, she was the very soul of our family'.

Rinchen Khando feels uniquely privileged to have shared those last months with her beloved Amala. 'I benefited so much from being with her,' she says, 'she was an education in herself. As the mother of the Dalai Lama, she could have gone anywhere, done anything, acted like a queen. But right from the first, she rejected the trappings of power. She never forgot her roots. And she never forgot the poor or those who were in any kind of pain.'

They do not forget her either. While she lived, Kashmir Cottage was accorded the reverence that always accrues to a holy place. That aura still clings to it. Though since her death it has reverted to being a guest-house, her spirit lingers on. As one old man said to Rinchen, five years or more after Amala had died, 'We always felt Kashmir Cottage was special because of her, and that it would cease to be so when she had gone. But, young lady, I have to tell you you're a very lucky woman, because nothing has changed. She's still here.'[10]

Later that same year, Kundun lost the surrogate 'mother' of his childhood, the head of his household, Lobsang Jinpa, always known as Ponpo, the Boss. This kindly monk had taken care of him from the day when, as a small, bewildered boy, he had come to Lhasa to take possession of the Lion Throne. 'He fed me,' says Kundun simply. 'Most mammals consider the creature that feeds them as the most important in their lives. That was the way I felt about Ponpo. I knew my teachers were more important than my cook, but emotionally the strongest bond was with him. He was my mother, my father, my entire family. When my mother died I was sad, but I didn't cry. But when Ponpo died and I looked down on his dead body, I wept.'[11]

Next it was Pema's turn to weep. In February 1984, she had gone to southern India for the official inauguration of a new Tibetan Children's Village in Byllakuppe and had spent the rest of the winter holiday in Bangalore where her husband, Lhundup Gyalpo, having run a successful Tibetan restaurant for eleven years, had just opened a second. In March she returned with the three children (now 17, 15 and 11) to Dharamsala in time for the opening of the new school term. At about two o'clock one morning, early in May, she was wakened from sleep by shouts and a loud knocking on the window. It was Gyalo Thondup's wife, Dekyi Dolkar, announcing that Lhundup Gyalpo's body had been discovered in a burned-out car in Bangalore. In a state of shock, Pema woke the children and told them, struggling to stay calm for their sakes. Gyalo Thondup drove them to Bangalore, and took Pema straight to the police station to see her husband's remains. Rumours were already rife about the death: nobody being sure whether it was accident, murder or suicide. Lhundup Gyalpo had set out at night in his car and that was all anybody knew until next morning when the burned-out car was identified by his assistant. When the funeral rites had been performed, and all the prayers were said, Gyalo Thondup and his wife suggested that Pema should hire a detective to investigate. But Kundun advised that the desire for revenge could only be destructive, and in the end she decided not to proceed. Many people criticized her decision, 'few of them understanding,' she wrote, 'my desire to protect the children and avoid any unsavoury publicity for our family.'[12] Instead, she returned to Dharamsala and to the demanding work of the TCV.

Lobsang Samten's personality had undergone a sea change. 'When he came back from Tibet,' says Namlha, 'all his enthusiasm, life, energy, jokiness had gone. He was like a zombie.' While Namlha watched helplessly, he lapsed into a permanent depression. 'We Tibetans talk about a disturbance of the wind energy,' she says, 'when both mind and body are in the grip of stress.' For about a year after his return, people would seek him out for news of their families. When these people came, the information he gave was always sad, their relatives were in prison, murdered or dead of starvation; this or that monastery had been destroyed. He used to talk about it and we all sat there and wept. It seems to me that we never stopped crying that first year. It was difficult for all of us; but Lobsang it destroyed: he began to drink heavily and to suffer from violent mood swings.'[13]

In 1980, a Director was needed for the Tibetan Medical Institute in McLeod Ganj, with its Medical College in Dharamsala and clinics all over India and Nepal. There was no one with the required qualifications to run this combination of hospital, pharmacy and medical school for traditional Tibetan medicine, but as Lobsang had had some experience of administration, had worked for the Tibetan Government and done some fundraising in the USA, he was appointed Director, with Namlha as his English secretary and interpreter and eventually as Assistant Director in the foreign department. They moved from the Tibetan Children's Village to a small café/guest-house in McLeod. Lobsang, however, was a shadow of his former self and 'all his bubbly energy had gone.' 'He had been such a happy person,' adds Kundun, 'always telling jokes. But after going to Tibet, he just fell into an almost chronic depression.'[14]

Lobsang immersed himself in the work of the Medical Institute, trying to ward off the terrible nightmares. But in 1984, even as he was drawing up plans for a new Medical Institute in Delhi, he warned Namlha that he did not have long to live. Tibetans often have astrology charts made, to ascertain their lifespans. Namlha had had one done for herself and for the children, but Lobsang 'didn't hold with that kind of thing, he said it was weird'. Nevertheless, he knew his time was up.

In April 1985, they were offered a three-roomed apartment to rent in the Namgyal Monastery in McLeod. Lobsang, recovering from a gastric attack, took no interest in the move, not caring which room was which, nor even about where he would sleep. But one day in May, on impulse, he suggested inviting the family to a party: Pema and her three children came, Khando and Rapten. 'A friend happened to drop by and took a photograph of us all – it was the very last time we would be together.' 'It was a wonderful evening,' Khando remembers. 'Lobsang seemed to be his old self, cheerful, teasing us all, cracking his terrible dirty jokes. We were doubled up with laughter.'

Soon afterwards, Lobsang and Namlha began commuting to Delhi to set up a clinic and look for land on which to build a new Medical Institute. (Both of their children were in Delhi, Tenzin reading Political Science at St Stephen's College, and Chuki, who had graduated in Psychology at Chandigarh University, at secretarial school.) They spent two months setting up an exhibition of Tibetan Medicine at Tibet House in Delhi, trudging around in the sweltering heat of the city for eight or nine hours each day in search of a suitable place for a clinic. Eventually they found a house, bought furniture, appointed staff and opened for business: on the very first day, about two or three hundred Indians came for treatment. Lobsang's work in Delhi was almost done, though he still had to finalize an arrangement with the Indian Government concerning the purchase of land for the Institute. At this juncture, Kundun arrived in Delhi, on his way to Switzerland.

'I had decided to take Lobsang along,' he says. 'He wanted to come, but at the last minute told me he ought to stay in Delhi to clinch the business about the land. When I came back, he was still waiting for the man to turn up. I was returning to Dharamsala by overnight train and asked him if he'd like to travel with me.' Lobsang and Namlha had already decided to go back to Dharamsala and catch up with the backlog of work, before returning to Delhi. They were booked on to next day's bus. Kundun's offer was a godsend. 'I was delighted,' says Namlha, 'Lobsang was very tired and stressed-out, and travelling up in His Holiness's special coach would at least ensure he had somewhere to lie down. I left on the bus next morning, and they were due to leave that evening.'

But Lobsang didn't arrive. Just before leaving, he had discovered that the man dealing with the land business was due in Delhi in ten days' time. He decided to wait for him.

Namlha attacked the daunting backlog of work at the Institute. When Inge, a German friend visiting Dharamsala, suggested they should travel down to Delhi together for Lobsang's birthday on 1 September, she reluctantly refused. 'Besides, as I told Inge, I needed to be on my own for a while. Lobsang and I had never once been apart in our entire married life (except when he went to Tibet) and for some unexplained reason I felt I must experience what it was like to live alone. Inge told me not to be morbid, but my mind was made up.'

Lobsang wrote to say he would be coming home soon, but couldn't say when. At first Namlha was unconcerned. Only after a week had gone by did she begin to worry. On Monday she phoned Chuki in Delhi. 'I asked her how [Lobsang] was, and she told me he was getting over some kind of flu virus. He had been to see a doctor and was now staying with Gyalo Thondup's wife in Delhi. I was shocked but relieved. My sister-in-law was very motherly and practical, so he'd be in good hands. I asked Chuki to go and see her father and call me if necessary. But I could no longer concentrate on work. I was not in the habit of making personal calls from the office, but next day I rang Dekyi Dolkar...who told me Lobsang had developed jaundice. I dropped everything and ran.'

According to Kundun, one of Lobsang's friends misguidedly 'gave him rum or brandy or something to treat the flu, and that made everything worse, turned the 'flu to fever and then to jaundice. From then on, his condition began to deteriorate rapidly.'

Catching the night bus from Dharamsala that same day (Tuesday), Namlha went straight to her sister-in-law's apartment. 'I found Lobsang in the dining-room, wearing a white kurta pyjama and reading the newspaper. He looked terribly thin and exhausted, almost lifeless. When he saw me, he dropped his paper, came and hugged me and burst into tears. I hugged him back, stammering out through my own tears that he was ill and ought to be in bed. He went to bed, but each day insisted on coming down to meals because – like his mother – he didn't want to be a bother to anyone. On Sunday afternoon, he was unable to get off the toilet and called me to help. I cleaned him up and called for my brother who was in the house. Together we wrestled him back to bed, he was a dead weight. Later that evening, when I tried to get him to take his medicine, he became violent. He'd always had a temper, but it was never more than a momentary thing. This time, he pushed me away – hard. Something was terribly wrong. My sister-in-law and I went for a doctor. There was a Tibetan one nearby, but Lobsang refused to see him. We looked for the Indian doctor, but it was Sunday and he was out for the day. There was nothing for it but to return home and wait.'

The Indian doctor came at about eight and ordered Lobsang to hospital. But where to take him on a Sunday evening? They took him to the only hospital Namlha knew, the Catholic Holy Family Hospital. When they arrived, Lobsang was delirious and uncontrollably violent. 'There were three young doctors and two nurses, but none of them could handle him. He had lapsed into a coma, from which hour after hour he would wake up and cry aloud in pain – but he wouldn't let the doctors come near. I went and whispered prayers in his ear. When he relapsed into coma, I would go out and help the nurses with five or six terminal cases who were constantly crying for water. In the room that night, I lay down on a shawl, but I couldn't sleep.'

Next morning, the Bureau of Tibet in Delhi informed the Indian Government of Lobsang's condition and he was transferred to the All-India Medical Centre. There he lapsed into a final deep coma – which lasted for thirteen days. Kundun still reproaches himself for not being with him at the end. 'I sent my own physician, Wangyal, to him,' he says sadly, 'but there was nothing he could do. I couldn't stop myself thinking, over and over again, if only Lobsang had come to Switzerland with me, none of this would have happened. If I'd insisted on his getting the train with me from Delhi, it wouldn't have happened. There was so much negligence. Lobsang was alone and exhausted when he got sick, and he didn't take steps to look after himself until it was too late.'

Pema had arrived in Delhi to be with Namlha – and Chuki. Lobsang's son, Tenzin, was so distressed that he had not been seen at his university hostel for two days. Tempa (Gyalo Thondup's younger son, a doctor) had come from Darjeeling to be with the family.

In the early afternoon of 28 September 1985, Pema was out shopping, Chuki was with her mother, Tenzin was still incommunicado. Namlha was resting, intending to go as usual to the hospital at five. At three o'clock, she became unaccountably agitated and knew she must go to Lobsang without delay. Tempa drove her and Chuki to the hospital. 'As I walked into the hospital, I saw Pema queuing for the telephone. She said, "Something has happened to Lobsang, I was trying to ring you." My son, Tenzin, had just arrived too. We went up together, and there we were, Pema, the children, me – and Lobsang. It was as though he had known I would come and had waited for me. As I got to his side, he breathed his last.'

The doctors wanted the body removed immediately, as they needed the bed. But the family wished the Buddhist after-death ritual to be followed. 'His Holiness had sent two people to help. Rinpoche [Tendzin Choegyal] had come with them, but he was so upset that we felt he should not stay and sent him back to Dharamsala with one of the secretaries. With the help of one of His Holiness's helpers, I washed Lobsang's body all over with the remains of some holy water which he had sent. Then we dressed him in a white kurta pyjama that I had bought for him in Bombay two years earlier. A Rinpoche from Tibet House said the last rites. It was stiflingly hot in Delhi. My mother suggested that we should have the body cremated there. But when I rang His Holiness, I was given the message that I must take the body to Dharamsala that very night.'

Lobsang Samten was cremated in Dharamsala. It was, Kundun says today, 'one of the very saddest times of my life. I think it is no exaggeration to say that Lobsang died of a broken heart. He simply couldn't understand how the Chinese could be so indifferent to the sufferings they had caused in Tibet.'[15]

For Namlha, there was overwhelming grief. She and Lobsang had been married for twenty-three years and in that time had scarcely ever been apart. 'Ours was a love-match,' she says, 'and we were the best of friends as well as lovers. When he died, a part of me died too.'

In October, she was asked to take over Lobsang's post as Director of the Medical Institute. Appalled at the suggestion, she refused, protesting that she was quite unequal to such a heavy responsibility, but offering to help the new Director all she could. The physicians from the Institute said they had already written to His Holiness and to the Kashag, and, if she continued to refuse, the entire staff of the Medical Institute would stage a sit-in in her apartment. Namlha was petrified. 'I asked them to wait a few days, as I didn't want to make a big issue of it. I went to see His Holiness's Private Secretary to ask him if a divination could be done, to determine whether or not I would be suitable for the job.'

She then left, with Chuki and her uncle, Jigme Taring, for Bodh Gaya. 'I went there to pray for Lobsang. I felt completely empty. My uncle said he thought I should not live alone, because I'd never been used to it, but I told him I should simply have to learn.'

Namlha was still in Bodh Gaya when news of her appointment as Director of the Medical Institute came through. 'When I received that letter, I went to the main temple with Chuki, and there, in front of the statue of the Buddha I promised to do my best and prayed for blessings on the work.'

She took up the appointment on 1 January 1986. 'It was difficult and strange,' she says, 'but the very worst thing of all was sitting in the chair that had been Lobsang's.'

NOTES
1. Author interview with Rinchen Khando, 1993.
2. Norbu, *Tibet Is My Country*, p. 269.
3. *Tibet Is My Country*, p. 274.
4. Tibetans were being allowed out of Tibet to visit relatives in India, but only on condition that they left a son, daughter, husband, parent behind as hostage.
5. Author interview with HH the Dalai Lama, 1994.
6. Conversation with Tendzin Choegyal and Rinchen Khando, 1994.
7. Author interview with Khando Chazotsang, Utah, February 1996.

8. Conversation with Rinchen Khando, October 1994, in the room where the Great Mother died.

9. Author interview with HH the Dalai Lama, October 1994.

10. Author interview with Rinchen Khando, 1993.

11. Author interview with HH the Dalai Lama, 1994.

12. Jetsun Pema, *Tibet, Mon Histoire.*

13. Author interview with Namlha Taklha, Dharamsala, 1993.

14. Author interview with HH the Dalai Lama, 1994.

15. Author interview with HH the Dalai Lama, June 1994.

25

Return to Darkness

On the whole, the...switch of policy in Tibet is just the crunchy end of the time-honoured stick-and-carrot treatment which China has, with a fair rate of success, applied to its Tibetan problem. What it has gained through force and terror it now hopes to consolidate by coercion and bribes.

Jamyang Norbu, 1980

Gyalo Thondup was a disappointed man. By 1983, he had visited Peking twelve times as Kundun's personal emissary. 'The Chinese wanted to trick us, giving us sweets as if we were three-year-old children. They were sure they could persuade us of the advantages of going back to Tibet.' As Deng was already back-tracking on the promises he had made (cancelling the request for teachers, for example), and as he was tired of being a hate-figure in Dharamsala, GT once again retired hurt to Hong Kong. 'I told the Chinese it was a thankless task being a go-between. I said, "You kick me like a ball to Dharamsala and Dharamsala kicks me right back again. Both of you suspect me and I can't take any more." They tried to persuade me to carry on, saying things would get worse if I gave up. But I'd had enough. I told His Holiness that in future he could send his officials to Peking, not me.'¹

Kundun hoped to visit Tibet in 1985. To this end, he sent a delegation of three senior ministers – among them his Minister of Security, Phuntsok Tashi Taklha – to Peking to open a dialogue. It was a waste of time. The Chinese wanted one thing only – to get the Dalai Lama back. (They needed his help to develop Tibet. As they had told GT, 'One word from him would be worth a thousand from us.') Accordingly, they set their own agenda, refusing to discuss anything except the Dalai Lama's future political status, whether he would reside in Peking or Lhasa, by what route he would return, and so on. No amount of argument would persuade them that these were side-issues, says Phuntsok Tashi, 'far less important than improving the well-being and happiness of the Tibetan people. To them, there was no such thing as "a Tibet problem".'

Chinese immigrants began flooding into Tibet in 1983, raising for the first time the spectre of what the Dalai Lama called 'a final solution by stealth' in which Tibetans would be edged out in their own land. Chinese nationals, mainly the young and poorly-educated, were being encouraged – with irresistible incentives in pay, housing, special privileges and holidays – to leave their own over-populated areas and assist in 'developing the Tibetan Autonomous Republic'. For them there were rich pickings to be had. For the Tibetans it spelled disaster. In Lhasa, prices soared and thousands found themselves out of work, as even their traditional trades and crafts were taken over by the Chinese. Before long only the most unskilled, underpaid jobs were available for the Tibetans and most of them had to resort to street-hawking and begging. Kundun dropped his plans for a visit.

By May 1984, sixty thousand skilled and unskilled Chinese workers had arrived in Tibet. Many others followed as private individuals, and the new invasion showed every sign of gathering force. As active resistance to the intruders grew, so did a new wave of repression, arrests and public executions.

In September, a second attempt at dialogue with Peking had as little success as the first. Unsurprisingly, perhaps, since China was being asked to accept 'the historical status of Tibet and its right to self-determination, the right to reunification of the three traditional provinces of Tibet, the need for a relationship or alliance with China on an equal footing and the transformation of Tibet into a zone of peace'.[2]

In 1986, a year after Tibet had officially 'celebrated' twenty years as the Tibet Autonomous Region, Kundun's brother, Norbu, who made no secret of his loathing for Chinese colonialism, was refused a visa to visit friends and relatives in Tibet. An official at the Chinese Consulate General in New York cited Norbu's aggressive support for Tibetan Independence and the 'many things' he had said against China.

In this stalemate, the Kashag swallowed its pride and turned again, cap in hand, to Gyalo Thondup. 'For three years,' says GT virtuously, 'I had kept a very low profile. I didn't go near China. Then the Kashag began writing to me, asking me to come to Dharamsala. I said I had nothing to say to them. They replied that if I wouldn't come to them, they'd come to me in Delhi. They came and confessed that their relationship with China was at breaking-point. The Chinese had told them not to come back any more unless they were prepared to travel as "overseas Chinese", which of course they weren't. So, please would I try again. I agreed to see the Chinese Ambassador in Delhi about reopening the discussions. Peking replied "Gyalo Thondup is an old friend and, like any other member of the Yapshi family, will be welcome in China,"[3] so then I resumed my visits.'

During this period, GT's wife, Dekyi Dolkar, died. Many felt she had never recovered from the death of her daughter, Yangzom, in a motor-car accident in the Sahara four years earlier. Yangzom, who was married to Namlha's brother Jigme Tsarong, left a young son, and after her death Dekyi Dolkar took the boy home with her and brought him up as her own. But her health was already declining and in 1986 she was diagnosed as having cancer of the pancreas. Though her sons flew her to New York for surgery, it was too late, and she died on the operating table. Despite her Chinese birth, she was mourned by the Tibetans as a true Tibetan who devoted her life to their cause. For Tendzin Choegyal, she had been a truly formative influence. 'I miss her still,' he says, 'she was warm, understanding, and utterly honest. When you talked to her, you felt you'd talked with a real human being. There was no deviousness in her.'

Over the next three years, GT resumed his visits to Peking. He claims that he told the Chinese repeatedly that their policies were morally and politically wrong. 'They accused Tibetan exiles of being splittists, but they were the real splittists – they had split off huge chunks of Tibet and absorbed them into China; they'd destroyed our culture and sucked up Tibet like a giant vacuum cleaner; they claimed to have liberated us, but Tibet was in chains. "You are worse than the Manchus," I said. "Mao wanted all the minorities to love each other and be happy within the Motherland. But look at the Tibetans, they're very unhappy and they hate you."'[4]

Indeed, many Tibetans were still braving the terrors of the high Himalaya to reach India or Nepal. All of them yearned to see the Dalai Lama, and as they had no option but to go to Dharamsala for screening (the Chinese being known to plant spies among them), their wish was usually granted. Kundun saw them in groups or individually, listened to them, wept with them, and grieved that he could help them so little. There were so many shortages, of accommodation, of water, of electricity – of money. As a guest of the Indian Government, he couldn't levy taxes, and was dependent on what he received from the host country, from donor agencies, private benefactors and donations made to him personally through his teachings and lectures. Among the refugees, salary earners contributed two per cent of their salaries, business men ten per cent of their takings and everybody else at least one rupee a month.

Dharamsala had flourished. The Government-in-Exile ran small hotels, guest-houses, restaurants, travel agencies, handicraft centres and an import/export business. The place was awash now with market-stalls offering anything from fine bronze Buddhas, Tibetan antiques and jewellery through to fluorescent socks and tawdry cotton T-shirts. The Tibetan Medical Centre offered traditional remedies, while the Delek Hospital, staffed by volunteer doctors from all over the world, provided more modern, Western treatments. In South India, Nepal, Bhutan, Switzerland, the USA and the UK also, Tibetan refugees were proving themselves to be survivors rather than victims.

Though much remained to be done, their achievements were remarkable. The eighty-two schools, for example, in the Indian sub-continent alone, thirty of them supported by the Government of India, forty-three entirely by the Tibetan Administration. The nine Tibetan Children's Villages, overseen by Pema, fed and clothed about eight thousand refugee children, two thousand of whom were in Dharamsala. They were arriving at the rate of about two hundred each year and the Homes were stretched to breaking point. Pema would never turn any child away even if they had to be housed in makeshift shacks, they would manage somehow. Things were changing, though, not least in the attitude of the TCV's supporters. The old days when donors gave money without being much concerned about the overall picture disappeared when Kundun began travelling and making personal contacts. People had become more interested in Tibet itself. Pema was finding that helpers were no longer concerned just for the immediate needs of the children, but also for 'our culture, our religion, our Tibetan identity. People seem to have realized that we have something to offer the world'.[5]

For six years Khando had successfully run the Tibetan Homes Foundation, Mussoorie, and all its branch programmes scattered around in India. Her predecessor, Mrs Taring, had adopted an old-fashioned, authoritarian approach, but Khando was different: 'Mine was a management style geared to consensus and an open-door policy. I was determined to hold open meetings with house-parents and older students, but I'm afraid that some of the house-parents really did not approve of the freedom with which the older students expressed their views on behalf of all the children. Initially when we had meetings, they all sat with their heads bowed, waiting for me to address them. One day I said, "Look, I don't think this kind of meeting is getting us anywhere. Frankly, it's a waste of time. For me, a meeting is about identifying difficulties, you telling me what you need, setting our priorities, and then all of us putting our heads together to see if we have the necessary resources and money. I'm learning too, you know."'

It was hard-going. But Kundun supported her. 'He kept telling me that difficulties and problems were inevitable and didn't matter as long as we did our best with a good conscience...His encouragement and the hard teamwork of the rest of the staff paid off, as slowly we developed the capacity to provide quality care and education for our children. Donations began to pour in, and with help from many different organizations and from the Government of India, we put up more buildings and made improvements to the existing ones. I really thrived in the new atmosphere.'[6]

One day in 1986 Pema walked down the mountainside to McLeod Ganj, and called on a cousin who lived near the Temple. The atmosphere was ominously still. Suddenly, a thunderous boom from the mountain reverberated through the valley. Within seconds, the earth began to shake and noise exploded all around them. 'I huddled against the door, my thoughts full of the children up at the Village. My cousin began praying aloud, and we could hear people shrieking outside.'[7] The quake (with a force of seven or eight on the Richter scale) lasted only a few seconds and when it was over Pema rushed to Kundun's residence from where she could telephone to see if the children were all right. In fact, three or four of the makeshift houses in the Village had collapsed, covering the children's beds with rubble. But to her intense relief, the children were all outside and there were no casualties.

Kundun had been reading when the earthquake hit. His house, built by the British at least eighty years earlier and only partially renovated, did not withstand the seismic shocks. Stones were dislodged from the space between the roof and the ceiling, and some of them fell inside the house. Huge cracks appeared in several of the walls. It was clear that something would have to be done. As news of the earthquake spread throughout the world, letters and donations poured in. Work began almost immediately on a new, shock-resistant residence for Kundun on the site of the old.

For Pema, there was an unforeseen outcome. During this period, she came into frequent contact with one of Kundun's Private Secretaries, Tempa Tsering, who in the late Seventies had been a firebrand President of the Tibetan Youth Congress, outspoken advocate of a greater militancy against the Chinese. Independence, he had proclaimed, 'wouldn't come on a plate. It had to be fought for and won.'[8] Under Tempa's embattled leadership The TYC had briefly flirted with the idea of terrorism – against Chinese embassies and personnel abroad. Some training got under way, the TYC expanded its contacts with underground groups inside Tibet, but in the end, its vow of loyalty to the Dalai Lama – and the more hopeful climate of the early 1980s – had caused Tempa Tsering to shelve his plans. Invited to become Secretary of the foreign section of the Private Office, with the prospect of travelling the world with Kundun, he became convinced instead that 'Tibet's unique hope lay not where the guerrillas had failed, but in the strength of the traditional society, now rebuilt and entering the world at large.'[9]

Pema had long been a pillar of that traditional society when she and Tempa Tsering decided to marry. Her decision exploded like a bombshell in Dharamsala, since Tempa Tsering was, to put it mildly, not liked either by the community in general or by the Yapshi family in particular. In her autobiography, Pema writes that the Tibetans did not expect the Dalai Lama's widowed sister to remarry, they would have preferred her to become a nun. But 'I did not attach too much importance to the opinion of others. Honesty is what counts; one must be true to oneself and not pretend to be other than one is.'[10] When she consulted her children, they told her it was her life and she must make her own decision. The marriage took place in New Delhi, with Gyalo Thondup giving the blessing. Shortly afterwards Tempa Tsering was transferred to Bangalore and Pema was separated from her new husband for months on end. Both of them accepted the situation as normal. The Tibetan cause had to come first.

In 1980, Tendzin Choegyal had accompanied Kundun on his first visit to Zanskar and Ladakh in the mountainous north-west of India. This was the area in which the monasteries of Ngari Rinpoche lay and though he had long since handed over control to the monks themselves, he was still ulti-mately responsible for them. Kundun, learning that the monasteries were in a state of neglect, now told his brother in no uncertain terms to do something about them. Tendzin Choegyal thereupon sent out a letter to all his monasteries, informing them that he was resuming a degree of con-trol. For the next few years, he sent a friend and colleague from army days to keep an eye on the monasteries' affairs. 'He was full of ideas. He built tourist hostels to generate income and set up co-operatives. Thanks to him, the monasteries in the Leh area bought some land, built houses on it, and rented them out. The arrangement worked quite well. The abbots thought I was eccentric but at least they knew I wasn't a crook.'[11]

After Amala's death, he and Rinchen had decided to support their family by reconverting Kashmir Cottage into a guest house. Rinchen pawned some of the family valuables to finance the renovation and the building of a new house close by for themselves. With Amala gone and the children growing up, she took up (unpaid) social work among Tibetan women with large families, and fundraising for nuns who were finding it difficult to survive. When the Tibetan Women's Association was revived in 1984, she was elected as its first President. The Association commemorated the courageous women who had risen against the Chinese during the Lhasa Uprising, many of whom were arrested and died in prison. In exile, small local groups of – mainly illiterate – women had gathered together to keep their memory alive. They had started small handicraft centres, but had few resources and no cohesion. The new Association was both national and international, with a network of representatives from twelve different regions of India and Nepal and with influential contacts in the USA, UK, Norway, Sweden and India. It aimed to keep alive the sense of belonging to a unified Tibet, and to preserve the Tibetan language and culture in an alien environment. 'Our women were in a strong position to do this,' avers Rinchen, 'because they were the ones who bring up the children. They needed to be made aware of their potential and the value of their own con-tribution. But we had a wider aim too: to make contact with women all over the world, so that we could tell them about what had been done to Tibet and work with them to bring peace to the world.'

To Rinchen's delight, Kundun asked if nuns could be included. 'I'd al-ways been interested in the lives of nuns, partly because when I was a child in Kham, I had a very kind and loving aunt who lived in a hermitage in a beautiful valley with a stream running by...But nuns had never received a proper education like the monks: that's why there isn't a single nun *geshe*[12] today. It really was high time we provided a decent system of education for them.' So, with a gift of money from the Council for Religious Affairs and from the refugees' fund, the Tibetan Women's Association incorporated a special Nuns' Project. A year or two later, when Tibet was again in turmoil and monks and nuns were at the forefront of resistance, the full force of Chinese revenge was directed against them. Many of them were tortured almost to the point of death; hundreds of survivors took the difficult and dangerous route to India and freedom. When sixty-four refugee nuns arrived on one day in Dharamsala with nowhere to put them, Rinchen sent an SOS to friends in the West for money for beds, then rented a large house behind Kashmir Cottage, and started planning a permanent nunnery and an Institute for Higher Studies. She was offered some land in the beautiful Kangra Valley and a friend donated the money with which to build on it. 'Our real hope,' explains Rinchen, 'is that when the nuns get their degrees, they will be able to return to Tibet and teach. And not only teach. Some of them will train as health workers and nurses. If all goes according to plan, they will be able to play a really useful role in our community.'[13]

Kundun had become a popular ambassador for his country, not least in the USA where during visits in 1979, 1981 and 1984, he had received many offers of support. In July 1985 the US Congress wrote to the President of the Chinese People's Assembly in Peking, approving the negotiations taking place between China and the Dalai Lama's representatives and asking for the Tibetans' requests to be given due consideration. That the Chinese would ignore the missive was a foregone conclusion. Nevertheless, Congress had served notice that it both recognized and upheld the Dalai Lama's cause. Other countries followed suit.

Early in 1987, Kundun was again in Washington, to address a Congressional sub-committee on Human Rights. Friends suggested that he might like to put forward a list of aims with which supporters of Tibet round the world might identify. Accordingly, on Capitol Hill on 21 September, Kundun proposed what came to be known as his Five-Point Peace Plan – a Buddhist Charter for Tibet:

1 Tibet should be designated a Zone of Peace, the entire plateau to be an area without weapons of destruction. Even the peaceful use of nuclear energy would be banned, because of the pollution it would cause. Tibet would become the world's biggest nature reserve, in which plant and animal life would be protected, the environment guarded from exploitation, and social development attuned to the needs and potential of the people. With peace actively promoted, Indian troops could abandon their defensive positions along the Himalayan borders and trust could be re-established. But the precondition of such trust would be the withdrawal of Chinese troops from Tibet. 'After the holocaust of the last three decades...only a withdrawal of Chinese troops could start a genuine process of reconciliation.'

2 China should abandon its population transfer – its Final Solution by stealth – which was threatening the very existence of Tibet. If this did not happen, Tibetans would 'soon be no more than a tourist attraction and a relic of a noble past'.

3 Human rights and democratic freedoms should be respected. Tibetans had become second-class citizens in their own country under a system of outright *apartheid*.

4 The environment should be restored. The wildlife of Tibet had been almost totally wiped out and irreparable damage done to what had once been an unspoiled wilderness sanctuary.

5 Serious negotiations should take place with the Chinese, concerning not only the future of Tibet but the relationship between the Tibetan and Chinese peoples.

This last proposal the Chinese interpreted as a call to 'independence in disguise'. Their fury found expression three days later in a mass political rally in Lhasa at which fifteen thousand people were compelled to watch the sentencing of eight Tibetan dissidents, three of them to death.

This reversion to terror tactics served only to push the Tibetans over the edge. On 27 September 1987, the first of more than eighty spontaneous non-violent uprisings erupted, spear-headed by monks and nuns and all demanding Tibetan independence. It was, as one woman who took part told the author, 'an absolutely universal rejection of the regime'. At first the authorities were caught off guard, but they soon recovered, introducing specially-trained riot squads who would shoot to kill, and beat people up without mercy. Over the next three years, there followed a savage programme of

murder, torture and intimidation unequalled since the Cultural Revolution and to which even the Chinese gave the name of 'merciless repression'.[14] The difference was that this time both the protests and their
suppression were witnessed by foreign tourists[15] and by the world's press.
No longer could anyone plead ignorance of the human-rights abuses being
perpetrated in Tibet.

With more and more Tibetans being killed, wounded or arrested every
day, the policy of non-violent resistance hung by a thread. Knowing that at
any moment the Tibetans might resort to violence, Kundun intensified his
search for a solution. While Western leaders called on China to resume
talks with the Tibetans, on 15 June 1988 he stood before the European Parliament in Strasbourg and enlarged on the theme of his Five-Point Peace
Plan. Reaching for the bottom line of what he was prepared to offer, he declared himself ready to abandon claims for full Tibetan independence and
to be willing to leave foreign policy and defence matters in the hands of
the Chinese. In effect, he was offering China 'suzerainty' in exchange for
the Tibetans' right to conduct their own internal affairs. It was an attempt
in good faith to find out what China was willing to concede.

Kundun made it clear that the final decision would be left to the Tibetan
people themselves. But the fall-out from Strasbourg was enormous and the
shock-waves are still reverberating today. The Chinese predictably de-
nounced it as 'splittist'. But their reaction was nothing to the fury of young
(and some not-so-young) Tibetans in Dharamsala and the exile communities world-wide. Individuals and groups protested openly, defying the Dalai
Lama to an unprecedented degree, wondering how such a spectacular sell-
out could ever have been contemplated. By what right could Tibetans in
Dharamsala hand over the very independence for which their fellow countrymen in Tibet were daily paying with their lives? Phuntsog Wangyal, a
prominent Tibetan in London, spoke for many. 'History has always believed
that Tibet was independent,' he said bitterly. 'His Holiness had always
talked about Independence. But with Strasbourg, suddenly a new chapter on
Tibet began: "not-Independence". Was that in his own best interests? Or in
the interests of history? To exchange Independence for whatever is on offer
now, at this moment?'[16] Kundun was blamed for wishful thinking, the
Kashag and various foreign advisers for giving him bad advice, and Gyalo
Thondup – for still carrying on his unofficial talks with the Chinese.

GT was indeed still talking to the Chinese, though to scant effect: 'They
kept on about our being splittists, even when I told them they were being

paranoid. They were suspicious of their own shadows, I said. They thought His Holiness was being exploited by the Americans and I couldn't convince them it wasn't true. Of course, what they really wanted was for His Holiness to say openly that Tibet was part of China. I told them that was impossible, because historically it wasn't true. Tibet had never been ruled by the Chinese.'[17] Norbu did not share the views of either GT or Kundun. 'My eldest brother disagrees with me fundamentally on this issue,' says Kundun.[18] 'He expresses his feelings quite forcefully and is very critical of my approach.'

'I don't believe in violence but I certainly don't think His Holiness is being tough enough,' agrees Norbu. 'China has absolutely no excuse for being in Tibet. We're not Chinese, we're Tibetans. If a thief comes to your house, you must drive him out, and China should get out of Tibet. We owe nothing to China, we have our own language, our own culture – if we talk, we have to talk as equals and not with China dictating the terms.'[19]

The killing did not stop for Strasbourg. The force of Tibetan resistance would be broken only by the brutal imposition of martial law after the last big riot in March 1989, less than three months before the more famous massacre on Peking's own Tiananmen Square. 'The idea of China imposing martial law in Lhasa was terrifying,' wrote Kundun.[20] 'It looked as if the Chinese must be about to turn the place into a slaughter-house, a Himalayan killing-fields. Two days later, on the thirtieth anniversary of the Tibetan People's Uprising, I therefore sent an appeal to Deng Xiao-ping, asking that he intervene personally to lift martial law and end the repression of innocent Tibetans. He did not reply.'

Martial law failed to crush the Tibetan spirit – calls for violent action were increasingly heard. When the Tibetan Youth Congress assembled in Dharamsala in the September after Strasbourg, the delegates were breathing fire. Kundun opened their deliberations, arguing that violence would only beget worse violence and the use of force would forfeit the sympathy of the outside world; but they were unwilling to listen. I saw him in the afternoon, when he was still bruised from the encounter. 'There they all were this morning,' he sighed, 'wanting to take up arms and fight the Chinese. It's very easy for them to talk, but when you come down to the practical details, it's impossible. For one thing, India wouldn't tolerate it. Nor America, Russia, France – nobody would help or supply weapons. And there's one more thing – if Tibetans turned to violence, they would no longer be special. Many countries now support us because we are fighting for our freedom through non-violence. That's something quite new on this planet and it is unique.'[21]

In the end, the young Tibetans did not make a call to arms, though they agonized over the decision. 'Every nation has the right to defend itself from annihilation,' the new President, Lhasang Tsering, told me emotionally as the Congress ended. 'We are talking about our very survival.' Later, he and many others would note that Strasbourg, in compromising on Independence, had opened up a tragic fault line in Tibetan society. 'We are traditionally divided over religion, provinces and many other issues, but we never before had two opinions on Independence. The Strasbourg Proposal divided us.'[22]

The world, however, approved Kundun's judgement, for in December of that year he was awarded the Nobel Prize for Peace. The Award cited his unwavering non-violence and tireless search for 'peaceful solutions based upon tolerance and mutual respect in order to preserve the historical and cultural heritage of his people'. Here was an implicit condemnation of China – which in June had dealt with its own people's aspirations by leaving them dead and dying on Tiananmen Square. China was stung and, protesting that the Nobel Committee's decision had 'hurt the Chinese people's feelings', imposed even more draconian restrictions on Tibet. Kundun saw the Award differently, as signifying the world's recognition of the value of compassion, love, and forgiveness even of one's enemies. In his acceptance speech on 10 December 1989, speaking as 'a simple monk from far-away Tibet', he drew the world's attention to his country's tragic fate and to its continuing non-violent resistance. The prize money (3 million kroner, $469,000, about £281,000) was used to set up a Foundation for Universal Responsibility: for needy people everywhere, particularly in his host-country, India; and for a number of peace projects throughout the world. The Chinese, for their part, ended this infamous year with another mandatory public rally in Lhasa at which eleven monks received jail sentences of up to nineteen years for the crime of campaigning for Tibetan Independence.

As for Gyalo Thondup, he had decided that discretion was the better part of valour. What was the point of bothering, he asked himself. 'No matter what I said to the Chinese, they didn't listen. And no matter what I said to the Tibetans, they did not listen either.' It was an impossible situation. From now on, he determined to 'emulate the three monkeys: hear all, see all, say nothing'.

NOTES

1. Author interview with Gyalo Thondup, New Delhi, July 1996.

2. 'Sino-Tibetan Negotiations since 1959', *Resistance and Reform in Tibet.*

3. In other words, no Cabinet Ministers. By underlining that the Yapshi family was welcome in China at any time, the Chinese may have intended to cause discord in Dharamsala.

4. Author interview with Gyalo Thondup, New Delhi, July 1996.

5. Author interview with Jetsun Pema, June 1994.

6. Author interview with Khando Chazotsang, Utah, February 1996.

7. Jetsun Pema.

8. Avedon, *In Exile from the Land of Snows*, chapter 5.

9. Author interview with Gyalo Thondup, New Delhi, July 1996.

10. Jetsun Pema, *Tibet, Mon Histoire.*

11. Author interview with Tendzin Choegyal, Dharamsala, October 1993.

12. Buddhist Doctor of Philosophy and teacher.

13. Author interview with Khando Chazotsang, Utah, February 1996.

14. For details of this period, see, among many other sources, my own *Tears of Blood*, HarperCollins, 1992.

15. Tourists had been allowed into Tibet after 1980.

16. Author interview with Phuntsog Wangyal, London, February 1996.

17. Author interview with Gyalo Thondup, Delhi, July 1995.

18. Author interview with HH the Dalai Lama, October 1994.

19. Author interview with Thubten Jigme Norbu, Dharamsala, July 1995.

20. Fourteenth Dalai Lama, *Freedom in Exile*, p. 288.

21. Author interview with HH the Dalai Lama, September 1989.

22. 'Talks with Lhasang Tsering', *Lungta* 7, 1993.

26

The Hazards of Democracy

A wise man calmly considers what is right and what is wrong, and faces different opinions with truth, non-violence and peace.

The Dhammapada

Tendzin Choegyal felt he was going mad. Beset alternately by depressions and panic attacks, his self-esteem was at an all-time low. It was while accompanying Kundun on his second visit to Zanskar and Ladakh in 1988 that he 'went from full-blown depression to full-blown mania'. As Kundun's Private Secretary, he was in charge of arrangements for the visit. 'In Zanskar,' comments His Holiness, 'many meetings had been organized. Tendzin Choegyal is a perfectionist and expected everything to go exactly according to plan, but, of course, things don't always turn out the way we want them to, and this was no exception. One major factor in what happened was his terrible temper, another was his extreme anxiety. When things went wrong, he lost control.'[1]

'I really hallucinated,' admits Choegyal. 'Usually your reason exercises some sort of control and makes you aware that part of you is fantasizing, but when you enter a manic phase, rationality is completely over-shadowed. There was one incident...without going into details, I behaved outrageously. I can only describe it by saying I was 'on a trip', without having taken any hallucinogens. It cost me no money, but I certainly paid with my reputation. After that, people used to shy away from me, as if I was possessed.'

Total nervous collapse ensued. 'It was his very worst period, when we were in Zanskar together,' reflects Kundun. 'He seemed to be completely out of control. I felt a kind of desperation and worried endlessly about what I could do to help. I tried telling him that many people suffer from that condition and that it could be treated, but it was no use.' Doctors confirmed that Choegyal was suffering from manic depression, and prescribed a course of Lithium tablets. The cure was effective, but in one sense came too late: his position as Private Secretary to Kundun had been fatally compromised. 'I resigned,' he says heavily, 'I felt it would be completely irresponsible of me to hang on to a job of such importance...I discussed it with His Holiness, and he told me to do as I saw fit.' It's all water under the bridge now, he shrugs.

'Resigning was a hard decision, but I think it was best for his peace of mind,' says the long-suffering Rinchen. 'The most important thing was that he should be happy. I never really despaired, but I must admit that it was difficult not to be depressed. At times I used to wonder if there would ever be an end to it, but I tried not to show him those feelings. In marriage you make promises for life, for the bad times as well as the good, and this was a time for hanging on and waiting.'

Choegyal himself made heroic efforts to control the destructive rage – the all-consuming wild-fire as the Buddhist texts describe it – which periodically possessed him and came near to destroying him. Rinchen worried about the children – 'I had to make them understand that their father loved them, that when he was angry and impatient he needed help not blame. The important thing was for us to work through these difficult times together, to discuss everything, share all the problems. And in fact he does deserve a lot of credit – he worked terribly hard on overcoming his problem after he resigned.'[2]

In January 1989 the Tenth Panchen Lama died. Since his release from prison in 1978 the Panchen had abandoned celibacy, married a Chinese woman in Peking and had a daughter by her. Publicly, he toed the party line, but the Chinese no longer trusted him. In 1985 they allowed him to visit Lhasa for the twentieth anniversary celebrations of the Tibet Autonomous Region, but though they did their best to hide the true state of affairs from him, the Panchen was not deceived. Seeing the sufferings of the Tibetans, he took up their cause with Peking: protesting about the degradation of the environment, the destruction of Tibetan culture and the devastating effect of large-scale immigration by the Han Chinese. When misery exploded into protest in 1987, he deplored the torture and the killings, and as the Chinese introduced ever more repressive measures to keep the Tibetans down, he insisted that such policies would invite cat astrophe. He warned other Tibetans to be wary. When Gyalo Thondup, for example, met him in Peking, 'He was circumspect when the Chinese were present, but when we were alone, do you know what he advised me? "Gyalo-la," he said, "think very hard before you agree to let the Dalai Lama return. You mustn't let him go back to Tibet." He was warning me not to fall into the Chinese trap.'[3]

When the Panchen Lama returned to Tibet in January 1989 for a special ceremony at his home monastery of Tashilhunpo, it was known that before leaving Peking he had had a showdown with the Communist leaders. What benefits had the Chinese ever brought to Tibet, he had demanded to know at a high-level meeting, hitting the table hard with his clenched fist? 'Take away my chair [i.e. in the Chinese National People's Congress],' he taunted the officials. 'It doesn't matter. My real position has nothing to do with you. It is not yours to take or give.'[4] In Tibet itself, at a meeting attended by Chinese officials, he went further – and probably sealed his death warrant. Whatever benefits the Chinese may have brought, he said, were not worth the terrible price the Tibetans had had to pay. A week later, seemingly in excellent health, he was at Tashilhunpo to consecrate a new *stupa* to the memory of past Panchen Lamas. After a party that evening for the workers who had built it, he retired early to bed. Next morning, as the assembled monks waited for him to perform the consecration, news came that he had died during the night. A heart attack, commiserated the Chinese. Nobody believed them.

Kundun was invited to attend the funeral in Peking, but refused. He knew that now the Panchen Lama had gone, the Chinese would be more intractable than ever. He also foresaw trouble ahead, when the time came to seek the reincarnation of the dead Panchen. How could the Chinese fail to exploit that situation for their own political ends?

In May 1990, as martial law in Lhasa was replaced by an even more punitive civilian regime, Kundun took another small step towards democracy for his people in exile. History was made when forty-six elected members of the Tibetan Assembly from all over the Tibetan diaspora came to Dharamsala to elect a new Kashag – the very first time that it had not been chosen by Kundun himself. He was impatient that the changes were still only skin-deep. 'We should be drawing up a document about electing the People's Deputies themselves more democratically, as well as allowing them to appoint the Cabinet,' he told me on that historic day, adding his long-felt hope that one day the Tibetans would accept that he himself is dispensable. 'The Tibetans,' he said ruefully, 'conceive of the Dalai Lama as the ultimate and necessary ruler of Tibet, but they will have to stop thinking like that. Otherwise we shall never have a truly democratic system. I have told them that I will remain as their leader as long as we are in exile, but when we have achieved our freedom, then I will no longer participate in Government. They must learn to do without me.'⁵ (In the following year, the Deputies reluctantly agreed to accept that one day their Supreme Ruler might be edged out. 'We actually took the clause out,' admits Tendzin Choegyal, who had emerged from his hibernation to be elected to the Assembly, 'but he made us put it back in, insisting that without it there would never be any democracy.')

One of those elected to the Kashag was Pema. It was an honour that she would have preferred to forego. She rushed up to the Private Office to explain that she did not want to be a Kalon, and had no aptitude for officialdom. It was explained to her that for the first time in the history of Tibet a woman had been elected to the Kashag, and she must rise to the occasion. In a panic, she rang her husband, Tempa Tsering, in Bangalore, and he counselled her to accept. She could always resign later if it didn't work out, he suggested.

On 12 May, Pema, with two other elected ministers, took the oath as the new Minister of Education. 'To be honest, I was very tense and unhappy,' she said. 'I had to read a text in Tibetan, and that terrified me. I wasn't familiar enough with the Tibetan script – I read English much more easily – and I made lots of mistakes.' Outside, a huge crowd waited to congratulate her and festoon her with white felicitation scarves. 'But I felt more like crying. I wanted to tell them that they'd made a bad choice, just when Tibet was facing such terrible problems. I knew nothing about politics, my skills were all in the field.' Though many of her former pupils wrote to say how happy they were about her election, she herself was wretched.

Matters went from bad to worse. On her first day in the Kashag office, she was horrified to find that all the documents were in Tibetan script, and she needed help to read them. Once they had been translated for her, she was able to reflect carefully on their contents, but she knew very well that she was a misfit. Instead of the hands-on work she excelled in at the TCV, she now had administrative responsibility for the education of all the children in exile, for the TCV itself, the Tibetan Homes Foundation, and the schools run jointly with the Indian Government.

A year later, she offered her resignation, but Kundun refused it, saying: 'We need you.'

In May 1991, Pema contacted Gyalo Thondup and asked him to break his three-year silence and advise Kundun on how things stood with China. The Assembly, meanwhile, celebrated its new freedom by electing GT to the Kashag. 'For some years,' says Kundun, 'the Assembly had been wanting my brother to be given more responsibility, to be given Cabinet rank, but I did not respond.'[6] Now, however, the decision was theirs to make. As Phuntsog Wangyal, one of the delegates, explains, 'It seemed that whenever something important was happening, like negotiations with China, suddenly GT would be on the scene – appearing out of nowhere. We never quite understood how it happened, he was supposed to be just a businessman in Hong Kong. None of us dared ask too many questions, but it was obvious he had important political connections. Within the Assembly, when things went wrong with China, everyone blamed GT, but if things went well, the Tibetan Government took the credit. Some of us decided it was time to stop using GT as a convenient whipping-boy. We should either ignore him altogether or give him a responsible position within the Government. So we brought him into the Kashag.'

Gyalo Thondup felt trapped. He was aware that he knew very little about the affairs of Tibet-in-exile, that in fact he did not really know many individual Tibetans. At first he thought of refusing the Kashag position, but he realized that if he did so many people would be upset. So he came to Dharamsala to test the waters – and decided to accept.

From the outset, he had many enemies in the Assembly. Over the years of negotiations, the Chinese had made not a single concession to Tibet, yet here he was, still advocating making a deal with them, at the expense of Tibetan independence. He had actually urged Tibetans to give up all claims to independence and return to Tibet to work things out. The trouble was that many, possibly most, of the ordinary Tibetans in exile still almost worshipped GT, both because of his past work for the Resistance and as His Holiness's older brother, the secular head of the Yapshi Taklha family. These people found it hard to believe that GT was not the authentic mouthpiece of Kundun, so anyone daring to oppose him must automatically be 'against the Dalai Lama'. While GT was fighting his corner in the Kashag, a rent-a-mob of students from the school for new arrivals from Tibet at Bir in the Kangra Valley was trucked in to Dharamsala, carrying placards and banners, and wearing head-bands proclaiming 'WE LOVE GYALO'. At the same time, there was an outbreak of fighting at Bir, with pro- and anti-Gyalo Thondup factions slogging it out with knives, rocks, sticks and even axes. The school had to be closed down for several months.

In 1992, while visiting the USA, Gyalo Thondup infuriated Tibetan exiles there by publicly berating them for their boycotts of Chinese goods and their campaign to have China's Most Favoured Nation status cancelled. If China lost its MFN status, said GT, forty thousand Chinese would lose their jobs in Guangdong Province alone. Since he believed Tibetan Independence to be a mere pipe-dream, he urged that a deal should be worked out as quickly as possible with the present Chinese administration. The resulting furore was predictable, but the Tibetans in the USA and Canada whose letters of protest were published in the Tibetan press, were threatened with violence and arson by those who supported GT.

A Commission was set up in Dharamsala to investigate GT's outrageous statements, but no one really believed it would get anywhere. The dangers of opposing GT were underlined when Pema Bhum, a writer recently arrived from Amdo, was accused of 'opposing the *dharma*' and received serious death threats. He had urged the students at Bir to stay out of factional politics, and at a public meeting of Amdowas had been the sole dissenter to a decision to withdraw from the democratic process altogether if the commission investigating GT were not called off. (When the present author asked GT about his supporters' tactics, he replied soothingly, 'Some of them behave quite badly, I agree. Our people don't always understand how complicated everything is, and besides there will always be some people determined to use a situation for their own ends.') In the end, the investigating commission crawled out of its responsibilities, clearing GT unreservedly, claiming that his remarks (which certainly did not represent Tibetan Government policy) were simply 'personal opinions'. 'Gyalo Thondup,' reflects a critic, 'affects a somewhat Olympian attitude in matters of statecraft, coolly making public statements absolutely contrary to Tibetan Government policies – and getting away with it.'[8]

In his last few months in office, Gyalo Thondup arranged talks with the Chinese leadership in both Taipei and Peking. He took two officials with him to Taipei and three to Peking. Incredibly, none of them spoke Chinese, the language in which the negotiations were conducted. 'This,' wrote Jamyang Norbu at the time, 'has raised the suspicion among many, including, I understand, the aides themselves, that the participation of these three officials was nothing more than window-dressing for Tibetan public opinion, behind which GT once again did exactly as he pleased.'[9]

Kundun admits that he has frequently been embarrassed by the behaviour of his maverick elder brother. By 1993, he had come to accept that his efforts to initiate a dialogue with the Chinese had been misplaced. Speaking at the Tibetan Institute of Performing Arts in April 1993, he admitted that absolutely no headway had been made. That on the contrary Chinese overtures actually concealed an insidious long-term plan for ensuring the end of Tibetans as a distinct nation and people. Tibet now faced its greatest danger in the ever-increasing immigration of Chinese into Tibet, and he called on all Tibetans to do everything they could to combat this threat.[10]

In the end, GT had to go. 'He did some good things, but he also made many mistakes. He is stubborn and he creates controversy wherever he goes,' says Kundun wearily. 'He ended by offering his resignation and I accepted it.'[11] 'He'd failed and knew he'd failed,' says Tendzin Choegyal. 'The game was up for him. I think he was manipulated by the Chinese. He took their bait, without even knowing that it was a bait.'

He resigned. Yet his brief reign in the Kashag was not all loss, claims Phuntsog Wangyal. 'It worked in a way, because for the first time in his life GT had to explain himself, had to be accountable. That was one of our achievements. He had to face parliamentary criticisms and we made him justify his actions. Previously he'd always got away with everything.'[12] By this time, Pema too had gone. In 1992 she had tried again to resign, again in vain. But in the following July she took matters into her own hands and sent a written letter of resignation to Kundun – 'in English, the language I know best'. Kundun accepted defeat and she returned with gratitude to her own world of the TCV. She was succeeded as Minister of Education by Tendzin Choegyal's wife, Rinchen Khando, who, as Minister of Health, had been the second woman to be elected to the Kashag.

Gyalo Thondup still believes he was much misunderstood. His two years in office in Dharamsala were blighted, he claims, by the feuding within the Tibetan community, by the regional divisions which both the Chinese and certain Indian politicians were all too ready to exploit. 'The Chinese do exploit the rivalry,' he says, 'they send funds to certain groups. And the Indians also have a finger in the pie. You see, neither China nor

India wants to see a strong set-up in Dharamsala, because then the Dalai Lama would be difficult for them to manipulate. They prefer to keep us semi-conscious rather than fully awake.' He is adamant that he resigned for health reasons – he has diabetes – and because he was exhausted. At the same time, he admits to having been 'very fed up. We're supposed to be here for a purpose, we're meant to be thinking about going back to Tibet. People in Tibet have a terribly low standard of living and we should be thinking of how to improve it when we go back. We give little thought to the education of Tibetans in Tibet. We are just wasting time.' His voice, already animated, rises dramatically. 'For the last few years I've been telling them, His Holiness is getting old, I'm getting old, our days are numbered and the Chinese are waiting for us to die. We must achieve something solid before His Holiness dies. If we don't, we shall become like the hundreds and thousands of Tibetans on the south side of the Himalayas, most of whom are by now hybrids, half-Indian, half-Tibetan. Our younger people here are going the same way. We must persuade some of them to return to Tibet, to make a contribution towards educating their fellow Tibetans. And we *must* try and deal with China. Even if we don't want to, we have to. But when I say this kind of thing, they accuse me of being pro-Chinese. It's a no-win situation – the trouble is the Chinese think I don't see their point of view at all.'[13]

GT, it may be surmised, has not yet spoken his last word on the subject. Meanwhile the stalemate continues.

NOTES

1. Author interview with HH the Dalai Lama, June 1994.
2. Author interview with Rinchen Khando, October 1993.
3. Author interview with Gyalo Thondup, New Delhi, July 1995.
4. Article in the *Far Eastern Review*, 1 June 1995, 'Designation of Panchen Lama stirs a storm', by Lincoln Kaye in Peking and Vijay Kranti in New Delhi.
5. Author interview with HH the Dalai Lama, May 1990.
6. Author interview with HH the Dalai Lama, June 1994.
7. Author interview with Gyalo Thondup, Delhi, July 1995.
8. Jamyang Norbu, 'Some Observations on the Independence Controversy' in *Lungta* 7. This article is the source of the above information.
9. Author interview with HH the Dalai Lama, June 1994.

10. HH the Dalai Lama speaking to TIPA, April 1993.

11. Author interview with HH the Dalai Lama, June 1994.

12. Author interview with Phuntsog Wangyal, February 1996.

13. Author interview with Gyalo Thondup, July 1995.

27

A Role for the Yapshi?

It appears the Chinese have won now
But the Dalai Lama still waits
in Time's vast momentariness
and in its infiniteness
for truth to triumph
From a poem by Professor
U. R. Ananthamurthy[1]

Tibetans do not set much store by birthdays, few of them being sure of when exactly they were born. But on 6 July 1995, wherever they were in the diaspora, they celebrated the sixtieth birthday of the Dalai Lama. The Yapshi were no exception: the whole family, brothers, sister, nephews, nieces, cousins and their spouses met in Dharamsala to celebrate the occasion with a special Long Life liturgy in Kundun's private temple. (There were, sadly, a few missing faces: Tsering Dolma, Lobsang Samten, GT's wife and daughter, and, most recently, Tenzin Ngawang. The latter, living in the States, had neglected his health to a degree that suggested he was weary of living, and early in 1994 his condition had worsened. Phuntsok Tashi brought him back home to Dharamsala, where he died a few months later.)

There was a larger shadow over the birthday celebrations that July. Relations with China had recently taken a nose-dive over what can only be called the Case of the Two Panchen Lamas. Briefly, what happened was this. Since the death of the Tenth Panchen Lama in 1989, all help offered by Kundun in the search for the next reincarnation had been rejected by the Chinese as 'outside interference'. Gyalo Thondup, as usual, was on the scene. 'I had kept on raising this issue with various Ministers,' he says,[2] 'requesting them to advise the Chinese leadership about the right procedures to be followed. These procedures, I told the Chinese, must be undertaken with the knowledge of His Holiness, otherwise there would be a lot of misunderstandings.' In 1993, the action accelerated. 'In July, Chatral Rinpoche, the Abbot of Tashilhunpo Monastery and Chairman of the Chinese Government's Selection Committee, came to Beijing to see me and gave me a letter for His Holiness. I brought the letter to India. In the letter, Chatral Rinpoche asked His Holiness for prayers and help in the search for the new Panchen Lama. The signs, he said, indicated that the reincarnation had already taken place – in Tibet. His Holiness immediately asked the Chinese to allow Chatral Rinpoche to come to India for discussions. I handed that letter personally to the Chinese Ambassador in Delhi. It was ignored.'

Over the next two years, Kundun made several attempts to discuss the matter with the Chinese, but in vain.

Meanwhile the search went on, with around thirty names of possible candidates being submitted from inside and outside Tibet. After a number of tests, oracles and divinations, Kundun finally chose six-year-old Gendun Choekyi Nyima as the authentic reincarnation. And on 13 May 1995, it was decided to go public with the recognition. Gyalo Thondup takes up the story:

On 13 May, His Holiness's Secretary telephoned me about the decision to make the announcement on the 14th. I was instructed to tell the Chinese. It was Saturday, and the 14th therefore was a Sunday. This presented me with a very big problem, since on the Sunday all the offices would be closed, and although I had a hot line to various Ministers, I didn't have their home telephone numbers. It took me hours to find the numbers and get through to them. When I did, they were all absolutely furious. They shouted at me, saying that His Holiness had not consulted the Chinese Government and was playing politics. They insisted he was breaking the rule whereby in former times the Emperor (and now the Chinese Government) had the final say in the selection. And so on. I told them to calm down – we'd tried to consult them at every step of the way, I said, but they'd always ignored us. I said it was unfair of them to suggest that His Holiness was playing politics – he was under a lot of pressure from the lamas in both Tibet and India, pushing him to make a decision, and if he was really playing politics, wouldn't he have selected a boy from India, instead of one from Nagchuka with whom he could have no contact?...'Anyway,' I said, 'you're all atheists, you don't believe in any of this, so why should you care about selecting the Panchen Lama?' They went on being angry, but they were worried men. They knew they'd got themselves into a mess and didn't know how to get out of it. I warned them to be very careful how they handled the situation. 'If you handle this badly,' I said, 'you'll become a laughing stock in the eyes of the world. People have heard about the search for the Panchen Lama, they're watching you.' They didn't take any notice, of course. On 17 May, they began reviling His Holiness and blackening his name.³

On 18 May, Chatral Rinpoche was arrested and flown to Peking, charged with having been in contact with the Dalai Lama over the matter. A new wave of repression and intimidation hit Tibet, with a ban on gatherings of more than three or four people and another on any discussion about the Panchen Lama's reincarnation. Over fifty monks and laypeople were detained in custody.⁴ Monks and nuns were confined to their monasteries, and religious leaders were forced to prepare written and oral statements denouncing the Dalai Lama and Chatral Rinpoche. The six-year-old reincarnation and his parents were taken from their home to Peking, and have not been heard of since.

In November, the Chinese men-in-suits chose another six-year-old, Gyaltsen Norbu, whose parents just happened to be Communist cadres. He was selected by the Golden Urn method at the Jokhang Temple in Lhasa and installed as the Eleventh Panchen at Tashilhunpo monastery in the presence of monks who had been coerced into attending. He too was then spirited away to Peking. Doubtless, the Chinese will take no chances with him – they will not risk a repetition of what happened with his predecessor. Given the fact that the Dalai and Panchen Lamas have to recognize each other's reincarnations – a tradition the Chinese were quite happy to ignore in the present instance – he is their passport to the future, a watertight guarantee that, when the present Dalai Lama dies, Tibet will become truly theirs. If this Fourteenth Dalai Lama finally declares, as he well may, that he is the last of his line, then, if all goes to plan, the Chinese puppet Panchen will be the undisputed – if captive – ruler of the land they call the Western Treasure House.

In Dharamsala for the birthday celebrations in July, GT aired his general sense of frustration. 'There are too many people here who think they're somebody,' he accuses. 'I'm always telling them we're nobodies, vagabonds, beggars, who need one day to go back to Tibet and must be ready.' He recalls the words of an old Chinese friend, a businessman from Shanghai and close friend of Jiang Ze-min, the Chinese Premier. 'This old man said to me, "You Tibetans are very naïve. The Chinese Communists are just waiting, counting the days till the Dalai Lama dies. When he does, the Tibetans are finished. Whatever has to be done must be done *now*, while he is still alive. Gyalo-la, don't miss the opportunity.' Gyalo Thondup takes the warning seriously. Tibet is always on his mind, but the conclusion he arrives at is that its future is bound up with China. He has obviously discussed the question at the highest levels in the Chinese leadership, in a way that must surely alarm the Tibetans. 'I told them, if I come back to China, I will participate in the Government, but I will not be a rubber-stamp. There have been enough puppets in our history – don't expect His Holiness and myself to be rubber-stamps for you. If you want Tibet to remain part of China you must treat us as equals. For a start, we want the whole Tibetan-speaking area – Amdo, Kham and Central Tibet – to be reunified.'

It is this sort of talk, off-the-top-of-his-head, over-confident, arrogant, bombastic, that maddens the Tibetans and not only those who hold to the idea of independence-or-nothing. To them, particularly the younger ones, it illustrates that Gyalo Thondup is out of touch with his own people, that he thinks like a Chinese and to all intents and purposes *is* Chinese. The criticisms sadden his sister, Pema, for whom GT has always been both father-figure and friend. 'He had so much to offer the Tibetan cause, and at the time when we most needed help, we had much cause to be grateful to him,' she sighs. But she cannot deny that GT, with his high-handedness and craving for power, has always been his own worst enemy. 'He's so stubborn, he won't listen to anybody else. So of course, he's made many enemies.' 'He thinks,' says a normally placid observer, 'that he's the only person who can solve the Tibetan problem and that he must solve it before he dies.'

GT, sixty-eight now and disillusioned with Tibetans and Chinese alike, has put himself on the back-burner once again – resuming his role of mystery man and 'China-watcher' in Hong Kong. 'I've told the Chinese Ministers I'm not going back to Beijing unless they can come up with some

positive suggestions.' He did not hesitate to lay the blame for the continuing stalemate on Deng Xiao-ping and his closest cronies, though he knew
well that one day he might pay for such outspokenness. 'If Deng is still
alive when the Chinese take over Honk Kong,' he said cheerfully, 'he'll
probably have my head.'

Two years later, Deng is dead – and the situation in China is wide open.
GT may be in less danger of losing his head, but he is tired and has once
again 'categorically retired'. Then, lest anyone should think that is his
final word, he hastens to qualify it. 'Of course,' he says, 'if His Holiness
were to ask me to come back again, how could I refuse?'⁵

Norbu takes a more long-term view of the situation than his brother. 'If
we talk to the Chinese,' he says, 'it should be as equals, not with China
dictating the terms. I know what the Chinese are like. We Tibetans
shouldn't yield an inch on regaining our independence. We have to have
the hope of returning one day, but who knows when? Maybe in ten years
time, maybe a hundred, maybe not for several generations.'⁶ Tibetans who
share this viewpoint must prepare themselves for a long struggle, the outcome of which they will not live to see. 'I'm retired now,' Norbu shrugs
patiently, as if to underline his attitude. 'I just pull up the weeds. Well, I
pull them up one day and next day they're back.' It is true that most of his
life is now spent quietly. He lives on the premises of a Centre for Religious
Studies which he started after his retirement in 1987. 'He is a very spiritual person and very simple,' comments Tendzin Choegyal. 'The very fact
that he hasn't come up with some fancy Dharma Centre in the States
speaks volumes. He could have commanded a huge following, but he was
strong-minded enough to resist the temptation.'

Certainly Norbu is too honest and blunt to be a politician, and he too
makes enemies among the Tibetans. 'They think I'm a reactionary,' he
says, 'I come on a bit too strong for their tastes.' But he has the courage of
his convictions. On 16 March 1995, this 75-year-old patriot with a pace-
maker completed a 'Trek for Tibet', walking 75 miles through rural Indiana to draw attention to his country's plight. Addressing a press
conference afterwards, he did not pull his punches. 'The time for negotiat-
ing with the thief, that is the Chinese Government, has passed,' he asserted. 'We Tibetans must stand up and loudly state, CHINA, GET OUT OF
TIBET. We must also shout TIBET MUST BE INDEPENDENT. He professed

his solidarity with Kundun. 'I do not advocate violence,' he said, while emphasizing the need for a tough approach. 'I speak for justice that is grounded in compassion. We must be more aggressive when fighting the Chinese Government – not with military weapons of destruction, but with political, legal and economic weapons.' Announcing the formation of a new International Tibetan Independence Movement with himself as Chairman, Norbu promised that in the following year he would march from Washington DC to the UN Building in New York. 'Until then,' he pleaded, 'I call upon all Tibetans to speak up and listen to their teacher, the Great Compassionate One, His Holiness, the Fourteenth Dalai Lama. Tell my brother what you think. Take more personal responsibility for Tibet's future. Our greatest danger is that we Tibetans will become too comfortable in exile, and will forget that we ever had our own country. Our strength lies in our wisdom, our generosity, our ability to act. Fight for justice with compassion in your heart, and Tibet will be independent once again.'[7]

Exactly a year later, 76-year-old Norbu completed the 25-day march from Washington to New York. Before leaving Washington, he stood outside the city's Chinese Embassy to address a large crowd:

> I am very pleased to speak to you today where the diplomats and agents of the People's Republic of China can hear us and see us. It is important that we speak up here, so that people inside the Chinese Embassy can know that no matter what methods they use to suppress the desires of the Tibetan people, the Tibetan struggle for independence will always continue. It will not end until the legitimate hopes and desires, that is, their inalienable right to independence, not some sort of 'autonomy' within China, is eventually realized.

He ended with a passionate peroration:

> We cannot and will not fly half of the Tibetan flag. Our entire flag must be flown all over the world, including at the United Nations. We will not occupy one-half of a seat at the United Nations. We have the right to a full seat.[8]

'The important thing for Norbu,' says Phuntsog Wangyal, who himself holds this view and believes that His Holiness secretly does too, 'is that this Dalai Lama should not put his seal of approval on anything less than total independence. He must not go down in history as the Dalai Lama who gave away Tibet. Norbu loves him too much to let that happen, and so do I.'[9]

As might be expected, the women of the Yapshi family are involved less with rhetoric than with the day-to-day business of nurture and survival. Pema, having completed over thirty years service in the Tibetan Children's Villages, still lives in Dharamsala in a school that is literally the size of a village, with twelve hundred residential pupils and about one hundred day scholars; and caring for ten thousand more Tibetan children throughout the diaspora. To mark her thirty year achievement, in 1994 the National Assembly gave her the official title of Amala, Mother of Tibet. She often thinks back to those early days when there was no money, no staff, no equipment, no food, no clothing, no shelter – and realizes that the threat now is of a different order. 'Nowadays our problem is how to educate our young, how to bring them up as true Tibetans, what values we should be trying to instil into their minds. We *must* maintain our culture, our identity as Tibetans must not be lost and it is the children who will preserve it. They are the seed-grains of the future. But how to preserve our identity in the face of outside pressures and influences? It's not a question of whether we have slanty eyes or wear Tibetan dress, our Tibetan-ness has to be interior. We have a special culture: we take whatever happens, however awful, in our stride – and we go on smiling. How do we get our children to understand that?'[10]

Khando has temporarily left the scene – partly to prevent burn-out and partly to provide herself and her family with a breathing-space (and a College education for their daughters). She and Rapten are in America, in Utah. She had returned to Dharamsala in 1987, knowing in her heart that she would never make it there. 'When I returned I was asked to work at the Council for Home Affairs as Additional General Secretary, and I plunged into it headlong, determined to make a go of it. But I was up against a lot of male chauvinists – small-time politicians who stay alive by manipulating the weaknesses of a society – and an enormous amount of prejudice. I was too independent, too outspoken, too impatient with their out-dated Anglo-Indian bureaucracy, too Western in my attitudes – and, worst of all, a WOMAN! Then I became General Secretary of Information and International Relations and when that didn't work out, certain people were so keen to take over my job that I did not even get the chance to clear my desk! I'd had enough. The fight had gone out of me.'

Rapten's parents had died, their children were growing up. Working in the Government service for all those years, they had made no money and had no independent means. Kundun had occasionally stepped in to help with the children's education, but both she and Rapten felt that the time had come to move on, to emigrate. 'We agonized over the decision,' says Khando, 'alone, together, with relatives and friends. But when Rapten filled in the immigration forms, I knew His Holiness would know that I too was leaving. When I went to break the news to him I felt very sad, as though I was letting him and the family down by breaking away from all the things I had worked so hard for in the last thirty odd years. If he was disappointed, he did not show it, but I know he understood and felt my unhappiness, as he used the intimate form of address he has always used with me and said "Yes, I know, and I understand completely." I had to struggle not to cry, it was a very emotional moment. Later on, of course, when I was already in the States and went to meet him, he joked about it. "Well," he teased, "the consumer society obviously agrees with you. You've put on a lot of weight."

Khando and Rapten both have found jobs in the Utah Valley State College, advising American and foreign students, working with the faculty and staff to internationalize the campus. There are about sixty Tibetans in the Salt Lake City area – 'all the immigrants keep in touch and help and support each other'. Their own house is always full of people, their own and the children's many friends, and a constant stream of relatives and visiting friends. Khando swears that they come in the first place out of simple curiosity as to why the Chazotsangs chose to come to Utah!

'Life's odd, isn't it?' she muses. 'Here was this Tibetan girl, whose parents were born into a farming family in Amdo, then were elevated to become the highest family in the land, surrounded by every luxury and privilege. Then she was sent away from home and put into an Irish Roman Catholic convent...A refugee in India, despatched to England to lead another kind of privileged life. Then back again among the Tibetans, the hard, hard work, the traumas of learning about the torture and death in Tibet, the frustration and the anger. And finally, fetching up in Salt Lake with many more friends, some of whom are wonderful Mormons. Everything in that Tibetan girl's life has enlarged her horizons and added depth to her experience.'

What has belonging to the Yapshi family meant to her? 'Well, it's a privilege, of course. A privilege and a great joy to be related to such a great, compassionate and marvellous person as the Dalai Lama. But it's also a responsibility and sometimes a heartache. If I hadn't been a Yapshi, I might not have had the opportunities I was given, but then people can sometimes accuse you of being too much of a Yapshi, when that is simply not true...I used to be embarrassed by the adulation, I used to plead with people not to prostrate to me. That sort of thing somehow seemed demeaning to everybody concerned, although I know it was done out of respect for His Holiness. The latter is always reminding us to practise compassion in our lives at every moment, and to try and put others before self. I'm trying very hard to do that – because it makes a lot of sense to me.'

And what of Tendzin Choegyal, still known to most of his compatriots as Ngari Rinpoche and venerated accordingly? The veneration irritates and unsettles him. 'Sooner or later,' he says, 'people will find out it was all a mistake.' He really does not believe in the *tulku* system, and finds the present mania for creating new ones distasteful. 'I think it appeals to people who don't really know what Buddhism is about,' he complains. 'It's a kind of spiritual materialism. Real Buddhism means interior change, but no one wants to be bothered with that.'

On Kundun's insistence, he has been back again to Ladakh, since his breakdown eight years ago. 'His Holiness says I am Ngari Rinpoche whether I like it or not, whether I believe it or not, and I must accept that. He tells me, "Forget about the religious side of things if you must, just go and advise them on practical matters. And if they ask you about the spiritual life, just tell them what you can." The trouble is, I can't be what they want me to be: a colourful personality dressed in exotic robes, sitting on an ornate throne and mouthing a lot of nothings. When I go there, I feel I'm expected to be some kind of Moses, even if they see me driving a Land Rover rather than a camel. But I can't be. They think themselves blessed because I'm Ngari Rinpoche and I'm there with them, but they don't really understand a word I say. It's what I said earlier: true Buddhism has nothing to do with blind faith, it is about transforming the mind.'

Even Kundun is surprised by the intensity of his younger brother's search for the spiritual life these days. Seeking a deeper meaning in life is, he claims, all that really matters; he has no other ambition. Sometimes he thinks he would like to look after the mentally ill or mentally handicapped or the depressed, but most of all he would like to be some kind of contemplative. With his love of people, his capacity to immerse himself in their lives, he would have to be an extremely mobile contemplative, with time off for stimulating conversation. One writer on Tibet commented that 'many who have been fortunate enough to have long conversations with him are convinced that he is actually one of the best teachers that they have ever encountered'.[11] Many friends would echo that, but, with few exceptions, they would probably be Westerners. Tendzin Choegyal is a born-again Westerner, fully convinced that in no previous life could he have been Tibetan.

With his own people, he is frequently at odds. Partly it is the old gold-fish bowl syndrome, the constantly being in the public eye, the object of envy and sometimes of malice. Partly it is his own inability to suffer fools gladly, his intolerable desire for things to be as they should be and mani-festly are not. Nowhere were these two strands more in evidence than during the five years he served as a member of the National Assembly. 'His impatience and high-handedness earn him many enemies,' reflects his friend, Tenzin Geyche. 'He loses his temper easily and people get hurt. Then, of course, they think he's arrogant and spoiled. Those who remember his father in Lhasa think that Tendzin Choegyal inherited even more of his bad temper than the others.'[12] Tendzin Choegyal did not enjoy his five years in the Assembly and will not be standing for re-election. He is scathing about the experience: 'It's chaotic,' he says, 'they fight over small issues and disregard the more important ones. Essentially they do nothing at all.'

Because he cares so deeply about the *dharma*, it angers him that many of the monks and nuns in the Tibetan community seem not to care about it at all. There are far too many monks, he claims – adding that His Holiness has said so too. 'The majority of monks and nuns in our community seem to do nothing but wear the robes. They don't seem to have the faintest idea that a monk is supposed to be on the path to becoming a realized being.' Tenzin Geyche tries to soften the tirade, though by and large he too agrees. 'Some of the younger ones are a disgrace,' he admits. 'They don't understand the vocation they have chosen and some of them behave very badly indeed. When you see monks going out to watch videos, riding motorbikes, standing around on street corners and going with women, that's very bad. But the picture isn't quite as black as Rinpoche makes out. There are still many very holy and excellent monks about.'

Though Tendzin Choegyal is frequently depressed, three things save him from total despair. One is an impish sense of humour that endears him to his many friends and rarely deserts him, except perhaps in the darkest moments. The second is his closeness to Kundun, the brother he resembles in so many ways, and whom he loves, admires and respects above all other human beings. To some extent, Choegyal is Kundun's right-hand man, or as the latter describes him, his 'man of action', practical and talented in many directions, an engineer or perhaps an inventor *manqué*. It is said that before he died, the Great Thirteenth wrote to his friend and fellow-student, the Fifteenth Ngari Rinpoche, 'In our next incarnations, we shall be very much closer to each other.' There is no denying the special relationship between the two brothers, alike in their ideas, their interests and in their engaging capacity for laughter. ('Kundun is many people in one person,' says Choegyal typically, 'someone from whom I receive great teachings, political guidance, personal encouragement, and occasionally a few rockets.')

The third and most important saving grace is his increasing dependence on the *dharma*. This is reflected in a poem he has written:

He [the Buddha] gave us the gift
of the path called *dharma*
that opens our eyes
to perceive the world with joy.[13]

And lastly to Kundun himself. In his sixties now, he seems to have the energy and dynamism of one half his age. He is a seemingly inexhaustible ambassador for his country, jetting across the world with breathtaking frequency, yet emerging from these marathons with his famous smile, plunging instantly into the talks and teachings demanded of him. These days in the West, he has become almost a cult figure, taken up by a host of famous actors, directors and politicians. Yet, although the Western media like occasionally to debunk him as a fashionable, trendy guru, those who come to scoff often stay to admire. In a *Sunday Times* article featuring the Dalai Lama in a gallery of men with 'allure', its author's conclusions were less glib than might have been expected. 'I once heard him give a talk on "The Virtues of Compassion",' wrote the journalist,[14] 'and, although I had come with a sceptical attitude, I found myself getting more and more wise and compassionate by the minute.' Here, she decided, was 'one of the saintliest men in the world'.

Kundun is hopeful that the democracy he has tried so hard to introduce to his people in exile has at last taken root, though he knows that the real test will come if and when he and his people return to Tibet. The idea that in that event he himself will bow out of any political role is hard for the Tibetans to swallow. They don't quite believe him, but he is determined. 'I have my reasons,' he says, 'and they have nothing to do with any loss of interest in Tibetan affairs.' Meanwhile, he remains the undisputed leader of his people, though, as Tendzin Choegyal says, 'one hundred per cent of our Tibetans hero-worship His Holiness, yet only about ten per cent listen to what he is saying.' Some say that people only tell him what they think he wants to hear and that he does not really know what they are thinking. This is not for want of encouragement on his part, but, as Phuntsog Wangyal says, 'If people speak their minds, they will immediately be cast out by the community, *in his name*. They won't take the risk of that happening.' Kundun agrees that 'very few are willing to speak out against me on certain issues', but claims that 'on most matters they're only too ready to complain'. Meanwhile, he sees many of the young people in exile adopting Western, consumer-orientated values, and worries that what made Tibetans special is fast disappearing.

In spite of everything they have done, he firmly refuses to hate the Chinese – though he admits it's quite a struggle. 'I can curse and rave in private but I do not allow hatred to rise in my heart. I tell myself constantly that whatever the Chinese have done, maybe it is not their fault. If I ever allow myself to believe that such and such a person does not deserve happiness, then my *bodhisattva* vow would be broken.'[15] He tells a story which has moved him deeply, of a monk who came to Dharamsala in 1980 after twenty years in a Chinese prison. In all those years, he told Kundun, the greatest danger he faced was that he might lose his compassion for the Chinese. 'Now, I think that's wonderful,' exclaims Kundun. 'I have the feeling that in his place I'd have let rage engulf me. Either that, or' – and here he bursts into the familiar, sometimes disconcerting gales of laughter – 'I might have done a Yes, Minister, saying yes, yes, of course, oh sure, to whatever the Chinese suggested.' He believes that had he been put to the test he would have been nowhere near as brave as the last Panchen Lama, whom he describes lovingly as 'a true freedom fighter'.

Optimism is strong in him, and he is confident of returning to Tibet within a few years. 'The present totalitarian system cannot last much longer. There will be change, either total collapse or evolutionary change. I hope it will be evolutionary – it'll be less chaotic. If there were to be conflict in that huge country, the bloodshed would be enormous.' His astrological chart tells him that he will live to the age of 122, but his dreams suggest the figure 113. 'I know that's highly unscientific,' he chuckles, adding that he himself thinks he'll live to be ninety. (Which may be some consolation to his bodyguard and to the security personnel provided by the Indian Government to protect a life which is constantly under threat.)

If Kundun does end his days in Tibet, he knows exactly where he will go: the Reting Monastery, home of the disgraced Regent who first discovered him to be the Fourteenth Dalai Lama. 'We passed through there when I was coming from Amdo,' he reminisces, 'and again as we returned from China in 1954. In the main temple, standing in front of the principal statue, I was overcome with a sense of the great teacher who had founded this monastery over one thousand years ago, Drom, disciple of the Indian scholar-saint, Atisha. With that feeling came tears – I cried and cried as though I would never stop. It was one of the most powerful emotional experiences of my whole life, and after it was over I knew I would spend my last days in the little forest surrounding that holy place. I still believe I shall do that.'

It may be that he is too optimistic. Since 1994, when the West stopped putting pressure on China to improve its human rights record, the Chinese have tightened their control over Tibet and declared all-out war on the Dalai Lama. The Tibetan People's Congress openly admits it. 'Let everyone in the Tibetan Autonomous Region understand clearly,' they announced in the spring of 1996, 'that the struggle against the Dalai Lama group is a long-term, bitter, complex, you-die-I-live political battle with no possibility of compromise.'[16] They couldn't say clearer than that. In probably the severest crackdown since the Cultural Revolution, officials throughout Tibet have been ordered 'to fight tooth and nail', against the Dalai Lama, the 'Number One criminal' who is bent on splitting the Chinese Motherland. The Tibetan independence movement is described as a snake, and the Dalai Lama as 'the serpent's head', which must be cut off.[17] Once again all photographic representations of him – and of the authentic Panchen Lama – have been banned. Not only from Government offices and public places, but from monasteries, temples, schools and private homes. From Lhasa come reports of monks and nuns being beaten up – and shot – in struggles with the police over the ban. House-to-house and school-to-school searches have been taking place – and resistance is growing. Fresh waves of unrest threaten to engulf Tibet.

Perhaps even more dangerous in the long term, China's new Tibet policy[18] calls for greater indoctrination of Tibetan children in schools, while urging ever more Chinese to come to Tibet. Tibetan children studying in India and elsewhere have been ordered home. The prognosis is hardly hopeful. But then, the same could have been said of the situation in the Soviet Union and Eastern Europe in 1989. Miracles still do happen. Political change must come to China – and one can only pray that it will not be too late to save Tibet. Must one then agree with Gyalo Thondup that it is better to be pragmatic and seek a serious accommodation with China, making a return from exile possible and assuring some kind of normality for Tibet in the near future? Or should one, like Norbu, insist on nothing less than total liberation, even if it takes ten, twenty, a hundred, even a thousand years? Caught between the polarized views of his elder brothers, the Fourteenth Dalai Lama still seeks the middle way of dialogue and non-violence. Which of them is right will be for history alone to judge.

The Great Thirteenth expressed the hope that in his next incarnation he would have brothers and sisters to help him in his work. His successor has seen that hope richly fulfilled. His siblings – like siblings in any family – may not always see eye to eye with him, and may even differ quite force-fully. But his goals are always their goals and their lives, like his, are dedi-cated to achieving them. He knows that, whatever the disagreements, the love and the loyalty of his Yapshi family will always be beyond question.

NOTES

1. Published in *Tibetan Bulletin*, January–February 1995.
2. Author interview with GT, New Delhi, July 1995.
3. Author interview with GT, July 1995.
4. See: 'The Panchen Lama: Politics intruding on a religious discovery', DIIR Pub-lications, Dharamsala; and Amnesty International report, 18 January 1996, which used earlier documents: 'Three detained in Panchen Lama controversy', ASA 17/40/95 and 'Crackdown on Tibetan dissent continues', ASA 17/74/95.
5. All the above from author interview with Gyalo Thondup in New Delhi (1995) and Jetsun Pema in Dharamsala (1994).
6. Author interview with Thubten Jigme Norbu, Dharamsala, July 1995.
7. *Today* Press Conference, 16 March 1995, Indianopolis.
8. Reported in *Tibetan Bulletin*, March–April 1996.
9. Author interview with Phuntsog Wangyal, London, 1996.
10. Author interview with Jetsun Pema, Dharamsala, June 1994.

11. Roger Hicks, *Hidden Tibet*, Element Books, 1988.
12. Author interview with Tenzin Geyche Tethong, 1993.
13. Tendzin Choegyal, unpublished poem, 'The New Path', September 1995.
14. Rhoda Koenig, 'Allure Boys', *The Sunday Times*, 12 May 1996.
15. Author interview with HH the Dalai Lama, 1995.
16. Sunanda K. Datta-Ray, 'Diplomacy Key to Beijing's 'war' with Dalai Lama', *The Straits Times* (Singapore) 7 June, 1996.
17. See: 'Cutting off the Serpent's Head: Tightening Control in Tibet 1994–95', Tibet Information Network (London) and Human Rights Watch/Asia (USA), 1996.
18. The Third National Forum for Work on Tibet, held in Peking, July 1994.

Bibliography

Avedon, John, *An Interview with the Dalai Lama*, Littlebird
  Publications, 1980.
——, *In Exile from the Land of Snows*, Michael Joseph, 1984.
Barnett, Robert, & Akiner, Shirin, eds., *Resistance and Reform in Tibet*,
  Hurst, 1994.
Chapman, F. Spencer, *Lhasa the Holy City*, New Delhi, Bodhi Leaves,
  1992 (First published London, 1940).
Craig, Mary, *Tears of Blood: A Cry for Tibet*, HarperCollins 1992; Fount
  Paperbacks 1993.
'Cutting off the Serpent's Head: Tightening Control in Tibet, 1994–95',
  Tibet Information Network and Human Rights
  Watch/Asia, 1996.
Dalai Lama, His Holiness the, *My Land and My People*, New York,
  Potala, 1962.
——, *Freedom in Exile: The Autobiography of the Dalai Lama of Tibet*,
  Hodder & Stoughton, 1990.
——, *HH the Dalai Lama: Speeches, Statements, Articles and Interviews
  1987–95*, Dharamsala, DIIR, 1995.
Dhondup, K., *The Water Bird and Other Years*, New Delhi,
  Rangwang, 1986.
Ford, Robert, *Captured in Tibet*, OUP 1990 (First published by Harrap, 1957).
Goldstein, Melvyn C., *A History of Modern Tibet, 1913–1951: The
  Demise of the Lamaist State*, University of California Press, 1989.
Goodman, Michael Harris, *The Last Dalai Lama*, Shambhala, 1987.
Harrer, Heinrich, *Seven Years in Tibet*, Paladin/Grafton, 1988
  (First published Rupert Hart-Davis, 1953).
Jetsun Pema, *Tibet, Mon Histoire*, Paris, Éditions Ramsay, 1996.
Murphy, Dervla, *Tibetan Foothold*, John Murray, 1966; Pan, 1969.
Norbu, Jamyang, *Warriors of Tibet*, Wisdom, 1979.
——, *Illusion and Reality: Essays on the Tibetan and Chinese Political
  Scene from 1978 to 1989*, Tibetan Youth Congress Books, 1989.

Norbu, Thubten Jigme, with Harrer, Heinrich, *Tibet Is My Country*, Wisdom, 1986.

Norbu, Thubten Jigme, with Turnbull, Colin, *Tibet*, Chatto & Windus, 1969; Penguin, 1976.

Ra, Raghu (photographs), & Perkins, Jane (text), *Tibet in Exile*, Cassell, 1990.

Richardson, Hugh E., *Tibet and its History*, Shambhala, 1984.

Shakabpa, W. D., *Tibet: A Political History*, Potala Books, 1984.

Taring, Rinchen Dolma, *Daughter of Tibet*, John Murray, 1970.

Tucci, Giuseppe, *To Lhasa and Beyond: Diary of the Expedition to Tibet in the year 1928*, Snow Lion Publications, 1983 (first published 1956).

Index

Although Taklha is the Yapshi family name, few of its members actually use it. I have also had a general problem over the use of Tibetan surnames. Some use their second or third given names as a surname, e.g. Choegyal, Norbu, Taklha, Taring; others – even within the same branch of the family – do not use a surname at all. (And among those whose first name is Tenzin, some prefer to spell it thus, others with a 'd'.) I have tried to be consistent, but it is never easy and not always possible, and if in some cases I have made the wrong decision, I can only apologize.

Bhrikuti, Queen (Nepalese wife of
King Songtsen Gampo) 4
Bir 352
Birla House (Mussoorie) 232, 233,
235
Bloomington (Indiana) 245, 276-7,
294
Bodh Gaya 239, 249, 323, 325, 332
bodhisattva 3, 8n, 367
Bomdila (Assam) 227, 228
British India (Government of Great
Britain in India) 1, 11, 18, 20,
52n, 61, 67n, 73, 75, 76-7,
107-8, 123, 154n, 172; after
1947 173n
British (later Indian) Trade Mission
in Lhasa 61, 70, 76, 81n, 87, 88,
101, 118, 124, 126, 158
Buddha Jayanti (1956) chapter 16
passim
Buddhism in Tibet – *see* Mahayana
Buddhism
Buxa Duar camp (Bengal) 237-8
Byllakuppe (S. India), refugee
settlement 245, 273, 281

Calcutta 130, 133, 134, 150, 159,
172, 190, 191, 192, 201, 202,
204, 250, 259, 265
Caroe, Olaf 78, 81n, 88
Central Intelligence Agency (CIA):
and Norbu 159, 201; and Gyalo
Thondup 172, 201, 206; and
the Tibetan guerrillas 207, 248,
249, 252, 253, 281; and the SFF
252
Chakrata 298
Chamdo 139, 140, 143, 152, 177

Chandzo Jampa, 89, 90
Changseshar (Yapshi house in
Lhasa) 85, 113, 114-15, 120
Chapman, F. Spencer 87, 116, 193
Chatral Rinpoche 357, 358
Chazotsang, Khando Tsering
(daughter of Tsering Dolma and
Phuntsok Tashi): childhood in
Lhasa 114-16, 157; and Tsering
Dolma 165, 192, 264, 265-7;
and Phuntsok Tashi 276; at
school in India 150, 161, 190-1,
231, 232, 252; with the
Thondups in Darjeeling 190-1,
207, 231; incident at Chinese
Embassy, New Delhi (1955)
191; at Buddha Jayanti (1956)
202; greets her refugee family
(1959) 231; and further
education 265; in Geneva 275;
and Kundun 300-1, 338, 363;
and Amala 275, 323; and the
Mussoorie Homes Foundation
300-1, 337-8; in Dharamsala
(1987) 362; in Utah 362-4
Chazotsang, Rapten (m. Khando
Tsering) 265, 275, 276, 300,
301, 315, 316, 317, 318, 323,
362, 363
Che la Pass 220
Chenrezig, patron deity of Tibet 3,
69, 96
Chen-yi, Marshal 186
Chiang Chin-wu, General 152, 165,
166-8, 177, 196, 199, 208
Chiang Kai-shek, General 7, 18;
and Chinese Communist Party
7, 119; and the Civil War in

Preparatory Committee for the
Autonomous Region of Tibet,
(PCART) 178, 186, 196, 199, 206
Pullen, Judy 268
Pu Yi, the 'Last Emperor' of
imperial China 219, 225n

Radio Lhasa 141, 221, 222
Rai Bahadur Norbhu 16, 85, 106–7
Rame monastery 221
Rangzom Monastery, Ladakh: and
Ngari Rinpoche (Tendzin
Choegyal) 279
Reform Party, the 249, 251
reforms in Tibet 1–2, 166–7, 168–9
Reting monastery 368
Reting Rinpoche (Regent of Tibet)
87, 232; elected Regent after
death of Thirteenth Dalai
Lama 8; and Fourteenth Dalai
Lama 12–13, 71; and the Kung
116, 120; and Gyalo Thondup
116; growing opposition to, and
resignation 79–80, 98; and
Taktra 98, 108–9, 121; arrest
and death in Potala prison
121–2, 232
Richardson, Hugh (official
representative of British and
Indian Governments in Lhasa,
1936–1950) 58, 68, 71, 84, 87,
106, 126, 127, 128n, 130, 140,
141, 146, 155, 156, 165, 237;
and the Dalai Lama's ransom
61; and the death of Reting
122; in charge of British
Mission in Lhasa (1937)
79, 128n

Rigya 69, 70
roads (built by Chinese in Tibet)
176–7, 181, 182, 183–4, 188n,
247, 253

Sabo Pass 221
St Joseph's College, Darjeeling 190,
257, 283
St Joseph's Convent, Kalimpong
150, 285
Sakyapa sect 258
Scotch Plains (New Jersey) 291–3
Seattle University 258, 286
Se la Pass 170
Self-Help Centres in India and Nepal
238, 246, 272, 286, 290, 340
Sera Je College 121–2
Sera monastery 7, 15, 121
Seventeen-Point Agreement with
China (1951) 150–1, 153, 164,
165, 166, 178, 187, 204, 216,
228, 234
Shakabpa, W. D. 86, 198
Shanghai 131, 132
Shartsong hermitage 15, 43, 44, 46,
50, 51, 135
Shastri, Lal Bahadur 272, 273
Sheriff, George 116, 128n
Sikkim 154n, 158, 172–3, 192, 201,
233–4, 239, 247, 248, 252;
treasure in 243–4, 249
Sikkim, Maharajah of 75, 148, 158,
172, 198
Siliguri 231
Siling (capital of Amdo) 18, 19, 28,
48, 61, 69, 89, 90, 185; and the
Chinese Communists 135, 137,
185

vegetarianism among the Tibetans
52n, 159; and Kundun 273
Volunteer Army to Defend
Buddhism – *see* Chushi
Gangdrug

Wangdu, General Gyatso 281, 297
war between India and Pakistan
(1965) 272
Wen Chang, Queen (Chinese wife
of King Songtsen Gampo) 4
Wu Chang 65, 76–7, 80–1n

Xinhua, New China News Agency
232, 306, 308

Yangtse River 91, 143
Yapshi Taklha family 83, 167,
209–10, 212, 255, 290, 298,
303, 304, 308, 328, 336, 339,
346n, 351, 356, 362, 363–4,
365; and Khando 363–4
Yarphel Padatsang 243
'yellow parachute' 207, 249, 281
Younghusband, Colonel (Sir)
Francis 42, 52n

Zhu Dan – *see* Thondup, Dekyi
Dolkar